MEMORIES
And
OBSERVATIONS
A Memoir
by
Hugh Murphy

The Wealthy - in the following pages refers to the aristocracy which is not supposed to exist in Ireland. These are the people who never did a day's work in their lives and control and manipulate the Democratic Process. They suck the life blood from the people and what's left is divided between Vulture Funds and Parasites.

TABLE OF CONTENTS

CHAPTER ONE

My first memory is being aged about two or three, being violently lifted up and flung into a corner. My crime was that I had pulled my father's arm while he was sleeping. I was screaming my head off and being comforted my mother and my older sister.

My next memories about the same age, along with my younger brother, Chris, in the company of two of my Aunts, Peggy and Kathleen, was leaving my Granny and Granddad's house. My mother Tilly, another aunt, Eileen, and my granny kissed us goodbye. My granny, Peggy and Kathleen were reed thin, but aunt Mary, Eileen and my mother were plumper. There had been six sisters but Jean had died when she was very young and was never spoken about. Aunt Peggy and Kathleen were taking myself, and my younger brother Chris to the Circus and we were really excited.

My granddad was a very enterprising man. The house his family lived in was a green grocers shop, that sold everything, and was the last dwelling at the bottom of Mayfair Street. This was situated off the Old Park Road in Belfast. Granddad also had a horse and cart that he kept in a stable around the corner. In the summer would go around the streets selling fresh vegetables.

Quite often he'd stop outside our house in New Dock Street for a cup of tea. When he did this he'd give all the children an apple. When we'd eaten the apple down to the core the horse would crunch the rest. Five or six of us would sit beside granddad as he drove up the street and then jump off the cart as he turned the corner. In the winter his horse wore a coat and he sold Coal Bricks. These were bricks made out of coal dust and sand that were slow burning. A hard crust formed and beneath it the fire kept going all night. In the morning a thrust with a poker and some fresh coat saw it roaring into life.

Grandad had also served his time as a Sign Writer and every Sunday w hen we visited, he would be writing signs in his shop. I remember him showing me how to do an apostrophe and telling me that it was a full stop with a wee tail on it. I to this day I can still remember the smell of the paint on the freshly painted signs.

When Aunt Peggy opened the front door, the bell rang and we exited into the freezing cold. Mayfair Street was in an area called 'The Bone' because - or so I've been told that there used to be a large Bone-yard there. This was used to grind up bones for fertilizer - and is very close to an area called Ardoyne.
We walked down an alleyway where granddad kept his horse and emerged into Flax Street. There we we got a bus to the circus. I can't remember much about the circus, only the fact that the lions terrified us. We returned to my granny's for fish and chips and our Da arrived in a taxi because it was snowing. The faces were kissed of us and we went home.

We lived in an area of the Docks that was known as Sailortown, for obvious reasons, because most of the men went to sea. It was sandwiched between York Street, and Garmoyle Street with Whitla Street and the Docks Wall at one end. Nelson Street ran up the middle cutting through major thoroughfares like Dock Street, Earl Street, Henry Street, etc. Between these major streets was nestled a warren of working class two up and two down houses.

On several of the major streets grain mills were situated, for making flour and with Gallagher's Tobacco Factory on York Street, the smell that greeted the Sailortown inhabitants every morning was fantastic.

Nelson Street also divided the streets on religious lines, with Catholics at one end and Protestants at he other. This configuration occurred many years before, in the 1920's when because of Sectarianism, Protestant and Catholics exchanged houses.

Every Twelfth of July the Protestants would light a big bonfire on Nelson Street, between upper and lower New Dock Street.
To be honest, I don't remember any major conflict between religions, but knew well of the dangers. The stories about the murder of Catholics, in the early 1920's and how Catholics were thrown into the water at the Shipyard and being pelted with rivets as they swam for their lives, were never far from our thoughts.

In the back yard of every house in New Dock Street, facing each other, small doors had been set into the walls. These were so that Catholics could go up and down the street without being shot at. In the front wall of John Wards house was a furrow made by the track of a bullet. A man going up Garmoyle Street had to cross New Dock Street. John's house was the first in the Street and a man peeped around the corner and pulled his head back just in time.

On the gable walls of most houses on the Protestant side of Nelson Street, depicted, in full colour, was a painting of King Billy crossing the Boyne. On the painting at the corner of Fleet Street there was also a list of names, stating, 'THEIR ONLY

CRIME WAS LOYALTY'. I passed this painting every day and enquired what it meant. I was told, in the 1920's, England was 'rightly' accused on the world stage and especially in America, of not only allowing the murder of Catholics but actually participating in them. Eventually, the new Northern Ireland Government, who 'tongue in cheek' had condemned the murders, were forced to bring in policemen from the country, who were backed up by the military.

When a Protestant mob invaded the Catholic Streets of Sailortown, with flaming torches, intent on burning the Catholics out, the country policemen and soldiers levelled their rifles at them. The mob thought this was just for show and kept coming. Then, after three warnings and a volley of shots over their heads, which didn't deter them, the order was given - 'to shoot to kill'.

This was the only thing that stopped the slaughter of Catholics, and hence the list on the wall. Even as a young boy I was aware that the Belfast RUC was a wholly sectarian armed force. However, these killings put an end to the troubles of the 1920's. And as it turned out, most of the dead were Scotch-men. By the 1950's things had quietened down and discrimination instead of murders ruled the day.

My first experience of the RUC was, when aged just eight I was arrested and charged with trespassing on UTA - Ulster Transport Authority Property. What transpired was - myself, Chris and five other children followed a 'choo choo' train that crossed Duncrue Street, from the Docks into the UTA goods yard.

I remember like it was yesterday, standing in front of the fire station in Whitla Street and watching this monster of a train spitting smoke exit the Docks and enter the gate of the goods yard. Ignoring the traffic and the blaring horns we ran across Whitla Street and followed the train through the gates. Overawed, we walked behind it and touched it as it belched smoke and steam and followed it until it stopped.

When the train driver saw us he shouted to 'get the hell outter here', which we quickly did. We were returning along the tracks, between the rails jumping from sleeper to sleeper, when suddenly we were attacked by five or six very large RUC Men.

I was grabbed by the back of my neck and lifted off my feet. I couldn't breathe and was struggling, then the RUC man swung me against a red brick wall knocking me unconscious. Only since moving to Dublin twenty years ago and now aged 75, do I not have to quell the panic that rises when I see a policeman? To this day I still have nightmares about hitting that red brick wall. We were arrested and taken to York Street police station were we questioned about were we lived. They shouted at us-Protestant or Catholic end? When we answered 'Catholic' we were put in a cell and our parents sent for. We sat for hours in a filthy smelly cell that smelled of urine until our parents arrived. When I told my parents how I got the bloody nose and scrapped face - even though my friends confirmed what I said, I was told to forget about it or it would be worse for me.

That next night, I was taken back to York Street Police Station to be finger-printed. As it turned out, I was the only one aged over eight years of age {two days in fact} 'the so-called "age of reason" at which I was supposed to know the difference between 'Right and Wrong'.

I was charged and convicted in the children's court of trespassing, and fined Five Shillings. The judge laughed at the RUC man who gave evidence against me, he actually said I should be charged with trying to de-rail the train. I remember the frosty silence from my father, both before and after my appearance in court. He like the police actually blamed me.

I don't remember being beaten for the railway incident but the memories of being whipped on many other occasions are seared into my memory. Along with my two younger brothers, Chris and Harry, in mum and dad's room, we ran running around naked and screaming as our father lashed us with his thick leather belt. I remember vividly thinking, what's the use of running, there was no-where to run to as the door was locked and he had the key. So I stopped running and stood still. That lock figures large in my nightmares.

It was big and square with an old fashioned large key.
As I stood there absorbing the pain, my mother and older sister were banging on the door pleading with him to stop. Strangely, this was the only time he allowed us into the upstairs front room. On this occasion, whatever heinous crime we'd committed, he used the buckle end on us.
This resulted in a lump being lifted out of my neck.

Obviously, with me standing still, enraged him further - but seeing what the belt buckle had done, without missing a stroke he changed hands with the belt. {He was ambidextrous} and continued. He concentrated on me and whipped me with a vengeance. The blood flowed down my front and back and the pain and got worse - building until a red explosion happened inside my head.

When I came around I was in the back room, being attended to by my mother and sister, Peggy.
I could hear the other two sobbing in the bunk above my head. As mum washed my neck she said to tell the Teachers that I'd fell on the yard walls and cut my neck on the glass. This referred to the yard walls between the streets where the children played, and which we ran along like monkeys. In earlier times, to stop their homes being invaded, people had implanted broken bottles into cement, along the top of their walls. However, over the years they had been worn down to

stumps.

Between the beatings, we had a normal life. But after this one, the head-mistress of Earl Street School which we attended, Miss O'Bern, had me brought to her office. When I entered, Standing on table with his short trousers around his ankles was Chris. A large women and a small man were examining him. They turned to me.

The woman took the padding from my neck and examined the cut. The small man said: "that's infected". The big woman whose breasts blocked out the sun, wanted to know how I'd got the cut. I replied as I'd been told. "I fell on a yard wall', I said. "And hit a broken bottle". She looked at me disbelievingly.

"Nothings going to happen to you, so tell me the truth."
I said again, "I was playing on the yard walls a fell onto the glass." They expressed annoyance and the small man with the pointy nose, said:
"Who told you to say that".
Chris was about to say, 'My Mammy' but I got in first and said loudly
"Nobody"! Chris nodded and also said "nobody".
The big woman lifted me onto a chair, and I winced. She opened my shirt took down my short trousers, and gasped. The thin man counted the bruises and wrote the result in a notebook. They both angrily wanted to know who had done this to us. This frightened us and we started to cry. Miss O'Bern hugged us and dressed us and said to the big woman
'look how clean their underpants are'. They were very white in the sun.

The big woman assured us that we'd done nothing wrong and we were to tell the nice man what happened to us. I didn't thing he looked very nice, with his pointy nose and glasses with no legs on them. I repeated, "we were playing on the yard walls". The large woman hugged Chris and said to miss O'Bern, "we'll look into this".

Chris was my brother but was also my best friend. He never said very much and was always smiling, but he looked very sad, as was I because we didn't know what was happening. We obviously suspected that these were the 'Cruelty People', who took you away if you told tales.
We were sent back our classrooms and for me the day passed in a blur.

At one stage, my teacher, Miss Mulligan, asked me what was wrong and why I was scowling.
That afternoon when school got out, the boy's all charged onto Earl Street and down Garmoyle Street. The girls, with my older sister Peggy, with their skipping ropes, crossed the street into Dock Street. They played outside Fyffes Warehouse beside the Dock Gates where the Dockers gathered every morning. During the summer when we went to 8' O'Clock Mass, the old women would shout at them to 'get out of the way'.

The boys ran onto to the empty site at the corner of Dock Street. This was where we played every day, until they built a Garage. Eventually when hunger got the better of us, we headed home. We continued on down Garmoyle Street, past Fleet Street, Ship Street, Marine Street and turned into New Dock Street. Our house was half-way down on the right hand side, and parked outside it was a large black car. This was unusual.

We'd never before had seen a car in our street. Even the milkman and the baker had horse and carts.
With trepidation we approached the car and touched it, before entering our house. Seated at our table was the large women who'd undressed us. She was bouncing a baby on her knee, either John or Tilda. and sitting by the fire was the small pointy

nosed man with the funny glasses on. I wondered what kept them on.We both ran to our mum who hugged us. The big woman smiled and her face lit up. She looked really different.

She took from her pocket a bag of sweets, 'cough drops' she called them, and held out the bag to us. They were red and white and we took one each.

Mum took a big loaf from the bread bin and sawed off the end. When the doorstop fell, she turned the loaf around as sawed off the other end.

From the kitchen cabinet she took a large jar of strawberry jam - and reversing the big knife scooped the Jam onto the bread. With deft and well practised moves she spread the jam and handed them to us. "Now go out and play, I've got things to talk about".

We took the 'Jam Pieces' and left. The big woman was still smiling.

Puzzled,we walked up the street, eating, with our noses covered in Jam.

Chris asked, "who are they and what do they want". Shaking my head, I said, "I don't know but we're going to find out".

"How"? He asked.

"We'll hide in Billy Gault's hall until we see my Da go into the house, then we'll run down and listen". We hadn't long to wait. Soon our Da came down the street, looking at the car. As soon as he entered the house we ran down. No sooner had we arrived when we heard him shout, "Get out! Get the fuck out before I throw you out".

The big woman calmly replied: "If you put a hand on us or on either of your children again, you'll be jailed for Assault, which is what you deserve.

The funny wee man spoke and said, "We are officers of the Court and are on official business".

Our Da Shouted. "No one will tell me how to discipline my

children and especially not you do-gooders. Did you never hear of, "spare the rod and spoil the child".

The big woman spoke up. "Mr Murphy that is patent nonsense and is used by bullies, to excuse the beating of children.

However, you are entirely right in your assumption that it is not against the law, if - you claim that it is in the child's best interest, and-.

Angry and with venom he replied: "Why else would I do it"?

The wee man replied. "While we have limited powers to stop you, I presume know about, 'The National Society For The Protection Of Cruelty To Children, and our office in High Street.

Our Da shouted: "Get fucking out". This was unusual because he never cursed.

She replied. "We are going, but if it is ever again reported to us that these children have bruises on them, I will photograph them, and display your name and their photos in our Rogues Gallery, window".

The wee man spoke again. "Obviously you know about the photos outside our office, and everyone will know exactly what you're doing".

There was silence from inside. So we quickly moved and hid behind the car. We heard the sound of the inside door opening and banging shut.

As we peeped around the car we saw our Da storming up the street.

Big Bella Hasty, who lived across the street, called us over and brought us in. Bella was a good woman and was nice to us. Her house always smelled of 'toffee apples' that she would make for the kids of the street.

She only had one son, Jimmy, who was a great dribbler with a football often beating five or six of us at a time with a football.

His career as a professional footballer was severally inhibited when he started work in Jennymount Mill. Aged only 15, on his first morning he had his arm pulled off my a machine. Although he did play professionally for a few local clubs, he could've been the forerunner of George Best.

What's going on Bella asked? "Who owns the big car"? Before I could stop him, Chris replied. "It's the cruetly people". "Good, about time". She said. "Sit down there till they go". She poured two cups of Lucozade and gave them to us. We only ever got Lucozade in her house.

As we watched out the window, Susie Docherty and Colette McAtamaty, two friends of my sister Peggy skipped past with their ropes, both were looking at the car. Colette lived around the corner in Marine Street and Susie further up our street. Her brother Jimmy was a bit older than me.

The girls had cornered me the day before, and asked who was the best singer - Elvis Presley, or Tommy Steele? I had no idea who they were talking about and guessed - Elvis Presley. Susie cheered, but Colette threw up her arms in disgust and said, "what would you know" - and stormed off. I heard somewhere that Susie had become a Nun.

Collette's mum had died and left a young family, her dad Eddie Joe, called 'The Boson' came home from sea to look after them.

As they skipped away, the big woman and the wee man came out of our house. He got behind the wheel and started the engine, while she walked around and got in beside him. He could hardly see over the steering wheel. The car drove off and we ran over to our house. The smell of petrol was very strong in the street.

Mum had the John on her hip and a big frown on her face. She lay him down and on the settee and put a cushion in front of him. Very tenderly she examined the cut from the belt buckle on my neck, and asked,

"who's been looking at this"?

I replied, "The big women who was in here, but I told her what you said.

"That's good", she replied. "We don't want you da to go to Jail". This terrified me and Chris began to cry. Mum reassured him it wouldn't happen as long as we told nobody how we got hurt. That night we were wakened, by the sound of our da shouting and the smell of drink, which always accompanied the beatings. The three of us huddled together terrified, but nothing happened. After this the beatings stopped for a while but we were never again ordered to strip. This lessened the pain to our bodies but the belt raised lumps on our heads.

Earl Street School was over-crowded and in 1954 to relieve the pressure, an empty school down the Shore Road was obtained. We were told this was an ex Protestant School. It was situated at the corner of Bute Street facing a waste ground where they built the swimming pool a few years later. This was in a wholly Protestant area and obviously no-one in the Education Board had given any consideration thought as to how we were to get to and from the school.

The first day we arrived, we were greeted by a Mr McColgan, he was a white-haired gruff old man with many lines on his face. The school was large and freezing and he set us to work cleaning it up. He informed us it hadn't been unoccupied for thirty years. There were inches of dust on the floor with tiny mouse footprints everywhere.
Upon clearing out the cupboards we came upon a school register and jotters which were full of names and addresses of Catholic children.

I enquired of Mr McColgan - I thought this was a Protestant school. He sighed, and reluctantly replied - 'that the school we occupied had never been a Protestant School. The 'white lie' to hide the Truth was, so not to stoke sectarian hatred in us. The names in the register were of children who had been driven from their homes in surrounding areas. In many cases they were identified by their own grand-children.

With another large sigh he said, "the truth of the matter is that the school was built as a Catholic School.
It opened in 1897 and catered for boys and girls from the nearby streets. However, after the 1916 Rising in Dublin, antagonism towards Catholic's was fermented by wealthy Protestant Politicians and Leaders, both here and in England. They fostered discontent and bigotry among the poor, for their own financial benefit". None of the children had any idea what a 1916 Rising was, so he rather reluctantly informed us. Agog we sat around and listened as he related stories about the War of Independence which freed three quarters of the country and the Civil War after the signing of the Treaty.

"The wealthy Wealthy elite were afraid that if Revolution spread to the North, they would loose the life of privilege that their ilk had lost in the South, and which they wallowed in, all over the world".

All the boys questioned him at once. "What does 'ilk' mean and what did they wallow in", were the main ones. He gave us a potted history of the British Empire and how they used the Rich in every country they invaded to persecute their own people. They did this by foisting their religion and language upon the conquered- using the Elite to keep their own country-folk in subjection.

This tried and tested policy enabled the British to rule most of the known world and led to the fact that 'the sun never set on the British Empire. Several boys wanted to know, "why only three quarters of the country was freed".

He replied: "Because after they invaded Ireland in the 16th century they planted the country with English People.

He had to explain what

'Planted' meant, and continued. "Protestant People today are the descendants of the Planters who were given free land which was taken from the Irish People".

Half the boys said 'taken' and the other half said 'given.' McColgan said it was 'confiscated'. All the boy shouted, "what does that mean". With great reluctance he said, "all right stolen." The Butcher Cromwell coined a saying - "to hell or Connacht This meant to go to the far west of Ireland where the land was bad, or be killed here." He refused to answer who Cromwell was and why he was called a Butcher.

"look" he said. "When 1916 happened the descendants were going to lose everything so they kept the last part of the country were the Protestants were in a majority and partitioned the country with a border.

They only took the last quarter because the religion of the invaders was the largest here and they established the so-called country of Northern Ireland".

As the boys clamoured for answers he stated - "Look, I come from Banbridge which is Protestant area and we have to keep our heads down. In the past when any military action is taken like the murder of two RIC men - the well established tactic of the British, which they used the world over, is to slaughter the innocent - and for them the more innocent the better. This is why the McMahon family were slaughtered. Now if you want to know any more ask your parents they should be telling you all of this".

"Who are the McMahon family" all the boys shouted.

"Ask your parents" he retorted.

15

"But what about this school", asked one boy.

In exasperation he replied. "When Catholics were driven from their homes along the shore Road, the school fell into disuse. Look, an interesting fact about this terrible time is the fact, that it was not their Protestant neighbours who persecuted Catholics and drove them out or even the Orange Order Bigots - but a 'murder squad' of police directly controlled by the wealthy in the government. They in turn were controlled by the British government, who knew, unless they partitioned Ireland and made it look like a humanitarian gesture, then the British Empire was doomed".

None of us boys knew what this meant and he continued. "The murder squad was led by a District Inspector of the RIC named John Nixon who often participated in them. His reason for the Aron street killings was because a Constable Turner was shot dead. Although it seems from the downward angle of bullet that killed him, that he was actually shot from the roof of Brown Square Police Barracks. This was used as an excuse by Nixon and his cohorts to murder Catholics".

All the boys clamoured- "What were the Aron Street killings"? Clearly annoyed he replied, "Ask you parents. Another tactic of Nixon's was to shoot at the military from Catholic Areas to get them to retaliate.

However, when two Specials were shot dead by the IRA he machined gunned Catholic areas, smashed his way into their homes and shot dead the menfolk"

We were stunned into silence. "Who were the United Irishmen who my Grandad sings about and my Granny tells him to shut up" asked one boy.

Taking a deep breath McColgan answered. "That's going further back, they were a group of Irishmen, mostly Protestants who in 1798 wanted freedom from England and started a Rebellion. Now no more questions get to work and get this place cleaned up". With this he opened cupboards and starting pulling out papers.

We could only use the upstairs of the school as the bottom floor was flooded, and had to use a shaky fire escape to get to our classroom. At the start there were about sixty boys taught in a large room by McColgan.
There were sliding partitions which could be closed to make the room into three smaller ones. McColgan as the only teacher never used these, and divided us into three classes according to age. Myself and Chris were in different classes while Harry remained at Earl Street school.
In the winter the wind would blow up through the spaces between the floorboards. McGogan brought in a big roll of twine and a mallet and we spent a whole day hammering it into the cracks.

The attacks on us by the Protestant kids started in a small way, as we went up and down the Shore Road, then they increased in ferocity as the Marching Season approached. They were celebrating the victory of William of Orange's army, a Protestant Dutchman who became King of England. He defeated the army of James the first of England, a Catholic.
The attacks on us schoolchildren became a daily event. They even got brazen enough to attack us outside the school. When the people in Bute Street {all Protestants} objected, they'd waylay us on the Shore Road with several boys being bloodied.

Mr McGolgan told us about a Bridge that crossed the railway tracks and was a back way to our school, which led from Duncrue Street. We knew Duncrue Street well as we went up and down it every weekend on the way to the sea and our favourite playing fields at the Point, which jutted out into the sea. Years later I discovered that they were actually called 'The Point Fields'.

We checked out the Iron Bridge and discovered that McColgan was right.

This led into Milewater street which was a dead end because of the railway tracks. What we also discovered, was, that the path to the Iron Bridge actually continued on running between the railway tracks and Jennymount Mill, emerging into Jennymount Street. I looked at the only two houses remaining in the street and realised where I was. It was from one of them my Grandfather had escaped with his wife and two children, one of them my father - as a mob led by the RIC burned out Catholics. I had heard the story many times.

Every Saturday, we used to go to a Picture House on Duncairn Gardens, nick-named 'The Donkey'.
Then one day watching a Cowboy and Indian film, it occurred to us, that we could use the same tactics as the Indians. So the next day after Sunday after Mass the pupils got together and formed a battle plan.

The following day in class McColgan sensed something was up. He questioned several boys, trying to find out what was going on but all pleaded ignorance. At five to three McColgan said, "Right, wrap it up for today". As we left the grounds of the school the decoys gave their school bags to the others and went up Butte Street to the Shore Road. Here they knew they'd be ambushed. The rest hid in the two alleyways at the end of the street.

When the decoys reached the top of the street, they could see their would be attackers across the road on waste ground where the Grove Baths would later be built. Both groups threw stones at each other, then the Catholics feigned injury retreated. The ambushers charged after them and at the bottom of the street the ambushers were ambushed.

The full force of sixty yelling pupils from St Joseph's emerged from both alley ways and caught them in a pincer movement. Shocked, bloodied and demoralised they retreated back up the street. Mr McGolgan watched this from his window.

The attacks stopped after this, with just a few long-range catapult shots.From then on the Iron Bridge was a safe way to and from our school as it consisted only of offices, bus depots and no houses.
This bridge has since been replaced by a concrete structure that also spans the motorway into Belfast.
At home the beatings of myself and my two brothers continued but no marks were left. The lumps on our heads didn't show. My sister Peggy was preparing for the Eleven Plus. This was an exam which decided if you went to an elitist Grammar School or the ordinary Secondary School.

Peggy and one of her friends, were chosen by their Teacher from their class as capable of passing the test. This girl was from a mixed marriage and as discrimination was rife in everything, her name almost guaranteed she would pass. This is exactly what happened. Peggy was upset, especially as she had helped her friend with everything. Our Da ranted at the unfairness, but there was nothing could be done. Catholics knew to keep their heads down and their mouths shut.

The following year, when I was eleven I wanted to take it the exam.

However Mr McColgan ruled it out, saying, "We can't have one boy out of an entire school sitting the exam, what would that say about me? It's better if the whole school is put down as intellectually incapable, which they'll be delighted with. And anyway, your dad's a Docker and is getting more money than me, and you'll be a Docker too, so you don't need an education".

This was both true and untrue. I would've loved an education. That said, we were not 'poor', like many of my friends. We were always well fed and well clothed. Nothing fancy but we all had 'Sunday best' clothes which we wore for going to Mass. These were taken off and hung up as soon as we came home.

When I was about Ten my Da would go out shooting game with a Protestant friend he worked with. Through the influence of his friend with the Police, he applied for and got a gun licence, then bought a shotgun of his own. One Saturday he returned with four large rabbits and said they had to be 'hung' for a week then he'd skin them and we'd eat them.

However, after a few days the stink from them was unbelievable. My mum told me to take them and dump them in the Docks, which I did.
They didn't sink but floated away. There was a terrible row over this but he never lifted his hand to mum. Too afraid of Uncle Jackie who was a lorry driver and a massive size. Uncle Jackie had branched out on his own and would load and unload his lorry on his own. Compared to him, our Da was tiny in comparison.

After the summer holidays I attend St Patrick's Secondary School on the Antrim Road, with my friends. This had been built a few years before by the four Catholic Parishes in Belfast. The first few days were taken up by doing 'aptitude tests' which were designed to ascertain our level of education. The result decided which class we were allocated to and. I was separated from my friends. While Mr McColgan had a wide expanse of knowledge which he imparted to the class, sometimes with a well aimed hawthorn stick - what I was now being taught from a series of Teachers was fantastic.
However, what I was not prepared for was the ridicule from my peers.

The slagging I got because I was learning 'French' tore me apart. I couldn't handle this, and yearned again to be a 'part of the gang'. So I stopped doing homework and became non-attentive and disruptive in class. Very soon I was moved to my friends class, and in the following year we became unteachable. Many Teachers didn't even try. Two exceptions were 'Big Billy O'Neill' a History Teacher and Wee Harry Enright, the gym master. Wee Harry wanted the malcontent's {which we were named} to be taught the rudiments of a trade, something useful like bricklaying or plumbing, but he got nowhere.

He was often used a standin when some other teacher was off sick, or couldn't put up with the abuse from us. He had common sense and treated us with respect- and he got loads in return. Big Billy was also a great teacher, he believed that there was no such thing as a stupid child. He would fascinate us with the great events from world history, and on the days when we had him for the last period, we could be in class until five o'clock listening to him.

Our house in New Dock Street with only two bedrooms was overcrowded. My Da had applied to the Housing Trust, as it was then, for a new house. They had built houses in outlying areas like Rathcoole, which was a mixed area, and in Catholic areas like Turf Lodge, and Andersonstown. However, he never moved up the queue and he learned that 'new applicants' were being awarded houses in front of him. Then someone in the Pub one night advised him to give the local politician 'Gerry Fitt' a donation to his re-election fund. He came home and ranted about this, but in the end gave a large donation. This resulted in him being offered a four bedroom house in the estate of Andersonstown.

In those days when your family got smaller, you had to move to smaller accommodation. The family we replaced moved to a three bedroom house house, nearby. We moved on a very foggy night in the middle of winter, with our furniture stacked on top of Uncle Jackie's lorry. Myself, Chris, and Harry were perched on top, I can't remember where the others were but when we arrived in Corby Way, they were all present.

The people who'd vacated the house had taken all the light bulbs with them and we couldn't see a thing. Two neighbours lent us some light bulbs as the shops were all shut, and with great difficulty we eventually got moved in.

This was a cultural shift if ever there was one. Instead of going to school with our friends and neighbours, my brother Chris and I had to leave at half past seven, get two buses, one down the Glen Road and Falls Road and the other up the Antrim Road to arrive at St Patricks School for Nine O'Clock. This only lasted for one term, then, he was moved to a new Christian Brothers school that opened on the Glen Road.
It seems because I had only another term to go until I was 15, they didn't bother moving me. For the the last year at St Patrick's, they didn't even bother trying to educate us. Our class was used for emptying bins and brushing up.
Then planning permission was granted to extend the school out to the Somerton Road, which ran behind the school. So, we were used to clear the grounds out the back. This was to facilitate the chopping down of dozens of very large trees to accommodate the building of new classrooms. Armed with hatchets, crowbars and saws we'd a great time clearing the land.

However, every day a group of a dozen or so pupils from the Protestant School further down the Somerton Road, would cycle past shouting nasty sectarian abuse. I was able to stop any retaliation by saying 'just smile and wave at them'. Then one day digging out a large root, I struck myself on the ankle with a crowbar and could 4of4 hardly walk, so had to take the next day off.

When I limped back to school the following day, my class weren't working out the back so I went in search of them. Not able to find them I went to the office and enquired where they were. The secretary informed me, that they had attacked the Protestant school boys and they had all been expelled. I was shocked and enquired what I was to do. She got on the phone to the headmaster, Willie John Steele, and I was sent into his office.

He told me "that my class had assaulted the Protestant schoolboys and smashed up their bicycles. He wanted the other headmaster to press charges, as he had the names of all those involved, but his counterpart didn't want to make an issue of it".

So I asked, what was I to do, as I couldn't do the work out the back myself? He replied, "As its only a few weeks until the summer break, I should just stay away, as I was leaving anyway. To which I readily agreed. However, I added that I didn't want it recorded that I had been expelled with the class. He agreed, and said he'd put a note to this effect in the file on the matter. We then shook hands and he wished me well, saying "I suppose you're going to become a Docker" to which I agreed.

This was a complete about turn from his last encounter with me. On that occasion he had leapt from the assembly hall stage with his black gown splayed out behind him and swiping at me with his leather strap.

What led to his unseemly behaviour was, during morning prayers, one of my friends had undone the straps ties, holding the floor to ceiling curtains together and wrapped them around me. I shouted and fought my way out of the gathered curtains. When I eventually did so, Willie John looked at me from the stage- and said, "Murphy, I might've know. I believe you've moved up to Andersonstown, how much coal does you bath hold". This caused great laughter from the assembled pupils. So, I stood on a chair and held up my arms, and said: "Willie John - as an educated man, you should know - that it holds exactly the same amount as your own". At this the laughter doubled, and Willie John became airborne.

With his gown spread out behind him he looked every bit like a swooping Vulture. So I beat a hasty retreat.

That day in the summer of 1962 aged 15, I left St Patrick's School for Boy's on the Antrim Road in Belfast for the last time. This was a Friday. The following Monday I started work at the Docks as a non-union man.

I was big for my age - not that anyone cared. The standard practice for 'schoolboys' working at the Docks, of which there were plenty, was, if you did a man's work you're entitled to a man's wages. For years, when carrying bottles of tea to my father, on a Sunday, I watched the Dockers as they discharged, deep sea, cargo from ships, and knew well the rudiments of Manuel Labour. Weekend work was particularly lucrative, as Saturday afternoon and all day Sunday was paid at double time and double tonnage. I was quickly issued with my Insurance Cards, as without them I couldn't be paid. Because the Casual System was in vogue we carried our own 'cards' and the first employer we worked for in any given week stamped your card.

Years later on the week for my 18 birthday a sticker on my cards said: 'change to adult rate here'. For my first year working at the Docks I was 'schooled' at Dock Street corner. Schooled, was the term used when a foreman employed you by putting a small piece of metal or plastic-like material, called 'checks' into your hand. The Head-Line had their own specific 'checks' made of White Bakelite, the forerunner of today's Plastic, with the name - Head Line in black writing on them.

When a foreman had a money-making job at 'bag stuff' - which was either ground up Soya Beans, Lucas bean meal, or Fish-meal, which was ground up fish and stank to the high heaven, pandemonium was assured. This entailed much pushing and shoving to get the foreman's attention.

This spectacle, took place at eight of clock every morning. The heaving mass of hundreds of Dockers blocked traffic and impacted on the progress of people attending Mass. St Joseph's Chapel, was further down Dock Street and sandwiched between two flour mills. The Faithful had to negotiate through the pushing, shoving and swearing Dockers.

However, it got so bad that the Catholic Church intervened. After negotiation with the Harbour Commissioners an agreement was reached to erect a purpose built shed on Dufferin Road - inside the Dock Gates where the Dockers would be employed. A Docker, Johnny McAdorey , from New Dock Street, seeing it for the first time remarked it looks like a cow pen.

The name stuck and thereafter after it was known, as "The Pen". This had a raised platform on three sides, behind a crash barrier for the Foremen to stand on. This civilising of the employment Dockers removed it from the public's gaze. However, that said, with the foremen raised above the Dockers, there was now no reason for pushing or shoving as he could see everyone.

This was in the days of Manual Labour, when 'Bag stuff' had to be heaved out of the holds of ships on ropes, landed on large hand-trucks, and wheeled into Storage Sheds.

There it was man-handled into stacks which were called Piles. The speed and precision at which this hard work was carried out was unbelievable. Belfast was renowned the world over for having the fastest 'turn around' of Ships. Manual Labour ruled the day.

When aged sixteen, I was allowed to join the union. This was the ITGWU and the committee sat in front of a James Connolly Banner. On the way home I asked my Da why James Connolly and Jim Larkin's Socialism was not practised at the Docks. And he replied, "never mind about all that stuff just do your work and keep your mouth shut".

Naturally I was intrigued but he refused to elaborate. Unbeknown to him, I had formed my own opinions as to why these great men's principles were not being acted upon. At school we had a Teacher who swore us to secrecy over what he taught us - because it was not on the curriculum.

It was unbelievable to us, Belfast schoolboys, who'd grown up with the stories of sectarian murders that Larkin had united Catholic and Protestant in his famous 1907 strike. Our class was fully versed on 1913, Jim Larkin, the Dublin Lockout and the trials and tribulations of the Irish Poor.

We were also up to date on Larkin arriving in Belfast as organiser for the English based NUDL to Unionise the casually employed Dockers and Carters.

And he even got Constable Barret to threaten strike action by the police, because they were being used to protect imported strike-breakers?

However the Bigoted Unionist authorities to destroy this outbreak of solidarity between religions, stationed British Soldiers on the Falls Road to provoke Catholics tensions. This succeeded - and during rioting two people were shot dead and many others received gunshot wounds.

Larkin was on the Falls Road during the shootings and denounced the army, "who were only here because of a Strike in another part of Belfast".

The pro Unionist newspapers proclaimed that Larkin was not here because of trade unionism, but was, "part of a conspiracy against the Unionist cause in Ireland."
Sectarianism resumed and over Larkin's head the leader of the NUDL, James Sexton, bowed to pressure from the Northern Ireland Employers to agree a settlement. However, this was along sectarian lines and broke 'Larkin's Strike'.

The carters and coal fillers got wage rises while the Dockers got nothing - and had to apologise for causing the strike if they wanted to work again. The main plank of Larkin's demands was rubbished. The Employers got their way and they were entitled to employ non-union labour. As school children we were fascinated by the fact that Protestant and Catholic workers could shelve their differences and work together. This was the first time we realised that the British and Irish Wealthy used Sectarianism as their main plank of Repression - which resulted in low wages and no working conditions.

While defeated in Belfast Larkin went on to found other branches of the NUDL in Ireland. And when in Derry in 1908 he heard that the Dublin carters were on strike and needed him, so he gladly went. However, Sexton and the NUDL's National Executive wanted nothing to do with the Dublin strike - and when he ignored them - he was dismissed from the NUDL.

Then Larkin, with James Connolly, William O'Brian and others - in 1913 founded the Irish Transport & General Workers Union. This was based in Dublin and obviously had a large Catholic membership. However the Belfast Low Dockers remined true to Larkin, they left the NUDL and joined the new Union. With no clout and with no support from other Union's who were antagonistic towards it, the Union was on its own and had to comply with whatever the Belfast Employers wanted. This situation prevailed for years and in the end got worse.

CHAPTER TWO

In the North of Ireland after Ireland was divided - Catholics were murdered and driven from their homes. This is an accepted fact that was inspired by the politics of the British Government and fermented by the wealthy. The bitterness towards Catholics is 'touched upon' and documented in the Oscar winning film, 'BELFAST' by Kenneth Branagh.

This shows a Protestant father, in 1969, working in England, returning home, and taking his family from Mountcollyer Street - to escape the state inspired bitterness. Kenneth, at a very young age witnessed his Catholic neighbours being driven from their homes.

In this instance, in the late 1960's and early 1970's. Hired Thugs {not their neighbours} were driving Catholics out because of the success of the Civil Rights Movement. Obviously Kenneth, was too young to know anything about this? The wealthy ruling class could see that this was the thin end of the wedge, and their very way of life was under threat. First and foremost was the 'Religious Discrimination they engendered'. If they couldn't play one side off against the other, while paying them both low wages, Democracy would put manners on them. Obviously Kenneth Branagh researched the history of Mountcollyer Street and like a good dramatist doesn't want to put all his eggs in one basket? There is a lot more to this story than the simplistic one he has portrayed.

While this was obviously an emotional time for young Branagh when he experienced his Oscar winning Trauma - as an adult film-maker he knows it did not start in 1969. The proof that it was 'not' their Protestant neighbours who drove Catholics out of Mountcoyller Street, is proven by the fact that they were there in the first place. Catholic families obviously returned to live in the Street after - being driven out fifty years previously.
No doubt he is saving the earlier evictions from his street and the murder of Catholics - for the Prequel and the Pre - Prequel? These will obviously garner Branagh a lot more that one Oscar. No doubt these future films will cause influential Human Rights People in the world and especially in in Britain to question the British Policy of World Domination - and their barbaric tactics?

The murders and evictions employed in Mountcollyer Street and greater Belfast, and ' *not*' witnessed by the young Branagh or portrayed in his film, was just a continuation of Cromwell's tactics. Hopefully his 'follow up films will expose, where and how Great Britain became Great. The innocent peoples of the world were enslaved and had their blood spilled, to make it 'Great'. Actually that could be the title for the next film - GREAT BRITAIN with a question mark. While Kenneth's Oscar winning film pulled emotional heart-strings the reasons for the evictions and the Truth behind the Truths are not shown.

No doubt the British Establishment and lovers of Shakespeare, are very glad of this 'oversight'? Any time the Ruling Gentry felt threatened - as they did in the 1920's they played the Orange Card and used the likes of Nixon and later day bigots - to murder Catholics and drive them from their homes. At the time when our school was vacated Catholics were driven from

' *Mountcollyer Street*', Jennymount Street, Milewater Street, Shore Street, Weaver Street and North Derby Street. This was an attempt to bring about the diktat of James Craig - of a Protestant Parliament for a Protestant People. Westminster turned a blind eye to their methods of achieving this.

Terrible examples of the slaughter happened when Nixon and 'The Special Constabulary' led rioting mobs, shooting and looting through the Sailortown district of Belfast, burning out Catholics. In North Thomas Street, on June 11th 1921, a baby, Terence Murphy was shot dead in the arms of his mother. Kenneth Branagh could hardly make these horrible events more dramatic?

'The Irish News' on June 14**th 1921** reported, "Following terrible happenings in the Dock Street and North Thomas Street area on Sunday night, portions of the district presented a scene of desolation.
Catholics families living in isolated parts of the district where they were particularly at the mercy of the unionist mob were so terror stricken that they rose and fled their houses. The houses which they left are now derelict wrecks and their furniture and other belongings have been smashed to matchwood or carried away. The Streets most affected, are Nelson Street, Earl Street, North Thomas Street, Dock Lane and Quinn's place. In the Streets and narrow lane-ways scarcely a Catholic family
has been left, and it is doubtful if they will ever be permitted to return.

Patrick Milligan and Joseph Millar, both twenty four years old and both living in Dock Lane were murdered on the Saturday evening. Their wives claimed the assassins wore the uniforms of the Special Constabulary.

While the murders of these two young men were shocking,

what happened to Millar's famiy must rate as a war crime. During a sectarian attack on their street, Sarah Millar, the sister of Joseph, was blinded by splinters from a bomb. The same bomb blew of the hand of William Kane, an Uncle of Sarah and Joseph. Another sister was shot in the thigh. The figures for June were, 26 killed, 140 wounded and 216 Catholic homes destroyed.

On July 10th fifteen people were killed and 56 put into hospital. These terrible murders continued unabated, and while there were undoubted bigots among the murderers - the fact that The Rioters opened fire on Police who were sent to protect Catholic workers, entering and leaving Gallaher's tobacco factory - shows that they weren't local. There is no way Protestant gunmen from Belfast would fire upon Protestant Policemen, their friends and neighbours.

Rioting continued throughout the summer, and in August 23 people died and 165 were wounded, and during October while no-one was killed 56 people received gunshot or bomb wounds. Then, in November, women in offices at the Docks had to climb walls a scramble over roofs to escape from snipers. In an incident that would bring 'Tears from a stone', the mother of the murdered Joseph Millar, Margaret, was wounded, she died the next day. She was just one of 15 people to die that day, while 83 were seriously wounded. Rioting continued and saw the year out, with 7 killed and 23 injured in Ballymacarret.

The total for the year was 130 killed and 639 wounded.
Hopefully, Kenneth Branagh {now that he recognises that he is also Irish} will embark upon making films that show the truth - and the catastrophic 'real drama' behind the claims that 'Great Britain' civilised the world. And while not wanting to live in the past { he started it with his whitewash} the past cannot be ignored. Surely Branagh, a dramatist, who has travelled

far from his roots in Mountcoyller Street, cannot allow the - orchestrated
sentimentally in his film to override the Truth.

As a Belfast man he knows - that he has just scraped the surface of suffering from Mountcoyller Street, the Shore Road, Sailortown and greater Belfast. From the facts of Kenneth's research and the softly softly approach of his film - the next ones will be blockbusters.

He recognises that the vicious sectarian hatred engendered towards Catholics, was inspired by the British Government - and fermented by the 'well heeled' to keep them Financial Secure.

The Wealthy factory and business owners did not condemn the murders and bombing of Catholics - but actively encouraged them to keep down wages and living conditions. The Bigots done this overtly, but the Employers and Politicians did it by simply being members of the Despotic Orange Orders and marching with them.

By allowing Sectarian Murders and with the partitioning of Ireland - when the British Government set up the Northern Ireland State, in 1922 Both had a lot to gain. Britain stopped for a while, the disintegration of their Empire and Wealthy Protestants got the Protestant State established.

The following facts which Kenneth's research will have turned up are harrowing and deserve to be recorded on film. On February 13th 1922 a bomb thrown at children playing in Weaver Street killed two and wounded 18 others. Four more were to die later in hospital. That same night Paddy Lambe, the owner of a pub, The Blacksmith Arms, at the corner of Trafalgar Street, who had a wife and six children, was shot dead. And on the day of his funeral shots were fired at the hearse.

In May, the driving out of Catholics from Mountcollyer Street, and other streets along the shore road began. These included, Shore Street, Milewater Street, Weaver Street, North Derby Street and Jennymount Street. One Hundred and forty eight families including my own Grandfather and Grandmother, my father, and my Uncle Mark, were driven from their homes. The fact that Catholics in later years, were prepared to move back into streets they were driven out of, proves that they knew it was not their neighbours doing, but was the actions of paid imported Thugs. Instead of stopping these terrible events - the Police and 'The Specials', often led them.

The terrified people fled to wholly Catholic areas - although in these areas they were also not safe from Nixon and his murder gangs. In what became known as 'The Arnon Street Massacre', on 1st April 1922 after RIC Constable George Turner was shot dead - a murder squad drove to the Catholic Carrick Hill area. In Stanope Street an armoured car riddled the houses and the Police broke down a front door with a sledgehammer.

Inside the house they found Joseph McCRory and shot him dead. When they broke into more houses they could not find any men to shoot.

However, upon breaking into a house in Park Street, No 26 they found Bernard McKenna, the father of seven children and shot him eight times.

The murder gang continued searching for men to shoot and at No 16 Aron Street found William Spallin, who that very day had buried his wife, who had been murdered as well. William Spallin was 70 years old and was in bed with his grandchild and was shot dead.
At No 12 lived the Walsh family. Joseph Walsh was in bed with his son Michael, 7 and his daughter Brigid aged 2. They opened

fire on them all, Michael was shot a number of times and died a short time later. Brigid survived. Joseph was dragged downstairs and his head smashed in with a sledgehammer. Frank Walsh 14 was shot but survived, as did Joseph Walsh's brother who had hidden outside with two other children. The names of the members of this murder gang, and indeed all the murderers was well known but they continued with impunity.

Just a few months later, in July, after the killing in Millfield of two Specials, Nixon raked the area with machine guns and rampaged through the houses killing any local men they could find. The tally for that night was fourteen dead. However Nixon didn't only shoot male Catholics. Many independent eyewitnesses testified that he shot at women as and children as well. On the Crumlin Road he shot dead a girl named Skillen who was aged just four and in Upper Library Street shot dead a baby boy who was in the arms of his sister. Another member of this murder squad Head Constable Giff, was particularly sadistic. Before killing his victims he would use his bayonet on them, mocking the injuries of Christ's hands and feet, on the cross.

On the night September 26th 1920 two murder gangs under the command of County Inspector Harrison left Springfield Road Barracks.

They first burst into the home of Edward Trodden on the Falls Road and murdered him.
The other smashed their way into James Gaynor house and murdered him in his bedroom. Before leaving Giff mutilated the body with his bayonet and beat the dead man's mother. Again the names of the murders are well known and have went down in History.

On Saturday 12 June 1921 Nixon ordered that the driver of an armoured Patrol Car be replaced by Constable Glass and

Sergeant Clarke. With Nixon on board they picked up a murder gang and drove to 28 Cardigan Drive, the home of Alexander McBride. Mr McBride dressed in his nightshirt was taken to the fields at Ligoniel and gunned down. After murdering McBride Nixon and his murder gang went to the home of Malachy Halfpenny.

After battering down the front door they dragged him from his bed and took him to the armoured car. He was beaten with rifle butts and Giff stabbed his feet with his bayonet. When the vehicle came to a stop they dragged him out and riddled him with bullets, shooting him seventeen times. Besides stabbing Halfpenny's feet Giff had used the bayonet to rip out his testicles. Two of this murder squad, Sergeant Clarke and Sergeant Clover were killed by the IRA. The remainder continued to kill Catholics.

On 23rd April 1921, the day after the IRA had killed two Auxiliary Policemen men, the British Counter Insurgency tactics to slaughter civilians swung into action. A murder gang led by Nixon and Harris went to 64 Clonard Gardens, the home of the Duffin family. Here they murdered two brothers, Patrick and Daniel.
However, when they had left the nearby Springfield road barrack they had been followed by the station dog. After the killings they left by the back door leaving the dog inside - and realised this upon returning to the station. Nixon returned to the murder house to get the dog and was seen by numerous eye witnesses.

These atrocities were paid for by the Wealthy, who saw the success of the Rebels in the South of Ireland, as a threat to themselves. Even members, of the newly formed RUC which was a Protestant Police Force, were not safe. If even seen talking to a Catholic you were a target.

A Constable O'Rourke was talking to a the Catholic Curate, of St Joseph's Church - Fr. James McGrath and two other people in Garmoyle Street, when a bomb was thrown into their midst. It only partially exploded sending shrapnel into the Priests leg. Had they all been killed this would have been blamed on the IRA.

Then on 24th March 1922, One of the worst sectarian episodes of wanton murder occurred. Owen McMahon and his three sons and a man who worked for him were murdered in their home at Kinnaird Terrace on the Antrim Road.Two other sons survived their injuries. The murderers collected the womenfolk and put them in a back room then dragged the men at gunpoint downstairs. When they had collected all the men - they were told to pray for their souls and then shot dead.

However the shots aimed at the youngest boy, Thomas, missed and he ran screaming all around the room. More shots were fired at him but also missed and he escaped the room. The murderers fled the scene. Young Thomas was found later hiding under a sofa.

The gunmen who carried out this terrible deed were continuing the activities of the British Empire when it conquered the world. This policy of genocide which was intended to quash any semblance of resistance from a native people - was particularly effective when the most innocent were slaughtered? There was a massive Funeral for the McMahon family and a similar one for the other murder victim Edward McKinney from Buncrana in Co. Donegal. This County is one of the three that the Unionist Government wouldn't take because there were too many Catholics in it.

Because of the bad press that the British Government was getting, especially in America over the murders in Belfast, it set out on a face-saving exercise. It replaced the R.I.C. with a supposed new police-force named the R.U.C.However the A, B, and C specials were retained and unbelievably the leaders of the murder squads Nixon and Harrison kept their senior positions in the "new force".

Tensions simmered for a while, then, when Catholics wanted to book the Ulster Hall for an exhibition on Catholic Missionaries, all hell broke loose.

Reverent Hanna, or Roaring Hanna, the predecessor of Ian Paisley with the support of the Ulster Protestant League, a militant protestant organisation began rabble rousing. At a meeting in the Ulster Hall he advised his audience to, 'get to work and stop the hiring of the Hall to Catholics'. While his sidekick in bigotry a Mrs. Harnett, suggested that young men should get training in shooting. "Let us stir up feeling" she said. "These Six Counties of ours are about the only Protestant stronghold in the British Empire". On the way home from this meeting a gang attacked houses in Dock Street.

Many Protestant Leaders, including the Dean of Belfast condemned these actions. While these terrible events happened one hundred years ago, they are brought to the present day, every year on the 12th of July.

On this date hundreds of thousands of Protestants in the Orange Order parade all over the gerrymandered 'six counties' of Ulster. Because of the Irish Diaspora world-wide the names of the murderers were well known and moves were afoot by the British Government to get them out of the RUC. Nixon and the other known murderers were asked to resign.

They all refused. Nixon was offered a similar job to his own, with the Canadian Police but refused it. So he was suspended. On 28 Febuary Nixon was sacked but with a full pension as were his cohorts.

The Orangemen celebrate the victory of William of Orange in 1690 on the twelfth of July.
He defeated the Catholic King James outside Drogheda. This happened at the river Boyne in Ireland. Personally, like many others, I believe, if that's what they want to do, let them do it as long as they don't hurt anyone.

Unfortunately this celebrating has led to drunken bonfires on the 'Eleventh Night', where effigies of the Pope and the Irish Flag are ceremoniously burned. While the Orange-men parade through their respective cities and towns, shenanigans often occur outside Catholic Churches. The irony of this is lost on the Bigots. The Protestant Religion broke away from Catholic Church so they could have tolerance in Religious Practice, and their behaviour belittles all involved. The yobs dancing around in a circle don't realise, this is a perfect metaphor for themselves.

Often Orange Order bands take buses to Catholic areas, like Ardoyne, and the Garvarky Road in Portadown, so they can march through Catholic areas. That said, however, the orange parades are a large Tourist Attraction which the Orange Order are delighted with. Even if the British tourists are mystified, never having heard of King Billy, or the Battle of the Boyne. On one occasion an Englishman was threatened with extreme violence when he suggested that they 'were living in the past'. One slightly drunken bystander proclaimed "but its our British Culture".

What many Protestants don't realise, is that while the Catholic Church was once a powerful force in Ireland, the recent scandals have reduced it to something of a Joke. Only the very old at deaths door bother to go to Mass. Very few Catholics believe in it any more - and the thought that you could burn in Hell for all eternity for not going to Mass, has become ridiculous. The term Catholic, has largely lost its meaning - and simply means, that they are not Protestant in their thinking. I.e. - that they don't look to England or Great Britain as the Motherland? However, quite recently with Brexit, Protestants are seeing that the British government doesn't care about them - except maybe to complain about the Billions of pounds they're costing the exchequer every year.

It seems that ordinary British People, over the centuries having been exposed to different Peoples and different Cultures have overcome their "White and us are Right attitude" - but not so the upper echelons of the British Government. They want to hold onto the first and last remnant of Their Empire. This is where the Unionist Leaders get their false superior attitude from.

No doubt if Kenneth Branagh reads this, he will, like many other civilised people in England, ask "where were the Police when these attacks in Mountcollyer Street and other places were taking place"?

They were as usual, leading the Sectarian mob. This sectarian behaviour has continued to this day and why they attacked the peaceful Civil Rights Marches in 1969. This has been verified by numerous TV recordings of Marches, especially in Belfast and Derry and shows them being attacked by the RUC. While this behaviour became public
knowledge, their treatment of individual women they arrested was scandalous. Anyone doubting this should read the book by Catholic Priests, Fr. Denis Faul and Fr. Raymond Murray, published in 1978 named - THE CASTLEREAGH FILE which shows RUC brutality in 1976 to 1977. The pages 137 to 147 are particularly repulsive, because they show the arrest and interrogation of women and children. Also of interest will be a book by the Belfast, Central Citizens Defence Committee

printed 1973, named "THE BLACK PAPER, THE STORY OF THE POLICE". For anyone wishing to see how a Sectarian Police Force works and how 'not' to police your people this is fundamental reading.

Fulsome praise must go to Joe Baker an ex Sailortown man - who produced a booklet entitled THE McMAHON FAMILY MURDERS to remember the terrible deeds inflicted on the Catholics with the founding of the Northern Ireland State in 1922. My only quibble is.- why Joe stopped his exposure of collusion and murder by the State, in 1922.

Seeing that Ken Branagh was so affected at one neighbour being evicted, surely he will be shocked at murders and the truth in these publications. Hopefully the 'World Wide' cinematic and theatre going public can look forward to a lot more Truthful Drama from Kenneth's locally of Mountcollyer Street and the Shore Road. If he decides to follow the route of truth and justice - he'll discover that Belfast'has a terrible past that deserves to be exposed. When these 'Truths' are shown on the big screen. Many more Oscars await him.

By the late 1960's Catholics led by enlightened Protestants wanted an end to the Apartheid System that existed in the manufactured false entity of Northern Ireland. This prevailed in Employment, Housing - and in the
'gerrymandered' voting system. Where instead of one man having one vote, a Protestant business men could have up to fifty. The Civil Rights Movement had distinct shades of the 'United Irishmen', who wanted Catholic, Protestant and dissenter to be to control their own affairs. Both, wanted everyone, no-matter what religion they were, to be treated equally no matter what religion they were - and their aims were to be entirely peaceful. Unlike the United Irishmen who believed only armed rebellion would would succeed in having the British leave these shores.

Things came to a head for the civil rights movement, when a single Protestant mother was deemed to be more in need of a house, than a Catholic family of ten children, and the rest is History.

Alongside all this our progressive history teacher informed us, that the Irish TUC and the Congress of Trade Unions had come together to form, The Irish Congress of Trade Unions. This was an attempt to abolish sectarianism in the workplace, however, because Protestant Unions in Belfast were antagonistic to Irish Unions in general, they would not affiliate with the ICTU. They still held to the dictum of, "A protestant Parliament for a Protestant People - which they actually had. However, under pressure from their head offices in Britain who were opposed to discrimination in the work-place - a compromise was reached. Which was - that, in Belfast they established a Northern Ireland Committee of ICTU, which the Protestant Unions and ITGWU in Belfast joined. This was just window-dressing and capitulation on behalf of ITGWU because they never had a say in Trade Union affairs, for the simple reason they weren't wanted and had no clout.

Because of the heavy handed tactics of the police in Belfast and Derry, plus the filmed and televised beatings of civil rights marchers, which led to the in the 'Battle of the Bogside' which culminated in victory for the people of Derry. This saw British soldiers appearing on the streets of the North. Initially, they were seen as protectors of Catholics from the murderous and sectarian RUC. However, this didn't last long. The Wealthy, worried that British soldiers were supporting the demise of 'The Union' convinced Whitehall to take a more vigorous approach to protecting the northern state. This brutality sparked off the 'Troubles'.

Belfast is regulated on religious lines and because of the murderous activities of loyalist paramilitaries, which led to

'The 'Shankill Butchers' who literally roamed Catholic areas kidnapped individuals and Butchered them. {See the book by a Journalist on same} In working class areas large so called 'Peace Walls' were built to divide the Catholic and Protestant communities. However in more affluent areas like the Malone Road, wealthy Protestants have no problem living alongside their equally wealthy Catholic neighbours.

Some years ago in a cafe in Belfast I encountered an American woman, and her husband. When she lowered her voice we chatted over coffee. I asked her husband 'were they here searching for their roots'. She replied, pointed, and proudly proclaimed "he has Irish ancestry but "I am pure British and proud of it". She launched into an appraisal of how good Britain was for the world, not least for the English Language which was universally spoken" I smiled at this and would have said nothing, but when she paused for breath she asked "what was I smirking at"?

I smiled again and replied, "I wasn't smirking I was smiling at your grandiose description of how far the English Language has reached. As far as I know it is only spoken on Earth". Her husband laughed and she silenced him with a withering look. Taking a deep breath she fastened the same look onto me, and said: "It's a figure of speech and you can't deny that we "British, civilised the known world".

Again I smiled, not wanting to antagonise the woman but answered.

"Pardon me but you have just made two glaring contradictions."

Drawing herself up to her full height glared at me, which was scary, and hissed. "Just what are the contradictions".

"Well first and foremost I'm sorry to disillusion but - you cannot civilise the Peoples of the World by enslaving them - and - be Pure British as there is no such thing?

White in the face and almost apoplectic with silent rage she lowered her voice and spoke with deliberation. " I am pure

British I can trace my family back for generations. My great, great grandfather was a General in the British Army at the time of the Boston Tea Party ".

"That may indeed be the case but there is no such thing as Pure British you are"-

Interrupting me he fixed her blue eyes on me. "I don't just claim it I am!".

"Look" I calmly said, "With no disrespect to you or the ordinary British People, but you and they are an amalgamation of various Saxon - I.e German Tribes - the Angles, the Jutes and the Saxons. The name of England comes from Angle-land, which was a portion of the land they

invaded and named after themselves. In shock with her head shaking she remained quiet, so I containued. "in the third century after the Romans left, The German tribes and their descendants fought with each other and the Vikings - until in 1066 when William the Conqueror invaded England. He was the French King and defeated Harold's army at Hastings. However, what must be noted, is that the French People are also descended from the Angle-Saxons so you can see - there is no such thing as Pure British. One way or another, either down the French or the English line you are descended from the German People?

Shocked the woman stuttered. "You you you're making that up."

"It's History" I replied "look it up".

They both frantically tapped their smart phones and while reading, the husband smiled broadly and replied. "You're right!". In the dictionary it says just that. England was in invaded by the Angles, the Saxon's and the Jutes".

Unable to hide my smile, I asked. "I wonder what happened to the Jutes".

Like a pricked balloon the woman shrank in her chair. "I'm German" she said".

Smiling the husband said: "Where we come from in the States, pure British is worn as a badge of honour".

She pointed at her husband and hissed. "Don't you breathe a word of this back home".

The husband placed his forefinger under his nose gave the Hitler salute and said: "Ya Vole mine Furether". We both laughed as his wife stormed off.
While the barbarity of Britannia ruling the waves and the slaughter and murder of indigenous people the world over - has been well documented
- the activities of the "Mother of Parliaments" in Ireland has been treated as troublesome housekeeping. Since the atrocities of Oliver Cromwell to more recent times this has been the case. However with the apology from the British Prime Minister over the murders in Derry on 'Bloody Sunday' *{the most recent Bloody Sunday}* not the Croke Park one - things are beginning to change.

In every country Britain invaded, murder and brutality was their calling card. They planted Colonialists to oversee their despotic rule and encouraged the Wealthy they had conquered to run it for them. They did this by allowing them to keep their lands. Hence the wealthy few controlled their country for them, paid homage, allowed their country to be stripped of natural resources and supplied soldiers for the continuation of their maniacal desire to rule the world.

Cromwell's brutal conquest of Ireland paved the way for the more recent atrocities by them. In one instance of many, Cromwell took deadly retribution against the people of Drogheda who opposed him and slaughtered men, women and children for opposing him.

These are historical facts which can't be denied - but are being ignored.

Today in Ireland their has arisen a class of intellectuals

who deny History. These detractors of the Truth are led by Professor Diramid Ferriter, professor of modern history at UCD. University Collage Dublin., In this instance he and his followers are corrupting 'Irish History'.

CHAPTER THREE

On the night I got into the union in1962 - there were four Dockers 'up before the committee', for what I have no idea, but they were all fined Ten Pounds, which in 1962 was a large amount of money. I inquired from my father what they were being fined for. He didn't know what the others were fined for, but one man, Jimmy Walls was fined ten Pounds for working elsewhere than the Docks. As I was to learn the 10 pound was standard practice and the least that the Union fined anyone, but with Jimmy's case there was a twist. Several years before he had 'sloped' this was the term used - when Dockers would take the good money making bag work from a ship, and move on to another money-making job.

I was confused because this was standard practice that my father, along with his friends, 'sloped' several times a week. This left non-union men used to finish what had become a 'Time Job'. He explained, that Jimmy had done this on a Monday, which was not allowed. He explained that the Employers had pressurised the committee to make a rule - that, if you worked on a Sunday you must return to that ship on Monday. And because Jimmy sloped, the Union claimed the money he earned working until eleven o'clock on the Saturday and Sunday Night.

I was shocked and began to wonder was getting into the Union such a good idea? I enquired of my father, 'so why was Jimmy not fined ten pounds like the others, instead of having his wages taken'? He shrugged, saying: "It looks like they were using him to teach everyone else a lesson and anyway, he didn't slope, he didn't go to work on Monday because he'd nobody to mine his kids. His pregnant wife was rushed to hospital in the middle of the night, but the Union maintained that he still should have gone back to his Job. I was astounded at the unfeeling of the Union.

He added, "Jimmy even got a letter from the Royal Victoria Hospital confirming that his wife was admitted in the middle of the night, but they tore it up and threw it at him, saying, "them Doctors will say anything you want them to say".

"Jimmy, disgusted, refused to pay, left the Docks and went driving a lorry for several years, but when the firm folded he was forced back. And - if a Docker worked elsewhere he had to pay ten pounds to the Union plus paying the Union dues he didn't pay while he was away before he was allowed to allowed to return to the Docks".

I was astounded - then shortly afterwards similar example of skewed Union Discipline happened to a friend of mine. Hugh Dempsey who also lived in New Dock Street and was a good friend of mine. He along Alec Loughran got into the union on the same night as myself. Hugh had knocked off work at 5 'O'Clock { *an unknown occurrence*} and the Union ordered, that his pay for that day be paid to the man who replaced him.

This was absolutely crazy and I complained to the Union Committee about it. I got no satisfaction so wrote to Dublin but never got a reply from them. I also wrote to the Northern Ireland Committee complaining about the union behaviour at the Docks, but was also ignored. In particular I wanted to know where they stood on the ten pound fines that were dished out like confetti.

When I learned that the Northern Ireland Committee had been awarded ten thousand pounds a year from the Stormont Government, I realised I'd been wasting my time. However, I lambasted this cosy arrangement and questioned - how could we expect our Union to behave like Connolly and Larkin's Union, when the ruling body of Unions in the North was in the pay of a repressive regime like Stormont? The Docks Aped in many ways the discrimination that flourished in the artificial and gerrymandered six county's of Northern Ireland, however, the Docks committee were all Catholics.

As a fully fledged Docker I was now entitled to be employed in the Pen where a discriminating normality was maintained. I.e. shut your mouth, do as you're told and you'll get work. In their wildest dreams the Union Founders could not have imagined that the Belfast Branch of the trade union they founded - would become an employers plaything. The only difference between Union and Non-Union was that I now didn't have to rush in like a wild savage and take whatever job I could get from the Foremen - not even knowing what the Job was. Instead, now I could pick 4of4
and choose which 'time jobs' I went to. It seems that the 1907 agreement to destroy Larkin's strike is why - even up to the 1970's that non-union labour was still allowed to be employed at Belfast Docks.

Every so often work would dry up and by the Thursday most of the Ships had been discharged so many Dockers were idle. When I stated to the Union Committee that employing non-union men the answer was, their answer was - "the ships can't wait". To which I replied the logical answer, "well, if they're being employed why not get them into the Union and use the greater numbers to expand the Union's power and activities".

49

This was never answered. However I had the distinct feeling that if men who had no past relations on the Union Committee, and no connection to the Union - then the Committee would lose their power to control the Dockers.

When I questioned the Committee on what the letters OBU on our union badge meant - none of them had the foggiest idea. When I enlightened them, that it was the initials of JIm Larkin' favourite slogan: 'One Big Union', and what he wanted ITGWU to be, they refused to believe me and thought it was childish to suggest this.

The ignorance by the Union Committee of Larkin and Connolly founding the Union they belonged to, was astounding. This was fostered by the paid Officials. If anyone inquired about Union Matters {myself in particular} the response was, "never mind, that doesn't concern you - or the inks not dry on your union card". I got fed up listening to this and seeing the good money which could be earned for 'bag work' I threw myself whole-heartily into making money and having a good time.

To be schooled for work, Dockers stood in front of a Foreman, and he picked who he wanted. With time work anyone could do it. However, with bag work only the most fittest and hard-working were employed. Of these their were plenty, and I had to make a name for myself as a good worker. After a few bag boats and hard work this was done.

The only people who could join the Union were, 'supposedly' the sons of Dockers but over the years a few absolute strangers appeared from nowhere, and rumours were rife of back-handers to the committee.

Although no-one would dare say it out loud. These men hadn't a clue about Dock work, even the worst non-union were far better than them.

From my early days, I saw the deference given to union committee men, who always got the best work. However, now as a fully fledged, Docker I came under the union's diabolical control, and I did not like it one bit.

When still a non-union man I had freedom, to work at the Cross Channel ships, if I wanted to. As the name suggests these ships just crossed the channel from England and moored at the top end of the Docks beside the Queens Bridge. This was in the city centre. However once I was in the ITGWU I was restricted by Union Rules and could only work at the Low Docks i.e. the lower end of the port.

These so-called rules were obviously designed by the Employers and implemented by both Unions, to keep the Dockers apart. The Cross Channel Union was was mostly Protestant with a few Catholics, while our Union was mostly Catholic with a few Protestants. I can honestly say there was no sectarian hatred at the Docks. I knew some Catholics who worked at the cross channel and they reported the same thing applied there. The cross-channel Dockers were well paid, and as the saying goes, 'worked like Christians' at a more sedate rate than us, who worked like Heathens.

However, mechanisation was already on the horizon. Actually, I remember the first time I saw a forklift truck. It was in the early nineteen sixties and owned by an enterprising man from the New Lodge Road, named Gerry Storey. In his spare time Gerry trained young boxers at the Holy Family Gym. Gerry established himself in a little wooden office behind the canteen and at the start, work for him was very slow. Often he could be found in the canteen where he willingly explained the working of his Forklift to young Dockers.

He maintained that Forklifts were the way forward and that mechanisation would eventually replace hand trucks, which we found hard to believe. However, not only was he right, but even he couldn't have envisaged the destruction that was coming down the line with containers.

This is not to say that the firms at the Docks were in the Stone Age, far from it, the Headline had a fleet of electric trucks that were 'state of the art'. These were mostly used to deliver the working gear needed for each gang – depending upon the cargo in each Ship and hatch. Such as rope-slings, wires, double purchase heavy duty wires, crown heads etc.

However, on occasion when there was a glut of work and no hand trucks available, electric trucks would be used to move cargo from the quayside into the sheds. They were not ideal for bag stuff as a Docker had to jump up onto the truck to catch the 'bite' - when the Heave landed. This was to stop the heave spilling all over the place. The electric trucks would be charged over-night in the old Fyffes warehouse which the Headline had bought.

At this point manual labour was still cheaper that mechanisation and one Stevedore firm, Smith Coggins, introduced hand trucks with ball bearing wheels. Previous to this, to make the wheels turn efficiently, the old wooden trucks with cast iron wheels had to be upended, the wheels removed and the axles cleaned and oiled by the Dockers. Not to do so meant the wheels seized up and refused to turn. The oil was begged from the engineer of the ship that was being discharged.

Eventually the Head Line followed suit and introduced their own, hand-trucks with ball-bearing wheels. These were a treat to push and pull but over time forklift trucks replaced them.

The smaller firms like O'Connor and McCann, Guy Burn's and McCausland's, stuck to the old Wooden Trucks for a long time. However, they eventually followed the larger firms and went onto Forklifts, having by-passed ball-bearing trucks altogether.

An example of Dockers discharging 'bag stuff' from the hold of a ship, being winched ashore and landed on Hand-Trucks can be seen at the start of UTV's 2007 programme 'Death Trap On The Docks'. This was made to highlight the disgraceful way Dockers working at Asbestos and suffering from Asbestosis were treated by the Union. However, the video isn't a true representation of Dockers working at 'bag stuff' - because all is calm and sedate. Nothing could be further from the truth - as the speed at which Dockers worked is not shown or conveyed. What can be plainly seen is the size of the bags that the dockers were lifting. They weighed a 'hundred and a half each' - I.e a hundredweight and a half 4of4
which was 12 stone.

After the funeral of a Docker, we were sitting in a pub and someone remarked, that it was a pity that our working lives at the Docks, was not recorded on film'. Someone remarked, 'no one would believe it, they'd think the film was speeded up'. Bag work was about making money and many multiples of the daily rate was earned.
In those days animal feeding stuff came in bags, mostly Ground Nuts from South America, or India, and Soya Bean meal from the Plains of America, shipped out through the Great Lakes.

I'm not sure if Ground nuts were so-called because they grew on the ground, or because they were nuts that were ground together into a pulp rolled flat, broken up and loaded into bags. The Soya bean was also ground down and came in eight stone, one hundredweight bag's and shipped across the Atlantic in the 'Head Boats'. These belonged to the Head Line. They were so called because they were named after headlands in Ireland. I.e. The Rathlin Head, Torr Head, Ballygally Head etc.
'Bag stuff' was discharged by a gang of 26 men. Most ships [especially the head boats] had very fast Clark Chapman Winch's or the equivalent.

The 'deck men' consisted of two winch men and a 'hatch-man', who directed the winch men with his hands, whether to slack out or heave up.

Six men worked in the hold loading the bags onto a rope sling. {see the video} This was called a Heave and when hooked onto the cargo hook, left the hatch at great speed. On the quay nine men worked, three to a truck. They landed the heave onto a hand truck which had a man between the shafts like a horse. They pushed and pulled the Heave into a large storage shed where it was quickly unloaded. And like clockwork they rushed out to get their next heave.

Dockers, in their normal course of work used hand-hooks to facilitate the moving of cargo, and with bag stuff needed 'wee hooks'. These were small, nestled in the hand, and were used for pulling and lifting the bags.
Dockers in the hold slinging bag-stuff would use half hook's which were about six inches long with a thick handle and ideal for loading heavy bags onto rope slings. Speed in unloading bag stuff was were the money was made. On the other hand, 'time jobs' which as the name suggests were in no hurry to be discharged.

These cargo's usually were bales of Russian Flax, large cubes of Rubber and loose planks of Timber. The Timber boats were time consuming and could last for a month or more, and were easy-going Jobs. They were usually manned by older Dockers past their prime and non union men. The rate for a time job was obviously a lot less than for bag work. Big hooks were necessary when slinging timber or cases of tobacco and could be up to eighteen inches in length. Old retired Dockers to make a few pounds would fashion these hooks from metal spikes gathered from a local scrap yard.

Even from my school days I knew, that just over an hour's

work at a bag boat earned more that working all day at a time job. Large pay packets were commonplace and earned regularly by the top gangs. These were loyal to one foreman and continually 'followed' him. However, besides the 'constant gangs' who were, Feeny's gang, McKenna's gang - etc, there was an elite of 'bag men' who moved around working for every foreman.

This happened because the main foremen had two gangs each, and when the elite took the best out of a job they 'sloped' i.e. moved onto the next good job.

There was great rivalry between these 'elite' bag men and the foreman's 'constant gang' as hey tried to outdo each other in tonnage moved and money earned. The banter in the pub afterwards if the constant gang was out-done was brilliant. The worst thing about the constant gang was that every job to them was a treated as a bag job. They saw no difference and worked full pelt at the most mundane of jobs, when there was no need - and no extra money involved. This ensured that their Foreman could be counted on to turn a ship around in the shortest possible time, thus saving the employers money on 'Berthing fees'.

At the Docks the worst thing anyone could do was to work in the rain - yet the constant gangs did this as a matter of course. The saying was: 'you don't get the Industrial Injuries for Pleurisy'. This was a payment made to anyone who was hurt through the course of their work. There was an old saying which I never fully understood, which was - 'Who's going to bell the cat'? This meant, whomsoever knocked the gang off and 'stood in', was 'left out' i.e. not employed for the next good job.

Another aggravating factor was: while the 'main gang' were prepared to work in the rain - the cargo was ' *not getting wet*'.

However, once a Docker put his health before money and 'stood in' the rest had to follow suit. Once this happened the vindictive foreman ordered that the hatch had to be covered up. Often this was simply done with a large tarpaulin called a Tent. This was suspended over the hatch from the cargo hook and secured around it by ropes ties. However very often, as a punishment, depending on how annoyed the foreman was, he could order a full 'covering up'.

This was a dangerous practice in lashing rain, with King and Queen Beam's winched from the leeward side and lowered into slots on the side of the hatch. Then, heavy wooden soaking wet hatch covers were manually fitted into place. The whole thing was then covered by a heavy tarpaulin and secured with long metal flanges and wooden wedges. For the Dockers it often wasn't worthwhile - and easier just to work in the rain. Plus, they didn't put in jeopardy their position for the next 'good job'.

The top foreman for the Head Line - which was the main employer, was Jimmy Feeney, he was an old man and hard as nails, who sacked me on one occasion. I was in the wrong and suffering from a bad hangover.

The Head Line foremen stood on the back platform in the Pen, arranged by issue of importance, with Jimmy Feeney being the first. With these top foremen the Dockers stood well back and treated them with respect.

These foremen had little concern for union rules or bad weather and were a law onto themselves. Years later when I was driving a taxi on the Falls Road - who did I see with a lollipop leading schoolchildren across the road at Daly's Garage, only Jimmy Feeney.

I waited until the children were safely across then pretended to drive at him. I shouted good naturedly "ya oul bastard you sacked me"! He threw the lollipop down and stormed off. Sadly he took it to heart and never came back.

At the upper levels in the Port there was animosity between the unions with each vying to take work from each other. One such ship was a new Roll on Roll off weekly service from England, nicknamed 'The Ramp'
due to the floating ramp which the lorries used to access the ship.

It was a filthy job where every lorry had to be fastened down with 'bottle screws'. These were heavy duty metal cylindrical screws about two feet long with a hook at one end and knob at the other. They could be extended or retracted by rotating the long inner screws. This was done by twisting the outer shell of the screw. The knob was placed into a raised plate on the Lorry Deck which had four receptacles, and the most suitable on was used. The hook was then attached to a wheel or suitable position on the lorry and the bottle screw tightened up.

This was done with a spike through a hole for that purpose.
After every lorry was secured, a sailor with a lump hammer would walk around the lorry hitting the 'bottle screws' with the hammer to make sure They were tight and the lorry wouldn't move during the crossing.

I remember an altercation in a Pub, "Wee Tommy's" in Corporation Street, which was an extension of Garmoyle street, and close to the Cross Channel Docks. This had nothing to do with Religion. Several cross-channel dockers accused the Low Dockers of being very low. The cross-channel Union had got the contract for the 'Ramp' and was paid by the tonnage they discharged and loaded, which was obviously considerable. Plus, besides the large wages they received, and due to the oil and grease beneath the lorry's - they also got an allowance for new working clothes.

However, after only two ships, the cross-channel lost the contract and it was given to the Low Dockers. All we got was a days pay and five shillings dirty money. The cross-channel Dockers annoyed at loosing this lucrative job were right, our Union were very Low.The cross channel dockers could not believe that the we knew nothing about this scandalous and anti worker situation And to crown it all, the cross-channel Dockers doing the accusing, were Catholics.

There was a fear in my father and among the fathers of my friends, that we keep our mouth's shut and not offend the Union. While I understood this fear was well founded as the Union had absolute power over the Dockers - it was generally only used if a Docker questioned their word or failed to pay his union dues on time. One case where the diabolical control was used sparingly - was at the weekly Dutch Boat, known as the 'beer boat'. Which as the name suggest were full to the brim with Beer. This ship imported Carlsberg Specials and Pills diabetic beer in
bottles that were shipped in wooden crates.

In the hold the crates would be loaded onto 'Trays' which were square wooden platforms and heaved out of the hatch. Besides the beer, the Dutch Boat carried boxes of Chopped Ham and Pork that were in little cans with a small key for opening them. They were delicious. Also in the Dutch Boat were working men's boots which had an integrated sole and heel, but weren't very water-proof.

The Dutch Boat was well know for the excessive drinking of cargo, but no one cared, especially the union, who along with everyone else participated in this weekly festival of drinking and merry-making. Often sing-songs were organised in the hold. This occurred because there was a massive over shipment of Beer sent every week. This was along the lines of a Bakers Dozen. Because of 'breakages' many thousand extra bottles of beer than ordered were sent - and a good time was had by all.

One Foreman a really decent guy, interrupted a sing-song and shouted down the hold, "I'm counting to three, and if you don't hook a heave on you're all sacked". The sing-song stopped and the foreman counted, one... two... two and a half - at this everyone in the hold erupted into laughter. But they did hook on a heave.

Often at the end of the night several Dockers had to be heaved ashore on a Tray.

This festival of drinking ended when the Brewery Firm, Carlsberg, began shipping the beer in large round containers about twelve foot high and the same around. One Docker, annoyed at this devised a way of still getting at the beer. However he had to wait until the containers were ashore and placed outside the cargo shed. He'd discovered - that at the bottom of each Container was a small hatch which contained an outlet spout and a lever. He opened the hatch sat down and placed a large clean plastic bag around the spout. With a crow bar his friend gently tapped the lever open until the beer leaked out. When the bag was filled he tapped the lever closed.

After doing this several times they both were very drunk. Deciding to have one last bag before going home they started again. However, the drunken friend stuck the lever too hard and the Carlsberg Special, under pressure burst out with tremendous force.

It struck the Docker holding the bag and propelled him twenty feet, over the cobble stones and a mountain of foam obliterated everything.

Drunkenly the friend calling his name into the foam. A voice emerged saying. 'Fuck you my arse is in raw flesh and full of stones'. The next morning in the Pen the Chairman ranted about this destruction of cargo and he promised that through hell or high water he'd stamp out the drunken behaviour.

The Docks was a dangerous place to work with injuries common-place with several deaths. One particular dangerous cargo was bales of rubber shipped in the Blue Funnel Boats. These started off as three foot square cubes weighing about four hundredweight, but were loaded into the ship while still hot. During the voyage they would melt into each other forming grotesque shapes that had to be crow-barred apart.

These were loaded four at time onto trays and because of the melted shapes were very unstable. Many times while being heaved out of the hold, from a great height they'd roll of the tray and back into the hold.

When the hatch-man shouted -"Lookout below, the Dockers would run behind a stanchion for safety. When the falling bale stuck the the other bales it would bounce at great speed like a giant ping pong ball around the hatch. Six Dockers would move around the stanchion as the bale of rubber smashed the thick stringers apart. Stringers were heavy wooden planks used to keep the cargo off the metal sides of the ship. The Dockers continually moved around the stanchion keeping it between them, the flying splinters and the bouncing rubber until it finally remained still.

The deeper the Dockers got into the bales of rubber the more difficult it was to prise them apart and then can hooks had to be used. These were a set of four hooks that were hooked around an individual bale and heaved out. Everyone ran to safety behind the stanchions. Slowly with great resistance the bale was pulled from the rest. Many times the hooks tore through the rubber and now the flying can hooks added to the dangers. Thankfully no-one was ever killed.

About 1965 there was 'foot and mouth' scare. Lorries going out the Dock gates had to drive through a trough of disinfecting fluid formed by two ridges of asphalt. A South African Ship was unloading at the Sinclair Wharf with a multitude of cargo's including bags of Bran.

However in the 'In-between decks' known as the 'Tween decks' i.e. there was a cargo of copper ingots. These were about three foot long and tapered at the ends. Some Dockers would throw these into the lower hold, where they were placed in a half empty a bag of Bran.

This was placed in a heave taken ashore driven out the Dock gates and sold to a local scrap dealer. Things were going so well that they decided to send two or there ingots at one time, however, they had to stop this and go back to one.

What transpired was, the car carrying three in the boot could not drive out of the foot and mouth, disinfectant trough. The driver in panic saw the Harbour Policemen approaching and called for passers by to give him a push. They did but it still wouldn't move over the trench and traffic was building up behind the car. The harbour policemen took control and called on the lorry drivers to come and push the car, which they did, with the policemen joining in. When it rolled out of the trench everyone cheered. The Dockers With relief.

On another occasion a South African Ship and a Beer Boat were lying beside each other in the York Dock. The South African Boat was laden with Altar Wine and several thousand tons of Bran. The Bran was particularly fine which made it difficult to breathe. When rain started the hatch was covered with a Tent. Soon a barter system was in operation, with alter wine being swapped for Carlsberg Specials.

The Alter Wine was very thick and sweet and had to be watered down. Then someone thought of using the Carlsberg Specials to water it down, and 'Snakebite' was invented. They partied into the night. When the rain stopped at two O'Clock in the morning - work was resumed and the Dutch Boat Dockers went home.

In the 1960's the Union showed just how powerful and dictatorial they could be. However, in these cases it had nothing to do with their slavish mentality towards the Employers. In two separate cases, three Dockers were deprived of their livelihoods and sacked from the Docks. They were Shortt, Quinn and Turner. The first two were sacked for an incidence that happened in Connolly Hall.

The Committee leaked a story that they were 'up' before the committee on a Tuesday night, arrived half drunk
and attacked several committee men. Whatever transpired these two young men were deprived of their livelihoods by the Union Committee, who were well known for being economical with the truth.

In the second incidence, in Sammy Turners case, at which I actually was present - and in a sad way, by trying to help contributed to Turner's sacking. What transpired that night stands Trade Unionism on its head.

We were working a midnight shift at Stormont Wharf, slinging Square Timber. These are whole trees that had been squared off. This job required little work and only myself and Peter [Peachy] Black had returned to work. However, about two in the morning, Sammy [Swalla]
Turner arrived back, very drunk. He was staggering all over the deck load and at one point we were lucky to jump on him as he almost went over the side. Dragging him back he cursed us up and down, and we had just saved his life.

"You're too drunk to work", I said, "away into the Foc'sle Head and sleep it off". This is a small area in the bows of every ship. In the days of wooden ships this was a fortified castle, named the 'Forecastle'. This had a cannon and would be manned by a sailor with a bucket of grapeshot - prepared for any eventuality. However, in the present day this area on most ships is used as a paint locker and the name Forecastle was shortened to Foc'sle. Swalla, drunk agreed and he staggered up the deck load, ducked his head and went in. He had no sooner entered the Foc'sle Head when a small dark-skinned seaman ran out screaming gibberish. Swalla staggered out confused with eyes rolling and was completely disoriented.

The screaming of the Seaman attracted the attention of two committee men who were on the quay.
One of whom was Bobby Dickey, a future chairman. They came on board and quietened the Seaman while we steadied Swalla. In broken and excited English the seaman stated, "Me sleep he rob, me sleep he rob". The committee men took this at face value and ordered Swalla off the ship. He protested, and I protested, But when they stated that he was 'Up' on Tuesday Night for entering a seaman's cabin, Swalla enraged, head-butted Bobby Dickey and punched them both. At Swalla's trial by the Union - which I was not allowed to attend, he was deprived of his livelihood and sacked from the Docks. I wanted to appear as a witness for him and to tell what really had transpired but was not allowed. In fact I only heard about his sacking a week afte it happened, from his younger brother.

The irony of Connolly Hall on the Antrim Road, in which so many wrongs were committed in the name of Irish Trade Unionism – is the fact, that the Dockers actually owned the building. The previous union rooms were over a money-lenders in Donegal Street. He opened late on Tuesday nights so any Docker who hadn't got the money to pay his fines could borrow it. This was necessary because they couldn't work until the fines were paid. However, In the 1960's Arglass Fitzsimons organised a series of 'Dockers Dances' to raise the money to buy

Connolly Hall.

From our 'not on the curriculum' History lessons at school I knew this was not how Trade Unionism was supposed to work. In the Pen I tried to get the Dockers to object to Swalla's sacking but they refused to do anything. In fact it was said to me many times, to "keep your mouth shut or you'll be next".
Connolly Hall was sold about fifteen years ago after having lain empty for a long time. A question must be asked, "Who got the money for it"?

Rumours abounded about the last union chairman, who bought a new house up the Antrim Road, at the time. In the heyday of the Docks, it was hammered into the Dockers by their fathers, to keep on the right side of the Union. There was on my father's behalf a personal reason for him to fear the Union. It emanated from my grandfather's time. He had gone against the union's wishes and fought for, and got Sugar paid by the ton. The union stood by while he was blacklisted and he never earned another penny at it.

It was drummed into the young Dockers to always do what the Union said, and be ahead with our union dues. To keep them off our backs.
Arglass Fitzsimons was most helpful in this regard, by reminding everyone when their dues needed to be paid. Sadly, Arglass passed away and the Union fined with impunity.
Most young Dockers worked for a Head Line foreman - Tony McCafferty.
He was last in the pecking order of foremen and had 'time jobs 'most of 4of4
the time. Tony was an easygoing foreman and his gang of young Dockers were nicknamed 'F' Troop, after a popular TV series of the 60's, set in the'Wild-West' of America, in cowboy times.
This featured a haphazard troop of US soldiers who could do

nothing right. One day we were discharging a cargo of animal skins, that stank to the high heaven, and was infested with God knows what. However our main bone of contention was the large rats about a foot long that scurried out from every bale we turned over. In panic they scuttled up the stringers over our heads and then would fall on top of us.

We stopped work and sent for the committee. We wanted danger money for doing the job. However, because we'd stopped work which was a 'cardinal sin' the then Chairman himself along with his cronies attended. I put our case to him, and, he could see for himself the size of the rats from the few we'd killed. Actually, this Chairman was a direct representative of the employers and in fact was an employer himself. He worked for the Grain Silos, doing what - I have no idea. Besides being Union Chairman, he would employ a 'Sampler', whose job was to fill a small white bag with grain and to give it to him. This was then tested for water and mould content, and to see if was fit for human consumption.

The Sampler was then required to sit in the canteen all day, in case another sample was required. In regard to the foul and stinking bales and the rats, as usual, our not "Independent Chairman" wheeled out the usual platitudes I.e. that the employer was away or unavailable for a few days and we should go back to work and let the committee deal with it.

I laughed at this and in no uncertain terms told him we weren't falling for that, and wanted the matter settled right now. To say I was treated with disdain is no under-statement and my length in the union, hurled at me by his cronies. To cut a long story short, we were told we'd be up before the committee if we didn't start work immediately. These threats frightened the other young Dockers, who climbed back into the hatch.

When I enquired about 'Danger Money' I was told we were

getting nothing, but we'd be given large shovels to kill the rats. Previously I'd shovelled a large rat into the bag. As the Chairman and the committee were leaving, I joined them. The chairman asked "where are you going with that"?

"To the 'First Aid in Fire Station", I replied. "I want it on record what you're making us work with". The Fire Station was outside the Dock Gates. He nearly took a fit, "Alright, alright" he exclaimed. "You can have five pounds on top of your days pay". They young Dockers cheered.
Delighted, I threw the rat into the Dock. Subsequently we never received the five pounds, and when I inquired about it was told "you're not getting it and you're lucky you're not up before the committee for trying to Blackmail the Union.

Because of the anti worker stance of the Union, a long time committee man and a good Catholic, who later became Chairman, I ask him for a rule book. He laughed and said: "It would need to be as big as the Bible to fit all our rules into it".
To this I replied, "No you're wrong, if it contains the rules that benefit Dockers, it will be a very thin book indeed". With that he called me a communist and walked off. It should be noted here, that while injuries were common place, no first aid or any medical facilities were ever present at the Docks. The Union Committee ran, and controlled the Docks for the employer and the well-being of the Dockers was very low on their list.

The worst situation of all prevailed when Jim Austin became Chairman.
He neither drank nor smoked and was very hard on anyone who did.
Small and slight of stature, I saw him ordering men almost twice his size back to work or they'd be up before the committee - where they knew they'd be lucky to get off with a Ten pound fine. The main grievance of the Dockers was once the ship they were working on had sailed, the prospect of

achieving redress for whatever wrong had transpired, was nil.

This was obvious to the committee who promised to look into the matter but never did. The Union mantra was 'work was not allowed to be stopped - for any reason'.

Skulduggery regularly took place with the Union being up to their neck in it. One such occurrence was in the mid 1960's - many tons of an expensive fertiliser 'Fishmeal' was going missing. An undercover stake out was set up by the harbour police and the people involved were caught red handed. However, one man, a cod foreman well down the ranks took the rap and was sentenced to several years in Jail.

However, just after his release the fist container ship to arrive in Belfast started a regular service. This guaranteed very large wage packets as the Dockers were on 24 hour standby. And lo and behold the 'just released lowly ranked foreman' who took the rap for the fertilizer' was given the Job as foreman. As per usual, he employed his family and those with Union connections.

One man, the nephew of the Branch Secretary walked away after a few weeks, leaving the son of the Union Chairman, his friend and the Foreman's family to be accused of Nepotism. Not that they cared as they were never near the Pen to be insulted. During the Fishmeal stakeout, the Harbour Police had observed an old Docker, Mugs McStravick, rolling out a barrel of grapes from the back of a storage shed. He sat on the barrel and lit a cigarette.

This Docker was well known to the Harbour Police as a smuggler, but they never could catch him. He would often arrange diversions to tie them up while he got his contraband smuggled out of the Docks. No doubt they suspected he knew they were watching him - and this was simply another diversion - and seeing they never could get him for smuggling, they arrested him for stealing the barrel of grapes - for which he was Jailed.

On his return he was greeted by the Dockers singing the popular song, 'Roll out the Barrel, we'll have a barrel of fun'. This was all good natured as everyone knew he was Jailed in the wrong.

However, the mirth faded when the Union insisted, as per usual, that anyone convicted for stealing at the Docks had to serve the same sentence away from the Docks. This was most unfair as everyone knew Mug's wasn't stealing the grapes.

Mugs complained and asked where was the difference him and the 'just released' Cod Foreman who was given the job of bossing the container boat. Mugs was killed at the Docks several years later when a heave of bag stuff was lowered on top of him.

As a young man I developed a love for the hard work and for the money, and like many others, was soon indulging in Tailor made suits and hand-made shoes. As I progressed through my teens, however, I began to see that while my friends and I were making good living, the Union Committee were making an even better one, and doing little or no work for it. Because of the anti worker stance of the Union I wanted to attend a union meeting - only to be told that there wasn't any.

When I protested and stated the obvious, that there was a committee meeting every Tuesday Night, I was told, "but that's not for you - that's for us to maintain discipline". This was in the mid 1960's when I again sent complaining letters to head office in Dublin.

My main reason for wanting to attend a Union meeting, was, because it was an accepted fact that Dockers had to work any hours the employers required.

A normal day could entail working, from 8 0' Clock in the

morning until twenty past eleven at night - or until the ship was unloaded, if it was for sea. I questioned several committee men 'why Hugh Dempsey had worked all day and lost his day's pay, but never received a straight answer. And after several years I was still continually reminded that the ink on my Union card was hardly dry, which was actually said in the form of a threat. Rather smugly I was told to bring it up my complaints at the AGM. This was the only Union meeting that the Dockers were allowed to attend.

I had never attended an AGM in the months leading up to my first one, practically every day something happened which caused the Union to side with the employers against the Dockers. So when the AGM took place, I was determined to stand for the union committee, and indeed the election was the first order of business. As soon as nominations were declared open, in less than five seconds the twelve sitting committee men shouted their nominations for each other and nominations were closed.

There was uproar in the hall as apparently this was a usual occurrence. From this fine example of Trade Union Democracy - things got progressively worse. At least half of the members left in disgust and shouting matches were the order of the day, with nothing at all being spoken about or resolved. I attended several AGM' s, with the same result, and after every fiasco, wrote to head office telling them what had transpired.

Then in 1969 I was ejected from the AGM for insulting a senior official from Dublin. I Can't remember his name but he was waxing lyrical about how "the Belfast Docks was on the cusp of a new beginning, whereby due to the hard work and due diligence by our Union we would soon be getting Decasualised". This was the first time it was mentioned and no-one had any idea what he was talking about. While the Dockers looked at each other in confusion, he explained that "Head Office was determined to eradicate the curse of Casual

Labour in Ireland - because the use of non-union Labour was keeping wages low".

The Dockers were delighted to hear this.
He continued, crowing about the fact, that we had come so far with 'industrial relations' and that there was no stopping the forward march of mankind - seeing that a man had just walked on the moon. To great laughter someone shouted, "was he in the Union?"

The Union official replied, "He may well have been because our members are everywhere". This encouraged more laugher which I interrupted, stating: "That's all well and good but when is the Union at Belfast Docks going to be on the side of the Dockers. There's only one Union Meeting a year for Dockers to raise their complaints, this one!

They can put men on the moon but when are we going to get showers and washing facilities. All we have is an old fashioned stand pipe, and when are we going to get Rule Books"!
St Mary's hall erupted with cheering and the Union Official looked baffled.

When the cheering subsided he looked at me and asked: "What are you talking about? This is your Union, you can have as many union meetings and as many rule books as you want".

This caused much laughter and several caustic comments from the Dockers, the best one being: "Tell that to the man in the moon" - to more laughter. I pointed at the committee and said to the Dublin Official: "You
- can say that to us but tell it to them". This caused more cheering.

Flustered, the Dublin Official spoke to the Chairman and the leading committee men beside him, but they ignored him. It looked like he was asking 'what is he talking about'?

Clearly upset he addressed the meeting again. "You the Belfast Dockers are the backbone of this Union. Since before the Lockout the Dublin Dockers could be relied upon to stage Sympathetic Strikes whenever Jim Larkin required it". At this point I interrupted him. "You're talking
nonsense, there'll never be a strike here because the Union are in the Employers pocket and no one here has any idea what you're talking about. At Belfast Docks, where Larkin had his great strike, Trade Unionism does not exist - and will never exist, when you're more concerned with a man on the moon that with the Union at Belfast Docks."
The Dockers cheered again. Flustered, the Dublin Official looked at the committee men with contempt - then continued with his prepared speech.

"However" he said. "And to be fair, in Guinness Brewery, Larkin could make no inroads there, because they treated their workers with decency and respect." This caused great laughter from the Dockers with many shouting 'Give us some of that'.

Bewildered, he continued and tried to get the Dockers on his side. "In every other industry, especially the Trams and the Independent newspaper, Larkin's and his Union would not work alongside non-union workers!" This was delivered with gusto. Instead of the cheer he expected, this caused absolute silence, which obviously baffled him.

Seeing his confusion I enlightened him. "Look, while Jim Larkin and the Dublin trade unionists would not work with non-union men, here, they're used by the Union and Employers to keep us in our place, and the mad union rules don't apply to them". The Dockers loudly agreed. Clearly stunned at what he was hearing, the union official drank a glass of waterand walked away from the Chairman and the committee. "What are the mad Union Rules". he asked"?

As one voice the assembled Dockers shouted "Ten Pound Fines."
Several of the Committee and their sons were sitting in the first few rows.
They jumped up shouting " we must have discipline"! A shouting match ensued which alarmed the Union Rep from Dublin. He raised his arms and the men slowly quietened down. "There are no mad union rules!
Every Union Member must be treated with respect and paid a fair wage.
This is what led directly to the Lockout"!
Someone shouted, "Tell us the one about the three bears". Everyone shouted agreement and cheered.

Baffled the Dublin Official continued.
"This Union, my Union, your Union has always demanded that non-union men be encouraged to join the Union, and not used by the Employers to divide and conquer the working class"!
From the emphasis on his last few words and the clenched fist salute, it was obvious the Dublin Official expected a rousing cheer. Instead, the Dockers laughed their heads off and jeered him. Perplexed he paced the stage looking with anger at the Committee. Holding up his arms he stated: "This Union is dedicated to the Irish People and to abolish Poverty by getting every worker to join the Union".

I couldn't take any more of this nonsense and stood up and said:
"Obviously you haven't done your homework. Here, we work alongside non-union men. They can come and go as they please, and are not subjected to the mad union rules that you say don't exist. For example, they don't get fined if they're off hurt and fall behind with their union dues".
The hall erupted cheering and the Dublin Official's mouth

dropped open.

I was as surprised as the Dublin Official that I had been able to say so much about the situation at Belfast Docks. So I shouted, "This is a Mickey Mouse Union and is only for their benefit" and pointed at he committee. Obviously the committee had heard enough. Six of them swooped on me and frogmarched from the building. The Dublin Official shouted, "stop, I want to hear what he's saying".
I shouted in reply, "Read the letters I'm sending to Liberty Hall every week".

My feet hardly touched the ground as I was propelled towards he doors, with me shouting. "The Union and the Employers use non-union men to keep us down! We need a decent canteen to eat in, cause the one we have has been there since the first world war and the tables are crawling with maggots, Jim Larkin would be ashamed of this Union".

The Dublin Official looked on, open-mouthed as the hall erupted in protest. When the Union refused to bring me back most Dockers walked out. Needless to say, when the official got back to Dublin, nothing changed at Belfast Docks. However, with his statement about Decasualisation he had prepared the ground for another trade union atrocity. From this fine example of Trade Union Democracy things got progressively worse.

I continually wrote to Liberty Hall asking for a rule book, but was refused one.
See letters. I previously had been told by an academic from Queen's University, that this was the basic right and necessity of every union member - and that I should have been given one when I joined the union. I persisted, trying to get a rule book, but to no avail. Head Office told me to get it from the Belfast Branch, and the Branch kept telling me that they hadn't got

any as Dublin wouldn't supply them.

See letters to this effect, from head office and them returning a five shilling postal order for a rule book. Under the Casual System, the Union continued to control Dockers, and for any offence, a Ten Pound fine was the norm. Far from being unique this was official Union policy. The first letter in the corruptoconnor website that accompanies this book proves this and shows that Liberty Hall knew full well what was going on at Belfast Docks. Actually this proves that both agreed with the 'Fines' and that it was union policy - which the Belfast Branch eagerly participated in.

At Belfast Docks the Union operated a dual system whereby it was both an open and closed shop. When there was plenty of work it was open to all and sundry to avail of it, but when there was a scarcity only union members were employed. However when the Union Committee ordered the foremen not to employ a particular person. [*as happened with Sammy Turner*] he was not employed. The union would not allow him to work – even as a non-union man and he had to leave the Docks. Shortt and Quinn didn't even try because they knew what to expect.

For over 50 years I have been trying to expose the nonsensical impositions of this Union, whereby they sacked Union Members - myself included. However in my case I was the first victim of the newly formed Union and Employers Court. This was one of the unknown conditions of the new Decasualisation Scheme. One of which was - that non-union men would no longer be employed. To be honest I found this strange, as the dictatorial aspect and collaboration between the union and employers extended to the use of non-union men.

When I was aged about 17, during a glut of work,I brought a friend, 'Frank Young' same age, who lived up the street in

Corby Way, to the Docks and got him started as a 'non-union man'. As previously stated, the Employer you worked for on a Monday took the money for your insurance stamp. However it transpired that every day that Frank worked, money was taken for his stamp. When I went to the employers concerned on his behalf, I was assured this would stop and the money be paid back, but it never was.

Over the weeks this amounted to a considerable amount of money and I persevered. On speaking to other non-union men I learned that this was was done on them all, and the price they paid for being allowed to work.
I thought this most unfair and was determined to stop it – but was told on the quiet by a clerk at one of the companies taking the money to desist, as it was the Union who was getting the money.

While there was no sectarianism at the Docks, it was never very far away. Some years after the docks collapsed, an ex Docker and an old neighbour from New Dock Street, Jim Browne, who bought Pat King's shop on Garmoyle Street, was shot dead by Protestant gunmen. And several years later, Bobby Monaghan who bought O'Rourkes Pub, also in Garmoyle Street was shot dead in Rathcoole.

CHAPTER FOUR

In 1970 a Young Docker named Martin Lynch appeared. He was on his Dad's button, which meant, if a Docker is off injured or sick, his son or brother could work on his Dockers Button until he returned. Lynch had progressive ideas, which aligned with my own, regarding Union Democracy. He was involved with several community groups and seeing he had access to a hand cranked printing machine, we started 'The Dockers Voice'.

This was a weekly news-sheet which highlighted the worst anti union activities imposed on the Dockers by the Union in the previous week. The first four editions were written by Lynch and on the first morning of its appearance, we walked around the Pen shouting, "Read the Dockers Voice, the paper of the downtrodden Dockers".
The Union Committee went ballistic and tried to pull the paper off us.

We had intended to sell the paper for one penny to cover the cost of the paper and ink, but because of the hostility from the committee, who were determined the Dockers would not read the paper, we threw them into the air. While the Chairman ranted "this is a communist rag and anyone who reads it will be excommunicated" - the Dockers dived on the papers with many hiding them in their coats.

After six editions of the 'Dockers Voice' the Dockers began to question the anti-worker behaviour of the Union - but the Union struck back. They stated that Lynch was an undesirable and rescinded his right to work on his dad's button. This meant he was forced to leave the Docks, because foremen wouldn't be allowed to employ him, even as a non-union man.

I was disappointed and thought this was the end of the 'Dockers Voice'.

However, due to my belief in trade union democracy,'The Socialist Labour League got in touch and promised to print the paper. On my first meeting with their Belfast Rep - John Magee - in the Pen, he introduced himself and asked: "What did I think of the Union sacking the young Dockers". I had no idea what he was talking about but soon learned, that the Union intended - before Decasualisation to sack all the young Dockers. To say I was stunned would be an understatement. Their Dad's had been informed about this but told to keep quiet - in case their son could be sneaked in.

John Magee had learned this from one of the young Dockers that was to be sacked.

I can't remember his first name, but he was Dinny Docherty's younger brother. I challenged the Union Committee about this but they wouldn't speak of it, saying it was none of my business. However, now seeing I had editorial control of the Dockers Voice, I got stuck into the Union for their betrayal of Trade Unionism. I brought out a special edition on Decasualisation - with interviews from several Young Dockers who were naturally heartbroken at being sacked by the Union. I contacted other Union's to complain about the Union sacking the young Dockers for the employers, but was always told: "What does your rule book say". Which was a polite way of saying, 'we don't want to become involved'. I couldn't answer anyway as I had no rule book. When I said this I was looked at with disbelief.

Many times I complained to Head Office and ICTU about the Union doing the Employers Dirty Work and the Ten Pound fines but was continually ignored. That these fines and sackings were used to control the Dockers and placate the employers. I was once fined Ten Pounds for insulting a Head Line Rep, a Mr James. It was at a Time Job 'The Ghent Boat'. He shouted down the hold and gave me an order to put bales of flax up against some tall boxes of sheet glass, in case they would fall over.

This was nonsense as the glass was contained in wooden a frame at least three feet wide and an elephant couldn't have pushed it over. I refused and told him in very' un-parliamentary language' where to go.

Brian McCann, the 'singing Tallyman' and Committee Man, wanted me to apologise, and I told him, in the same 'language' what to do with himself. McCann demanded that I be brought before the committee and punished. In due course I was so ordered and refused to go - however, in my absence I was fined Ten Pounds which I refused to pay. I told Mr James, that "If Brian McCann and the Union Committee, suspend me, or lift my wages to deduct the fine from - you and the Head Line will be explaining yourselves in the Courts". The matter was quietly dropped.

Lifting your wages was a common practice by the Union, until Mugs McStravick complained to a policeman that he had been robbed. The policeman accompanied him to the wages office, where the clerk, insisted that Mugs was mistaken and that wages had not been made up yet.

Mugs pointed his finger and said, "You are a liar you told me half an hour ago that the Union had lifted my wages". Mug's wages were duly returned to the wages office. Regarding the fines by the Union, Head Office in Dublin and ICTU maintained that these fines never took place.

The letter from Head Office, dated 11/8/1971 proves this is untrue. The letters states that a ten pound fine imposed by the Belfast Branch, on myself should be paid forthwith. In this instance I was fined for defending myself against a drunken foreman.

Needless to say I never paid any of these fines, and threatened them with a solicitor if they suspended me for not paying them. However, the Dockers not realising that the Union couldn't fine them money, did pay, in great numbers. When I told them not to pay but to see a solicitor, the Union stated: "don't listen to him, he pays his fines, he's just trying to get you into trouble".

Because of my insistence that the Union should behave like a Trade Union I was shunned, and foremen instructed not to employ me for money-making jobs. Thus my earning capacity was substantially reduced. The committee and the Union chairman, Jim Austin plugged Decasualisation at every turn, and how great it would be - to be treated with respect. Both maintained that anyone who was against it was stuck in the past and wedded to the behaviour of the Drunken Dockers. To quieten dissent they stated: "that the Dockers would have a guaranteed week's wages, and would be brought into the 20th century".

This seemed like a good idea to many, who had in the last few years, saw their wages dwindle. This was due to a greater sucking capacity by the new West Twin Silo, which could handle heavier cargoes. These cargoes would previously have come in bags and not a penny of compensation was ever paid to the Dockers for losing this work. To make sure of this, the Union Chairman, Jim Austin, was appointed as foreman at the New Silo, and as a matter of course employed all his own family.

With bag work 'going up the pipe' plus a creeping takeover of conventional cargo's by containers this was sounding the death knell for manual labour.

While none of this happened overnight - there were many months and occasions when it seemed nothing would change - as conventional work and the money flowed. Defending his new job as the Silo Foreman the chairman maintained this was not a betrayal of the Union but would enhance its standing with the employers.

When asked about compensation for the loss of 'bag work' he maintained "we cannot stop progress" and continued to beat the old drum of that "drunken behaviour would spell disaster". He actually seemed delighted when his dire predictions were eventually realised. The steady march of containers continued to eat into the manual labour of dock work.

However, at the start they still needed Dockers to hook them on, albeit in greatly reduced in numbers. Eventually, with the invention of new cranes, that had an ingenious device that hooked on itself - this put paid to Dockers jobs and Manual Labour.

In the run up to Decasualisation - 1971, the Chairman, Jim Austin and the committee were frantically selling the idea of the new scheme, and for once it seemed as if they were genuinely on the Dockers side.

However, at a meeting called to give the details about the structure of the new scheme, the Dockers were told nothing - other, than it was actually happening. We were given a four page document entitled 'Decasualisation: Basic Rules and Conditions' that gave no insight whatsoever into what was about to happen. In retrospect, it seems the meeting was organised so the Union and Employers could say that this meeting 'actually took place'. So they could say claim that the Dockers agreed to the Rules of the new scheme. None of which were contained in their publication?

The booklet actually says "all rules have not been formulated yet and we should follow the Union's lead". As usual, this was the Employers speaking out of the Union's mouth.

The Chairman opened the meeting by saying "it's a bad night and we all want to get home to a big fire so I won't detain you long" He then launched into his usual good living diatribe, stating: "The only thing that's going to change is the fact that - for the first time in the history of the Docks we will be treated with the respect we deserve, because, the drunken behaviour will no longer be tolerated."

I interrupted him saying: "That is confounded lies, everything is going to change! You and this so-called Committee are doing the Employers dirty work by sacking the Young Dockers and have turned this Union into a laughing stock.
Who ever heard of a Trade Union sacking its own members, or fining them massive amounts of money into the bargain"!

The Chairman Jim Austin, as always remained calm. "We must have discipline" - he declared. "The young Dockers were told when they got into the Union - that their time at the Docks would be limited. We made them fully aware that any Docker, not in the Union before 1968 would not be included in the new Decasualisation Scheme"
Several Dockers jumped to their feet shouting, "Liar, liar.

I was told nothing and my son was told nothing". One

Docker, shouted, Decasualisation was unheard of when my son got into the Union, so don't be coming out with that oul guff. To which everyone agreed.Calmly the Chairman replied, "Whether you like it or not this is a fact". Another Docker replied with a string of expletives - "I was with my son and you told us nothing! This is all your sick idea to control us and to suck up to the employers and the Church". He continued with another unprintable string of expletives.

The chairman waited for the verbal attack to end, then using his 'Divide and conquer tactics' stated: "Whether you like it or not the Employers believe there are too many men, and your sons can't be allowed to jeopardise Decasualisation, which I've worked very hard to get, for us all".

This caused uproar in the hall, with the Dockers - and those with son's getting put out, shouting at each other. His tactics for the Employers had worked again. 'The Docker, who attended with his son, shouted. 'You're turned this Union into a Monkeys Union that jumps through hoops for the employers'.

The Chairman replied: "Whether you like it or not the Employers have always controlled us, but this time they will have to pay to do so".The Dockers' whose sons were sacked by the Union, protested, and shouted: "No - its our sons who paid with their jobs". After another unimaginable and unprintable catalogue of remarks, as to what the Union committee and Chairman could do to themselves - about fifty Dockers walked out.

I pleaded with them not to go, but sickened at the treatment their son's had got - they continued out the door hurling insults at the 'Chairman and the Puppet Union'. The chairman continued, singing the praises of Decasualisation while the committee and their Lackeys cheered.

"The fact is" he stated, "that we are a vital industry and are treated worse that slaves - and that is going to stop" While he spoke I was hastily scanning the four page booklet we'd been given on the way in, entitled: **THE BELFAST AND NORTH OF IRELAND FEDERATION OF EMPLOYERS DOCKS EMPLOYERS PAY ORGANISATION DECASUALISATION SCHEME BASIC RULES AND CONDITIONS JANUARY 1972**
Holding up the booklet I jumped to my feet and shouted: "Mr Chairman: This is a con job! 'Stated here - in this nonsense and erroneously named 'Basic Rules and Conditions', it states' in black and white just what you and the employers are up to"!

The chairman's brothers and the committee were incensed, and shouted, "this is the only way forward for the Docks Industry". The chairman, as usual, totally calm stood up and waited for the clamour to subside. "Men"
he said, "Murphy, the Communist, has accused me, and your Union Committee of conning you. He wants to deprive you of a decent standard of living, and - to impose at the Docks what he and his ilk have done on the great Catholic Country that Russia once was. They murdered priests and did unspeakable things to Nuns who were then martyred for their faith".

The chairman's brothers and the committee cheered and agreed.Unable to listen to this nonsense any more I addressed the Dockers. "Men this is nonsense and a red herring to get you to accept whatever the Union and Employers want you to accept". I held up the booklet and waved it.

"Right here is a diabolical statement from the Union and Employers that no 'real' trade unionist would ever think of agreeing to. Read it, read it!
This is utter madness. It plainly states - now listen to this and take in what it means - it says that… "As the complete rule book

relating to Decasualisation will not be finalised and ready for issue at the start of the Scheme, I.e. the week beginning the 17th of January 1972, it is
necessary that the main rules are strictly adhered to, **until all the rules are made known**"!

The chairman jumped to his feet and quick witted as usual, said: "That is a simple statement of fact, and when Murphy said this was a Red Herring, the only thing he got right was the colour". At this the committee and his family cheered.

I shouted, holding up the booklet. "Men, him and the Union as usual have sold us out again. It says here - "the following is a summary of the basic rules and the fullest co-operation is required to ensure that these rules are followed from the outset. Just what am I missing! What are these rules to be"?

The Chairman interrupted me. "See men, Murphy like all Communists doesn't want to follow the rules".

'Ok' I replied, "Tell me one rule you want me to follow". The Chairman stuttered. "I… I… the rules have not been decided yet".
"Exactly" I shouted. "Men listen to this diabolical statement from the employers {Reading} 'We are assured by the Union that strict enforcement of the Rules of the Scheme will have their full backing". -
Neither we - nor you, the Union Chairman know what these rules will be.
There was uproar in the hall.
The chairman calmly waited for the shouting to subside and stated: "Why would we not agree with them?
It also says that rule books with full details will be issued as soon as possible".

Stunned, I replied: "As you well know you sell out bastard,

they can put whatever they like into the Rule Books and you've already agreed to them.

There was uproar as what I said sank in - with the Dockers agreeing with me. They shouted: "Murphy's right, they can put whatever they want into the rules". Some questioned - "Where in the rules does it say, or will it say that the Ten Pound fines have been abolished. Many Dockers shouted - "We want to know what we're agreeing to"?

The committee tried to quell dissent but they were ignored. The chairman walked to the front of the stage and waited until the shouting stopped and said: "There's Murphy the Docks Lawyer, again finding fault and nit-picking. They just don't have the time to write them all down. But I will assure you - we will be treated with the utmost respect".

Pandemonium reigned with many shouting "What are the rules, what are the rules, do you even know"? One Docker, whose son was sacked by the Union shouted: "We' sold our sons and for what! They sacked them without any rules, what will they do on us when they have them"!

Unfortunately we soon found out.

The chairman stood silent for several minutes until the clamour had died down.

"Only Murphy with his twisted mind could read into those words what was not intended".

I leapt to my feet and said "twisted? you would know all about that. How could you be - a Union Chairman and a Foreman at the West Twin Silo, that's corruption for a start! And for you, as a Union Chairman to sit there and say... the employers have no time to invent rules that will effect our whole working lives, is a sell out of basic trade union principles. Again!

And you should be ashamed of yourself".

The Dockers loudly agreed and chanted, throw it out throw it out.

Flustered the Chairman's eyes darted from side to side as he looked for answer. He walked to the front of the stage and with arms outstretched, he pleaded: "Men, for God's sake see sense, this is the only way forward".

Someone shouted, "will the ten pound fines be abolished"?
"Yes! I believe they will be-but the fines will have nothing to do with me".

This incensed the Dockers who shouted, "You're the chairman it's you who does the fining"! His terminology seemed strange, and only later did it make sense. The Dockers realising that they'd been conned "shouted
'Sell out, sell out, we never wanted it". It really looked like they were going to reject Decasualisation.
The chairman stood rubbing his hands together until the shouting stopped. "Men, as Union Chairman I agreed on your behalf, no-one is selling you out". My friends shouted, "We don't want employers rules, we want fair rules not Employers Rules".

I Shouted! "Yes, its utter nonsense to agree to something when we don't know what it is".

The chairman replied: "And we know were, your loyalties lie, with perverted Socialism". As usual he soft-soaped the Dockers. "Men, everything I do is for your benefit, nothing major is going to change, except that you will come to work in your good clothes and change into your working clothes, provided by the employers. Then you'll hang your good clothes in your locker, and at the end of the day you'll change out of your working clothes, have a hot shower and dressed like a Christian go home - or out for the night". This caused cheers from the committee and their lackeys.

"Right men, that's it" said the chairman, "We've had enough talk about it, the new scheme starts on the 17th of January". At this he left the stage.

I shouted, "what about a contract of employment, our employers can't be trusted, they promise the earth then when the ship sails they deliver nothing".
Incensed the chairman pointed at me "Don't you slander our employers!

We have decent Employers". With that he joined his family and cronies, and the meeting was over.

However, In light of what subsequently transpired it's a wonder his lies didn't choke him. The Chairman had lied through his teeth. it was what he left out and didn't say that was monumental. Not only would the Employers implement and make up new rules as and when it suited them, but - that it would be himself that would be implementing them.

Knowing that a disgraceful betrayal of Trade Unionism and sell out of Dockers had taken place, I produced a 'Special Edition' of the Dockers Voice in which I high-lighted the sell-out by the Union. I photo-copied this and four page so-called Rules and Conditions on the photocopying
machine in the GPO, in Royal Avenue - and with copies of the 'Dockers Voice' sent them to Head office in Dublin and to the ICTU. I asked them both to explain how a Trade Union could engage in such nefarious practices. I was hoping against hope that some semblance of Connolly and Larkin's Trade Unionism still existed in the Union Leadership and ICTU. Sadly it did not.

After the Decasualisation meeting the union quickly moved against me.

Obviously they didn't want me and the Dockers Voice included in the Decasualisation Scheme - whereby I'd be in a position to expose every pro-employer tactic and sanction on the Dockers. To this end the Union sent me a letter {See letter 25th November 1971} In this the Belfast Branch pretended that trade union democracy existed at Belfast Docks.

They claimed that the Dock Section Committee recommended to the Branch Committee, { *which didn't exist and was actually themselves*} that I be expelled from the Union and thus from my job as a Docker.

Seeing that I was in regular contact with Head Office and ICTU, albeit it, mostly on a one sided basis, I photocopied the letter and sent it to them both.

While I showed them every week in the Dockers Voice, the sham trade unionism that existed at Belfast Docks, this deception was different. The Union in Belfast was actually pulling the wool over the eyes of the Unions head office and ICTU, in Dublin? I asked them both, to have the Belfast Union Office confirm to them by return of post, the names and addresses of BOTH the Branch Committee and Dock Section Committee members - to ascertain for themselves that these two committees did **not** exist.

For the Belfast Branch to resort to these underhand tactics meant that my complaints - at some level in Dublin were being believed and taken seriously. Along with the letter I again included the Dockers Voice which showed the farce of the Decasualisation Meeting, - plus the employers 'non rulebook', This proved that the Employers were drawing up rules for Union Members to adhere to - that not even the Union Officials know what they are to be?
While some elements in Head Office and ICTU, because of the

proof I supplied, believed me - this was 'not' because they suddenly found principles. As proven by their silence and subsequent cover up it was because they saw a court case in the offing. This would expose their hypocrisy to the world and change would be demanded by genuine trade union members in Dublin. The proof of this is in the fact: that the Corruption of Trade Unionism with Decasualisation continued unabated.

I heard no more from the union in Belfast about my expulsion from the Union, and *was* included in the Decasualisation Scheme.

In my private life, from the mid to late 60's my personal life was going down the tubes. In my teenage years I'd began to drink heavily and often slept in the sheds at the Docks. Later I'd come to realise that these episodes were sparked by unconscious memories that I was trying to block out. With another Docker, who was as wired up as I was, when mad drunk we broke into a shop and a Pub.

I was sentenced to four months in prison. On the was released that very night I wasarrested again for being drunk and disorderly-and sentenced to another month in prison. I had no idea what was wrong with me - but when I was released tried to pull myself together. When I didn't drink the red fog in my head stayed away.

For a while 'not drinking' worked and I got married - then my mum died and the nightmares of the beatings returned.
The only time I could sleep was when I was drunk, otherwise the screams of my mum and my sister outside the bedroom door had me banging my head against the wall.
With no-where to live we moved into my wife's Parents house and she had our daughter in the local hospital.

Because my wife's father had a 'Lung Complaint' we were given

'Priority' on the housing list and allocated a flat in a multi-story block of flats in Rushpark. This was a beautiful area just beyond the Doak Road in Newtownabbey. My drinking continued but I was more or less able to function. Then slowly I began to sink. My nights sleeping in the Dock Sheds became more frequent.

Then one day, working at bag-stuff at a Ship berthed at Sinclair Wharf, my workmates were planning a night out and invited me along. I hadn't been home for two or three nights and went home to get showered and changed. As soon as I got in my wife wanted to know where I'd been, I
told her I was working, which she didn't believe and a row started. So instead of having a shower I just put on a clean shirt and a suit and left the flat.

By half past eight I was in the Glenshesk on Castle Street, and by the time my friends arrived I was quite drunk. Even though the pub filled up, there was a large space around me. On one occasion when I walked into the gents toilet I slipped and banged my head. One of the people I was with, Liam McCormack, helped me to my feet. The floor was covered in piss as the drain had become blocked with cigarette butts.
I was soaked in piss which just added to the smell of bag stuff already emanating from me.

That's all I remember, until I wakened in the City Hospital a week later.

Apparently I had been found unconscious at the bottom of steps in the city centre. When I got out of bed I staggered and fell. The nurses and a doctor rushed to lift me up. They told me to get up easy and returned me to the bed. I sat for a while and tried again with the same result. Not only could I not walk but I couldn't speak properly either and just mumbled.

Also, my left arm and leg started to shake uncontrollably. The hospital did a battery of tests on me and could find nothing wrong. So they sent me to Claremont Hospital which dealt with neurological illnesses, for a lumber puncture. This entailed using a long needle extract spinal fluid from my backbone, and caused the worst headache I ever had in my life. After a week they told me this was clear and they didn't know why I had no balance, was shaking and had Tremors, so they discharged me with a walking stick and a crutch.

I feared the worst. I thought they were sending me home to die. This was because some of the people in the hospital were in a shocking bad way. A man in my ward was completely paralysed and in the middle of the night he would get the shakes so bad that the iron bed would rattle like a machine gun.

Even with the walking stick I still looked drunk and my Family Doctor the first time he saw me, said: "you're a disgrace coming here in that state". I mumbled and thrust the letter from the hospital at him - which he read and apologised.

Because I was off work, I got a weekly rebate on my tax. I would go to the DEPO - Dock Employers Pay Office every week to collect it - and then into the pub to drink it. This state of affairs continued for several months then I was put off the sick and had to return to work. I still had difficulty walking and on a Monday Morning arrived in the Pen. All I wanted was a slow time job to get me used to working again. However, the Bag men were milling around where O'Connor and McCann's foremen stood.

They'd heard that Mickey Collins, the son of Pat, was schooling a bag boat. As he was a new foreman they weren't sure where he'd stand on the foreman's platform. At two minutes to eight Mickey entered the Pen and walked along the platform. He stopped just about where his father stood. The bag men swooped and gathered in front of him, taking me with them. As Mickey schooled his gang I saw him looking at me, wondering was I fit enough for the job. As it turned out, he gave me the last check.

By the time I arrived at the boat he had all his holdsmen, and I was in a truck with Liam McCormack and Peter McGinn. Both good workers.
However, after the first heave it was apparent that I was staggering too much and couldn't walk fast enough to get back out for the next heave. So Liam had a brainwave and put in the shafts of the truck. With the shafts to hold onto I was able to work and walk quickly.

Mickey Collins was into cranes in a big way, and this ship had a new straddle crane which moved up and down the deck. Mickey was delighted with it and we earned good money for the three days the job lasted. Putting me off the 'Sick' was the best thing that could've happened to me, as I quickly regained my balance and the shaking stopped.

After the first day back working, and could hardly move. When washing my face, my two arms cramped and I was in agony. I called to my wife who ran into the bathroom - and she had to pull my two arms down.

After that baptism of fire I was more or less back to my old self, but with one difference, I could not smoke a cigarette. If I did so my left arm would shake and the balance would go and I was staggering all over the place. However life was beginning to look good again.

Then one night about half eleven, just as we were about to go to bed, the doorbell rang. I peeped out the spy-hole and saw my father and my uncle Paddy. Knowing something was wrong and dreading the worst, I opened the door. "Come in", I said,

"What's up". They entered the hall in silence, then Uncle Paddy said, "John's dead".

Stunned, I stuttered, "What, what, what happened to him"? Paddy looked at me, it was obvious he didn't want to answer, but he said, "Chris killed him". I felt like I'd been hit in the chest with a sledgehammer and fell against the wall. The walls were spinning and they were talking but I couldn't understand a word. I opened the door and almost threw them out. Walking up the hall I felt my stomach heave, and just made it into the bathroom where I threw my guts up. I never slept a wink that night.

I went to Townhall Street police station the next day to see Chris, and the policeman searched me before allowing me into his cell. Upon seeing me, he cried out. "Hughie, Hughie I'm sorry I didn't mean it! He was playing loud music and wakened me. I don't even remember doing it, I just saw a big red cloud and him lying there". Until he said this I was going to punch his head in. This is exactly what happened to me with Harry. Thankfully he was faster than me and got away. Shaking, I sat down on the wooden bunk. Chris said: "get me something so I can kill myself". I shook hands with him and left, with tears streaming down my face.

The next few days and the funeral are a blur. No matter how much alcohol I consumed, I could not get drunk. At the Docks I just worked and got drunk, then Decasualisation was implemented.

The Union Chairman had negotiated a supposedly life changing way of being employed for the Dockers, and as I predicted, had sold us out.

However, not even in my wildest dreams could I have realised the depth of his betrayal. For the implementation of the

Decasualisation Scheme, Yellow Boxes had been painted on the floor of The Pen with, with a central walkway. On the first morning the Dockers were milling around not knowing what was going to happen. Then the union Chairman holding a clipboard, along with a Mr Nesbitt, the new director, lately from Liverpool Docks, emerged from a newly built office at the end of the Pen.

Upon exiting the office, the Chairman pulled down a steel shutter, Then he and Nesbitt walked down the painted central aisle. They issued new Dock {Depo} numbers and instructed Dockers which box to stand in. It took about an hour before they got everything in order and the Dockers in the required boxes. Nesbitt then departed into the new office and to everyone amazement, the Chairman started to allocate work to the Dockers. Still in the dark, I thought he was, as usual being helpful to the Employers. I stopped him and said: "What are you playing at let the new guy do his job"?

Unbelievably, he dropped a bombshell and said, "I have left the Union and taken the job as Assistant Labour Controller with the Employers". And he continued allocating work to the Dockers. Astounded - my jaw dropped open and I stood speechless. It took a while for me to absorb this shocking information but the sight of our Union Chairman, sending-equally amazed Dockers to work - confirmed that I was not hallucinating.

Gathering my thought's as best I could, I shouted, "Stop. Stop". I ran to the Foreman's platform and jumped up, shouting: "Men! Our Chairman has sold us out! He's joined the Employers! No wonder he didn't want the rules to be known because its him that going to write them! Men, we must throw out this scheme, its null and void because an Employer has drawn it up".

The Dockers were as astounded as I was and they went ballistic and converged on the Chairman demanding an explanation.

I intervened to stop him being torn limb from limb. "Leave him alone men don't touch him, just throw this mad scheme of the employers out". I should have kept quiet. The now ex Union Chairman pushed his way through them and climbed onto the opposite Foreman's platform. He stood silent, clipboard against his chest, while every name under the sun was hurled at him. When the abuse subsided, as usual he sweet-talked the Dockers.

"Men, he shouted, "maybe I should've kept you informed of my decision to leave the Union, but I didn't want to give Murphy, and his lazy friends any information that would jeopardise my position with the Employers".

This was answered with contempt from the Dockers, but he continued2.
"Men, as you well know I will always be on your side and have your best interests at heart. I want you, to again be, the top earners in Belfast.
But to achieve this we must have some ground rules, and that means no more drinking at work and that we show respect to our Employers who are really decent people and want you all to be happy in your work".

The Dockers answered this with howls of contempt".
With arms out stretched he implored them. "Think of the benefits to your wives and children, there will be no more living from hand to mouth because they will know they are guaranteed a wage at the end of the week".

The committee and his family were spread out among the Dockers and they shouted agreement. I could see the Dockers were again falling under his spell and agreeing with him, and was astounded that they were again falling for his nonsense. I shouted, "Don't listen to him he could sell snow to the Eskimos! Throw this madness out"!

The ex Chairman smiled warmly and said: "The minimum fall back wage is the least you will get when there's no work, but that's only a safety net, you will still be earning very good money with 'bag stuff.

A few 'bag men' disagreed and one who was notorious for working in the rain shouted- "that's lies, it's all going up the pipe at your Silo". Many Dockers agreed with this.
The ex Chairman replied: "that's just the ebb and flow of cargo in and out of the Port and obviously - for your benefit - I have given up my position at the Silo"
The Dockers argued among themselves, many were confused at this information and didn't know what to believe.
"And before Murphy brings it up, I will not be more favourable to my family or to the committee, who have been wrongly labelled in the past. I have no axe to grind and everyone will be treated fairly. The next in line will get the next job. I am one of you. Everything I do is for your benefit".

Several Dockers protested, but it was obvious most were believing him. I protested. "Don't fall for this nonsense, he has sold us out again'.

The ex Chairman obviously knew the Dockers better than I did, as he continued to con them. Men" he continued. "Do you think I don't know what its like to go home on the bus stinking to high heaven with fish-meal on my clothes? I want you to be treated with respect and to hold your heads up among the workers of Belfast. Men accept this new deal so that you and your families will flourish from this new way of working.

Everything I do is for your benefit - and you know that"!

The committee men shouted go to work go to work!, While some were reluctant and opposed them many complied and got into their new boxes.

I shouted, "Men, our Union Chairman cannot overnight become an employer and Labour Controller. Look what he did when he was made foreman at the West Twin Silo, he employed his family and left out his best friend and workmate, who he'd been working with for years". I could see my words were falling on deaf ears, but I continued: "Men, we have no contract of employment and that's a fact and the young Dockers have no job and that's a fact. We cannot allow him once again to use the Union to further his own aims and those of his family at our expense".

Some Dockers approved of what I said - and shouted support but many were fooled. The ex chairman raised his hands and the shouting stopped. "Men, who among us has not make mistakes, we all do, but at the time we made those mistakes - we did not do so for malicious reasons? We did those things in good faith with the best intentions in the world, and thought they were for the greater good. Let us accept that this is a great move for us all - and as we move forward into prosperity Don't listen to these people who want to remain in the scandalous casual system and that has been outlawed the world over. Go to work and".

I interrupted him shouting, "don't listen to him! We have no contract of employment and that's a fact. The Employers can do whatever they like to us".

He counteracted with, "Men! I am only the assistant labour controller. I will, just like you have to take orders and do some things I would rather not do, but, for the benefit of our families this a small price to pay. Listen to the voice of reason from good God fearing people like the committee and or Employers us and not a crowd of Atheists who want to run the Docks".

A distinct murmur of approval emanated from the Dockers. "I shouted:

"Men how many times will we allow this man to sell us out? The only people that ever profit from his climb to power are him and his family. If we allow this they can do whatever they want on us"?

Shaking his head, he conned them again. Looking at me he said "Murphy, if you want a contract of employment I will get you one, it is only a piece of paper".

Incensed, I replied: "But what will it say? That we agree to whatever they want to do on us and pay us exactly what they want because you've agreed to"!

Shaking his head the ex Chairman addressed the Dockers. "Men, you know I'm one of you amd ow don't tell anyone I said this, and I hope your man isn't listening in there, but, the Employers will only do what you allow them to do, now get into your boxes and I will send you to work".

This was nonsense - and a nod to supposedly how militant they were.

This convinced the Dockers to accept his and the Employers semblance of Decasualisation. Like sheep the majority got into their boxes and accepted the sell-out and corruption of Trade Unionism. About one hundred men were reluctant but they were in the minority and had to follow suit. Several shouted to me, "Write about this in the Dockers Voice".

Actually, this did show the militancy of the Dockers. There had been only one strike at Belfast Deep Sea Docks since Larkin's Strike, in 1907. This was during the 'Twelfth Fortnight' when the North of Ireland literally closed down.

The ex chairman claimed he was only the 'assistant' but this was a joke as he was in total control, which the Dockers soon realised. The system of getting employed had changed, and was now in full control of the ex Union Chairman. He strutted about on his own, sending who he wanted to the best and the worst jobs. Needless to say I was singled out for the worst possible jobs. For several months little changed.

I continued to write to Head office in Dublin, and the ICTU about the corruption of Trade Union was ignored. They refused to acknowledge this Deviancy, or accept that both their organisations were contributing to the corruption of trade unionism and Connolly and Larkins Union. How and why they engaged in this behaviour beggars belief. Obviously, their attitudes have resulted in today's apathetic behaviour towards trade unions - which began 100 years ago when Jim Larkin was sacked.

One thing that changed at the Docks was that Dockers didn't have to go into the Pen every morning to be re-schooled and were now compelled to finish the ship they were working on. Something the employers had always wanted. Obviously, I kept sending the 'Dockers Voice' to head office and ICTU but to no avail.

In October 1972, After being schooled by 'The Judas Goat' a name I christened the ex chairman with, in the Dockers Voice, he handed me a letter and walked off grinning. It was from a 'Joint Disciplinary Committee' that 'I' or no-one had ever heard of. A crowd of my friends gathered round as I opened the letter. It stated that 'after my appearance before the committee, I had been suspended for two days without pay'.

This was utter nonsense, I had never attended any Committee meeting, Joint or otherwise. Incensed, myself and my friends went to the office and banged on the metal roll up shutter.

When the shutter went up I challenged the ex chairman to

explain what was going on. He played dumb and pretended he didn't know what was in the letter. All present wanted to know just what this Joint Committee was, and I specifically denied ever having attended any committee meeting with them.

The ex Chairman stated that: "while not knowing it was in operation The Joint Disciplinary Committee had been agreed by the Union prior to the Dockers going into Decasualisation". Everyone present shouted, "But that was you ya bastard you were the Union and the only one who wanted it". He quickly pulled down the shutter.

We discussed what we should do in respect of this Joint Committee and any other letters they sent out, and all agreed that we would ignore the letters.
I pointed out that this letter was a ploy to get the JDC established, recognised and accepted in Dockers minds - thereby legitimising, this diabolic betrayal of Trade Unionism. I also pointed out that the Union and Employers had always disciplined us, with ten pound fines, but previously, the employers input had happened behind the scenes.

I banged on the shutter shouting for him to open up. The ex Chairman's voice was heard saying, "I will put in your appeal". And he sarcastically suggested that I contact my Trade Union. Armed with the JDC letter we went to a ship where several Committee men were working, and challenged them. They claimed they were as much in the Dark as I was, but agreed totally with it.

Astounded, we demanded, "How can you agree with something that you know nothing about, and who gave the Union permission to join with the Employers against their fellow workers"?

The committee men insisted, that from now on 'the union'

would have a say in disciplinary all procedures. I retorted, "And what would you call Ten pound fines". With heads down they refused to look at us, but one, repeated the ex Chairman's mantra."We must have discipline". Angry we left and spread the word among the Dockers about the Joint Committee.

The following day the ex Union chairman posted a notice on the bulletin board. This had the disgusting letter heading of the "Joint Disciplinary Committee".
And below it a message which stated, that all rules must be followed to the letter. This was impossible as there were still no rules to follow, although the employers obviously had already drawn them up - and would use them, as and when required. Eventually they produced a book of rules as thick as the Bible

The employers and the ex Union Chairman added to these rules as they went along, and needless to say they were always in the employers favour. We soon learned the four page 'Basic Rules and Conditions' we were given at the Decasualisation meeting was a con job.

I pulled down the notice with the scandalous heading, photocopied it, and forwarded this betrayal of Trade Unionism to head office and ICTU. I also included the most recent Dockers Voice. This lambasted our ex union chairman, but as usual, what I told them about Belfast Docks was ignored. As were my letters to the Major Irish newspapers, including the Irish Times. I questioned how the Union could behave in such a treacherous manner. They also ignored me.

When I complained to ICTU about the ex Chairman's activities, and the capitulation of the Union - they didn't care one hoot about the betrayal of Trade Unionism. Or in fact - that the Belfast Union Committee were partaking in this betrayal - as indeed was ICTU and ITGWU by their Silence.

For several months nothing changed at the Docks but the letters kept coming - handed out to anyone who voiced disagreement with the 'unification' of the Union and the Employers. What later transpired and also not told to the Dockers, was that the Joint Disciplinary Committee which the ex Union Chairman and Employers had agreed to form, was in fact, a private court system for disciplining the Dockers.

The initial letters from the JDC were warnings about the Dockers behaviour - then they turned into 'summons letters' for the Dockers to attend the Unon and Employers Court that sat once a week in the Stella Maris Seaman's Hostel. This was the first time in recorded Trade Union History that a Trade Union disciplined and sacked its own members, for and with the Employers. To start the ball rolling the ex Chairman targeted weak Dockers who he knew would attend the J.D.C. - and at the start they were just reprimanded and given a warning as to their future conduct.

Every week and sometimes several times a week the ex chairman would hand me a letter. At the start I would tear them up and throw them at him but eventually I just refused to take them. The Union Committee become the employers Policemen. They always had been, but now it was out in the open. They would report [what they termed] breeches of discipline to the ex union Chairman, labour controller, who would decide if the full wrath of the employers and himself would be applied to the supposed wrongdoer.

It was he who was the prime mover in the Union and Employers Court and essentially the prosecutor, but always low key - whispering in the employers ears. And here is the disgusting banner heading of the Union and Employers Court - which every Trade Unionist in Ireland should be ashamed of.

NORTHERN IRELAND FEDERATION OF EMPLOYERS AND IRISH TRANSPORT & GENERAL WORKERS UNION JOINT DISCIPLINARY COMMITTEE.

All these years later, I find myself open to the suggestion, that 'if' Belfast Docks was not the testing ground for the "Partnership" between the Irish Government, Employers and the Unions - which came into being years later - with the only thing missing being the JDC' - then, the only other explanation 'is' that a massive conspiracy of corruption was in existence by the union leadership and the Employers in Dublin and Belfast?

This theory gains credence with the cover up started by Jack 'O Connor, when still Union President - and which continues to this day. When Containers and 'Roll on Roll off' made Belfast Dockers obsolete, what also became redundant was the storage sheds that stretched up the River Lagan into the City Center and only ended at the Queen's Bridge.

While not being a believer in Conspiracy Theories, a sceptic would argue that the obvious reason to remove Belfast Dockers was the fact, that the Docks could be developed for multi-story office and leisure activities - which has indeed happened.
Had Decasualisation **not** been forced onto the Belfast Dockers the Casual System and the Docks Sheds would have existed for many more years without being redeveloped? I wonder, even after all this time, could the bank accounts of the SILENT union officials in head office and ICTU be investigated?

While this theory sounds preposterous - it can be the only reason why the Dublin Union Hierarchy would sell out the Belfast Branch of its own Union. If the Belfast Dockers had thought for one minute, that their own Union and Union Chairman was not on their side, they would never have accepted Decasualisation. Obviously corruption controlled head office and ICTU fifty years ago - why else would they sell out the Branch that had stuck by them through thick and thin with no support from Head Office - because they were in a 'different country'.

In The 'Dockers Voice' at the time I was not fully aware of the enormity of the sell-out - just that we were being sold out and could not understand why? In the Dockers Voice I aired my complaints about the betrayal that Decasualisation was - to all and sundry in Dublin and Belfast. One grievance was, that while the young Dockers had been
sacked by the Union, Dockers were still expected to work men short.

The more I wrote about the wrongs of the scheme the more letters I received from the ex union chairman. They either stated: I was to appear before the JDC on such a date, or thanking me for putting in my appeal against a JDC decision they'd imposed upon me.
This was utter nonsense as I never attended any of the so-called disciplinary committee meetings.

Some of the letters I photocopied and sent to head office and ICTU. As usual they were ignored.{See Letters} The Truth of the matter is, head office and ICTU by their silence - gave carte Blanche to the Union at Belfast Docks to sell out the Dockers. It is unbelievable to believe they did this without an ulterior motive. It obviously gives credence to the conspiracy of wealthy far-sighted wealthy manipulators controlling the Union Leaders. Again I ask, could their bank accounts be investigated?

I had not given my Union permission to sit with employers to discipline me, or any union member - and would not have done so - had I been asked.
However, by their silence, then and now, Head Office in Liberty Hall and ICTU have been corrupted. This is a fact and why

none of the people I've mentioned will sue me. Back then I believed, there was no earthly reason why the inheritors of James Connolly and Jim Larkin's mantle would agree to this abject betrayal of the Trade Union they founded.

It therefore was beyond my comprehension and never even entered my head that they were bought off. Even at this late stage I would appreciate an answer from SIPTU and ICTU. I don't want to believe that the union leaders at the time were corrupt? There has to be an answer as to why… they stood Irish History on its head, betrayed the original ITGWU that fought for the rights and lives of Dublin citizens during the Lockout. Seeing that they're no longer around to answer for themselves, maybe the the cover up so-called historian previously mentioned will give his opinion on the matter - and not as usual remain silent.It's not as if these were the dark days of Union bashing, when William Martin Murphy ruled the roost in Dublin - and Larkin's Union was beaten and starved into submission.

In fact Ireland was a progressive country and had joined the Common Market. At the Docks a blatant and unsubtle example of divide and conquer was in vogue. While I tore up the letters from the employers, the more timid Dockers attended the JDC, and accepted the punishments handed out. These ranged from one to three days suspension without pay. Obviously the acceptance of this betrayal of Trade Unionism established the 'Joint Disciplinary Committee' - which no Docker or union member had agreed to - or even knew anything about - as the bona fide authority at the Docks.

On one occasion in the Pen, the situation became explosive. During an altercation between the ex union chairman and myself. He took exception to me ridiculing him in the Dockers Voice and naming him a 'Judas Goat'. He threatened to sue me and to loud cheering I told him to go ahead.

I explained to him exactly what a Judas Goat is. - I.e. a goat that mingles with the others, rubbing up against them - then leads them quietly to be slaughtered, while he nips through a doorway.

This caused much cheering from the assembled Dockers, especially when I pointed at the ex Chairman and asked him to show me the difference? The ex chairman for the first time anyone could recall got angry. Apparently the nickname had reached the ears of his neighbours children, who were "Baaaaa" at his family.

Obviously his wife and family were distressed. He wanted me to print an apology and a story about the good things he'd achieved at the Docks.

With a straight face I replied. "I cannot do that because my Journalistic Principles demand that I always print the Truth" This caused great laughter. Red-faced and annoyed he walked away shouting "Get into your boxes". Several, who had sons sacked by the Union "Baaaaaad" at him.

The next morning, whether it was on the orders of Employers and the JDC, or for the sake of his own self respect - the ex Chairman refused to employ me. He stated that "I had been suspended for two days without pay for 'insulting behaviour'. I jumped up on the Foreman's platform and shouted to the Dockers "Men, The Judas Goat has refused to employ me". Upon hearing this, my friends circled the goat, chanting "if he doesn't work we don't work".

Even the more timid Dockers joined in the chanting. The ex Chairman scurried into his office, and could be seen through the hatch on the phone.

Soon he emerged shouting "get into your boxes, I've got it resolved. Murphy's allowed to work until the next meeting in the Stella Maris".

For a long time nothing happened, save the betrayal of normal trade union practices. Then, one morning the ex Chairman accompanied by two committee men, stopped in front of me. He produced a letter and instead of handing it to me, read it out. "This is an official warning, you are not complying with orders from The Joint Disciplinary Committee and unless you desist disciplinary action will be taken against you".He handed me the letter, turned and walked away. "I shouted after him. "You can stick that letter and the Asbestos boats where the sun don't shine".

This warning came after I had tried without success, to convince a gang of Dockers 'not' to discharge a cargo of Asbestos. I crunched up the letter up and threw it after them. A few years before, prior to Decasualisation we had been completely ignorant about the dangers of this Asbestos, but according to Paddy the Turk, the Union and employers knew that it caused cancer. The first time I heard about it, was - when along with five others we had been in the hold of a ship slinging bags of the stuff. It was in the form of a white powder. It got up our noses, and into our eyes ears and throats. Clouds of it filled the air and was blown across the Herdman Channel into North Belfast. God knows how many Belfast People have died from the Union's and employers determination to save the Employers money.
Anyway to cut a long story short - back then in the hold of the ship we could hardly see never mind breathe. Just as a heave left the hatch, Paddy the Turk, with his scarf covering his mouth, in great excitement, shouted down to us, "Stop working at that get away from it, it gives you cancer". The excited behaviour of Paddy who was normally a placid sort of person convinced us to stop work and to leave the hatch. When the Judas Goat arrived, 'he was still Union Chairman at the time', with his lackeys, he ordered us to restart work. We

refused and Paddy told him "That stuff gives you cancer and you know all about it".

The union lackeys told Paddy to "fuck away of back to your own hatch or you'll be up before the committee". Addressing us, Paddy said "I've told you about it, on your own heads be it" and walked away.
"Look lads", said the Judas Goat, "how can dust kill you or cause cancer?
You know what Paddy's like he'll say anything to get you to stop work".

The Lackeys threatened that we'd be up on Tuesday night if we didn't restart work. This frightened the others who climbed down the ladder into the hold. I was reluctant to do so but my friend Liam, said, "Look, if Paddy's right the damage is already been done, we've been working at it for hours". This made sense and I went down the ladder.

Shortly after we resumed work, the Chairman threw into the hatch a shoebox filled with cloth masks, these were left over from a ship loading ritually slaughtered meat - the masks were so we wouldn't breathe on it.

When we put on the masks and started work they were less that useless. Because our noses were stuffed with Asbestos, when we breathed in, we sucked the mask into our mouths and couldn't breathe at all, so we threw them away. At lunchtime I went into Whitla Street Fire Station and checked out what Paddy had said, and was told every word was true.

On returning at one 0'Clock I informed the rest of the gang what I had learned, and I walked away. However no-one else did they were of the opinion that the damage was already done but in future they wouldn't work at it.
Surprisingly no action was taken against me for leaving the

job. This was an unknown occurrence at the Docks as I fully expected to be fined Ten Pounds. Maybe the fact that the Fire-station medic was was prepared to give evidence if disciplinary action was taken against me, stopped them.

Just a few years later, I wondered what had changed to make the JDC issue this warning letter? Were there ships sailing the seas laden with Asbestos that no-one would discharge and they were trying to bring them to Belfast? Details of the Asbestos scandal at Belfast Docks was highlighted by UTV with their 'entitled DEATH TRAP ON THE DOCKS, this is available on you-tube.

The scandalous behaviour of the Union towards dying Dockers and widows is shown in graphic detail.
The Union refused to comment on air and didn't want to talk about the Asbestos because they were complicit in making the Dockers discharge it. Also in the program Politicians and Doctors give their opinions that the so-called duty of care shown to the Dockers was grossly inadequate. An important point is: Shortly after this programme was broadcast, this highly popular programme was discontinued. Why...?

Employers and Trade Unions world-wide had known for decades of the dangers of asbestos fibres. In the programme this particular point is made by Solicitor Martin Hanna, who states, that the behaviour of Employers "could equate to Corporate Manslaughter". I will go further and ask - "surely, the Dockers Union and the ex Union Chairman are guilty of more than Corporate manslaughter - because they were aware of the danger and ordered Dockers to work at it - they and the Employers should be charged with Corporate Murder".What defence could they possibly put forward? The loss of profit?

Although this is a moot point as they are all long deceased. This may seem over the top, however, when juxtaposed with all other human rights and trade union violations they were guilty of - when they were supposed to be on the side of the Dockers, they must be exposed. This will also call into question the present day Union Officials who cover it up?

Such an investigation may even disclose if any Wealthy Southern Speculators were involved in the Docks Belfast Docks Scandal.

In the UTV Asbestos Programme, 'on camera', a Dublin Union Leader is questioned about his Union's reaction to Belfast dying Dockers. He states in no uncertain terms, "I told you I'm not going to comment any further".

The ex Union Chairman's words haunt me to this day: "It's only dust, how could that kill anyone"? The Union chairman who replaced him, when he joined the employers, stated, "You have to go sometime, look at that young Docker run over by a lorry, no one knows when it's going to be their turn". While anyone can be killed by an accident, it was no accident that the Union ordered Belfast Dockers to discharge Asbestos without protection. This was out and out Corruption.

After fighting for many years Arthur Rafferty and Billy Browne received compensation for contracting Asbestosis. The dead and dying Dockers may receive compensation but will never get Justice. Likewise, the widows of Billy Brown's two brothers who have already died from Asbestosis received lesser amounts. Billy Brown is over Eighty years old and is a good living Catholic. As a matter of urgency, a Legal Investigation which is interested in Justice should interview Billy. He is entirely lucid and can recite every atrocity imposed upon the Belfast Dockers by the Union. For the sake of 'truthfulness' - and the fact that Asbestos Dust was blown all over Belfast this must happen.

Why will no Human Rights Organisation demand that this

Inquiry be instigated?

I call on the Irish Government to do just this - and to stop covering up for the multimillionaires who owned the Asbestos.

As Decusalisation progressed, letters from the Joint Disciplinary Committee and suspensions without pay became common place. These were for infringements of the rules that Dockers knew nothing about.

However several timid Dockers began to question - why I was able to flaunt the authority of The JDC and insult the ex chairman in the Dockers Voice, with impunity. I told them. "Do what I do, don't attend the JDC, we never agreed to it, and in fact knew nothing about it". However, on their behalf I challenged the ex Chairman to produce the rules they were being suspended for breaking. To my surprise he produced a large book and smirking said: "tell anyone who wants to see the Rules, they just have to ask".

Astounded, and pointing at the book, I said: "You were the only person who agreed to that nonsense". Contrary to what the ex Chairman said at the Decasualisation Meeting, everything had changed. We were now locked into a straight jacket of his and the Employers making. The only thing that hadn't changed was his dictatorial attitude, and now with him in sole control of the allocation of work, the committee and his family still got the best jobs going.

With the Union and Employers united against the Dockers, everyone knew to keep quiet or they'd be never get any decent work.

However, they did write letters which I printed in the Dockers Voice - which were not signed and I made sure they were unidentifiable.

The so-called malcontent's like myself were given the worst paid and dirtiest jobs at the Docks. Needless to say the promised hot showers and washing facilities never materialised.

In my box it was obvious and well known from the start that I got the worst jobs going, so the Dockers got as far away from me as possible within the box, leaving me standing on my own. However, there was one exception. While I was campaigning about the lack of trade unionism and compulsory overtime in the Dockers Voice - a funny thing happened.

It had been rumoured for months that the Head Line were starting a new Container Service named, 'The Headterm'. On the morning it was to be schooled by the ex union chairman, the Dockers watched with great excitement his progress down the Pen.

Then to my amazement and to the amazement of everyone else, he schooled it in my box and I was one of the six men picked for this prestigious job. I smelled a rat immediately because the money was fantastic and like the only other Container Ship, it worked 24 hours. The company also installed telephones in the Dockers houses to make sure they were always available. I came in for much abuse, and friends even accused me of being bought off.

I said nothing, went to the Container Ship and worked all day hooking on containers. Then at Five 0' Clock I informed the foreman, Tommy Cunningham I was knocking off. "You can't knock off this Ship's for sea at two in the morning and there's another one starting". I informed him that I had other plans and walked down the gangplank.

The funny thing I referred to was - just how shallow did the ex Chairman think I was? Did he really think I was as lacking in principles as he so obviously is, and like him - could be bought off with a well paid job?

The following morning in the Pen the ex chairman refused to employ me, stating, that "I had voluntarily left my employment" and his hands were tied". Of course they were. My friends started chanting 'if he don't work we don't work' and the Dockers took up the chant. The ex Chairman and the committee had a whispered meeting and the end result was he relented, and employed me. However, he sent me to a really dirty smelly job loading bags of Fish-meal onto Lorries.

While suspension without pay was commonplace, it also entailed, that any suspended Docker lost his right to 'fall back pay' so when work was scarce he only got paid for the actual days worked. This made it worse than the casual system, at least with that you got the Dole when there was no work. This was one of the hidden rules employers and the Union had agreed to. The Dockers, sickened, had to accept this because speaking out just made it worse.
While I ridiculed the Union and Employers in the Dockers Voice, the more weasly Dockers asked, why I hadn't been suspended by the Court?

I informed them again not to participate in this farce of trade unionism, and that our Union had no right to suspend them. I also pointed out that the Employers and Union were playing a divide and conquer game, which by their questioning of me was working - and in due course they would make their move against me. I hadn't long to wait.

The following week, in the Pen, with only about a hundred Dockers present, the ex chairman handed me two letters, one dated 24th of October 1973, stating I had been suspended for two days. And the other was what I'd been expecting. It was dated the 25th of October 1973 - a day later, telling me that I had been sacked. This shows the devious thinking of the

Employers and the Union and how frightened they were of the Dockers Voice.

I jumped up onto the Foreman's platform waving the letter, and shouted, "there you are men! This so called Trade Union cannot sink any lower, their corrupt and illegal Union and Employers Court formed by him", I pointed at the ex Union Chairman". That Judas Goat has sacked me!

The Judas Goat ran up and down shouting. 'Get into your boxes get into your boxes. The Dockers ignored him and demanded to know why I was Sacked?
Shocked at the hostility The ex chairman stuttered, "As, as as you know I don't speak for the Union any more".
"When did you ever", I retorted! I shouted, "Men, go out to every ship, get everyone to stop work and come in here. We'll get rid of this Decausalisation farce once and for all". The Dockers agreed and ran out both doors, leaving me alone with The Judas Goat. Looking at him with contempt, I asked, "What sort of bastard are you".

Shaking he walked up the Pen into his office and saying to himself, "we must have discipline we must have discipline". I sat down and lit a cigarette. Shortly Dockers began to enter the Pen and demanded to know what had happened. I told them and showed them the letter. When the Pen was full I climbed onto the platform and walked to the middle of it.

I could see through the hatch, The Judas Goat standing inside his office, and pointed at him. "There men, is betrayal personified. He, as chairman of our union sold us out. He created this Joint Disciplinary Committee to curry favour with the employers and to sack anyone who exposed his betrayal of trade unionism".

The ex Chairman noisily pulled down his shutter with a loud

clatter.

"I have been unjustly sacked by this Union and Employers Court, and you all know it... It just as well could have been one of you, and, if you do nothing it won't be one of you - it will be all of you".

With a loud clatter the ex chairman opened the shutter. With telephone in hand he shouted through the hatch, "But you can appeal the sentence, it's not cast in stone".

The more timid Dockers leapt on this proposal.
"Yes, yes" they shouted, if you appeal and its shot down we'll go on strike until you're reinstated". Half the men agreed with this. Keeping my frustration under control, I tried, with common sense to change their minds. "Men, if I appeal - that is guaranteeing that I '*will*' be sacked -
because my doing so I am accepting that my Union has the right to collaborate with the Employers to sack me. Which it has not! it's supposed to defend me!"

A few Dockers cheered. I could see the money men itching to get back to work. Postponing strike action suited them. After almost two weeks of time jobs, a ship loaded with Bag Stuff had started that morning. The Bag Men argued amongst themselves, with one saying some saying we could shift 400 ton today.

The consensus was, that I should appeal, and given this show of strength they would think twice before carrying out my sacking. I tried to convince them otherwise but to no avail, they seemed not able to grasp the concept I had just explained. Reluctantly, I and my supporters had to agree. As the Dockers returned to work I approached the Judas Goat's hatch. He had a smile on his face.

"Right" I said, "For all the good it'll do, I want to appeal".

'You have to do it in writing'.

'Give me a pen and paper'.

'Get your own'. he replied

I walked into the old canteen next door and got a pen from one of the women, and asked had she any paper. She looked below the counter and came up with a brown paper bag.

I sat down and wrote the following:

'I - Hugh Murphy wish to appeal against the unfair, unjust, and diabolical decision to sack me from the Docks. This illegal decision has been reached by an unholy alliance that exists between my Employers and my Trade Union. This calls itself, "The Joint Disciplinary Committee".

While I expect nothing more from my Employers, I expected the Docks Section Committee Men, if 'men' is the appropriate term, to behave like trade unionists and not grasping Employers. That said, this in no way excuses their traitorous behaviour. They have come under the malign influence of the ex Union Chairman - who sold out the Dockers and joined the Employers as labour Controller. He pretends to be, an old time Holy-Joe, but in reality is just a greedy bastard, and because of his actions I have nick-named him verbally and in print - in The Dockers Voice, a Judas Goat'.

I returned to the Pen and gave the paper bag to the ex chairman. He read it and went apoplectic with rage and screamed "I won't accept this"!

I walked away saying "You do as you please but it's the truth and the only appeal you'll get from me".

In due course I received a letter from the Appeal Tribunal confirming that my appeal had been set for the 9th November 1974 at 11-30. In the run up to my appeal I telephoned and wrote many times to head office and ICTU - pleading with them to send a representative to observe the anti trade union practice of ITGWU and the Employers in Belfast - but as usual this was ignored.

CHAPTER FIVE

O n the morning of my appeal I entered the dining room of the Stella Maris, at the appointed time. Seated was a Mr Bennet or so the card in front of him said. It was a bit grubby and I had a suspicion it was left over from some other meeting, plus Bobby Dickey Stan, Alan, and The Judas Goat. Mr Bennet and the Goat wore suits and ties. The Goat spoke first, saying, "So you've decided to honour us with your presence".

I replied "Fuck up Iscariot"! And looking at Alan and Stan, asked; "what are you two doing here, you're Dockers! This is a joke and pointed at the Judas Goat, said: Decasualisation is a joke and the only people profiting from it, are him and his family".

Shaking the Goat replied. "Everyone profits from being treated with respect, and if you followed the rules you wouldn't be here and you'll deserve everything you get".
I looked at him with contempt. "Tell that to the Young Dockers that you put on the dole, everyone, of them followed your daft sell out rules".

Standing up the Judas Goat pointed a shaking finger at me. "It was the Union that put them out and, and they knew from getting in that their days were numbered".

'Liar', I countered: "You were the Union and you still are. What about Shortt, Quinn and Turner? What right have you and these Mickey Mouse Monkeys got to deprive me, or any Docker of our livelihoods and the means to feed our families"

Bobby Dickey and Stan and jumped up shouting but were calmed by the Judas Goat. "He's trying to get you to attack him and upset everything, don't let him do it. Give him nothing to complain to Dublin about". He smiled and said: "You'll get nothing here to put in The Dockers Voice"
So, I retorted, "you're admitting this appeal is a farce and I am going to be sacked". Stony faced the Goat looked at me, while Bobby Dickey and Stan grinned. Mr Bennet broke the silence, saying, "The outcome of this Tribunal has not been pre-determined. Stan and Alan looked puzzled. so I enlightened them. "He's pretending that you and the Judas Goat haven't made up your minds to sack me".

Clearly out of his depth Stan replied: "Why else do you think you're here".

I couldn't help but laugh. "And for the record, Mr ex union chairman, I didn't give my Union permission to sack me or the Young Dockers' or to set up this Union and Employers Court"

Clearly annoyed, Mr Bennet shifted uncomfortably in his seat and said: "This is not a Union and Employers Court. No doubt there is animosity here of which I know nothing, and don't wish to know. You obviously have many things to discuss, but can you do it elsewhere so we can get down to the business in hand".

"Who are you" I asked "and the business in hand, of this corrupt Court, as you well know, is to sack me with as little fuss as possible, while putting on it, a veneer of fair play, by pretending that those two are here to represent me"

"Wouldn't be guilty of it" said Stan.

"Now young man, let us not presume the verdict without first hearing the evidence".

'Exactly, who are you and what has this to do with you', I asked.

"I am an accountant, and have been appointed by the Joint Disciplinary Committee to ensure that you have been dismissed within the law, and to hear your appeal against this decision".

An accountant I replied?. "Are you a qualified Judge with a law degree?

If so, how can a Trade Union sack its own members? What's your name and what company do you work for"?

Looking at me replied "That is none of your business".

Laughing I said: "So you're continuing the farce of the Union's secret courts". The Judas Goat Bobby Dickey and Stan, were getting uncomfortable at this line of questioning. Dickey forcefully inquired, "Are we going to hear this case or not"?

Indeed, 'Judge Dickey' I replied. "And come to think of it, what legal training have you two eejits got, sure you can hardly read or write".

Incensed they jumped to their feet, pulling their big hooks from their belts.

"Stop, stop" implored the the Judas Goat. "He's trying to stop this tribunal and to show us as bully boys".

I laughed. "Many a true word is said in jest".

Clearly annoyed the Judas Goat said: "You keep a civil tongue in your head. You might at least have got cleaned up, before coming here".

Indeed, I sarcastically replied. 'Where, in the non-existent Shower Block you promised, you conniving little bastard. You want me to come in clean to a secret Court when there's nowhere to wash, and you want me to show respect to a secret judge in a secret court while being threatened by two monosyllabic goons? Tell me, what exactly am I missing"!

Stan and Alan jumped up shouting but with difficulty were calmed by the Goat.
Clearly upset the accountant had got very white in the face, I continued. "Look, Mr Accountant, this farce is because I wouldn't work at Asbestos and be bought off with a Container boat while these two were bought off with drink and power."

Dickey and Stan fingered their big hooks, as did I."Come on you scum bastards show exactly what you'll do for the Judas Goat and his sell out Union"?

The Judas Goat had great difficulty in stopping them. "Don't let him get to you, if you hurt him we'll never get rid of him".
Glaring, Dickey replied,
"I'll stick my hook in his head and we'll thrown him in the dock".

Shaking like a leaf the accountant poured a glass of water. "I have never met with such aggression in my life, I will have to call the police".

I nodded. "Please do and the lot of you will be arrested for impersonating a Judge in a Court of Law".
Stony faced the accountant said: 'This is not a farce but properly constituted legal procedure as outlined by'-.
Disgusted I interrupted him again. "Who are you to decide whether I keep my job or not?

Glowering at me the Judas Goat said: "One more word and we'll proceed without you".

I laughed. "It's a charade and matters not one iota whether I'm here or not".
Clearly annoyed the accountant replied: 'This is not a charade but a lawfully constituted panel to'-

Pointing my finger I interrupted him and said: "Lawful! I ask again what legal training have you got? Are you a Lawyer"?'.

Obviously the Judas Goat could see where this was going. If the accountant walked out their Tribunal would collapse so he said: "Stop questioning him you're doing yourself no favours".

Exasperated I re[plied: 'Will you stop pussy-footing about, this joke of a Tribunal is just here to sack me, so get on with it'!

Spreading his arms the accountant said: "Young man, this is nothing personal, I hope you understand that".

Amazed, I said "I understand that you and these clowns are trying to justify your pathetic corruption"?
The ex chairman Bobby Dickey and Stan jumped up, all shouting. "We are not corrupt". Pointing his finger at me Stan shouted: "You deserve all you get"!

Shaking my head I replied: "No Stan I don't, what right have you or these monkeys got to sack me". They all protested and I pointed at the ex chairman and said: "Can you Stan and the fools on the Docks Committee not see, 'he's' using you to rubber stamp dictatorship and the sell out of Union Principles".

Bobby Dickey shouted "He is not and we are not"
Clearly annoyed the Judas Goat interjected: "The membership

gave me the right to make decisions on their behalf". I pointed at the ex union chairman. "Not to sell out! You were the only one who wanted Decasualisation".

He snapped back. "I was not, there was plenty who wanted it".

I held up my hands. "Sorry, I'll rephrase that, you were the only one besides the Employers and your monkeys who wanted it".

Clearly upset at the home truths I was imparting, Stan resorted to type and said: "Call me a monkey again and I'll stick this hook in your head'.

The ex chairman looked at him and said: "Let it go we'll settle this without any violence, so there's no come-backs".

Looking at me he said: "Because of the seriousness of the events that have transpired, and the fact that you've refused to engage with The Joint Disciplinary Committee, and indeed on many occasions have shown outright and utter contempt for it - we have decided to dispense with the original charges, and-'.

I interrupted him with mock delight, stating, "So I've been acquitted"!

He glowered at me and continued. "We have decided to replace them with the simpler charge of - contempt - for The Joint Disciplinary Committee, and attempting to bring it into disrepute".

I replied saying: "You did that without my help".

"Shut up and let him finish". Said Stan.

The Judas Goat continued: "Firstly by refusing to attend its meetings when lawfully summoned, and secondly by spreading false malicious gossip in your Rag, that any Docks Committee member who sat on it, with the employers was betraying Trade Unionism'.

"They are", I shouted. "Lawfully summoned"? Why are you pretending that this farce is legal? Get a grip. My Union and the Employers cannot conspire together to sack me - the Young Dockers and the string of Dockers you've lined up to go, once you get rid of me".

The Judas Goat smirked. "If what we're doing is illegal, why then is head office in Dublin and the Irish Congress of Trade Unions ignoring what you tell them? Incidentally head office is in full agreement with everything I do because we've gotten rid of the casual system".

"Of course they are, but why - is the question? I send them the Dockers Voice every week and they still agree with you. What sort of trade unionists are they to ignore your corruption! This... is beyond my comprehension and ignoring it does not make it legal. It just means that they are as corrupt as what you are".

Bobby Dickey interrupted me: "Your beliefs won't be allowed to ruin the Docks".

The accountant slammed his cup down on the table. "Stop this nonsense how do you plead"?

Taken aback I asked. "What no Bible, I want a Bible to swear on".

The Judas Goat looked serious and stated: "You're making a mockery out of this, but I will not allow you to drag Christianity down with you".

I replied. "No - you and this Mickey Mouse Trade Union, this Mickey Mouse Tribunal and this Mickey Mouse Court of Law are doing that - and you couldn't make it up".

Stan jumped to his feet shouting. "How do you plead"?

"Insanity! I plead insanity for coming here and allowing your fools to sit in judgement on me, but because the cowardly Dockers wanted it I had to agree to it!"

The Judas Goat smirked. "You're getting a fair trial in accordance with Trade Union Law and the Law of the land".
I looked at him with contempt. "That is confounded lies and you know it.

Get on with it so I can go back to the men".

The accountant looked at me with a mixture of contempt and sadness.

"Do you actually think they'll support you"?
I nodded. 'Yes, because it's not just my job they're protecting but they're own.

He smiled. "You've a lot to learn about men, give them a way out and they'll take it".

I shook my head. "Not in this case, they must support me".

The ex chairman looked at me and laughed. "Dockers with core values who don't smoke or drink will always succeed".

I nodded. "You mean the ones like you who sell out, but, can't sleep at night".

He smiled a condescending smile. "In your book it's selling

out in mine its progress. Get it into your head you were sacked because you refused to attend the Joint Disciplinary Committee meetings. You could have ruined everything".

I looked at him and shook my head. "You have turned this once great Trade Union into a Lapdog union, with scum like yourself and these two prepared to do anything for the Employers".

Seething, Stan and Bobby Dickey glared hatred. Upset the accountant declared: "If there is any violence I am leaving, we must discuss this in a reasonable manner'".

The ex chairman calmed the committee men saying: "He wants this hearing declared null and void and that will happen if you touch him".

The accountant poured a glass of water and continued: "Mr Murphy, we… are here to dispense Justice and to decide if the Joint Disciplinary Committee acted lawfully when it removed your name from the Decasualisation Register, and I have heard nothing here to disagree with that decision - so it must stand". With nodding heads they all agreed.

Looking at him I sajd: "The lunatics are running the Asylum, these three corrupt bastards are running the Docks, and have prostituted the principles of genuine trade unionism".

Shaking the Judas Goat stood up. "You have brought it on yourself and deserve all you get. The finding of this Appeals Tribunal is that the original sentence stands, and you are dismissed from your employment at Belfast Docks. You will receive confirmation of this decision in the post and a date when to collect your P45 your national insurance cards and any outstanding wages due".

I approached the table. "We'll see about that". And I walked out.

As I emerged onto Garmoyle Street I was formulating in my head the letter I would send to head office about the mockery of trade unionism that had just taken place. Obviously my letters to Head Office and ICTU plus weekly copies of the Dockers Voice to both, were having an effect – but so far it was a negative one. Instead of them demanding that the Belfast Branch adhere to basic Trade Union principles, they kept quiet? This convinced me that there was a wider conspiracy at work.

Every Docker was aware that I was appearing before the committee and the following morning the Pen was packed. Upon entering a loud cheer went up. I mounted the platform and stated: "There's nothing to cheer about, I have been sacked"! The supporting roar gladdened my heart.

Above the heads of the Dockers, across the Pen, something was different, and then it struck me. The old constant gangs of the Headline Foremen were standing in their old positions, with the foremen in the middle of them. I took this as a positive sign and that they were also supporting me. I waited for uproar to quieten down

"Men", I said, "the Belfast Branch of this once great Union have insulted James Connolly, Jim Larkin and the men and women, who in 1913 sacrificed everything, even their lives to join the ITGWU. They refused to sign a pledge forced upon them by the Dublin Employers that they'd have nothing to do with Larkin's Union - and were locked out from their employment. This was the start of the infamous Dublin Lockout.
They had principles but aided and abetted by the Catholic Church were starved into submission".
I sensed right away a change of mood when I mentioned the Church.

"At the Belfast Docks today, by stealth, and with the aid of 'The

Judas Goat' the Employers have turned the Union Committee into the disciplinary arm of the Employers, and we, like the workers of Dublin will not stand for that. If they get away with 'framing' and sacking me then not one of your jobs is safe".
The Dockers cheered.

"We must make a stand and show them what we're made of. Just like the men and women of 1913 in Dublin, we will not allow the Employers to dictate to us and to rule our lives. We must strike until my sacking - and your eventual sacking is prevented. By standing together as members of Connolly and Larkin's Union - we will strike until our Trade Union treats our despicable Employers like decent Employers. Lets go".

The Dockers cheered and poured out of the Pen, chanting 'one out all out - one out all out. However, not all walked out. The Foremen with their old gangs of men remained behind. This amounted to many hundreds of men and I realised that the rot had already set in. Over the next three days, the union, the Foremen and their old gangs insidiously spread the gossip that I and my supporters were communists, the new chairman, Charlie Taggart announced that the Union were going to sack me themselves for writing 'The Dockers Voice.
At Friday lunchtime when the Judas Goat schooled Weekend Work, the strike was effectively broken. For three days - well two and half days - the Belfast Dockers had the principles of James Connolly and Jim Larkin, but when The Judas Goat shouted - 'Get into your boxes there's plenty of weekend work', led by the Foremen's old gangs, they did just that.

Thoroughly sickened at the behaviour of The Dockers, myself and about one hundred Dockers gathered in the Canteen. We decided over the weekend to try and persuade the others to behave like men. However, they were brain-washed by the Union Committee that I was a Communist who agreed with the rape and murder of Catholic Nuns. On Monday morning their was absolute silence in the Pen. I stood on the foreman's platform - watching - as the Judas Goat employed them.

My supporters didn't know what to do, so I told them, "you may get into your boxes or you'll be next". Reluctantly they did so. Disgusted I walked up the road and out the Dock gates.

Incidentally, and my mind boggles at this. The Judas Goat, after selling out the Dockers and the Union and joining the Employers as Labour Controller, he was allowed to remain a lifelong Union member. This confirms that Head Office in Dublin and the ICTU were up to their necks in this sell-out of Trade Union Principles.

Even after the Decasualsation Scheme was collapsed and the Dockers reverted back to the casual system, the Judas Goat remained as the Dockers employer - and still a union member.

My Union had always been pro-employer and made sly deals with them, but this always happened behind the scenes, and well away from the Dockers eyes. However, the Betrayal of 'The Judas Goat' and the establishing of the 'Union and Employers Court' over the eight years that Decasualisation existed - speeded up the demise of manual labour at the Docks. Over time, the introduction of Containers would've done this anyway, but the 'problem' of the Dockers would have remained. While the 'Court' was used to whittle down their numbers, the return to the Casual System with just a few ships being discharged each week would have seriously curtailed the redevelopment of the Docks.

The documentation relating to the manipulation of Union Head Office in Dublin is shown in the corruptoconnor website that accompanies this book. This proof is in the form of replies from head office in Dublin, and ICTU. They prove that they ignored the perversion of Trade Unionism that was taking place by the Belfast Branch and by the Judas Goat. I couldn't believe they were up to their eyeballs in it? The Lies and Promises lasted eight years - and in that time every trade union principle ever devised for the protection of workers was trampled upon.

However, the Ten Pound Fines were discontinued - but the Union still policed the Docks for the Employers with the 'Union and Employers Court'. This scandalous betrayal of Irish Trade Unionism and the slavish worship of the Employers by the Union Committee - allowed them to still wallow in their Corrupt Power over the Dockers.

In the covering up of this scandal, ICTU and the leaders of SIPTU {to the present day} are betraying the Principles of James Connolly and Jim Larkin. ' *Tongue in Cheek*' they pretend to honour them . The deplorable actions at Belfast Docks showed the Wealthy Employers ' *then and now*'
that everything they believe about Union Leadership is true - i.e that **THE UNION LEADERSHIP IS FOR SALE**. In hindsight its obvious that the Decasualisation Scheme was just a ruse to get rid of the Dockers. Is it any wonder that SIPTU and ICTU and the Wealthy want to keep this behaviour hidden?

CHAPTER SIX

After I was illegally sacked when I went to sign on the Dole I was told I wouldn't be considered for employment benefit because I had been sacked. When I informed the Dole Officials that I had done nothing wrong but had been rail-roaded and sacked by a Union and Employers Court, they laughed and treated me like I was mad.

However, when I provided the documentation that proved the unique circumstances of all I maintained, they gave me forms to fill in to take my case to an Industrial Tribunal and to appeal the decision Dole's decision. They also suggested that I contact a solicitor and made several copies of the documentation, for me.

Following their advice the next day I walked into the offices of Campbell and O'Rawe's. They were the solicitors who dealt with Dockers injury claims. Initially the solicitor I met, Desmond Deary, was supportive, see letter dated 15 February 1974.

But matters between us deteriorated. The questions he asked after I gave him the Joint Disciplinary Committee's papers, which he required for the barrister - showed that he'd been got at. So I left him approached several others. Some took my papers to read them - and when they wouldn't take action I had difficulty getting back my file. It became obvious they'd also been got at.

I subsequently attended an Unemployment Appeals Tribunal where the panel were supportive of the Union and Employers in their questioning, and refused to consider the documentation I provided. Their decision was - that I had refused to follow orders and therefore had contributed to my own sacking, so I was still refused unemployment benefit. However, when I appealed this decision to a higher panel and brought along four Dockers who substantiated my case about 'The Joint Disciplinary Committee'.

The appeal board questioned my friends and myself about our Contract of Employment and what it contained? They were amazed when told that we didn't have one, because or ex chairman said "we have decent employers". I received their decision by Post a week later which ruled in my favour, stating: that, "I had not been sacked for misconduct in the industrial sense".

They also told me to take my case to an Industrial Tribunal as they'd never heard of a Union collaborating with Employers to sack union members and included the forms to fill in.
However, it transpired that because I was no longer in employment, I was not entitled to bring the case, so my father took it for me. On the day of the Tribunal the Judas Goat-Labour Controller, Jim Austin turned up with a solicitor who tried to argue that my father had no case because the Dockers were not in continuous employment.

The Tribunal Chairman dismissed this out of hand, holding up and reading from the large book of rules that the Judas Goat had submitted. He commented. "If they are not in continuous employment, just who are all these rules for – and why would the Dockers abide by them? And added, 'I am not here to be fooled by 'red herrings'.

Upon hearing this I showed him the four page book of rules that the Dockers received, and stated: "This is all we were given at the start of the scheme, the rest which he's just produced were made up afterwards, by him, our ex Union Chairman" who joined the Employers and sacked me".

The Tribunal Chairman looked at Jim Austin and said with astonishment and said - you were the Union Chairman?

The solicitor interrupted him saying "That is not relevant."

The Tribunal Chairman replied: "I decide what is relevant here. Looking at me he said: "Young man this tribunal is only here to ascertain if the Docks employers conformed to the law when it employed the Dockers.
I acknowledge you have a grievance but it cannot be resolved here. The law as it now stands can only decide if your father had a Contract of Employment. Now having said that, and while I am not speaking about your specific case, it would seem from the papers that your father submitted from your previous employer, 'Depo Limited', that the Dockers have been treated unfairly in the extreme. Words practicably fail me. I have never in my life heard of an amalgamation of Trade Union and Employers, disciplining and sacking union members". Obviously your father nor the Belfast Dockers had a contract of employment.

The Employers solicitor stood up and objected. "Excuse me but you have no right to say that and you are relying on evidence from someone who is not the object of the Tribunal".

The Tribunal Chairman glared at him. "I have every right to say this because I am commenting on the evidence, of which you have copies, and they are very relevant. Am I to take it that you dispute these letters from the Joint Disciplinary Committee are not true"?

The solicitor shook his head. "No, no it's your assumption that I'm objecting to, it prejudges the-".

Bristling the Chairman replied. "I am assuming nothing I am commenting on the evidence from the Employers *{holds up papers}* presented by this Docker, which is sadly lacking from the Employers, and proves the fact, that they did not have a Contract of Employment when they were Employed.

The solicitor stood up. The fact that they were employed is in itself a Contract!
"Do not split hairs" replied the chairman. "It would seem that the Dock Employers including him, *{pointing at JIm Austin}* believe - by putting their actions in writing, no matter how diabolical, that that makes them legal. They fool themselves and if you as their solicitor have not informed them of this, then you are seriously at fault".

The solicitor stuttered. "I have been given no instruction about this from the Employers" "And I can understand why" Looking directly at the ex Union Chairman, he said: "Mr Austin, as the previous chairman of Mr Murphy's trade union I offer this advice. You cannot ride two horses and when this case gets into a courtroom you and the Employers should engage the best Barristers possible? Jumping up enthusiastically I said, "I agree, but I can't get a solicitor".

The Chairman smiled shrugged and replied. "I can only speak to your father, "It's patently obvious from the papers presented, that the Dockers did 'not' have a contract of employment and the law states that no one can be legally dismissed without one".

Almost choking I pointed at the ex Chairman. "I wanted one but when he was chairman of the Union he said we didn't need

one because we had decent employers".
Looking at the Jim Austin, with almost disgust he remarked, "Given his subsequent actions, he would say that".

Austin shrank into his chair as the Tribunal Chairman glowered at him.

"And while it gives me no pleasure to say this, within the Law as it now stands, I'm only entitled to ask questions to clarify a point. What sort of Trade Union were you in... that allowed you to change sides and help you to sack Union Members?

Myself and my father cheered.

The solicitor jumped to his feet and said: "you don't have to answer that".

My father interjected and said: He boasts that he still is in the Union. Jim Austin had turned as white as a sheet.

Astounded, the Chairman asked, "are you"?.

"You don't have to answer that", said the solicitor.

The tribunal smiled "I wasn't expecting an answer and what sort of Union allowed Dockers who had worked all their lives at the Docks to be only employed since the formation of the Decasualisation Scheme, a few years ago"?
There was absolute silence.

The Chairman shook his head and continued. "This matter and the behaviour of the Union must be challenged in a court of Law. However, and within the bounds of the law I am entitled to ask a question. Mr Austin, as the previous Union Chairman and now Labour Controller, what system was is in place under the Casual System for the payment of the Dockers?

The ex Union Chairman replied, "they were paid by DEPO, the Dock Employers Pay Office". The Tribunal Chairman slowly nodded. "And is that still the case", he asked.

The ex Chairman stuttered. "I, I don't understand the question.

The Tribunal Chairman smiled. "Of course you do, that's why you're stuttering. Has the method of paying the Dockers fundamentally changed. Or are they paid from the same office with the same staff" and do they receive Holiday Pay?

Ex Chairman remained silent. .

I am not going to repeat myself, is the answer to both questions yes or no"?

Jim Austin reluctantly replied, "Yes".

"Well then", said the Chairman, "as a simple point of law, when an employer, employs anyone, and pays them without quibble, and gives them holiday entitlements then it would be a very foolish man to imply that - they are ' *not*' entitled to a Written Contract of Employment"?

Jim Austin shrank in his chair, like a punctured balloon.

The Chairman continued. "A contract is an agreement between people to do something for something. And its quite obvious to me that Dockers who worked all their lives at the Docks should be protected by a Contract - and to be suitably rewarded for their long service.

The solicitor jumped up. "This is not what this Tribunal is about and is irrelevant."

The Chairman replied: "You are entirely right - but its not irrelevant because it gives the background to this devious behaviour of the Docks Employers." Looking at me with almost pity the Tribunal Chairman's voice softened.

"Young man... and again I am not commenting upon your individual case; however you should take note of what was just said in evidence, because it speaks volumes. And as a general observation I say this – a trade union can only sack its own members if it directly employs them. If it does not employ them it cannot sack them. That is simple common sense. So, 'if'... and I am bound by the law to say 'if"...
your trade union had a hand, act or part in your dismissal, sorry... anyone's dismissal... then they have committed a criminal act - that is - to deprive that individual of his livelihood and I would suggest that - the said individual, and any others similarly affected, see a solicitor as soon as possible".

The Tribunal Chairman held up a pamphlet. He gave it to an usher who gave it to Jim Austin and said. "The basic requirements for a contract of employment are in this booklet, the Belfast Dockers did not have one. I suggest you read it. "From now on Mr Austin, all sackings or dismissals must conform to Section {1} of the Industrial Relations Act - do you understand that". The Judas Goat - Labour Controller nodded.

I jumped to my feet shouting. "So you're saying that I'm not sacked"! The Tribunal Chairman replied: "I did not say that, I said: without a contract of employment no-one can be legitimately sacked. If... this applies to you then it applies to you and it is not lawful. Anyone - and I repeat anyone - finding themselves in this position should see a solicitor immediately."

I thanked the Tribunal Chairman. Turning to the ex union chairman Labour Controller I said: "see you on Monday morning". However, on Monday morning I was waylaid by Bobby Dickey. Fingering his big hook he advised not to go into the Pen. I told him to fuck off and that he didn't scare me. But when he said, "But what about yer Da, do you want him fished out of the Docks with his pockets full of stones"

Even though he was an old bastard and had somewhat redeemed himself, I didn't want to see this happen to him.
For the first time I realised what they were capable of, and frightened for him - so I decided to stick to the legal route.

My file www.siptupresidentjackoconnorexposed.com which accompanies this book, contains some of the replies I received from head office in Dublin and the Irish Congress of Trade Union proves all I maintain. Of particular interest is one from the then General Secretary of ITGWU, Michael Mullen dated 15TH July 1974 - who states in no uncertain terms, "that the contents of my insulting letters will not keep him awake at night".

While not wishing to speak ill of the dead, this betrayal of Trade Unionism did not keep him awake either. Obviously this was why the Northern Ireland Government was funding the Northern Committee of ICTU to the tune of ten thousand pounds a year. To keep them quiet.

Obviously the business men in government also wanted to see the redevelopment of the Belfast Docklands - and the hurdle of the trade unions was their first target.

My home life in Rushpark became difficult. This was a Protestant area and crowds of young people from nearby Rathcoole would pass by the block of flats were I lived. They were on their way down to the seaside which was just across the road. One day one of they remarked, pointing at me, "That's a Fenian Bastard" This is a derogatory term many

Protestants call Catholics, and how he knew this I'll never know.

At this time Sailortown was emptied of people, as they were going to knock it down to build a new bridge at the end of the M2 Motorway.

This was a deliberate act to abolish a thriving working class area. The bridge crossed Whilta Street and was unnecessary - a simple bend in the road taking in a slice of the harbour estate would have sufficed and saved millions. However, I started drinking again and things at home became turbulent. Very drunk one night I kicked in the front door of our old house in New Dock Street and found a bed upstairs in the front room. The nightmares I had in that room were something shocking. My head was all over the place. Things were difficult when I went home and I'd go off the drink for a few days but it didn't last.

Then I started to get handwritten letters pushed through the letter box calling me Catholic scum and telling me to get out or be burned out.

Catholics were being evicted from their homes all over Belfast so rather than wait for the inevitable to happen and as we were on the fifth floor it would be impossible for us to escape. I got my Da to hire a van and we moved to his house house in Andersonstown, furniture and all. The house was bursting at the seams and while the move was necessary it done my head in and the memories of Chris and John tormented me.

Still living in the house were my two younger brothers and my sister.

With my wife and child we moved into my old back bedroom, which was a tight squeeze. For the three weeks we were there the atmosphere in the house was toxic. With no-where to move especially at mealtimes, things came to a head when my

Da and my wife 'had words'. Unable to stand this I went to the local pub and got drunk.

Not wanting to go back to the house and to just to clear my head I walked up the Glen Road and into the Lenadoon Estate. British Army Jeeps were everywhere.
Near the end of Lenadoon Avenue, a barbed wire fence across a field separated the Protestant end of the Estate from Catholics. After I passed the field I noticed a house with curtains blowing out of all the windows.

On closer inspection I saw the walls above the front door and downstairs window were smoke-blackened. Intrigued, I walked down the garden path and pushed the front door, it opened and I walked in. The smell of smoke was everywhere. I tried the lights but they didn't work but I saw several candles on the fireplace. The wind was blowing through the house, but I managed to keep my lighter lit for long enough to see, that while the walls were smoke-damaged and a few broken windows there was no major damage. Delighted, I went back to my Da's house and told him to get the van again, as I'd found a house for us.

The next day while he went for the van I rounded up a few friends to help with the move. My wife wanted to see the house but I said no, for two reasons.
I was afraid when she saw the state of it she wouldn't move in, and secondly, I didn't want to alert any other potential squatters who had their eye on the house. Once we got in with our furniture we weren't moving out.

When he arrived with the van, in double quick time we loaded it and drove up to Lenadoon. As we parked on the green outside the house I could see several men working in the house. One was putting a lock on the front door while the others were replacing the broken windows.

Furious, I stormed down the path and told the one at the front door to "Fuck off this is my house". Shocked, he replied - "We're only working here". And he handed me the front door keys.

Relieved, I shouted "Right Lads get it unloaded." My wife and daughter, who was a toddler, were first down the path, both were loaded down with brushes and cleaning materials. My wife looked around as they came in, and went straight upstairs. My friends carried a table and chairs in and took them through to the kitchen which was unmarked.

Quickly all the furniture was carried in and kept away from the smoke damaged walls. The workmen had just finished putting the new windows in when an electrician arrived with something in his hand. It was the main fuse, and when he fitted it, the lights came on. As we had to leave our gas cooker in the flat, my Da had brought a small two ring electric cooker so we all had a cup of black tea.

However, one of the workmen produced a bottle of milk and shared it with us. Besides the smoke damage and the broken windows, the only other damage was a burn on the living room floor, in the exact shape of a smoothing Iron. Years later my daughter met the woman who'd lived in the house when it was fire-bombed. She had been Ironing clothes at the time and the mark on the floor was when she dropped the Iron. My daughter remarked, that she hoped us squatting in her house didn't upset her plans to move back in.

The woman replied, after what happened to her and the shock she'd got, there was no chance of her moving back into that house. What had transpired was, they'd burned each house at the end of the row, hoping that the entire block would be destroyed.

With the electric back on I soon had the TV working. I looked at my wife and saw she was crying. "What's wrong", I asked. My daughter climbed onto her knees and hugged her.

She replied, "This time yesterday I had no hope - and now I'm looking out my own front window. I smiled and looked out the window - and saw a patrol of Brits coming down the path. Determined not to go without a fight, I answered the door."What do you want". I said.

The second Brit, who was an officer answered. "You are illegally occupying this dwelling". He was smiling - so I replied, 'and you're illegally occupying this country'. Still smiling, he said, "Are you not going to invite us in?
"No". I said.

Shaking his head he said. "Another obnoxious Paddy - I know you've just moved in but if you see or hear of any illegal behaviour would you get in touch with us".

"No problem", I replied. Only this morning I saw six or seven men with guns coming out of a house. Delighted the officer inquired, "where did they go"?

With a deadpan face, I said. "they got into two jeeps drove into the Fort down the road". His lips curled and he walked away. I watched them go, but they didn't go very far. Surprised, I watched them go into a mini-fort which they'd established about a hundred yards away in two houses. I learned later that they'd evicted the families and taken over their houses and turned them into a mini-fort.

The houses were covered in wire netting, and the windows blocked up with breeze blocks. I found out later that this was a common practice. They'd done the same with two blocks of flats further up Lenadoon Avenue. One was at the top of the hill from where they could see the whole estate. They also had done the same with another block of flats in nearby Corrib Avenue.

Over the next few days myself and my wife worked together and made the house habitable. We also got to know the neighbours and had our daughter enrolled at the local school. Every time I exited the front door, and seeing the Brit Fort nearby, I wondered how the the houses were fire-bombed - when were so close?

The lower end of the Lenadoon Estate, from halfway down Horn Drive was Protestant. They even had Loyalist Club behind the shops on the Suffolk Road. I can honestly say no-one ever intimidated them but they felt frightened and left. When they did so, Catholics were prevented by the British Army from occupying the vacated houses and they were bricked up for years. This situation prevailed until hundreds of homeless families invaded the estate. The soldiers would have to shoot them, but they didn't and pulled back, which allowed the homeless to inhabit the houses.

Because the Dockers had refused to support me and I was sacked from the Docks, my father declared he could not work with such lily livered people. He lifted his cards and left, after working there for thirty three years. For him doing this I could forgive the beatings - but I couldn't forget them and still had the nightmares. Now that we were both without employment, I scanned the Belfast Telepraph Newspaper for work.

I happened upon an ad which stated that the owner of a Black Taxi was looking to exchange it for a small car.
The Black Taxis had started on the Falls Road in 1969 they evolved from ordinary cars. What transpired was: when there was any form of civil disturbance or protest, the Protestant City Council withdrew the Buses from the Falls Road and Catholic Areas.

The entire population of Catholics in West Belfast had to walk home? Then enterprising car owners stared to ferry people up the roads for a fare of ten pence. Soon there was a fleet of cars plying the roads. Then, when Catholic Black Taxi Drivers were intimidated from the city centre taxi ranks they starting working on the Falls Road.

In England at the time, taxi drivers had to change their engines every ten years, so to save themselves the trouble, they just bought another taxi. Belfast's Falls Road was soon festooned with cheap Black Taxis from London, Liverpool and Glasgow.

I saw this Ad in the paper as a great opportunity and as my Da had a small car we rang the number. It transpired that man who owned the taxi had used it in England as a private car. When he came home he got a job as sales rep and needed an ordinary car. He gave us his address of the Antrim Road in North Belfast and we went over to see the Taxi.

While we examined it, he looked over my da's wee car. For a hundred pounds and my Da's car we could have the taxi. The deal was done. They exchanged tax books and off we drove. On the way down the Antrim Road my Da got used to driving the Taxi. He even stopped and reversed it and was very pleased with himself.

He stopped at Millfield, just before the Falls Road for me to have a go at driving it. I could drive, having driven fork lifts at the Docks but did not have a driving licence.
Getting behind the wheel, pushed the long gear-stick into first gear and slowly moved off. When I turned onto the Falls Road there was a small crowd of eight people waving for me to stop. I did so and they all piled into the back. Looking down into Castle Street I could see a crowd of people trying to get home. I pointed this out to my Da and he was delighted. At Dunville Park, the dividing window rapped and I stopped.

Two women got out and paid me ten pence each. As I gave my Da the money, I saw two Brit jeeps come out of the Springfield Road and set up a road block. "Climb over" I got out, went around and go into the passenger seat. We moved up to the lights and when they turned green moved across the intersection. The Brits were stopping traffic going in each direction and waved at my Da to stop. The Brit looked in at the passengers and said to my Da, 'Licence'? My Da handed him his licence which he gave a cursory look and said, "go ahead".

At the Childrens hospital most of the passengers got out and paid him.

He was delighted. This started a new chapter in his life which he threw himself into with gusto. The Taxi proved to be very robust and a real gem. It sailed through the PSV test, which only him-self and the genuine taxi drivers from the city centre bothered with. And to be completely legal he took the PSV test, and passed it. An enterprising insurance broker had established himself on the Glen road and insured th the Black Taxis for 13 pounds a week and were insured for 'Road Traffic Act only'.
With liability to no-one. I.e. you travelled in them at your own risk. This situation prevailed until the British Government paid the English Insurance Company to pull out of Northern Ireland. By this time the FTA, the Falls Taxi Association had been established for the running of the taxis.

When the Insurance Company pulled out, the FTA in a revolutionary move, established its own Insurance Company. Every member would make a down payment and pay five pounds a week. For this they would get fire and theft and passenger liability but no insurance for themselves.

The Police refused to recognise this insurance, and often

threatened to prosecute any driver they stopped, but no action was ever taken.

Regarding myself, I soon passed my driving test and would drive the taxi at night and every weekend. This experience helped me to pass my PSV test. Then a case where I'd been hurt at the Docks came to court and I was awarded 18 hundred pounds. With this I bought a Black Taxi of my own and joined the Falls Taxi Association.

However, as usual, when things were going well I started to drink again.

One night in 1975 I was half drunk while turning onto the Glen Road, the nearside front wheel went into a pothole, which wasn't unusual as the glen road was full of pot holes. However, further down the road I was stopped by a Brit Patrol.

There was a plain-clothes policeman with them and he accused me of running in to his car, which I denied. Upon smelling the drink of me, he arrested me for drunk driving.

Before the case came to Court I received in the post my past criminal record and was astounded. There were three pages of offences, serious physical assaults and house-breakings that I knew nothing about and had never done. I went to a solicitor but he refused to challenge them, saying "if I get on the wrong side of the police by questioning them, I may leave the country" - so I defended myself. I pleaded guilty to the drunken driving but denied crashing into the policeman's car.

The policeman gave graphic detail about having to take evasive action to save his life but I still crashed into his car, causing several thousand pounds worth of damage. He produced the garage bills to support his arguments. I told the Judge he was a liar and that there was not even a scratch on my Taxi. The policeman replied, "that a Black Taxi compared to his car is huge vehicle". That may be the case, I said, "But it is not a Tank, how was there no damage to my taxi"? The Judge asked the policeman for a report on the damage to my Taxi and He and he had to admit there wasn't one - so the Judge threw out his claims.

I was duely convicted of drunk driving and banned from driving for twelve months.

When I asked the Judge what I should do about the false record he told me to get a solicitor to challenge it.. When I told him about the solicitor's refusal he told me to "keep trying".

For the year of my driving ban I was hardly sober and things were very difficult at home. When the suspension was up I went back driving on the Falls Road. From the start Police and Brits began to pick on me.

Hardly a day passed without me being stopped and checked out. There was an Army post in Cuper Street beside the Falls Road Baths. At this junction they placed large concrete blocks at each side of the Falls Road with tubular gates between them. At least once a day they fastened these shut with a chain and padlock. This caused serious traffic back-ups.

I would mount the pavement in my Taxi drive to the barrier and smash open the padlock with a hammer. Because of this they would harras me and stop and search my Taxi and passengers on every journey. It got so bad the people refused to travel in my taxi. This led to me working only at night. However after a period of night work I returned to working during the day - and they planted bullets in my Taxi.

This happened in 1979 I was going up the Whiterock Road when I was stopped by a Brit Patrol. They searched the Taxi then waved me on.

However, when going down the Monagh Road, just at the shops I was stopped again. During the search they found a white plastic bag which was not mine.They told me to open it but I refused and a Major, who was just passing by was called over. Now this is where it get interesting, because the Major and the soldier both claimed "to have "lifted the bag and emptied the contents onto the driving seat". Just after the 'find' was discovered they both made statements to this effect to the police. {See transcripts of the court-case on linkedin}

However at my trial the soldier changed his story to say that "the major had done the lifting and the empting out of the bag. It also transpired in Court that the bag was not only planted once, but was planted twice.
Because, when the Taxi was searched in 'Police Custody' the bag was found back below the seat - and no-one, neither the police nor the soldiers knew how it got there.
On the lead up to the trial I'd been informed several times that if I changed my plea to guilty I would receive a suspended sentence. This I refused to do, even when told that my judge was an ex British Soldier.

As the trial progressed and the soldiers swore my life away, my Barrister, Donal Deeney, later a high court judge destroyed the soldiers on the stand, especially, the soldier who had changed his story. When Mr Deeney said "so obviously you were wrong the first time"?

The soldier shook his he and maintained "he was not wrong and that it was the Major who lifted the bag and emptied it out onto the seat.
Mr Deeney said: "so your were wrong at the time".

The soldier shook his head. "No I was right" he kept insisting that both his versions of finding the ammunition were true. I.e. that 'he' had emptied out the bag onto the driving seat and that the one he had just given under oath - that the Major had done this, were both true. Mr Deeney rightly ridiculed this duplicity and to save the soldier any more embarrassment the judge suggested "that it was getting late and we should break for lunch".

The judge stood up, everyone rose and the judge left the court-room.

Then in the full hearing of everyone, the prosecutor Mr Adair, who was an ordinary barrister roped in for the job, asked the soldier - "Why did you change your story"

To the amazement of everyone he told the truth, and replied, "Because the Major told me to".

Everyone was shocked even the two screws who took me down to the cells couldn't believe what they had just heard. Likewise, I was in shock at the unbelievable occurrence. What had made this British soldier tell the truth - and what difference would it have on the trial? Could it continue when one of the witnesses had just admitted to telling lies under oath?

I couldn't eat the food they gave me and needed a drink, badly. At 2 'O Clock I was brought back into the court and shortly the judge swept in.

The clerk shouted "all stand" and we all stood up and when the judge sits, we all sat down. Entwining his hands the Judge spoke and said, "Now where were we"?

Mr Adair the Prosecutor stood up. "Your honour, a matter has arisen that demands, that myself and my learned colleague having some discussion, short discussion".

The Judge looked puzzled and asked, "why is that"?

To be fair Mr Adair looked a little embarrassed. "I would rather not say at this point your honour, but It is something which is most unusual in the circumstances that has arisen".

The courtroom was agog with interest My barrister Mr Deeney, looked surprised. It seemed the prosecutor was doing his job for him.

A little peeved, the Judge said, "Well... five minutes... and no more".

Mr Adair replied, "I'm much obliged, your honour".

The prosecutor and barrister met centre court and put their heads together and had an animated whispered discussion. As they whispered together here was an eerie Silence in the Open Courtroom. The judge looking disgusted twiddled his thumbs. The stenographer looked baffled, with her hands poised above keys of her machine, unable to type because she couldn't hear what's being said.
However, after several minutes, the Prosecutor addressed the judge, and asked. "May we approach the bench, you honour?

Grim-faced, the judge nodded his head. "You may". Obviously, he knew what was transpiring in his Courtroom was unprecedented. The prosecutor led the way to the judge, and for several minutes the three engaged in a heated, and animated conversation. If this was not so serious it would have been very funny, because they argued in whispers.

With her hands poised to type, the stenographer cocked her ear but could hear nothing. The prosecutor and barrister returned to their places and the Judge, with a face like thunder spoke. "At this point... I propose to stop this trial it would seem that the bag containing the articles discovered was placed in the Taxi by person or persons unknown. While this Silence in Open Court is unbelievable, it is exactly what transpired at my trial and can be checked out by anyone who wishes to read the transcript. This is available on the web in my Documents on Linkedin.

When I went back to work after the Trial the harassment got worse. It became obvious I was never going to get peace working as a Black Taxi Driver.

For a while I went on the drink, then, seeing I had a PSV licence I sold my Black Taxi, bought a car and went Pirate Taxing.
This went well for several years because I'd park the car and go on benders, often not remembering where I'd let my car. I was Drinking even more, and used driving the Taxi to fund it. Although by now I was into play-writing and would write every morning with a raging hang-over.
Then one day just after Christmas I brought a woman, {about ten years younger than me} with three young kids to her house.

She was loaded down with bags, having just spent Christmas with her parents. Her youngest was just a few months old and snow was on the ground. As pulled up outside her house, beside a coal lorry. I stuffed her bags into the child's pram and carried it down her path. She had difficulty walking on the slippery ground carrying the baby. We stood freezing as she fumbled with one hand putting the key in the lock, her hands were shaking from the cold.

When I carried the laden pram into her hall the freezing cold hit me in the face. It was actually colder in the house than it was outside. As she was paying me, I said to her, "you'd better get the fire lit or that child will freeze".

She burst into tears. If only I'd walked away then - but being a sucker for tears, I asked "what's wrong"? She shook her head and didn't speak, but the oldest of the boys, aged about six, spoke up. "We've no money for coal".

Shocked, I said "that child will die from exposure". She was holding out the fare to me, which was all small change. I pushed it back told her to keep it, and walked out.

The lorry driver was getting into his Coal Lorry when a thought struck me and I called him. "Would you throw two bags of coal into that house".

Aye, he said, "I will if you pay me"?

"Of course I'll pay you", how much is it.

"Three thirty a bag"

I gave him a tenner. "Put in three" I said.

Smiling, he said, "No problem".

I drove away and thought no more about it. However, three weeks later the girl on the Taxi desk contacted me on the radio. She said a blond woman left a tenner for the driver who drives a Diesel Mazda. "Are you getting us a bad name by doing free runs"?

I laughed. "No way, I said".

She replied. "Well she wants you to pick her up from her mum's tonight, about eight".

"Can't do it, send someone else, I'm picking my daughter up".

"Will I tell her that"?

Puzzled, I asked, "Why would you"?

She smiled and replied, "She seemed very interested in you".

"No", I emphatically replied. "I've enough on my plate".

However, unknown to me, the girl on the desk and this young woman with the children had struck up a rapport. Every time she required a taxi it was me that was sent. I didn't realise this at the time and got to know her very well. She would pay me long before we got to her mother's house which I found strange. On one occasion when she was staying for the weekend, I carried her buggy with the child still in it, into the house.

Her mother asked, "did I want a cup of tea"? Surprised, I declined.

On the return journey on Sunday night I remarked on this. She replied, "that's my mum she offers tea to everyone who comes to the house".

When we arrived at her house she gave me a fiver and told me to keep the change. Which, I did. For a few weeks I didn't see her, then late one night as I was about to knock off, I got a call on the radio to pick up at her house. When I arrived, as it was late I didn't sound the horn but flashed the lights. She exited the house and wobbled as she came up the garden path. "Hugh", She slurred. "My sister is a bit drunk, could you help me get her into your car?
"No problem", I replied and got out. On the way down the path she fell against me and caught her. "I think you've had a skinfull as well", I said.

She laughed. "We'd a great night". Inside the house her sister was dancing to a slow record. "This is Hugh, he's going to take you home"

"No, it's too early" she said.

I could see she wasn't as drunk as I'd been led to believe, so I said, "that's ok, phone the depo when you're ready". I turned and left the house. When I started the car and turned on the headlight, I saw her sister coming up the path. She climbed in beside me and said, "What's got up your nose, and where are you going"?

I looked at her puzzled. "I'm going home, I've been working from Six O'Clock and I'm shattered. What's it got to do with you?

"Home", she asked, "Are you not coming back here?

"What would I come back here for?"

"You're living with her, aren't you?"

Stunned, I replied, "No I am not, who told you that"?

"She did, and she's told mum and dad and everyone else. Are you not?"
"Correct", I said. "I definitely am not". I opened my door and said, "I'm getting this sorted out right now!"

She gripped my arm. "No, don't not while she's drunk, you never know what she'll do! Please please don't go in!
Her impassioned pleas convinced me, so I closed the door and drove off.

I dropped her at her own house and went home. For the next few weeks I worked away and heard nothing, but the fact that the woman had told people I was living with her rankled with me. Then on my night off, I heard over the radio that several taxis were picking up at her house.
Later that night I went to her house and saw the front door open. I walked in and she and her sister were present.

I immediately asked, "What have you been saying about me"? She started screaming "Get out Get out". I sat down on the settee and said "calm down, calm down. Look, it may have been partly my fault, because I helped you out with the coal, and you got the wrong end of the stick.
Has no-one never been nice to you before"?

She burst out crying and sat down on the settee, running her hands between the cushions.

"Have you lost something"? I asked?
She let out a scream, pulled a large kitchen knife from between the cushions and stabbed me three times in my left shoulder.

I threw her aside and ran from the house. Apparently she fell against a counter top and banged her face. As I drove away I was stopped by the police and the army. When the Policeman smelled drink he arrested me for drunk driving. The police doctor who certified me drunk also noted the three stab wounds in my left shoulder and told me to go to Hospital to get them stitched. Which I wish I had done? It took a long time for the Drink Driving case to come to court, and it resulted in me losing my licence for five years.

However, about a month after I lost my licence, I was charged with assaulting this woman and fined 100 pounds and had to pay her 100 pounds compensation. The Police Doctors report on my wounds was produced in Court, but was ignored by the Judge. The woman denied she stabbed me, but her witness a neighbour contradicted her and said she'd saw the knife in her hand. It should be noted that her sister refused to go to the Court.

I couldn't understand why these two cases didn't happen at once, then realisation dawned. The RUC waited to see if I would go to the hospital with my wounds, which, much to my regret, I hadn't. Even though I told the Police Doctor how I'd got them, this gave the police an avenue to pursue me for assaulting her.

Her sister told me later she had put make up and mascara on her face so she looked bruised, and took photos for the police. Because of her witnesses contradicting her story, I appealed the case but the night before, I'd got so drunk I couldn't attend the Court.

So the sentence stood. The irony is - the reason I'd got drunk and didn't attend my appeal, was because of a party by Tinderbox Theatre Company. This was held to celebrate their successful staging of the readings of six new plays, which included my first play 'Daddy'. This is about the after effects of child abuse and on two adult sisters.

The fact that the RUC "said" they believed the woman's version of events, despite my stab wounds, had severe repercussions on the man she later married. She stabbed him through the heart and he was very lucky to survive. Afterwards, she signed herself into a mental health facility named Purdysburn, in Belfast. Her husband wouldn't press charges so she was never charged. However, while this man obviously didn't know of his wife's murderous tendencies, the RUC obviously did and it almost cost this man his life. While this happened 40 years ago, this man will have had serious complications from being stabbed in the heart. And even at this late stage, if still alive, is entitled to compensation.

This is not to mention the serious miscarriage of Justice that the RUC engaged in. An important point here is - while this happened in the mid eighties, besides being convicted of Drink Driving was the last time I was in a Courtroom. Before that the drunken behaviour that saw me Jailed was obviously the result of my traumatic childhood. Obviously this contradicts the false records of severe and violent criminal behaviour the RUC invented and allocated to me. This criminality by the police, proved that the RUC had not changed.

The morals of the Policeman who slammed me into the wall and finger-printed me when I was eight years old were still to the fore. While their actions in leading sectarian mobs was restricted, the manipulation of the law and the inventing of fictitious criminal records flourished.

Obviously they knew about of my acquittal in 1980 and were punishing me for it. Ten years later in1990 I received a pittance in compensation. I have tried several times to have the false criminal record exposed and destroyed but to no solicitor will take on this case On one occasion when I'd been on the drink or a week, I returned home to my wife, her sister was present, so I went straight to bed.

Apparently 'someone' phoned the Police and I was put out of the house. When the police put me out, I sat on the green and wouldn't move. So they threw me into their Jeep and dumped me down the Falls Road. My wife found me a few days later and brought me home. My only recollection of this time was waking up and my wife spoon-feeding me vegetable soup. .

CHAPTER SEVEN

In the the late1980's, walking up Castle Street, I met Martin Lynch again. It was he who had written and printed the first four editions of the Dockers Voice. He informed me that he'd written a stage-play entitled
'Dockers' and it was going on at the Lyric in Belfast. I congratulated him and said, "Did you expose the Union and Employers Court, in your play"?

I was astounded when he claimed he knew nothing about it - which I found strange, as his brother still worked at the Docks and had been as opposed to the Court as I was. And because of the demise of the Decasualisation Scheme and the introduction of Containers the Dockers were lucky to get two or three days work a week.
"That's play number two" he said.

To cut a long story short - we went for a pint and I brought him up to date about the union's betrayal of workers, the Court and my sacking.
Half drunk, we parted company and I promised I would go to see his play. However, because I knew my old work mates would be attending, I waited for a while before going, I wasn't sure if I could keep quiet about their betrayal of myself and finally themselves.

Lynch's play was big disappointment. While it showed the bully boy tactic's of the Union, it portrayed the Docks of twenty years previous. Not one word was said about the union doing the employers dirty work. I couldn't understand why he ignored the fundamental betrayal of trade unionism by the ex union chairman - and was dumbfounded that he didn't show the sacking of Union members by Union members.

This was surprising because when he was sacked - it was the Union acting alone who who sacked him. At the time when I had questioned the Union as to why Lynch lost his job - they denied the reason was the Dockers Voice but because of the 1968 Union Rule. I thought after telling him about the Union and Employers Court he would at least 'join up the dots' put in a scene about the Union's betrayal of the Dockers. If only to bring the play up to date.
Sadly his play "Dockers" was, and is simply an employers whitewash.

Not surprisingly, there has been no 'Dockers' number two. His play was aplauded by critics for its 'naturalism' whereby the 'F' word was liberally sprinkled into the most mundane of conversations - which the middle class audiences found hilarious. This confirmed their belief that working class plays have no dramatic content.
After seeing his play, I decided if he wouldn't write the Truth about Belfast Docks I would, and proceeded to do so.

Lynch became playwright in residence at the Lyric Theatre for a time and wrote several plays while there. After leaving the Lyric, he set up his own Theatre Company 'Point Fields' to stage his own plays.

However, the Northern Ireland Arts Council wouldn't fund his company without a board of directors and a constitution. And when his company wasn't the success he envisaged, he needed arts council support – and had to comply with the arts council regulations. Subsequently we met and I told him about my Docks play, then named 'One big Onion' and another,'Justice' which I had nearly finished and was about the farce of my trial and the framing of me. He said 'Great' and wanted to see them both.

He informed me that from now on his Company would only be staging working class plays and invited me to join his company. I hesitated and he continued, saying, it would be a 'New Writers Company, that would stage plays that the middle class were afraid of', including mine. So I agreed to join and he recruited three others as a board of directors with himself as chairman. One of those recruited was Joe Devlin who had just graduated in Theatre Studies from a University in England. Lynch appointed him Artistic Director, saying, "He was exactly what we needed". First generation middle class with a degree in Theatre.

After reading my Docks play, Lynch and Devlin both stated it was too soon for another play about the Docks. Unbeknownst to me they both had an ulterior motive for saying this. However, after reading my other play 'JUSTICE' which is a satire about the legal system, and with my acquittal and recent compensation which had given the play, 'legs' Devlin enthusiastically wanted to direct it, to which I agreed.

My play was staged, - back to back - with a play written by Owen McCafferty, which Lynch would direct, thereby making his début as a director. McCafferty was appointed company secretary. Our two plays were staged at OMAC, Old Museum Arts Centre, in Belfast. The most successful would be the play Lynch's revamped Theatre Company would take on Tour. My play won hands down and now with directors on board, Point Fields received Arts Council funding. A condition was the company had to submit a Written Constitution. While the company retained its original name, {to save money as the promotional material was already printed}. With Arts Council money we toured 'JUSTICE' in NI for three weeks and then to the Dublin and Belfast Theatre Festivals.

It was also 'bought in' and staged at the 'Tron' Theatre in Glasgow. This transpired in 1992.

However, far from being a treated as member of the company with a successful play behind me, and indeed the reason that the company was getting Arts Council funding - I was never included in company meetings and had no say about the direction the company was taking.
I then found out it was not just myself, who never attended meetings - as no meetings were ever held. Lynch ran the company for his own benefit.

For several seasons after my play was staged he produced nothing - even though arts council funding had being secured and was being paid to the company. Rumours abounded among theatre people, with letters in the Press, about how a theatre company in receipt of arts council funding could produce nothing.

Paradoxically, at a meeting in the Arts Club by interested parties in Theatre, to discuss ways of convincing the arts council to devote more money to theatre companies - I interrupted Lynch. He was waxing lyrically about the need for increased funding for independent companies.
"I said, I agree, but when a company is funded by the Arts Council, could we at least ascertain that the writer gets paid."

There was absolute silence then one Lady Director said: "but Hugh that is always the case".

Stunned, I looked at her and said: "well how come I got nothing, I had to go 'cap in hand' to the Stewart Parker Trust for the money to see my play in Glasgow". Lynch immediately replied: "Hugh myself and Owen {the secretary} have been looking into that, and we'll see if there's anything left in the kitty to pay you". Owen McCafferty looked at him, with his mouth hanging open.

Lynch continued. "Hugh, we didn't think it was fair, but it was your own wishes, that we were complying with - this what you wanted".

Dumbfounded, I asked "what are you talking about?"

Lynch replied. "You said and I'm quoting you," 'I don't want money I just want my play staged'. I was stunned and replied. "Yes I did say that, but that is completely out of context"? Pointing at McCafferty I said: "When we did his play and my play the company was broke and working on a profit share. That's when I said I want nothing and just want my play staged". Still pointing at McCafferty, said: "I took nothing and gave my share to the actors, but this winging little bastard said: "I want my money". Those were the conditions in which I said I wanted no money - that, long before arts council funding was secured and to pay the actors.

Lynch calmed the situation by saying: "at least that's now clear, seeing you want paid, Hugh, you will get your money". Which needless to say I never got. Things didn't improve regarding company meetings and I may as well not have existed? When I discovered that Lynch was using Arts Council money to pay for a co-production at the lyric, with his new play about The Spanish Civil War - which Devlin was to Direct, I resigned.

Obviously they were pursuing their own agenda. I learned later that two other directors resigned after me, one of whom was McCafferty.

He obviously knew, it was him who was going to be on the hook for any interference with the finances designed for new writers. As an excuse and to distance himself from the company McCafferty declared, he wanted to devote more time to his writing. The other Director, Joe Woods cited personal reasons.

This left Lynch and Devlin out on a limb. They both knew that an Arts Council funded company with no board of Directors - wouldn't last very long. {Which was why he couldn't get funding in the first place} They both, for a long time tried to recruit new directors, but without success - no-one in Belfast wanted to be associated with Nepotism. Then a director from Dublin a friend of the Devlin's, Andy Hynds joined the company but didn't last very long.

Because I had started the ball rolling by resigning, the gossip from Joe Devlin and his theatre friends reached a crescendo. He was now suggesting that I hated his father, and I only resigned from the company before I was sacked. This was nonsense on both counts. I did not hate his father - however there was a grain truth in what he said. His father, 'who was still living at the time' was the ex SDLP Politician Paddy Devlin, who for ten years until its demise had been the last Union Organiser at Belfast Docks. He actually wrote a play about the Docks while he was there. I can't remember its name, but it was staged at the now defunct Arts Theatre on Botanic Avenue and depicted a Loyalist bombing of the Pen - which did actually happen.
Paddy Devlin was an avowed Socialist and wrote a book about his Socialist Life, called 'Straight Left' however - he "forgot" to mention his time at the Belfast Docks. This to me does not spell a Socialist, who - is as proud of his defeats as of his victories - providing of course that he didn't sell out workers. Joe, his son, typed the book for him. My views about Paddy Devlin are in a letter printed in a local Belfast Paper, The Andersontown News, in 1980. [see letters in the corrupt oconnor web site]
While rehearsing my play, 'JUSTICE' which Joe was directing 'someone' brought my letter to his attention.

I told him every word was true but that his father was 'too little too late' to do anything about the corruption at the Docks. I cited my Docks play then named 'One Big Onion' to prove what I said. This only made matters worse as he then believed the villain in the play, who I named 'The Judas Goat', was his father - and nothing would convince him otherwise. Despite being told that his father didn't arrive at the Docks until after I was sacked and the Union and Employers Court by then was well established.

This led to friction between us, on one occasion, during rehearsals, I sacked him in public - in a packed cafe on the Ormeau Road in Belfast.

Unfortunately, members of another theatre company were present.

I relented, when almost in tears he pleaded, that "he was throwing the baby out with the bathwater and his career in Theatre would be over before it got started". I relented and gave him his job back - but he never
forgave me. Anyway, to cut a long story short, Point Fields limped along without directors until the Arts Council closed it down. Joe was particularly upset at and losing his prestigious job as Artistic Director - and incensed at the terminology in the letter from DENI, The Department of Education for Northern Ireland', which funds the Arts Council.

In their final paragraph they state - they "have ceased to fund Point fields Theatre Company and have had "no further dealings with the Directors of the company". When I showed this to Joe he went white with shock, burst into tears and claimed 'that they were labelling him a crook and that his life in Theatre was over'. Worried, I implored him not to do anything stupid.

Regarding Joe Devlin's and Lynch's financial manipulations, theatre people were now treating them with suspicion, believing that they'd diverted Public Money 'designed for new writers' to produce their own productions? However, what was lost in the mix was the fact that they 'were producing Theatre' - albeit their own.

While it may be argued that their closeness to the money end of things impinged upon the quality of productions, only an audience can be the judge of that. Actually, what these two are guilty of - if 'guilty' is the right terminology in these circumstances? Is that fact - that the practice they engaged in has allowed Theatre in Ireland to flourish.
Had they been open and above board from the start and defended the theatre they were producing - and not felt guilty about being paid, their company would still be in existence.

They couldn't get new directors because they were hiding what they were doing, so no-one believed them. This sounded the death knell for Point Fields. Who can fault them for wanting to be paid for their artistic endeavours? Everyone has to live and to eat. Had they been transparent, and paid everyone who deserved to be paid, they both would now be presiding over a world wide Famous Theatre Company - like Druid. This and many other companies are gracing stages in the West End and Broadway through the Largess of the Irish taxpayer.

Although its history now, these two had their own reasons 'not' staging my Docks play. Joe Devlin thought he was protecting the reputation of his father and Martin Lynch didn't want my Docks Play - with the diabolical Union and Employers Court - to overshadow his own Belfast Docks play.

However, as a past director I was also being ostracised by 'theatre people' and was being tarred with the same brush. I complained to the Arts Minister and took the answer I received from DENI as a complete vindication of my complaints. However Devlin took a different view and subsequently told a different story, ie that they were closed because of my misbehaviour.

Which was utter nonsense because I had absolutely nothng to do with the financial end of things - actually I had nothing to do with anything relating to the company. The gossip mongers in the Arts world are renowned and I received the cold shoulder from all and sundry.

This is now called Cancel Culture. See below the letter that vindicates me. This happened many years after I resigned.

DENI
DEPARTMENT OF EDUCATION
NORTHERN IRELAND

TO210/98

Mr Hugh Murphy
37 Lenadoon Avenue
BELFAST
BT11 9HB

10 June 1998

Dear Mr Murphy

You wrote to the Secretary of State recently about the Point Fields Theatre Company. Your letter has been passed to this Department for reply.

I understand that you wrote to the then Minister for the Arts about the same subject on 13 September 1996. The Department's reply of 15 October 1996 explained that Government funds in support of the arts in Northern Ireland are disbursed through the Arts Council of Northern Ireland, and that the Government does not fund arts organisations directly. In keeping with this "arm's length" principle in arts funding the Arts Council has complete independence in determining the allocation of resources. The points which you have raised in your letter are a matter for the Arts Council to consider.

The Department is aware of your correspondence with the Arts Council. I understand that the Council ceased to fund Point Fields during the 1996/97 financial year and has had no further dealings with the Directors of the Company.

I will send a copy of this letter to the Arts Council.

Yours sincerely

P J HIGGINS
Arts, Libraries, Museums and National Lottery Branch

BAL/COULTER L/90169

Maybe Willie White, Director of the Dublin Theatre Festival, Garry Hynds Director of Druid and Cian O'Brian of The Project from whom the censorship stems - will take note.

Shortly after 'Justice' was staged, I received an invitation from the Arts Council of Northern Ireland to attend a play-writing course at an Arts Centre set in a beautiful country setting and on the shores of a lake in Co. Monaghan. It was the previous home of Tyrone Guthrie a famous Theatre Director. Owen McCafferty was also invited, and for a week, with three or four others, received instruction in the practicalities of Playwriting from Joe Dowling. Joe later became the Director of The Tyrone Guthrie Theatre in America. My abiding memory of my two sojourns there - is of the openness of the artists and being able to speak freely about the anything, including my sacking by the Union and Employers Court and its persecution of Belfast Dockers.

Upon my return to Belfast, inspired by the people I'd met who were really interested in my Belfast Docks Play, I was determined to get it staged but no-one wanted to know. I kept coming up against Brick Walls and couldn't understand why? My play showed how the most famous Trade Union in the world betrayed its roots by joining with the Employers to persecute and sack its own members. At that time moves were afoot in Dublin to change the name of the union, and to abandon its revolutionary workers past. From what I was hearing from the Theatre People I'd met, especially in Dublin, that the Truth in Theatre was a much valued commodity.
This reinforced the genuine feelings I'd received when my play JUSTICE was in the Dublin Theatre Festival.
A catalyst happened within me - when in 1994, with the powerful change in Irish Dancing by Michael Flatelly and the performance by the River - dance Company. I was blown away and could see that in one fell swoop he had changed Irish Dancing forever.

Thus, because of the 'cold shoulder' I was getting from the theatre world in Belfast and the supposed openness and Independence and of Irish Theatre - I moved Dublin to pursue my writing career. However, when it came down to the nitty-gritties of actually staging my Belfast Docks play, 'cowardice' rather than truthfulness ruled the day and Censorship prevailed. This started in Dublin with the Abbey and spread throughout Ireland.

The Union and especially the Employers didn't want it to become known - that since its heyday the Union had behaved worse than William Martin did during the 'Lockout'. They 'rightly believed' that these facts would finish it altogether. Especially, seeing that the Union had fought in the GPO with James Connolly as the Citizens Army to free Ireland from British Rule.

The Wealthy who control the Union leaders did all in their power to keep 'hidden' their Dictatorship on the Unions. Especially the Belfast Branch where the Dockers were ordered to discharge Asbestos or be sacked. Just how and why the Union Leaders in Dublin became Corrupted, I have no idea?
Although if Asbestos was being discharged in Belfast at the time, it almost certainty was in Dublin as well. This could be why the Wealthy Employers in Dublin kept hidden the Asbestos Deaths. So my Docks play could have caused them serious financial compensation?

Years later when I heard Jack O'Connor would be speaking at the May Day Parade in Belfast, I attended - and bumped into my old friend John Magee. He had printed 'The Dockers Voice' for me. We stood talking while various trade unionists had their say from the back of a lorry.
When it was O'Connor's turn to speak, I climbed the ladder to the lorry and attempted to pull the mike from his hands.

He held on grimly, aided by the previous union speakers, one of whom was Jimmy Kelly, of the 'just formed' Unite Trade Union', but I managed to wrest it from them.

With the mike in my hand I turned to address the crowd, pointed at O'Connor and stated: "This man Jack O'Connor and his Union are in Partnership in Dublin with the government and the employers" - Then the mike was turned off. In disgust I threw the mike at O'Connor and tried to speak but my voice was making no impact. Then Patricia King came forward and put her arm around my shoulders, "You've made your point" she said. At this I admitted defeat, shrugged off her arm climbed back down the ladder.

I passed John Magee and said: " The dying Dockers and their families are having a protest in North Street". John gave me the thumbs up and said: "See you there".
An hour later, as the May Day parade passed, Dockers widows and those suffering from Asbestosis waved placards condemning SIPTU's behaviour towards them. Many in the parade cheered, but others remained silent. Among the silent was the Derry journalist Eamon McCann to whom I sent the documentary evidence of the union's betrayal, but I never heard a word from him. He like the other "open-minded" Journalists, believes that the Union can do no wrong?

Seeing that he comes from Derry and has experienced Repression, I'd have thought 'he' would be delighted to expose Trade Union Corruption.

Obviously for him a socialist - it's easy to accept Corruption when its done by Irish multi-millionaires - but not from Union Leaders who pay themselves a fortune.
The present day silence of SIPTU's leadership on this matter beggars belief and is deplorable. But why? None of them were around fifty years ago, so standing up for workers rights and

exposing past wrongdoing would be in their favour.

I asked this question in the Asbestos programme 'DEATH TRAP ON THE DOCKS' made by Chris Moore for UTV, but as usual the Union remained silent. This video shows dying Dockers - and the widows of those who have already died from Asbestosis – and the uncaring attitude of the Union Leadership towards them. Could the reason be: that the rumours about ships laden with Asbestos - sent from Dublin to Belfast to be discharged - actually have foundation?
In the programme, Politicians and Doctors tell their stories and give their opinions on the shameful entity that practised and masqueraded as a Trade Union at Belfast Docks.

Like nodding dogs, ICTU and Union Officials ignore the Union and Employers Court that was established in Belfast, and do all in their power to stop an in-depth investigation into this Corrupt Amalgamation.
By pretending that the Union and Belfast Employers acted honourably.

The ICTU cover up of this unholy alliance - and the reason behind it must be exposed. This façade is maintained and facilitated by the upper level of "unelected" bureaucrats in Government and the private sector - so the general-public is not aware of the depth and scale of the dictatorship imposed upon them by Wealth.

This Censorship and Scandal is aided and abetted by the so-called 'free press' who pretend Ireland is an open and honest society. Every fair minded person knows, it's disgusting in the extreme for a Union Chairman to change sides join the Employers and persecute his former workmates. However, for that ex chairman to order Dockers to discharge Asbestos without protection - and still remain a Union Member, is unbelievable.

Then, juxtaposed upon this, the ex union chairman is rewarded by Jack O'Connor the then Union President - his 50 year long service Union Badge. This shows and proves that Corruption ran the Union back then - and still does.

These facts are horrendous so the Wealthy will not allow them to become Public Knowledge - but what about the Taoiseach Micheal Martin? I told him about this to his face and he promised to speak to Jack O'Connor "whom he knows personally" and get back to me. I'm still waiting. This happened several years ago in the Square shopping centre - when he was canvassing for a prospective TD in a by election. If this scandal is exposed an obvious reaction would be, that SIPTU members would leave it in droves, and the Wealthy would lose their most important puppet.

Several years ago to stop industrial unrest, i.e. a living wage and good working conditions, the Wealthy employers, unions and the government formed a "Partnership". This kept industrial relations on an even keel for years. The only losers in this corrupt amalgamation of Wealth and principles {besides Asbestos sufferers} are the ordinary workers. That said, Jack O'Connor must have a very strong stomach, especially when he honoured Jim Austin.

The Wealthy really know how to rub SIPTU and ICTU's nose in it by keeping them down by operating the policy of - "He who pays the Piper calls the tune". Disgustingly, everyone at the top of SIPTU and ICTU know exactly what the sell out of Connolly and Larkin's Principles have done to the Union. I.e reduced it to an unfunny Joke. By selling out the Principles of these Great Men - the present Union Leaders have reduced themselves and their members "in the eyes of the Wealthy" to 'bought of non-entities.

Instead of a Union that looks after ordinary union members SIPTU has been reduced to Profit and Loss Points on a spread sheet of the Wealthy.

Is it any wonder that a leading SIPTU Official refused to comment on the Insight TV programme. It seems Chris Moore has stepped on the same toes that my play 'The Judas Goat' has stepped on - because soon after his investigative TV programme was aired - it was shut down.

In Dublin, the lackeys of the Wealthy who control in the state broadcaster continually claim that Ireland is a Democracy. Yet refuse to allow their flagships - RTE Investigates or Prime Time' to expose any scandal that would show the Truth. Their supposed 'Free Speech watchdogs'
hog-tie themselves with imagined defamation and law suits to quell dissent. However they are being disingenuous - because they - above all know - that Truth can never be Libellous.

However- using this precedent the state broadcaster devised a strategy to frighten the Private Stations like Virgin who may have had more courage than them. They deliberately liabled an individual and made a program about his supposed activates which were obviously nonsense - and they were sued. A large award was achieved by the innocent person, and cemented RTE's reputation as dogged pursuers of the Truth - even when they're wrong. Unlike the private stations it cost RTE nothing, as the taxpayer paid the damages.

Likewise, all the human rights groups in this 'so called Republic' jump through hoops and do the bidding of the Wealthy. This stops ordinary union members and the general-public from realising the depth of their money-mad scheming. The descendants of the Wealthy - who made millions from Asbestos believe that the dastardly actions of their grandfathers will never be exposed. The only People who will suffer - and have suffered are the Belfast People and Dockers condemned to a lifetime of sickness and a lingering Death.

Even 50 years ago the Wealthy Asbestos Importers used their money and status to buy of the solicitors and ultimately the law society. Only when a Union Official not tainted by corruption is disgusted by the sell out of workers - and under oath has to explain why this cover up took place - will the dead and dying learn the truth and get Justice.

The sell-out by the Union in the 50 years ago, is the thanks the Descendants of the Dockers who left the NUDL and joined Connolly and Larkin's Union got? While this happened over one 100 years ago, since then the Union in Dublin has become has become totally Corrupted.

Due to the people I'd met at the Tyrone Guthrie Centre, my horizons were definitely broadened. This reinforced the genuine feelings I'd received when my play JUSTICE was in the Dublin Theatre Festival.
What I was hearing from Theatre People was that the Truth - especially in Dublin Theatre was Paramount and a much valued commodity.

Unfortunately, as the saying goes 'Talk is cheap'.
A catalyst happened within me. When I saw the powerful change in Irish Dancing by Michael Flatelly and the performance by the Riverdance Company. I was blown away and could see that in one fell swoop he had changed Irish Dancing forever. Because of the 'cold shoulder' I was getting from the theatre world in Belfast and what I was hearing about the Independence of Theatre, down South - I moved to Dublin to pursue my writing career.

However, when it came down to the nifty-grittinesses of actually staging my Belfast Docks play, 'cowardice' rather than truthfulness ruled the day and Censorship prevailed. Then completely out of the blue came an invitation to to an interview by the Director of a company named 'Moonstone'. He was John McGrath and he had seen my play 'Justice' when it was on in Glasgow. He sent me flight tickets to attend the interview in Edinburgh. Several other Irish Writers were also invited to attend. I had breakfast with him and his partner, a lovely woman in his flat and he promised to be in touch within a few weeks.

John informed me that 'Moonstone' had a budget to get Dramatic Plays made into successful films. I was delighted to hear this - and lo and behold was told by phone several weeks late my play Justice had been chosen.
Things moved pretty quickly a was sent plane tickets to attend a writers course for a week in Ulvic Norway with many world class film directors. Due to their advice I turned my play into a screenplay. During the week one of the directors and instigators of Moonstone, Michael Caine paid a visit. He was very down to earth and told some very funny stories.

However, shortly after the course ended John McGrath was bitten by a sandfly while filming in the Sahara Desert, developed an infection and sadly died. As did the interest in my screenplay. The Luminaire Brothers took over Moonstone and when one of them was in Dublin he invited me to meet him the Westbury to discuss my script. We met and he told me funding was no longer available to the same degree but he would see what he could do.

He seemed interested in my work and when I told him about 'The Judas Goat' he wanted to know more - and asked had I documentation that proved my Union had collaborated with employers to sack Union members. Shortly after this meeting 'Moonstoon' was closed down.
As despicable as the sordid Trade Union scandal is, the attitude and behaviour of members of the Artistic Community in Dublin, both paid and unpaid was and is scandalous.

To further their own careers instead of standing up to and exposing censorship - the amalgamation of actors writers and directors, I joined - allowed the principles they once had, {or pretended to have} to be abandoned. They had a Reading of my Docks play that was well received, especially by the two founder members. The atmosphere after the Reading was electric with all members condemning the Union concerned and asking how they could get away with this.

Rumours were circulating that the group would produce my play themselves, just as they'd done for a Scottish writer. I left that night on a cloud, but afterwards was given the cold shoulder. I was mystified as to what was going on, then, I was told 'on the quiet' that Jack O'Connor had given the group founder a roasting. It transpired that he didn't know {which I found hard to believe} that ITGWU had morphed into SIPTU.

I thought everyone knew this. I was only then became aware of what was happening. However or the next number of years, nothing happened as I was looking after my dying wife. When I returned to the group, on the first night, a very nice young woman, who had organised the Reading of 'The Judas Goat, allowed me five minutes - ahead of an American Voice Coach, to address the assembled members.

I gave a short history on the betrayal of the Union and stated that I intended to stage 'The Judas Goat' myself, {To loud applause} I called for actors and many came forward and put their names and email addresses on a large envelope I was carrying. The nice young woman interrupted, saying: "don't worry I will put all details on our website, and we will hold auditions" which I was very pleased with.
She then handed the meeting over to the American Voice Coach who immediately remarked upon my distinct Belfast accent. I also participated in the Voice Workshop and

contributed several times at the request of the Voice Coach.

I quickly gathered that the group was staging ten short plays, in Liberty Hall and that a panel of judges, including Ray Yeates, of Dublin County Council arts department {whom I have never me} would pick five, to go to New York. This subsequently transpired and they were staged at The Origin Theatre - Hence the American voice coach.

The very next day, I received a call from the groups founder, informing me, that the young woman who allowed me address the group had no right to do so. And furthermore, "that seeing I had been absent for so long I would need to reapply for membership", which I duly did - and needless to say, it was refused. This obviously stopped me from recruiting actors and barred me from attending meetings. They also blocked my access to their website.

After gate-crashing one meeting, which was poorly attended I was told that the police would be called to remove me if I attempted to do so gain. When I objected, the 14 people present {with a show of hands} voted I be expelled, and not allowed back. I had intended to enter the New York competition but obviously could not do so.

While expecting censorship from SIPTU, the last place I expected it was from the so-called "enlightened Actors, Directors and producers" of Dublin. No-one can tell me that Jack O'Connor had nothing to do with my expulsion.

However, now, with the play going no further to get some traction I applied to BCI, as it was then, for funding for a screenplay version and much to my surprise was approved , but "that no money could be released until a reputable Film Maker was on board". A big surprise awaited me, even though the Artistic group was full to the brim with 'reputable film makers' I could not get one to come on board and make the film. Censorship Rules. I then applied to BCI for funding for another screenplay, which they also agreed to fund, however the same scenario applied. No film director would make this film either. No doubt Jack O'Connor was calling in his favours for allowing the group to use the Liberty Hall Theatre.

While censorship in Ireland is usually oblique and companies don't comment on why they won't stage a play, Druid Theatre Company is the opposite. They had 'The Judas Goat' {then still named One Big Onion} for three years before refusing to stage it. {See letters} Obviously this could only happen with the full knowledge of Garry Hynds who runs every aspect of Druid. In a letter, they asked me "not to tell anyone they refused to stage this play", which I ignored and told all and sundry of this 'request' - for all the good it done.

To try and circumvent this censorship I founded the Heart & Soul Theatre Company and staged two of my plays. 'Daddy' and 'The Grandeur of Delusions'. And if proof is needed, that spite, dictatorship and censorship is controlling whether or not I get a play into an Arts Council Funded Theatre, here it is. My producer had accepted Four dates at The Mick Lally Theatre, Druids studio space, which they offered for - 'The Grandeur of Delusions'.

This play, a two hander, is about the evils of addiction in a modern day context. It shows the actor talking to himself through his delusion - a lovely looking but horribly made up female. However, a few days later my producer received an email from The Mick Lally Theatre, stating - "After having a meeting on the subject those dates are no longer available".

Who in their right mind can deny that that Garry Hynd's well documented dictatorial attitude was not at work here?

I'm sure Mick Lally, a wonderful deceased Druid Actor - is turning in his grave. By a strange coincidence, Patrick Sutton of Smock Alley did exactly the same thing - but with silence. After I accepted the four dates that Sutton offered in an email - for some strange reason he went incommunicado. While I accept these facts alone don't prove a conspiracy, or even a bias towards me, other situations have occurred.

I applied in plenty of time to the Dublin Theatre Festival with 'The Grandeur of Delusions', and after a long wait I received an email from Willie White, stating that it was fully programmed.
By this I mean, who could possibly think that a conspiracy might exist between Willie White and Gary Hynes, just because she sits with Willie on the board of The Dublin Theatre Festival? I bet they will both swear under oath that my name or my play ever crossed their minds, or lips.

Cian O'Brien one of the Theatre Elite, is Director of 'The Project' in Dublin, {by email} thinks my Belfast Docks play, 'The Judas Goat' is a great play, but he refuses to stage it and uses the debatable excuse that, "the Project is a receiving house, only". I say debatable because, it is a very strange receiving house that refuses to give a price, or dates, for the hiring of its Theatre?

While this is another fact that doesn't prove conspiracy, corruption or censorship emanating from the Artistic 'lovies' in Ireland, I will just add it to the basket. The outlined facts speak for themselves. Everyone in the theatre world knows, Willie White, current Director of the Dublin Theatre Festival - was for many years, Director of the Project Theatre. He, no doubt wishes to see it, 'toe the proverbial line', so his time there wasn't wasted.

To add insult to the denying of the Truth, a large likeness of O'Brien was painted outside the Project Theatre - holding a large sign that said CENSORSHIP. This was in response to him being ordered to take down a poster that the Arts Council objected to. The hypocrisy from himself and the "enlightened" in Dublin is mind-blowing.

I also applied to the 'then' Director of the Fringe Festival. After a long wait, he replied by email and refused my entry, saying: "This year we are changing Direction". Whatever that means? Nelson, accepted several companies who were supported with grants, on the basis of an idea only - yet I supplied him with a fully rounded hard-hitting production, which depicts the evils of drug taking, alcoholism and addiction in a modern context, and is a two hander.

However, despite the censorship we experienced from the "Cultured", Heart & Soul managed to stage a short tour of nine dates with this play. Several people who work in Theatre, and who saw the production, remarked, this would be ideal fare for any Festival. Of course, none of the above proves a conspiracy of silence.

The reason Druid asked me, 'in writing', not to say anything about the refusal to stage my play is obvious. They did not want accused of the dictatorial censorship they are practising. This wouldn't go down well or be accepted in the US, where Druid regularly perform. It also wouldn't fit well with Actors Guild in America and would seriously belittle Druids achievements on the world stage.

Because of the behaviour of Garry Hynds and Druid - the Dublin Theatre Elite have enthusiastically rowe in behind her. Obviously for self-preservation and to keep the grants flowing, Druid don't want it to be known that they practice Censorship. It also wouldn't sit well with the Irish Taxpayers if they knew that their money was stopping world-wide audiences from knowing the depths of depravity to which Irish Trade

Unionism, Druid and Theatre in Ireland have sunk.

Who can deny the evidence of Censorship emanating from them. {See the emails} Hynes, White and O'Brien, plus, the frightened hypocrites from the lower ranks of Theatre through abject fear - acquiesce. There can no doubt the wealthy stuffed shirts in the Employers, Siptu and the unelected in Government are determined to keep 'The Judas Goat' from being staged.

This is so - 'not' to expose the Despotic Dublin Employers who ruled the Union in the not to distant past. This corruption was ordered by the Wealthy - who owned and imported the Asbestos, which killed an unknown amount of Belfast People, who just thought they'd got 'ordinary cancer'? Theatre people are not stupid and know they must agree with this practice and cover up, or be ostracised themselves.

While the malign influence of the Union, Employers, Lawyers, so-called Newspapers and silent government cowards exist - the Belfast Dead will never get Justice. The voice of Independent Protest and the Truth in Theatre is as dead as the Asbestos Victims. The most disgusting part of this Censorship is the fact - that it's achieved - while claiming to the world how Free, Liberal and Unrestrained Irish Theatre is.
What amazed me at the time, and still does, is the fact that Garry Hynes, felt so secure in her position at the very top of Irish Theatre, that she felt safe in putting their dictatorial decision to Censor 'The Judas Goat'- in writing? However, this is not the full story. Hynes knew full well that to stage it - would put her on a collision course with the Establishment - who for years have kept a lid on this scandal.

This is why it took three years for Hynds to decide what to do with it. She knew that staging and touring it, would jeopardise her cosy guaranteed funding arrangements with the government. So, for three years Hynds wrestled with her conscience - then the Truth and Independence of Theatre was flushed down the toilet. My play... 'The Judas Goat' was a Truth too far which would end her glittering career.

So like a good little girl, Hynds allowed the censors to stage-manage Druid - her supposed free-thinking Irish Theatre and fool the world with its supposed openness, solidarity, devil may care thinking and to achieve the pinnacle of success. All this by keeping quiet and not staging 'The Judas Goat'. An interesting addendum to this, is - she staged all of Shakespeare's Plays in Dublin, in one go - and the hypocrisy never crossed her mind. He risked his life to put the Truth on Stage and mocked the classic indulgently of the Wealthy - while she wouldn't even risk her grants?

I don't have access to expensive lawyers to take Willie White, numerous others or Garry Hynds to Court for practising Censorship, or to trawl through their emails. In fact I cannot afford to get a lawyer and pay for Justice in Ireland. {**Pun intended**} The most disturbing thing about her supposed non-censorship, non-conspiracy of silence and non compliance with Artistic Ethics, is - the weight, she and Druid hold within the artistic community. They can use Cancel Culture and convince all and sundry, not to take seriously my complaints. I have also complained many times to several Arts Minister plus senior Arts Council Officers and have been effectively, fobbed off.

By word of mouth everyone in the Theatre World has heard of my play and were afraid to have anything to do with it. Censorship continued in Dublin with the Abbey and spread throughout Ireland. The Union, spearheaded by the ICTU and SIPTU trampled underfoot the Principles of Trade Unionism and sold out. This dual aspect was part of the Wealthy's plan. They couldn't have a play in a main-stream Theatres that exposed and ridiculed their supposed militancy and the sell out of Connolly and Larkin's Principles. Especially one that showed their secret weapon - 'The Union and Employers Court' that ITGWU founded at Belfast Docks. Obviously they hoped to introduce into every large factory and workplace. See their letters to me showing they didn't want to know about it - obviously hoping it would take hold in the Republic.

Of course, SIPTU and ICTU will never accept these facts - and the present-day Wealthy will do all in their power to protect today's 'well paid' Puppets from the past corruption of their predecessors. A simple Litmus Test is - but if not true - why did ICTU and the ITGWU hierarchy not stop - the Union and Employers Court from operating at Belfast Docks.

CHAPTER EIGHT

S everal Solicitors took my papers and refused to act on my case against the Union and Employers Court. So Because of their inaction I had to sue them and could not get a solicitor to do so. I complained to the Belfast Law Society and they gave me a list of three solicitors who would sue other solicitors. The first was a Mr G McCann and he took the case.

Mr McCann introduced me to a junior solicitor who would be dealing with my case. For several months my case proceeded well - and I received updates every week.

In a letter dated 24 May 1983 to my new solicitor, the Belfast Employers state: "The Joint Disciplinary Committee was not abolished in 1978 but continued as part of the procedures until the Decasualisation ended on 8th of August 1980". So for eight years after I was illegally sacked by the "Union and Employers Court" - any semblance of Trade Unionism that Connolly and Larkin had instilled into the workers of Ireland was turned into an Employers Joke.

The undeniable documentary evidence in www.siptupresidentjackoconnorexposed.com at the end of this book shows that Jack O'Connor and the labour Leaders - just like their predecessors - when informed of this scandal covered it up. For many years after I was sacked, I wrote to Liberty Hall, RTE and every union branch and every newspaper in the south of Ireland - but eventually gave up.

My Trade Union since its heyday had sold out. Any information that showed it behaved worse than William Martin during the 'Dublin Lockout' - would have ordinary members calling for the heads of their well paid Leaders was covered up. Obviously money corrupts and because ICTU and Union Leaders paid and still pay themselves telephone number salaries they see themselves as the equal of the Employers. Actually they are a million times worse.

50 years ago the Union and Employers Court didn't take hold in any other Union Branch - however the Union Leaders at Belfast Docks without doubt persecuted the Belfast Dockers for the Wealthy. This cannot be denied. Even today, Union leaders in Dublin do all in their power to keep safe the "Wealthy Upper Class System" that prevails in Ireland.

Fifty years ago the descendants of the Belfast Employers took their revenge on Connolly and Larkin, for the 1907 strike, and corrupted their Union. Today there are only a few token members in Belfast.
Back then, what seriously got up the nose of the Wealthy, is the fact that ITGWU members, in Dublin, fought in 1916 as the Citizens Army, to free Ireland from British Rule. This seriously disrupted the master and slave conditions at the time and the Wealthy had to change tack. For fifty six years in Belfast they ingratiated themselves into the labour movement and slowly but surely took it over. Then, when they believed the time was ripe, in 1972 - introduced Decasualisation - and the Union and Employers Court at Belfast Docks.

While this worked well in Belfast - workers in the Republic were not so easily fooled. Union members refused to accept these lap-dog conditions. I believe this was because of my letters and the absolute proof I was sending - to all union branches in the South of Ireland. Those leading the union in

Liberty Hall realised the Truth - and knew if exposed it would wreck the Union, so they covered it up.

The Asbestos related deaths in Belfast are kept as hidden - as those who owned the Asbestos. For the past fifty years this Censorship has prevailed and makes a mockery of all the Human Rights Groups and so-called Historians in Ireland that I've made contact with.

On par today with the accepted silence - is the corruption of Democracy by the higher levels of the Civil Service, who are paid from workers taxes.

A glaring example is the disgusting 'wallowing in power' of Robert Watt.
He is the General Secretary of the Department of Heath, who doesn't know the details of Slainte Care, which his department has been tasked to implement. This, shows, just where his priorities lie. The unparalleled, unwarranted and undeserving increase in his salary for changing Departments has not caused him to look with any degree of gratitude upon the Irish People. Instead with his arrogance he continues to treat taxpayers like a cash cow.

Watt, with his combative nature to the PAC, stoutly defends his position - his repartee is just as vigorous in a Public House. While his snout is firmly in the trough of greed, many Children face a lifetime of deformity because there's no money to pay for operations that would rectify their medical conditions. Another cost-saving by his previous department is the shocking treatment of people with disabilities - and the unatic assertion that Blind People are not disabled.

Would someone have a titter of wit and sack him and his well paid cronies. And if they're so inclined to defend the indefensible, encourage them to do so? Let Watt and his cronies defend themselves in a Court of Law and show - why they are entitled to treat the Irish Government, the Irish People and the severally disabled with contempt. Watt and the other heads of departments 'with their Dictatorial Heads in the clouds' rule Ireland for their own benefit. This nonsense must stop.

They should be treated as they treat ordinary people.
Every government TD, unelected officials and Union Leaders know that sleaze runs the country and pander to it. As John McGuiness so eloquently put it, "Faceless bureaucrats run the country, while we, the elected TD's are just sock puppets".

They flaunt democracy and demand that Ireland is run their way and for the benefit of their class. This is why no 'one' is ever to blame but everyone's to blame. This keeps embarrassing facts hidden and instils into every aspect of Irish Life the culture of cronyism. While high salaries have stopped the crass behaviour of bribes being paid, "good behaviour" is rewarded by promotion and perks thus establishing an unspoken culture of 'touching the forelock'. The nod and wink from the Rich rules Ireland still.

The shocking scandal that a major bank that was bailed out for billions by the taxpayer and is still two thirds own by the government - was going to introduce "Cashless Banks" to save money shows just how these panderers to the Wealthy believe and think? The faceless bureaucrats in the Department of Finance - with the Banks decided on this course of action - without notifying the Finance Minister. However, when the "Sock Puppets" heard about it they decided this was a step too far and told the Banks to desist - which they did.

This example is just how the faceless control SIPTU and ICTU for the benefit of The Wealthy.

They ensure everything runs smoothly in industrial relations - even allowing Union to exert their influence with the odd strike, or threat of one, to keep the militants happy. The Wealthy have absolute control over Journalism, the Arts and the Law. This is particularly blatant with the so called "Free Press" who effectively self censor anything which would embarrass their "Wealthy Masters".

I use this term deliberately. I have complained to several Press Ombudsmen about the 'Free Press' ignoring the truth, but received the same reply. I.e.
"We can only respond to something that has been printed in a newspaper". So I ask, how does the Truth get out if they and all media censor it?

This cover up is particularly obvious by the non action of the Irish Times and its leading journalist Fintan O'Toole - in regard to the censoring of my stage play, 'The Judas Goat'. This shows the betrayal of the Union Chairman at Belfast Docks. On one hand they ignore the cover up of corruption by SIPTU, yet hypocritically cherry-pick which human rights abuse to expose. To save face the so-called Free Press will highlight massive wrongdoing in the HSE, knowing full well that no-one will be held to account or rightly blamed.

Besides O'toole, John Lee editor of 'The Daily Mail' and Alan English of the 'Independent' jump through hoops for the wealthy and refuse to report the facts, 'that Asbestos dust was blown all over Belfast'.
Censorship in all Irish newspapers has been rife for years - as they kow tow to the Irish employers who owned the Asbestos. Why will they not report the number of dead and dying Dockers and Belfast people afflicted by it? Of course the Irish Times, O'Toole and the others know full well that SIPTU when still ITGWU ordered its members to discharge it, or be sacked.

The present Irish Government is not fit for purpose. While Leo Varadkar dug his heels in and refused to sack a TD for drawing attention to official sleaze, he picked the wrong fight. He himself said "she exaggerated her injuries when she fell from the swing and gave different accounts of the incident". This coupled with the fact she swore she couldn't run for ages, yet shortly after she fell, 'bottles in hands' - completed a mini marathon.

Her political partners were outraged because she had committed the Cardinal Sin of being "found out".
Astoundingly she was removed from the Chair of the Housing Committee yet allowed her to remain as Chair of the M.I.C.- the Members Interests Committee, 'of all things'. This powerful committee makes sure that TD's adhere to the 'Code of Conduct' of members of the Dail – which states: "Members must in good faith, strive to maintain the public trust placed in them and exercise the influence gained from their membership of Dail Eireann to advance the public interest - and does not bring the integrity of their office or the Dail into serious disrepute".

I am not making this up - this is exactly what it says.
So how do the multitude of elected TD's to whom I've made contact with, ignore the Asbestos scandal. If they are required to have scruples, where are they?

Why does this ' *ignored*' code of conduct not also apply to civil servants and Secretary Generals who are they above The Law? While it would be a moot point, it would give future generations of historians something to get their teeth into while questioning the cover up of Asbestos Deaths.

Today, no-one will question the standards and ethics of the silent and elected Td's, or why Watt and the other Secretary Generals do not have to adhere to the same principles of

Democracy?

The contempt for elected TD's in the Oireactas - by the leading civil servants has become too much for ordinary people to stomach - but nothing can be done. Not even by the Chairs of important committees.

Hopefully the next government will put a stop to their despotic rule, and tell them - that they work for the Irish People, and not the other way around. When this no-nonsense approach to Government kicks in, it will apply equally to Watt and all other unelected Department Heads.

Especially those who cover up the Belfast Docks scandal. From fifty years ago to the present day, this scandalous behaviour was and is controlled and covered up by the Wealthy.
The Proof of this is the censoring of my play and writing by a previous Arts Minister, Josepha Madigan. She linked with me on linkedin, and I gave her a brief run-down on the deplorable state of the Arts. She replied, gave me her Oireachtas email address and asked me to contact her. Which I did and gave details of the censorship I'm experiencing, with my play 'The Judas Goat'.

I went to bed that night elated, believing that the Arts Minister was going to do something about it. However I was shocked when "she" censored me. When I attempted to log onto her account on linkedin, I couldn't find it - obviously she'd blocked me. No doubt Robert Watt - or his equivalent who controls the Arts Minister told her to desist.

However her request for me to contact her - on her Oireachtas email are still on my account. I then sent a long email to her Oireachtas address that I also copied to a multitude of TD's Then to my surprise she replied. This was a shock especially after her debacle on linkedin.

Obviously Josepha's Controllers believe - that, 'seeing censorship has worked so far, I will never be able to bring this matter to Public Attention' - so the Truth and the cover up will never be exposed. Josepha - as the Arts Minister's censored me. This gives credence to my claim that the uncivil servants are running the country for the wealthy and not the elected Irish governments.

WHY DID SHE ACT IN THIS COWARDLY MANNER AND COVER UP?

The simple answer is - because she and everyone else in the Arts know full well, that… if they don't ignore this catalogue of corruption their career will go down the tubes. When the Minister of Arts can be controlled in this manner its no wonder far lesser mortals in the Arts keep quiet? This is far beyond any fair minded person's comprehension and totality at odds within a Democratic State? Amazingly in her email Josepha does not deny that censorship exists in Irish Theatres, and states that "my comments and observations have once again been noted".

She reiterates that "We are not in a position to intervene in this matter, so cannot make any representations on your behalf". Why not? Josepha was elected by the Irish People, her Controllers were not. At least in replying to me she showed SOME independence and states: "We believe that engaging in protracted correspondence on these matters serves no purpose. The Department considers the matter to be closed and will not be responding to any further correspondence from you".

This proves that the Arts Department Secretary General and his cohorts control every Arts Minister - just like every other Department controls their respective Ministers. This lifts the veil on Irish Democracy and is an absolute disgrace. It is also an insult to the People who vote in elections.

Josepha Maddigan was elected by the people to govern the country - not to be told what to do. The mind boggles.

Just what was she afraid of? Actually, had she taken a different course of action and exposed this Corruption of Democracy she would have guaranteed her permanency in the Dail. To give Josepha an inkling of what her slavish adherence to Dictatorship entails - Billy Browne has Asbestosis it in his left lung, and his two Brothers have already died from it. The Belfast Dockers were ordered to discharge it by their Union and this is an undeniable fact.

Obviously, I didn't want the Arts Minister to 'just' respond in writing I wanted her to do something about it. This cover up of corruption stinks to the high heaven. If the Minister and subsequent Ministers will do nothing about the censoring of 'The Judas Goat' by the Wealthy, then the ordinary staff in the Arts Department and every government Department must stand up and be counted.

They must insist - that they will not collude with this crime against Free Speech and Democracy any longer. The Irish People are entitled to know what is being kept from them and why?

Plus, just who were the Wealthy Employers that owned the Asbestos and corrupted the once great IRISH TRANSPORT & GENERAL WORKERS UNION, that was founded by James Connolly and Jim Larkin. Elected Ministers in every Department should be aware, that it's their own reputations that are on the line, because they know full well who is running the country - and it is not them - and what is being covered up.

Even at this late stage, if Josepha Madigan will point the finger at those who controlled her - and become a Whistle-blowers for Democracy - she will guarantee that she will be re-elected. This is the very least that the Public should expect from someone whom they have elected to run the country.

In, correspondence I once asked the Justice Minister - who was Charlie Flanaghan at the time, "Is censorship against the Law"? No doubt he knew better than upset the apple-cart by truthfully answering me. Is this anyway for a Justice Minister to behave when asked... a fundamental question that specifically relates to Democracy and the administration of Justice? Because of recent revelations about the back-room boys who really run the country - I will give Charlie the benefit of the doubt.

Maybe the Machiavellian Manipulators in the Department of Justice didn't make him aware of my question?
I also asked the Toaiseach - then Leo Varadkar {on twitter} the same question, but was ignored. Obviously from his silence he would not incriminate himself. He boasts that he uses twitter himself and not his staff, so he undoubtedly got my tweet.

Also the multitude of TD's whom I've emailed, from all parties, don't want to know either - or know not to rock the boat. I hope Josepha, now that she's no longer the Arts Minister will reflect upon this matter. Just where is the Dail's Code of Conduct, here?

If common decency or the Rule of Law does not cause a TD to act in democratic fashion - some day - { *hopefully*} those who censor the Truth, will pay the penalty for corrupting Democracy.

This will only happen when a Court of Law holds them to account for manipulating government for the benefit of the Wealthy? How will Ministers answer when asked - why did you allow the unelected to cover up the truth and run the country?

I look forward to hearing the justifications for their inaction. This is an abject betrayal of the People who voted for them. Do TD's actually think that this standard of 'nod, nod - wink wink' - I know nothing - from Ministers is acceptable behaviour?

Josepha Madigan, when Arts Minister allowed the Wealthy to deny the Irish People the right to see theatre of their own choice. This Theatre exposed Corruption by the Wealthy and was being absolutely true to free and independent Theatre. Alas Josepha Madagian allowed her controllers on behalf of the Wealthy to Censor Irish Theatre and my play 'The Judas Goat'. Whoever is Robert Watt's counterpart in the Arts Department - he must be told to back off and to stop behaving like a cog in Orwell's 1984. Ireland is supposed to be a free Democratic Republic.

However, for the Wealthy and their Puppet TD's in the Dail - the question they don't want asked, is 'who controlled head office of the union, and ICTU when they established, 'the Union and Employers Court in Belfast'?
A truthful answer would point the finger at the Wealthy manipulators and why this was allowed to happen?
Belfast Dockers and Citizens Lives were - or should have been more important than Profit for the Wealthy? The fact that the Union and ICTU were fully informed about what was going on - by myself... yet they still allowed Belfast Dockers and innocent people to be exposed to a deadly cargo to protect the financial interests of the Wealthy. That is disgusting.

The name SIPTU must be consigned to the dustbin of history and the ITGWU brought back to its former glory. This will ensure that better pay and better conditions to workers prevails. When this happens and the Union 'yes men' and the 'controllers' of TD's exposed, they will be hard pressed to hang onto the to their positions. This will have ramifications for Robert Watt and his present day fellow manipulators of

Democracy.

As proven by the control exerted on Josepha Madagian, Democracy doesn't exist in Ireland. For their misdeeds past and present Controllers must be exposed. The only difference between Belfast and Dublin today, is the fact, that, in Belfast - Connolly and Larkin's once great trade union is a pathetic shadow and example of the once great trade union it was, 100 years ago.

And in Dublin the truth of this betrayal is kept from present day Union Members. The poor get poorer to make the rich richer. If Josepha Madaigan is ever again a Minister, she must 'not' be controlled. By Watt and his cronies.

At the end of this book, in the I include the documentary proof of all I maintain. Replies to my letters from the Union and ICTU show they knew of the persecution as it was taking place and ignored it.

The behaviour by the Wealthy goes far beyond the need to accumulate wealth and shows, they had a Political and Philosophical reason to regain what the had lost. While they couldn't completely control the country in a political sense, they could at least control every aspect of the lives of ordinary Citizens. With particular glee they manipulated and made a laughing stock of the Union that was part of their downfall - and destroyed it in Belfast.

I must point out something they seem to have missed. Leo Varadker is a medical doctor and took and oath to 'do no harm'. I respectfully suggest that he tells this to the ex Belfast Dockers and people dying from Asbestosis. As for the women who now hold the Ministries of Arts Law and Justice, I ask you, as caring human beings, how can you ignore the suffering of these families?

They died from a from a wholly preventable industrial disease because of greed. Only when various ministers ignore the clamps that the 'unelected' have imposed on Democracy, will Ireland become the Republic that James Connolly and the leaders of 1916 died for. This will allow the Irish People to see how much they were betrayed.

Below is my email to the former Arts Minister - and her disgraceful reply.

M Gmail

Hugh Murphy <murphy.hughmurphy.hugh@gmail.com>

Censorship

Hugh Murphy <murphy.hughmurphy.hugh@gmail.com>
To: josepha.madigan@oireachtas.ie

Mon, May 20, 2019 at 6:37 PM

What has happened to the independence of Theatre in Ireland? My censored play 'The Judas Goat' is an Irish On The Waterfront. This censoring has led to all my plays being censored - so not to give me any clout and able to demand that 'The Judas Goat' be staged - and for the "Free Press" who [self censor] to report on this unbelievable scandal. An early draft is on my profile page on linkedin. This play is set at Belfast Docks and is a true story. It shows how 50 years ago the Union chairman joined his union branch with the employers. He even ordered the Dockers to discharge Asbestos without protection to save the employers money. For documentary proof of the Union and Employers Court which termed itself 'The Joint Disciplinary Committee' see my posts and www.siptupresidentjackoconnorexposed.com You may have to type in the address as sometimes the link doesn't work] Then open UTV's programme 'Death Trap on the Docks' on youtube and see dying Dockers and widows relate their unbelievable stories. This was the first time in Trade Union history, anywhere in the world that a trade union persecuted, sacked and ordered to their death its own members and their families. And also the first time anywhere in the world that an employer was a trade union member. After forming the diabolical 'Union and Employers Court' the chairman left the union and joined the employers as Labour Controller and brought his corruption to an even more disgusting level. The Court scene is missing from the draft on my profile page which I tightened up considerably.] However and unbelievably the now ex union chairman was allowed to remain a Union Member - by both head office in Dublin and The Irish Congress of Trade Unions - so much so that ten years ago he received his 50 year long service badge from Jack O'Connor - the then Union president. The cover up of corruption beggars belief. Neither O'Connor or Norman Shannon, the Belfast solicitor who sat on my case for seven years, until it became Statute Barred will sue me for calling them Corrupt and putting their corruption on linkedin. [See my posts] The documentary evidence of the Court on the website is is what SIPTU, which ITGWU morphed into, [it is still the same Union] and the Employers are covering up. However, the banner heading of the Court says it all. NORTHERN IRELAND FEDERATION OF EMPLOYERS AND IRISH TRANSPORT AND GENERAL WORKERS UNION JOINT DISCIPLINARY COMMITTEE. Any wonder SIPTU officials are using their friends in the Arts to censor this play. Also on the website is a letter to Jack O'Connor from his own Belfast solicitor, one John O'Neill of Thompson McClures, Belfast, stating that his Union 'did' sack its own members at Belfast Docks. He also tries to exonerate the Union, by totally ignoring the fact that a Trade Union cannot Lawfully sack and persecute its own members. See also the letters from ICTU and the Union in the 1970's - proving they knew what was going on but choose to ignore it. Why, who bought them off and how much were they paid? Was it the same people who bought off Norman Shannon? See the Proof for yourself on the website. However the censorship has not

stopped me writing as I've just completed a trilogy of plays set in a
Hostel for the Homeless in Dublin. Regards, Hugh

An Roinn Cultúir,
Oidhreachta agus Gaeltachta
Department of Culture,
Heritage and the Gaeltacht

Oifig an Aire
Office of the
Minister

Mr Hugh Murphy

30 May 2019

Our Ref: CHG-MO-01152-2019

Dear Mr Murphy,

I refer to your correspondence of the 21 May in connection with censorship in Irish Theatres. Your comments and observations have once again been noted and we must reiterate that the Minister is not in a position to intervene in this matter, so cannot make any representations on your behalf.

As outlined in our previous response of 2 May 2018, we believe that engaging in protracted correspondence on these matters serves no purpose. The Department considers the matter to be definitively closed and will not be responding to any further correspondence from you in the future.

Yours sincerely,

Helen Francis
Private Secretary

Page   1 / 1

IRISH TRANSPORT & GENERAL WORKERS' UNION

General Secretary MICHAEL MULLEN

Telephone
49731 (10 LINES)
Telegrams
OBU DUBLIN

Head Office
LIBERTY HALL
DUBLIN 1

IN REPLY PLEASE QUOTE   F/11 dmcd

11th October, 1971

Mr. Hugh Murphy,
Rushpark,
Newtownabbey,
BELFAST.

A Chara,

With further reference to your letter of the 20th August, we wish to inform you that your appeal against the fine of ten pounds imposed on you by the Branch Committee of our Belfast Branch has been considered by the Appeals Committee of the National Executive Council.

Having considered all aspects of the case, the Executive has decided to confirm the decision of the Branch Committee and we regret, therefore, that your appeal has not been successful and the fine should be paid forthwith.

Sinne, le meas,
IRISH TRANSPORT AND GENERAL WORKERS' UNION

MICHAEL MULLEN
GENERAL SECRETARY

I informed the NEC that the Branch Committee and the Dock Section Committee were the same men 15 corrupt Dockers.

197

Over the years I have written to several Taoiseachs, many government ministers, a multitude of TD's, RTE, and the so-called "Free Press" plus three Presidents and brought this scandal to the attention of the highest ranking members of the legal profession - and have been mostly ignored.

Anyone whose conscience was pricked, like Pat Rabbitte... was silenced and corrupted. Below are several emails I sent. The first example is in the form of an open letter on linkedin.
THEY KNOW EXACTLY WHAT THEY DO
Published on May 9, 2018 on linkedin
Edit article
View stats
Status is online
Hugh Murphy
Writer at Heart & Soul Theatre Company 46 articles
ANOTHER OPEN LETTER TO MR JUSTICE PETER KELLY, WITH EMBEDDED ATTACHMENTS .

Dear Judge Kelly,
Judge Kelly, you obviously know what happens when good men do nothing. A case in point is the scandal right now with smear tests. So far almost 20 women have died and hundreds more are living under a death sentence. Now go back 50 years to Belfast Docks when the union chairman ordered Dockers to discharge Asbestos.
My play about the Belfast Docks scandal is being censored by SIPTU
members and supporters in the arts, which because of her actions the Arts Minister Josepha Madigan is colluding with. Proof of what I
maintain about the censoring of my writing, is the fact: that neither she nor Justice Minister Charlie Flanagan will answer this question,- "is censorship against the law". While having no proof of Flanagan's bias, other than his refusal to answer what any Justice Minister should and must know, I can

undoubtedly prove that the Arts Minister is not behaving like an independent Arts Minister.

Find below a post she sent me on linkedin, then shortly afterwards blocked me and deleted it. She obviously didn't know she couldn't delete 'her' post from my account. While on its own this doesn't prove censorship, but when juxtaposed with all I'm experiencing, including this email from the Irish Theatre Institute offering help then going silent - what other explanation can there be?

Apr 13

I've just noticed that you're active now, and therefore have received my post.

10:54 AM

Apr 16LinkedIn Member sent the following message at 9:54 AM

View LinkedIn Member's profile

Hi Hugh, Would you be able to send an email on this to me at josepha.madigan@oir.ie and I will endeavor to get an answer for your question. I don't check my LinkedIn messages regularly. Thanks, Josepha Madigan TD Minister for Culture, Heritage and the Gaeltacht

----

On Fri, Mar 16, 2018 at 12:10 PM

Irish Theatre Institute

Before the usual censorship regarding my writing sets in - Re 'The Judas Goat', I'm sending 'Salvation...? to you for advice on how best to circumvent the censorship I'm experiencing.

Because of the recent groundswell by women and them standing up for themselves - I'm looking forward to your advice.

Salvation...? has a cast of five women

Regards

Attachments area

Elaine Donnelly <edonnelly@irishtheatreinstitute.ie>

Jan 31

to Admin, me

Good evening Hugh,

Irish Theatre Institute does not offer script-reading as part of our artist programmes. As the organisation does not have legal expertise we may not be able to assist directly with queries around censorship but might be able to offer some suggestions on who to talk with. If you have any specific queries please feel free to contact us.

Best Regards,

Elaine

Eláine Donnelly

General Manager

Irish Theatre Institute | 17 Eustace Street | Temple Bar | Dublin 2

T: +353 1 670 4906

www.irishtheatreinstitute.ie

Reg. Charity No. CHY 20847

Company Registration Number: 338199

VAT Number: IE6358199D

Judge Kelly, In my last open letter I detailed the cover up of Jack O'Connor and SIPTU, whereby 40 to 50 years ago the union chairman persecuted fined and sacked Belfast Dockers who wouldn't discharge Asbestos, myself included. The same Chairman who became an employer was awarded his fifty year long service union badge by Jack O'Connor.

How was this possible? For Heaven's sake this man was an employer and he unbelievably remained a union member? This must be the only time in Trade Union History that this occurred and the man covering it up is standing for election.

My stage-play 'The Judas Goat' is about the events that took place at Belfast Docks and members and supporters of SIPTU have done everything in their power to keep this play of an Irish stage.

Judge Kelly, I'm addressing this letter to you for several reasons – one is that we met before and on that occasion you allowed me five minutes to make my points. This was in 2010 at a conference in the Hall of Surgeons to discuss changes to the Defamation Laws, at which you chaired the Q&A session. As one would expect, the hall was packed with the upper echelons of Dublin's barristers and solicitors. Also well represented was the "Free Press" with the champion of this fine body of "truth seekers" Geraldine Kennedy, then editor of Irish Times

on the panel - and it seemed, ready willing and able to dispense the know I shouldn't have been present, but seeing I had challenged Jack O'Connor three times to sue me for defamation – I believed that I should at least be aware of new developments. I will take this opportunity to apologise to the young ladies I bluffed my way past, by telling them their computer wouldn't accept my registration, and hope they didn't get into too much trouble.

Judge Kelly, you will recall that when you called for questions I was the first speaker – and I stunned yourself and the assembled legal people by stating, "I tried to get myself sued for defamation" by telling the truth. The silence was absolute. Then I outlined the circumstances of how Jack O'Connor's Union at Belfast Docks persecuted and sacked its own members myself included, and that the Union and employers established an illegal Union and Employers Court, which they termed 'The Joint Disciplinary Committee. [details on website] I was sacked because I wouldn't discharge Asbestos and encouraged other Dockers to do the same.

In utter silence, I related how the cover up by the "Free Press" and the Legal Profession had caused me to accuse O'Connor, three times, at public meetings of being corrupt and of covering up corruption. On the first occasion he threatened to "sue the arse off me" and engaged a Belfast Solicitor, one John O'Neill of Thompson McClures to do so.

As I related these shocking facts to you and the assembled barristers and solicitors - there is no doubt O'Connor got a shock when his solicitor, O'Neill of informed him by letter that what I said about the Belfast Branch was indeed, true.

Judge Kelly, this scandal is well documented on the web, and is being ignored by the very people who make a living from ferreting out injustice and questioning the motives of the holier than thou. You saw on the day, how Geraldine Kennedy refused to answer my questions, claiming she couldn't do so until she'd spoken to Fintan O'Toole – and is why the Irish Times and every so-called newspaper in the state refuse to cover this story. There's no doubt that this important conference was recorded, many times, as the back of the hall was festooned with truth-seeking camera wielding members of the Journalistic Profession.

I have numerous instances of the censoring of my writing - and the Belfast Docks play in particular. E.g. Druid, asked me in writing not to tell anyone they refused to stage this play - which I refused to do. However, when my producer booked four nights in the Mick Lally Theatre, Druids studio space, for my play 'The Grandeur of Delusions' - they emailed a week later and stated "after a meeting those dates are no longer available". Mick Lally, a deceased Druid actor must be turning in his grave.

By a strange coincidence - Patrick Sutton of Smock Alley did exactly the same thing - but with silence. After I accepted the four dates Sutton offered in an email, for some strange reason he went incommunicado. While I accept these facts alone don't prove a conspiracy or censorship many other situations have occurred.

Last year I applied in plenty of time to the Dublin Theatre Festival with 'The Grandeur of Delusions', and after a long wait I received an email from Willie White, stating that it was fully programmed. Earlier in the year, I applied to the 'then'

Director of the Fringe Festival. After a long wait, he replied by email and refused my entry, stating "This year we are changing Direction". Whatever that means? Nelson, accepted several companies into the Fringe, and who were supported on the basis of an idea only, yet I supplied him with a fully rounded hard-hitting production, which depicts the evils of Alcoholism and addiction in a modern context, and is a two hander.

Despite the refusals of the "Cultured", I managed to stage a short tour of nine dates with this play. The two actors got a standing ovation on the last night and several people who work in Theatre, and who have seen the production, remarked, this would be ideal fare for any Festival.

Of course, none of the above proves a conspiracy and neither does the fact that Cian O'Brian of The Project thinks, 'The Judas Goat' is a great play but refuses to stage it, using the debatable fact that The Project is a receiving house, only. I say debatable because, its a very strange receiving house that refuses to give a price, or dates for hiring of their Theatre. While this is another fact that doesn't prove conspiracy, corruption or censorship emanating from SIPTU, I will just add it to the basket.

However, as everyone knows, Willie White who is now Director of the Dublin Theatre Festival - was for a long time, the Director of the Project, and who no doubt wishes to see it toe, the proverbial line, so his time there wasn't wasted.

And Judge Kelly, who could possibly think that a conspiracy might exist between Willie White and Garry Hynes - just because she sits with Willie on the board of The Dublin Theatre Festival. I bet they will both swear under oath that my name never crossed either, of their minds, or lips.

Also, Dublin City Council supported me by giving me four weeks free rehearsal space for my play 'Daddy'. However when I submitted 'The Judas Goat' and asked for the same consideration, the arts director, Ray Yeates became frosty and made up several excuses not to do so, all of which contradicted DCC's much publicised Arts Plan. SIPTU has its fingers in many pies.

And just today I've been informed that my play Salvation, has been refused entry to the Dublin Fringe Festival - which I've been expecting, even though it has a new director. Because of the truth enshrined in 'The Judas Goat', I cannot get a play into any festival in Ireland. Salvation is an important play about the after effects of child abuse on two adult sisters and has a cast of five female actors.

At the start of 'January' it was refused entry to The Dublin Theatre Festival by Willie White, who stated, again "we are fully programmed", this was a full ten months before the festival begins.

The most disturbing thing about this non-censorship, non-conspiracy of silence and non- compliance with artistic ethics, is the fobbing off, of my complaints by arts council officers. Why does Shelia Pratcheke say "It has always been my lifelong decision not to interfere with decisions of artistic directors, though I do sympathise with your disappointment not to be chosen". She was speaking about the Dublin and Fringe Festivals. I also asked both Pratscheke and Orlaith McBride to refer my complaints to a full sitting of the Arts Council, but received no response.

To support my proposal I sent a copy of 'The Judas Goat' to each member of the Arts Council, [care of the Arts Council offices] but have received no reply from any of them. Why is this most serious matter being ignored, can they all be members and supporters of SIPTU?'The Judas Goat' is not attacking trade unions but shows what happens to uneducated workers and their families when the union chairman is corrupted by employers.

When we were having difficulty, without funding, securing rehearsal space for "The Grandeur of Delusions" I asked McBride for help in securing a room. She replied by email stating: "The Arts Council does not have space available for your requirements". I pointed out to her, given the scope of Arts Council funding to Filmbase and the IFI, where rooms are plentiful and available, this is complete and utter nonsense. While no person in the Arts will oppose SIPTU inspired Censorship South Dublin County Council were most accommodating in providing a room as a rehearsal space.

However, the worst scandal and the one which the union are doing all in their power to prevent becoming public knowledge – is the fact that Asbestos Dust blew all over Belfast. It's an undeniable fact that many Dockers and members of the public died from Asbestos related cancers without even knowing what caused their cancer. However a few Dockers have received compensation.

Judge Kelly, besides the people who actually caused the cancer deaths

- the next worst offenders are the so-called "Free Press". They know exactly what they do. Two weeks ago in the Sunday Times John Burns waxed lyrically on how "in the Dublin office of the Sunday Times we like nothing better than a philosophical discussion on the finer points of journalistic ethics. Happily, a chance for editors to stroke their chins and use phrases like "morally justified" and "ethically dubious" has just presented itself. Burns was throwing flowers at the supposed enlightened principles of Sunday Times journalists – and commenting on the 'Chatham House rules and delighting in the fact that Sunday Times was under no such restraints and would print what they want.

I publicly ask John Burns "where is the ethics of Sunday Times when its reporters will not report on a Trade Union that illegally joined forces with Belfast Docks Employers, set up a private court system to persecute its own members and ordered Dockers to discharge Asbestos or be sacked". And why will they not report that Jack O'Connor will not sue me for calling him corrupt, three times to his face at large public meetings. Burns then goes on to state, "the best definition of the Chatham House rule was given by Simon Walters, political editor of the Mail on Sunday. He said 'We Chatham up and put it in the paper'. Let the speaker beware. Three cheers for the champions of free speech, what hypocrisy!

The Mail on Sunday and Irish Daily Mail will not report on the Belfast Docks scandal or the cover up by O'Connor. No doubt burns is planning a move to The Mail on Sunday.

Will the fact that Jack O'Connor is standing for public office and obviously will use his trade union contacts to get elected – encourage John Burns and Simon Walters to report on the cover up he engaged in with SIPTU?

While he has fooled many people including John McGuinness, Michael Martin, Pat Rabbitte and a multitude of other Td's who are prepared to ignore this scandal – I... nor the people in Belfast dying from Asbestos related Cancers can forget.

Judge Kelly, I am simply asking you – if some brave new member of the

"free press" who doesn't know about the defamation conference, or what I said, asks you for a quote, give it. As you know, the facts are on

www.siptupresidentjackoconnorexposed.com – and the link siptu-conspiracy.pdf which is a copy of the website and easier to read, as you don't have to click on each page.

Hugh Murphy

nbox x

Personally I don't believe the letter above needs clarification. Although the die hard censors and SIPTU supporters in will remark just, like the singing Tally-man at Belfast Docks, Brian McCann when he sarcastically remarked About the Dockers Voice, 'that's all Murphy's own opinion".

Indeed it was my own opinion - but it was also the Truth. Because I was prepared to speak the Truth and not accept as normal, the fact, that my Trade Union had been collaborating with Employers for a long number of years, I was persecuted and sacked by my own Union and the Employers.

Public enquiry demanded into Docks 'can of worms'

Last week's Court of Appeal finding that eight Catholic dockers were discriminated against by the Port Authority is "only the tip of the iceberg".

by
tom mallon

That's the view of former docker Hugh Murphy who is pressing for a full judicial enquiry into employment practices at the docks for over 20 years.

"The dockers are all gone now," he said, "but the architects of the discrimination which plagued the docks are still around, some of them in the most senior of positions. It's not enough for the Port Authority to be fined for one instance of discrimination against eight Catholic dockers, the wrong-doers need to be brought to book. There's a whole can of worms here just waiting to be opened."

The Andersontown man says collusion between unions and management at the docks is "a sordid scandal."

"The part that Catholics played in keeping their co-religionists out of the docks has never been fully exposed. The reality is that Catholics in the ITGWU, SIPTU and Northern Ireland ICTU were either involved in the discrimination or turned a blind eye to it," said Mr Murphy. "The Fair Employment Commission needs to investigate the criminal conspiracy at the docks and ensure compensation is paid to all its victims."

Hugh Murphy has been campaigning for a public probe into conditions on the docks since he himself was sacked in 1974. "The unions and management came together to set up a Joint Disciplinary Committee to try dockers for infringements of the rules," he explained. "In reality, these were never written down and it was used to get rid of 'undesirables' who were protesting at the way the docks were run. In my own case, I was summoned to go before this 'court' - the first-ever time in labour history that unions and management had set up a joint disciplinary body. When I refused to go, I was given the heave-ho after 20 years of service. My father was so sickened by the whole affair that he finished and left after 33 years on the docks. The men went on strike for three days in protest but were talked back to work by the union officials."

The former docker is now writing a play about his experiences. His last work for the stage, *Justice was premiered* in Belfast last year and dealt with his imprisonment for possessing ammunition in his taxi. That conviction was subsequently overturned when it emerged the ammunition had been planted by British soldiers.

Last week, the Court of Appeal ruled that eight Catholic dockers were discriminated against in 1988 when they applied for work at the docks. The eight were among 29 Catholics who applied for work on the docks in November of that year. All 47 people shortlisted for the vacancies - by an all-Protestant shortlisting panel - were Protestants. Of the 18 eventually employed, one was in jail at the time of his appointment.

On New Year's Eve 1991, the FEC ruled that the eight had suffered unfair religious discrimination from the Port Employers' Authority.

Appeal last week endorsed the original finding and ruled that the failure to include Catholics on a shortlist for the 15 jobs was "a clear case of discrimination on the grounds of religious belief".

"That was only half the story," adds Hugh Murphy. "What happened once the Protestants came on to the docks was that Catholic dockers there had to train them because they had no experience. Once the training was finished, the Catholics were sacked."

"Dockers' discrimination ruling 'just the tip of the iceberg': Hugh Murphy

CHAPTER NINE

When Decasualisation was implemented - because the Union had been persecuting and fining Belfast Dockers large sums of money for years, the totally corrupt and anti-worker 'Union and Employers Court, was accepted as normal. Even when the Union began ordering Dockers to their deaths, they still did not object, however, I persevered and eventuality convinced them not to work at Asbestos, many were reluctant to do so. They would rather lose their lives than their Jobs.

Eventually I was rail-roaded and sacked by the Union and Employers Court. This article was in the Andersonstown News, Belfast in either 1992 or 93. The only newspaper in Ireland that would report on this scandal.

Obviously, West Belfast was outside the influence of the Wealty Dublin Employers and their Union Cronies.

The scandalous decision to allow the destruction of 'Sailortown' the dockside community to build a bridge at the end of a motorway, was nonsensical and served no purpose - other than to facilitate the destruction of this vibrant working class community. Most appallingly was the destruction of a large Victorian Fire Station, which had the large green dome of Oxidised Copper. {The nickname of Sailortown is self-explanatory} Had it been left alone, this Dockside area would rival Temple Bar in Dublin as a tourist attraction.

In fact Temple Bar with its antiquated shop fronts was designated to be a large bus station, until someone saw sense. This sense was sadly lacking in Belfast - which would have had one big difference. It would be a living breathing slice of life from times gone by - with Pub at every corner. Today, many could have been turned into cafe's and tea shops.

St Joseph's, the local Catholic Church was allowed to fall into disrepair and eventually decommissioned.

Belfast Docks in the early 1970's had not progressed beyond the master and slave mentality that flourished with Dublin Employers in 1913. For Connolly and Larkins Union to collude with 'Belfast Docks Employers' in the 1970's and establish a Union and Employers Court, was - and still is unbelievable? The Union betrayed in every standard of decency that Connolly and Larkin injected into the ITGWU before the Dublin Lockout.

In Belfast the Union was not protecting ordinary union members from unscrupulous employers - instead it was doing the opposite siding with employers and sacking them.

Head Office and ICTU knew about this - because before I was sacked I sent them both the Dockers Voice every week. Their silence - even today shows they won't expose the Wealthy by showing the corrupt way they were controlling the Union. {see letters} To every right thinking person these actions are disgusting in the extreme and shows the sort of people who run SIPTU, even today - and ICTU is no better. By their silence these present day Union Officials demean what Larkin fought against for all of his life, and what James Connolly actually gave his life to achieve.

When the Industrial Tribunal ruled that no-one could be sacked without a contract of employment I initially was elated however the non-action by the solicitors I engaged - led me to again seek solace in Alcohol. One of the hardest things to accept was that my Da was treating me with respect. Every-time I saw him I had to fight quell the anger that almost overwhelmed me. I could not understand the contradiction of his actions.

I returned to my old ways and lost my driving licence for a year. To this day when I put on a belt... those memories come flooding bacn and a red fog clouds my consciousness.

The first two solicitors who took my Docks Case did nothing with it. Obviously they were bought off by the Union and the Employers.

Because of this I had to sue the solicitors for inaction but could not get a solicitor who would sue other solicitors. So I complained to the Belfast Law Society. They informed me that if I was turned down by six solicitors, they would give me a list of solicitors to choose from.a {See Law Society letters}

When I showed that I had already exceeded this number, I was duly sent a list of three solicitors to choose from. The first on the list was a G - McCann and company. Mr McCann read my papers and agreed to take the case. I was duly appointed a junior solicitor - Norman Shannon, who did sterling work contacting all and sundry named in my case papers and I was entirely satisfied that my case was progressing well.

However - this good work stopped dead when Norman Shannon left Mr MCann and set up on his own. {See his letter} and took my case with him. The corruption that took place at Belfast Docks could have been stopped there and then - but

Norman Shannon was corrupted and bought off. Instead of fighting my case this corrupt lawyer sat on it for seven years until it became Statute Barred. This is not in doubt and is a matter of Public Record. **To compound this, the Belfast Law Society know they have a corrupt solicitor in their midst and ignore it.**

When I brought this to the Law Society's attention unbelievably they blamed me - stating I had waited too many years before making a complaint to them. As they well know - I trusted a member of "their Law Society" to take action on my behalf and to uphold the finest traditions of the 'Law Society'.

Obviously to them and Norman Shannon because of my "False Criminal Record" I am the lowest of the low and they can treat me as they wished.

Even though I have named and shamed Shannon on linkedin he will not sue me for calling him corrupt in 'print'. I will prove in Court that he is as guilty as ICTU, SIPTU, the Irish Employers and the Wealthy. These facts shows that the Belfast Law Society is as corrupt as Norman Shannon.

{See their letters to me} Shannon is now a high flying, Human Rights Lawyer and they will not bring their supposed Legal System into disrepute by exposing him - hence I ask this question – IS THERE A LAWYER IN IRELAND WHO WILL EXPOSE THIS CORRUPTION?

I know it's a contradiction in terms to label a legal system corrupt - but as the facts prove, the Northern Ireland law Society is the exception to the rule. To try and bring attention to this scandal I have written to many human rights people, including Almal Cooney several times, at Doughty Street Chambers but never received a reply.

To go back to the start of Shannon's corruption, even the most lowly, law clerk knows about the Quinn v Leatham case which went to the house of lords in 1901. Interested people will no doubt look it up. This is a very similar case to my own and involves a Trade Union. The lords ruling states: that "if two or more persons combine together without legal justification to injure another and by so doing cause him damage, then they are liable in an action for conspiracy.

This conspiracy is exactly what the Belfast Union Leaders, the ex Union chairman, the Employers, SIPTU, ICTU and the Wealthy have engaged in. They all conspired to cover up the Asbestos Deaths and the Illegal Union and Employers Court that sacked Belfast Dockers and myself. The Court put their corruption it in writing.

However - this is not the worst of it. What the Belfast Law Society is ignoring is the fact - that Shannon was not just a 'little corrupt'? He took no action to expose the fact that Belfast People were put in danger by being exposed to Asbestos Dust that was blown all over Belfast.

That Norman Shannon was bribed to allow my case is to become Statute Barred, is without doubt. No-one knows how many people this Deadly Dust has killed? A simply biopsy of everyone who dies from a Cancer would tell if their death was Asbestos related. Why is this not happening?

To this end the Belfast Law Society has also become corrupted by Wealth. It must cover up for Norman Shannon - for to expose him they will have to expose themselves because they were involved from the very start. This begs the question, why does the Law Society in Dublin behave like the Law Society in Belfast? Even though this happened 50 years ago, where are the principles of lawyers in Ireland - and what is the Stature of Limitations on corporate manslaughter? Where is the famous lawyers quote in all this - Justice delayed is Justice denied?

What transpired here is LEGAL CORRUPTION and the fact that it's a criminal conspiracy of monumental proportions should add weight to the demand that restrictions on the Statute of Limitations in this highly exceptional case be waived.

Norman Shannon started the ball rolling, by being bought off and allowing my case to become Statute Barred. This is obvious to anyone knowing the facts, so I ask: **Is there an 'independent non - bought off Irish lawyer brave enough to expose the corrupt Legal System that exists here?** I fear not, seeing no journalist or politician will risk the 'ire' of the establishment by exposing it either. Accepting that this is the case, is there a British one?

I ask this - seeing that the initial corruption of the legal system took place in Belfast. So, will the much praised British Legal System and their free press expose this corruption? The reason no such inquiry or reporting of this scandal has taken place, so far - is because the Wealthy have been manipulating - so-called Irish Democracy.

This is a unique, novel and a special case which raises several Points of Law, that will never be remedied in Ireland - and therefore must go to the European Court. The most glaring point and the most obvious - is: how can a trade union - and putting aside for one minute the antecedence of this one - persecute and sack its own members - and WHY?

Belfast Docks was the start and proves that Corruption follows Corruption and has infected the upper echelons of the Law Societies North and South. At the start of this saga of corruption, when I expressed anger and disgust that my case had become Statute Barred, to fool me, Norman Shannon engaged a barrister Barry MacDonald, to give his opinion on the matter.

However MacDonald was deviously misled by Shannon, He was only asked to give an opinion on the non-action of the solicitors previous to Shannon, and his employer Mr McCann - and nothing about Shannon's involvement after he set up on his own. Obviously MacDonald based his opinion on them. He was as fooled as I was.

Obviously, Norman Shannon did not tell MacDonald, that - he himself, had been sitting on the case for seven years and it was himself who should be sued for malpractice. The barrister was blissfully unaware that he was being used as a 'cat's paw'. This is glaringly obvious from Barry MacDonald's opinion. {Read it in the documents}

Another glaring fact is: when I pointed out to the Belfast Law Society that Shannon had used a barrister, to unwittingly pull the wool over my eyes, they did nothing. {Another cover up} And this is where the case gets interesting and proves absolutely that Shannon was acting corruptly. At that time he was still within the time limit for taking action on my behalf. I just wish Shannon had left my case with Mr McCann. Obviously he was offered so much money from the employers and the union, to set up in practice on his own, that greed got the better of him.

Why did the Law Society in Belfast, when presented with the evidence of Shannon's non-action and malpractice, not take action? They must be aware of the 1901 house of lords ruling about Conspiracy? They should have immediately suspended him from practice, pending an inquiry into his 'Legal Corruption' and bringing the Law into disrepute.

I raised the matter of Belfast Docks at another conference. This one was entitled: Emerging Human Rights Issues and took place at the Law Society, at which Michael Farrell was speaking. Shortly after I arrived, late - I took a microphone from a young lady as I passed her, and interrupted the Lady speaker to highlight the cover up of the Union at Belfast Docks whereby the Union sacked its own members. {I should have waited until Farrell was speaking}

This didn't go down well. I had just got to the point of describing how my union and employers formed a Union and Employers Court, which corruptly sacked the Belfast Dockers - when I was accosted by two young ladies, the mike pulled from my hands and I was pushed out. I protested: "Is this conference not about Human Rights" I was told from the stage that 'I was out of order and should leave'. I replied, "Is this conference not about Human Rights"? I was told "there are proper channel's to go through". To which I replied: "Yes and I get the run around. Why are all you Human Rights People covering up the denial of Human Rights at Belfast Docks where we literally ate Asbestos".

Rather that put my hands on the young women who had me by the elbows I allowed them to lead me out. On the way out we encountered an Irish Times journalist, {can't remember his name} upon seeing these young women escorting me out he asked - was he late? I launched into the denial of human rights in Ireland but was propelled towards the doors and put out. My outburst at the conference was because - without financial, I.e a lawyers help I cannot expose, or get the case of Belfast Dockers illegally sacked by an amalgamation of Union and Employers into a Courtroom.

An interesting fact about an unrelated case has come to my attention.

Norman Shannon told me "That my Docks case became Statute Barred because the 'other side' would not enter a defence so he could do nothing about it". I read in the Press, recently - about a "Notice of Motion to have Judgement in Default of Defence".

Which means, that, if no defence is entered then the case is won?

Obviously, Norman Shannon was aware, that 'as a layman' I knew nothing about this - and it proves that he was Bought Off. It also proves that the Belfast Law Society is… as Corrupt as Norman Shannon. I had previously told them what Shannon had said - not knowing about the 'Default of Defence' - and they did nothing about it. Why did they not question Norman Shannon on this, and suspend him? Instead they questioned me as to why I had left the matter for years before complaining. The simple answer is because I was fooled by a Corrupt Solicitor who is still practising.

By doing nothing about this scandal The Northern Ireland Law Society have proved they are more corrupt than Norman Shannon - who is still in Practice in Belfast.

In the present day, in a different but related issue, even if Ireland had said "We don't want on the Security Council" they would still have been appointed to it. The wealthy countries in NATO who spend Billions on security need a neutral country on their side.

The competition for Ireland to be elected was a con job, to convince Irish people that it was not a done deal. However, the Wiley People in the Department of Foreign Affairs saw that this could seriously affect Ireland's Neutral Status - so they came up with a plan which was to 'downplay' their application and treat the whole thing as a joke. With the joke being on those who thought they could use Ireland's Neutrality in such a scandalous manner.

Everyone knows the Irish are very humorous, and to send socks and frivolous items to New York in the Diplomatic Bag showed just how serious they took the application to join the Security Council.

The department of foreign affairs while being no stranger to white elephants, knew that the 125 thousand Euros, spent on free gift bags, mints, pencils and chocolates would be small beer if they were actually on the Council. The Department hoped that the mode of transport for State Secrets and funny socks in the Diplomatic bag, would convince the Big Players to reject their application. Not so.

Even if they'd danced around a camp-fire with their posteriors painted Green, their application would still be accepted. The reason being: that the big hitters in Europe was determined to plug the glaring gap that had opened in European Union's borders, with Brexit, and to make the Irish pay for the country wide, Open Border that now existed.

They should have just showed a clip from Father Ted. In a last ditch attempt to get the Security Council to change their minds, and to show how much they valued security - the Department of Foreign Affairs held a party to celebrate Ireland's election. Talk about the tears of a clown.
This party was held during 'Lockdown', when they partied with impunity disregarding Covid Regulations. Many photos of their supposed hilarity were shown to Big Phil - who had to resign for the same offence.
This Party was designed to show just how much the Department of Foreign Affairs believe in Security and a last ditch attempt to get them to change their minds about including Ireland.

The same modus operandi operated at Belfast Docks fifty years ago.

Everyone was aware that the Union was more employer than the Employers and a big joke was made of it - until it was too late. In this instance the, Union Chairman pursued his own agenda and told the Dockers that they needed Decasualsation –

while he feathered his own nest with the employers.

My play 'The Judas Goat' started life as 'One Big Onion' but I changed it to - 'The Judas Goat'. With the new title there was no mistaking the layers of corruption which I had incorporated into the previous title. Past directors at the Lyric, in Belfast, no doubt ordered by the Wealthy censored it. And likewise, Jimmy Fay from Dublin, the present Lyric Director, with his eye to future, {knowing who controls Theatre in Ireland} has also refused to engage with it. Obviously, so not to upset anyone who could stymie his career. I wanted this play staged first in Belfast - where the death of Trade Unionism first occurred - and where Larkin had his famous strike that united Religions.

Where is the much heralded and world famous supposed "Irish, free speech and Independence of Theatre"?
It obviously resides with the supposed morals and ethics of The Legal Profession which are utterly corrupt. The other so-called champions of Free Press 'The news -papers are also in the pockets of Wealthy and do their bidding.

In Ireland the People who laud Freedom of Expression are the worst deniers of it. Because Ireland is so small the Wealthy control Democracy and all media and the Theatre. This unscrupulous behaviour exists in every aspect of Irish Life and guarantees the censoring of 'The Judas Goat'. Obviously this has led to all my writing being censored. Ireland is run by Puppets for the benefit of the faceless Wealthy who look down upon the uneducated and poor like they're vermin - and white collar crime in Ireland is rarely punished. A case in point is the recent scandal of the national broadcaster, RTE who squandered tax-payers money like confetti.

This only came to light when it was exposed that Ryan Tubrity had been paid hundreds of thousands of euros to which he wasn't entitled to.

There was uproar and 'Tubs' was eventually sacked. Not for misappropriation through a secret Barter account, but because he refused to accept that he'd done any wrongdoing. However, RTE claim that its not in a position to compel him to return the money, which even

'Tubs' now admits he wasn't entitled to.

I would respectfully suggest that a word in his ear about his refusal to return the money - will lead to a charge of "obtaining money under false pretences", will have him banging on RTE's door to take it back.

I attended many conferences on human rights abuses over the years and have been put out of most of them - however one in particular sticks in my mind because I left it in disgust. It was in the Law Society and

'laughingly' named "JUSTICE, FOR SOME OR FOR ALL".

Someone in the Bar Council has a very perverse sense of humour. The conference was organised by the Bar Council to discuss its voluntary assistance scheme. This, supposedly is to offer barrister services free to voluntary organisations. These services include advice to the organisations themselves, as well as advice and representation for their clients.

The main speaker at the conference was Mary Robinson, ex President of Ireland and a champion of human rights around the world. When I arrived, I sat in the front row, beside a Traveller Rep and the homeless campaigner and priest, Peter McVerry. After being introduced, Mary Robinson's first words were: "There are four pillars of justice; the first is the rule of law and access to justice". I was ecstatic at hearing this. Her second pillar was property rights, "where people did not have the right to the land they lived on". When I heard her say that "the third 'pillar' was Labour Rights" - I was convinced that I was in the right place and something would now be done about the corruption at Belfast Docks.

Her fourth right was "the right to engage in business,where the poor could develop their own businesses, access credit and form contracts".

Mary then invited questions, with the words, "This meeting is for you".

What a joke!

She should have said: This conference is to cover up the activities of the Wealthy in Ireland. At her call for speakers I raised my hand.

The Barrister Turlough O'Donnell who was chairing the event directed a young lady to give me a mike. I immediately launched into the cover up by SIPTU - and Mary raised her hand and "said your mouth is too close to the mike". These were the only words she spoke. I moved the mike further from my mouth and continued to inform her and the large audience about SIPTU covering up the fact, that the Union at Belfast Docks had formed an illegal Union and Employers Court for persecuting Union Members.

I then asked her a direct question, which was "Mary, why does the Northern Ireland Human Rights Commission say they can do nothing about a Union in Belfast collaborating with Employers to sack its own members at Belfast Docks - because the head office of the Union is in Dublin? And - the Irish Human Rights Commission say "This matter does not come within the jurisdiction of the State because it occurred in the North of Ireland".

Mary Robinson tilted her head and looked like she was listening with rapt attention - although her gaze was to the large doors at the back of the room. So I continued: "Mary as you well know corruption is corruption and for the Irish Human Rights Commission to say: "It has now considered my request for an investigation in detail, taking into account the information and documentation provided by me, as analysed against relevant human rights standards, etc etc. AND, they regret to inform me that it has been decided '**not**' to accede to my request for an inquiry on the following grounds".

As I paused for breath I looked around and the audience were listening with rapt attention. So I continued: "The human rights commission say my request for an inquiry is not clearly linked to any of the Commission's functions under paragraphs [a] [c], [d]
or [e] of section 8 of the Human Rights Commission Act 2000"?

There was absolute silence in the hall as everyone waited for Mary Robinson to reply - but she remained silent still looking at the doors at the back of the hall. So I asked her- "How can you refuse to investigate human rights abuses one hundred miles up the road, yet you can investigate human rights abuses around the world"?

When I mentioned Human Rights Mary looked at me, sharply. Myself, and the audience thought she was going to interject, but she remained silent and turned gaze back to the large doors.
"Mary" I continued, "I am really delighted to hear what you just said about The Rule of Law' because in the report I got from IHRC, it is sadly lacking".

I expected Mary to speak but she remained silent. I was confused and thought the great champion of Human Rights cannot be a supporter of the Wealthy. She must be gathering her thoughts for a broadside on the IHRC. Or at the very lease a denouncement of a Trade union that sacked its own members. There was absolute silence in the Hall.

However, I waited, and waited. The great Mary Robinson, champion of the underdog remained absolutely silent and uttered not one word.

When it became obvious that Mary Robinson was not going to answer, Turlough O'Donnel waved to the young lady to take the mike from me.

As she did so I shouted into it, "Will you give me a barrister to fight my case and sue SIPTU for covering up corruption".

Turlough replied, "It doesn't work like that you have to go through one of the NGO's". During the tussle for the mike, Mary Robinson sat as silent as the grave. Had the corruption and cover up I just related happened thousands of miles instead of just up the road her response would have been very different.

I was shocked as the conference continued. I listened while the great an the good, like Noeline Blackwell, Peter McVerty and a Damien Peelo, who is a Traveller, and spoke eloquently about the denial of human rights in Ireland for his People. I wondered to myself what planet are these people on? They had just witnessed an ex President of Ireland and one time United Nations Commissioner for Human Rights, ignore clearly defined corruption in Ireland - and not say a a word about it?

For Mary Robinson to ignore what I had just told her - was the denying of life to the Asbestos sufferers in Belfast - and to me Freedom of Speech by refusing to accept the Truth.

Not a word out of protest came from the the speakers or the large audience who obviously had a belief in Human Rights or they wouldn't have been here.

Noeline Blackwell on the stage and raised some valid points about how the poor are the most regulated by the state, etc. Her hypocrisy and the ignoring of what I had just said beggared belief.

When Peter McVerty related a story about a young boy, who was jailed for stealing a bottle of orange valued at one Euro, the audience were suitably aghast. Especially when he related how in the past 10 years there have been over three thousand prosecutions for welfare fraud worth 43 million that led to 48 people being jailed.
And in the same period only 39 prosecutions for tax evasion, which cost two and quarter Billion, with only six being jailed.

I wondered, could this audience and the speakers, objectors to the status quo -not see, by their silence regarding the corruption I had just outlined - are allowing the injustices they complain about to take place?

Had Mary Robinson supported my demand for an inquiry into the Belfast Docks Corruption by IHRC and the removal of the people responsible for denying it, then all their complaints in due course would be taken care of.
This would happen - because the corrupt in every aspect of Irish life would be replaced by unafraid genuine people.
While the supposed objectors 'touch the fore-lock' and object in a nice way - the supposed 'great and good' attend 'talking shops' and do nothing - so nothing in Ireland will change. The Travellers rep from Pavee Point, boasted that they could not get a solicitor to represent them - but now had got their own. He didn't make clear if this was a Traveller or not. However, I later emailed Pavee Point and asked them to represent me, only to get a reply a few days later, stating 'we only represent Travellers'.
After the sarcastically named conference I phoned both Turlough O'Donnell and Flac, Free Legal Aid Centres. I spoke to

Turlough's Secretary, who I really think was his wife, who said things like 'he won't be home until after six'.

However she was really interested in what I said about the Union and we had a long conversation. When I rang back, Turlough answered. I told him about the disgraceful behaviour of the Union at Belfast Docks and that I had documentary evidence of it. He asked me if I would copy it and leave it into the Bar Council for him, which I gladly did. However several weeks later he said he couldn't help me.

And for all the help I got from Flac, I need not have bothered. I spoke to Noleene Blackwell who shouted into the phone, "You were at the conference I can't help you - I can't help you". 'I asked her to calm down and questioned why she couldn't help me'. Still excited, she again shouted - "and no other NGO will help you either"'.

I again calmly questioned her as to why she wouldn't help, and asked, 'how did she know no other NGO wouldn't help me? She stated: "I've got work to do" and hung up.

Over the years I've been getting this response from a multitude of Lawyers, Journalists, Human Rights workers and TD's, including government ministers and many Arts practitioners - and why I coined the terms, the AMID and the ATL's to reflect just who runs Ireland. I.E. The Arts Mafia In Dublin and The above the Laws.

The facts and documentation at the end of this book are there for all to see. Yet both Law Societies in Ireland refuse to act on this corruption and conspiracy, which was - and still is being orchestrated by SIPTU, ICTU and the Wealthy. The proof of what I maintain is the fact, that the Belfast Law Society was involved from the very start. It was 'they' who got me Mr McCann in the first place. They know full well about this

Travesty of the Law and will do nothing about it.

Because Noline Blackwell was working for Flac at the time, and because I cannot afford Justice in Ireland I wrote to Flac seeking representation and free legal aid. Michael Farrell - her boss in Flac - who, Justice wise
- can only be classed as a Joke - although not a laughable one. He is also a high flying Human Rights Lawyer in Dublin - who also covers up for Norman Shannon. Are lawyers not supposed to be above reproach and above this behaviour? In a series of letters to me he defended
Norman Shannon.

Farrell, besides being the leading solicitor with Flac at he time was also a senior lawyer with the Law Society, the IHRC as it was then, and a myriad of other Human Rights organisations. After the Irish Human Rights Commission acquired the 'E' Farrell complained that the Justice Minister sought to reappoint eight members to the IHREC, without an open competition. While he is entirely correct, this would suggest that the IHREC had dispensed with his services. Originally from Belfast and of a similar age to Norman Shannon. One would think that Farrell's supposed dedication to human rights would put him above reproach.

Michael Farrell first replied to me on 31 January 2011. {See his letters}
He began by stating: "I cannot accept your account of your conversation with my colleague Noeline Blackwell and it is not a good way to start a request for help, by adopting such a confrontational tone. You begin your letter by saying you cannot get a lawyer to fight your case but you do not say what your case is"? This was blatant lies on both counts.

Obviously Noeline Blackwell had told him what I had said to Mary Robinson. I only learned later of his involvement with

IHRC or I would have thrown his lies in his face.

He states: "You refer to the Irish Human Rights Commission, IHRC not willing to investigate this matter. I cannot reply on behalf of the IHRC but I will simply express my own opinion about this issue". It's obvious now that he was lying through his teeth and was covering up - because he could not give an unbiased and independent opinion - as he was then a leading solicitor with - and a member of IHRC.

The fact that he did not disclose this fact proves what I say. Just like Norman Shannon many years ago in Belfast he was pulling the Legal Wool over my eyes. Farrell then made a ridiculous point that IHRC had no jurisdiction in Northern Ireland, etc - and then in a Freudian Slip said: "The fact that IHRC has not investigated your complaints about SIPTU is not the result of any "COVER UP", my capitals - but simply because it is not in IHRC's remit".

This all sounds fine and dandy and is probably just what he told IHRC when he persuaded them not to support my application for an inquiry.

For this statement alone - denying his involvement - yet "speaking for them" he should be stripped of his right to practice as a Lawyer.

This is not the dark ages solicitors from both jurisdictions regularly take cases North and South. Farrell then gives his expert legal opinion on the matter, stating that - "IHRC's remit is basically to investigate and monitor state agencies, etc and not private companies".

This gobbly-gook totally ignores the facts. SIPTU is a trade union not a private company. That the Union engaged in a criminal conspiracy to deprive Belfast Dockers of their livelihoods -and sentenced some to their deaths, is covered up by SIPTU and everyone who knows about it.

Farrell, this statement proved by his non-action that he is a disgrace and a cover up Lawyer for SIPTU, Norman Shannon and the Wealthy. By Farrell, remaining in the legal arena and acting for Human Rights groups he is bringing the entire legal profession into Disrepute - by riding two horses.

Had been acting as a Human Rights Lawyer in any of his incarnations - he'd have taken this case into Court and sued SIPTU for corruption. Plus arguing - that the Human Rights and very 'lives' of Belfast Citizens was violated.

That the Dockers were ordered to discharge Asbestos without protection to save the Dock Employers money is an absolute disgrace.

The Wealthy who owned the Asbestos knew full well that deaths would occur and couldn't have cared less. Farrell was no doubt shocked at the corruption shown in Documentation from the Union and Employers Court that sacked me. Sacked because I wouldn't discharge Asbestos and did my utmost to get other Dockers to do the same.

Farrell knew - and knows if this becomes Public Knowledge, himself, the Wealthy and Norman Shannon would be disgraced - and could well face criminal charges. Even if Shannon invoked the Statute of Limitations -
which he knows well, his Practice and the human rights reputation he's built in Belfast would be utterly and rightly destroyed.

Furthermore, the Statute of Limitations does not apply for murder, with which Shannon could obviously be charged. Because he knew of the dangers - long before any Dockers died from it. The opinion of the three Browne brothers could be sought on this. Billy has it in one lung - and unfortunately Sean

and Frankie have already died from Asbestosis.
Their deaths are directly attributable to Norman Shannon's cover up.

This is why the unseen Rulers of Ireland do all in their power to keep a lid on this scandal.
They all know that the formation of the Union and Employers Court in Belfast stood on its head any semblance of trade union behaviour by the Union. They also know that the 'persecution' by the Court of Belfast Dockers was highly illegal, and stood on its head the very notion that the Trade Union was on the side of the workers at Belfast Docks.

Even if Farrell wondered what possessed the Union to join with employers, given its revolutionary past the damage was done. And for Shannon to cover it up is beyond comprehension. No doubt he was told it was for the greater good - not realising that his decision to become corrupted would lead to many avoidable deaths. The Employers must have offered him a lot... If this got into the public domain, Industrial Relations for years would be severally disrupted and might never see the employers gain the upper hand again.

The Wealthy behind it all know this scandal will shatter the reputations of all involved and obliterate the cosy arrangement that exists with the Union's today. No doubt Michael Farrell on the orders of the Wealthy was told to cover it up - so he used the Dublin legal system and the Human Rights bodies to do just that. As a matter of interest, several Justice Ministers many TD's and Michael Farrell are singing from the same hymn sheet. None of them will expose this corruption. This scandal mirrors Farrell's own journey - from being a 'Righteous Rebel' in Belfast to becoming a closed mouth 'Pillar of the Establishment' in Dublin.
His letter dated 8th March 2011 which gives an insight into his perverse and corrupt thinking. He refers to Belfast Solicitor,

John O'Neill's letter to me and and frankly, the disgusting lies contained in Farrell's letter are unbelievable. He states: "You took a case to a tribunal in Belfast but did **not** succeed". This is utter nonsense and more gobbledegook dressed up as Legalistic Opinion. In fact, two Tribunals ruled in my favour, the first on 20th February 1974 against the decision not to pay me unemployment benefit because I was sacked. It ruled - "that I was "not" dismissed for misbehaviour in the Industrial Sense". {See Farrel's letters}

And the second tribunal, as related earlier, ruled that the "Dockers had no Contract of Employment". The Tribunal Chairman in no uncertain manner stated, that "without a contract no-one could be sacked" - and henceforth "all dismissals must take place within the parameters of The Industrial Relations Act". **Which was ignored for eight years**. He advised "anyone" sacked by this 'Court' to consult a solicitor as soon as possible. This started me on the Legal Merry go Round.

There's something seriously wrong with Farrell's head if he denies this because I sent him John O'Neill's letter and all of the Union and Employers Court's corrupt documentation - or is there? Obviously Michael Farrell has gotten used to the good life and to curry favour with the Wealthy in Dublin is representing them. Has he told them blatant lies that he has everything under control and The Union and Employers Court will never be exposed?
Well so far he is right, even dead and dying Dockers - and Asbestos Dust blowing all over Belfast, can't expose it
However, does Farrell with his many Human Rights Roles think I can be fooled? Just because he puts a Corrupt Legal Spin on the letters I sent him - does not make them Legal.

Without a shadow of a doubt Belfast Solicitor John O'Neill,said in the letter which I'd forwarded to Farrell, that the **"Union**

with the employers did sack its own members at Belfast Docks". This letter can be seen on the 'corruptoconnor website and on facebook, twitter and linkedin. If Farrell feels confident enough to try and fool 'me' with these "despicable lies" what nonsense did he relate to the IHRC to convince them - not to have an inquiry into the corruption and denial of Human Rights at Belfast Docks.

In his letters Farrell continues to give perverted so-called legal advice, with still not a word about his involvement in IHRC. It is also beyond belief that Noeline Blackwell did not tell him what I had said at the Mary Robinson Conference, and utter nonsense for him to suggest otherwise.

Obviously she conversed with him in the Flac office because she worked there - and he actually confirmed this in his first letter to me. No doubt Farrell copied the letters he sent me, to the Wealthy - to show where his Loyalties reside.

Anyone reading his letters will be amazed at the corruption of Michael Farrell in this matter. He not only prostituted himself but has also prostituted the entire legal system in the Republic and should be driven out in disgrace. What possessed him to alter what John O'Neill said in his letter to Jack O'Connor. Does he think that I'm Doting and can be fooled - like both Law Society's.

Obviously he has convinced them to overlook the corruption of Norman Shannon, so not to bring their respective society's into disrepute? Because they've acquiesced they betray their profession, ingratiate themselves and slavishly conform to the diktats of Wealth. Is it any wonder that lawyers get a bad name among ordinary citizens.

While there is no legality here, there are plenty of deaths? Farrell was also vice chair and co chair of Irish Council for Civil liberties - who fobbed me off several times when I approached them. I had no idea he was also a leading member of this human rights body or I would not have bothered. With his finger in many pies he is acting corruptly and the worst part of this scenario, is - that the Human Rights groups in Ireland which have Farrell on their boards, are contaminated by his Legal Perversions.

Is this why Farrell wanted an open competition for appointment to the IHREC - so he can blind the interviewing panel with his long service on - many - many - human rights bodies? Or to have himself or one of his cronies, like Norman Shannon, appointed.

It's patently obvious that 50 years ago SIPTU and ICTU, acting for the Wealthy corrupted every law designed for the protection of Irish Workers and Citizens. Why did their highly paid Lawyers not inform the dictatorial union leaders what they were doing was illegal? The Union and Employers Court in Belfast lasted for eight years. In that time I wrote many letters to the Union and ICTU and was ignored.

Instead, after the Asbestos Deaths and the collapse of the Decasualisation Scheme they did everything possible to throw a cloak of legality over the corruption. Hopefully this case will eventually get into a Courtroom and the 'Union and Employers Court' that persecuted Dockers exposed. When this happens Michael Farrell, Norman Shannon Mary Robinson and many others, will have serious questions to answer.

It's obvious now why Michael Farrell is on so many human rights bodies - so he can continue use his legal expertise to pervert them. Especially if the dreaded Asbestos is ever mentioned. When these facts become Public Knowledge - Irish Trade Unionism and Irish Law will become a world wide laughing stock.

I raised this with this matter with Ken Murphy of the Law Society [recently retired] he no doubt was reacting to observations from Michael Farrell, who for a number of years has been a member of the Human Rights Committee of the Law Society. Obviously Murphy consulted him when I wanted taken on as a "friend of the society." I.e. pro-bono.

For the president of the Irish Law Society to dismiss me with such obvious lies - i.e. "that no such scheme exists", shows and reflects the contempt which Murphy and Farrell hold for the Law and the Truth. These Lies beggar belief.

I had read in the Irish Times the previous day that the Irish Law Society had taken on a gentleman as a 'Friend of the Society'. Thus pro bono - because he couldn't afford a Lawyer. For Ken Murphy and Michael Farrell to play fast and loose with the Truth shows the state that Irish Law is in. To do this, considering the fact that they both for many years championed its independence, proves that the Law, like themselves are just "Tools of the Wealthy". Anyone reading this who thinks any of the people I've mentioned will sue me, think again.

They won't - but I WISH THEY WOULD however, they're not that stupid. This is the only way I can get this case into a court of law AS I CANNOT AFFORD TO PAY
FOR JUSTICE. As all these Legal Eagles know - THE TRUTH IS NEVER DEFAMATORY.

No one with 'clout' will expose this scandal. Why? The retired Jack O'Connor nor any present day union official had anything to with the Belfast Docks 50 and 60 years ago. Had the Union and ICTU held their hands up years ago and admitted the wrong-doing of the union at Belfast Docks, they would not be facing a humiliating trashing of their own reputations.

Particularly relevant to this is the deselecting of Jack O'Connor, who had been boasting at every opportunity that he was standing for the Labour Party when he retired from the Union.

Obviously the Labour Party knew that I would be questioning him and at every public meeting and demanding he answer the question: "How can you represent anyone when your own Union ordered Belfast Dockers to their deaths by making them discharge Asbestos without protection - and sacked anyone who wouldn't do so". I was looking forward to this, as a way of getting attention for the sacked and dying ex Belfast Dockers. Regrettably, the Labour Party had heard about what I was planning and his 'much wanted' and 'much vaunted' Political Career stopped dead.

And while 'Poetic Justice' was served, his non-action on the Belfast Dockers fell by the wayside. There's no doubt O'Connor would've continued to serve the interests of the Wealthy in the Dail. While this was an 'own goal' for the Wealthy, they have plenty of others in the Dail prepared to deny the Truth. However, if Jack O'Connor was to come clean about the Belfast Docks Scandal - and admit that he was 'leaned on' by the Wealthy - he could run as an Independent and be elected. If O'Connor did this he would go down in History for doing the honourable thing.

The Wealthy control the dictatorial need, that... some individuals have, to use lesser mortals for their own aggrandizement.
This particularly applies in trade unions and must be stopped. This can be achieved by paying Union Leaders an average salary. The fact that money corrupts is a well established fact - and why the Docks Committee and the ex Union Chairman, Jim Austin, could be so ruthless, both before and after they joined the Employers. To knowingly expose Belfast Dockers and their families to the danger of Asbestos - flies in the face

of humanity and beggars belief. Union leaders must get back to representing their members and not the interests of the Employers.

Because of the Asbestos Deaths, what is mind-boggling - is why educated people in the Arts, Journalism, the Law and human rights, deny the Truth and cover it up? Many supposed champions of the downtrodden, who claim they want to right the wrongs in Irish Society, don't answer me. It is fear for their own livelihoods that keeps them silent For a long time I hoped that 'Theatre' would expose this blight on Irish Society - but I was wrong.

The leading participants, like Druid, fear that that any semblance of 'non conformity to corruption' will put in jeopardy their own positions. This is common knowledge and 'open minded' Artists know to keep their opinions to themselves if they wish to be employed.

While it's obvious no ordinary person in Theatre will speak out because they'll be censored and their life in the Arts ruined - this deplorable situation cannot be allowed to continue.
Someone in the Arts Council or Aosdana must speak up for the downtrodden - who through fear cannot speak for themselves. This will never happen while Garry Hynds, Willie White and the other 'nodding dogs' to Wealth have SIPTU's best interests at heart. They do all in their power to keep my plays, and in particular 'The Judas Goat' off an Irish stage. Hence I ask, where is the independence of the Arts Council and the Arts Minister?

To curtail the power of the Wealthy - an investigation must be held. By cowardly inaction the aforementioned and the rest collude with and perpetuate the present day attitude of 'Keep Quiet' and you'll keep your job. This ultimately proves that the Arts have the same Right Wing Fascist anti working class mentality that James Connolly and Jim Larkin fought against, for all of their lives.

During the tenure of Fiach MacConghail as Manager of 'The Abbey' our National Theatre, which is supposed to be a 'turmoil of discontent' would not stage 'The Judas Goat', or any of my plays. There's no doubt that the Wealthy gloried in the dumbing down of genuine drama and independent thought. The Abbey became like a music hall without the music.

The 'Wealthy' stamped their opinions and beliefs on what they believe Theatre to be - i.e.very quiet and middle of the road and most importantly 'not against them'. MacConghail, stifled controversial dramatic plays and closed down 'The Peacock', once the power house of new writing in Dublin. While on the main stage 'The Abbey' promoted Wealthy beliefs as the norm. Anyone with an ounce of sense knows that an Artistic Director is a necessary 'must' for any theatre. He, she or them, will obviously give Artistic Direction to the Theatre's endeavours. Unfortunately, this position was left vacant at the Abbey for many years, and MacConghail
filled the position himself.

Political decisions were allowed to take precedent over Artistic ones and to dictate policy. In the dark days the lack of money was used as a cloak to hide the dearth of cutting edge drama produced.

Obviously warning bells sounded in the Arts Council when the Abbey was lambasted on the world stage as a joke. This was for two reasons, the first, because of its output and second because MacConghail was from a political background with friends in high places. Hence, the Abbey stumbled along for years. No-one on the Arts Council was prepared to put in jeopardy their own position by speaking out against the mess the Abbey had become. Had he been sacked or at the very least, warned to pull his socks up - the disastrous years with him at the helm and the cowardly way they allowed him decide when 'he' would leave, could have been avoided.

Progressive Thinkers on the Arts Council had to wait until the time was right to act. In the meantime, while the bad reviews following each other like Banana Buses, {they come in bunches} with even the Tourists complaining - it looked like the 'non – artistic director' had run his course.

However, Fiach, the 'Manager' pulled a master stroke. This silenced his detractors and cemented his reputation with his old friends in the back room of politics. This was also a warning to the Arts Council not to mess with him, and gained him a few more years at the helm of The Abbey.

The master stroke or scandal {it depends on your viewpoint} - that transpired was - Garry Hynds was 'gazumped' by MacConghail, over Sean O'Casey's plays. 'Gazumped' was how Fintan O'Toole described the matter in the Irish Times. What transpired was - at a friendly meeting between Fiach and Hynd's at the Abbey, she stated she wanted to stage all of Sean O'Casey's plays in the Abbey.

This was what she'd done with Synge's plays in Dublin, and exactly what she was then doing at the time with Shakespeare's work. However, Fiach disappointed her and expressed no interest in such a proposal. Hynd's left the meeting obviously upset at the thwarting of her plans. However, the very next day when Hynd's approached O'Casey's daughter with the same proposal, she was told that Fiach had phoned the previous day and had been granted the Rights to her father's plays.

Hynds was rightfully livid - and Fintan O'Toole the leading Arts critic at the Irish Times was incensed at this underhand devious behaviour. Especially coming from, from such a respectable person as Fiach - who was in charge of our National Theatre and therefore the morals of the Nation?

Seeing he was such was a staunch supporter and admirer of Hynd's work, O'Toole took up the cudgels on her behalf. In the Irish Times he lambasted MacConghail for bringing the Abbey into disrepute and wrote several fine articles on how Artistic Integrity was in the pits.

Hynd's bull-dog determination to see difficult theatrical productions to a successful conclusion is known worldwide - and while being 'championed' by O'Toole and the Irish Times, the theatre going public's expectations for dramatic action of Shakespearian proportions, was sky high.

Just as the war of words reached boiling point and seemed to be heading for the Courts - with the theatre going public agog and lapping up the dastardly deeds happening at the Abbey - the situation unexpectedly calmed down. All went quiet on the Gazsumping front and animosities disappeared. Obviously, they had MacConghail on the ropes, so what happened to sooth their artistic egos? O'Toole, Hynds and MacConghail neither kissed and made up, or even shook their respective digits - but for some reason peace broke out. In an uncharacteristic manner Hynds and O'Toole backed off and let the matter drop. This surprised many, as the "Champions of Truth", had the full uncompromising support of the most important broadsheet in Ireland.

What transpired was vastly different from the expected hissy fit from Hynd's and O'Toole, and McConghail's departure from the Abbey, in disgrace never materialised.

Obviously, the theatre going public were baffled and the question asked - why did they save MacConghail's reputation in the Arts and let him off the hook? This was never answered?

However, I believe the reason is plain to see. Hynd's and

237

O'Toole were obviously told by the 'Wealthy' to cool it, and let the matter drop it, as too much information was being aired in public. Plus the fact, MacConghail's departure would jeopardise their well constructed plans for 'high brow middle of the road plays' that kept the lower classes out of the Abbey.

No doubt being told what to do offended and galled Hynd's and O'Toole. He demanded that the Freedom of the Press, like Democracy must be honoured. While she, like a demented Lady McBeth wanted blood - claiming - Truth, Justice and the Nobility of Theatre must be honoured.

With both moralising to high heaven and claiming: "We must prevent this 'Perversion of Theatre' from continuing and that MacConghail a dyed in the wool charlatan is driven from the Abbey". However, what I believe happened and their actions support it, is - that the Wealthy whispered in their respective ears and suggested they should look to their own reputations. Horrified at this slight on their characters and full of righteous indignation, they both wanted the 'Court of public opinion' to expose MacConghail - his reputation shattered, and the O'Casey plays awarded to Hynds.
Then the Wealthy dropped a bombshell. It was revealed to these two 'Champions of Theatre and Democracy' that Fiach MacConghail was in possession of information about their own cover up and refusal to expose corruption in Theatre. No doubt they both were aghast and insisted that this was nonsense - and that they would never behave in such a despicable and underhand manner as MacConghail.

However, when Hynes was shown copies of Druid's letters, which censored my Belfast Docks play - she was rendered speechless.

Needless to say, the word Asbestos leapt off the page. In a similar context when O'Toole was presented with emails sent to him at Irish Times - showing that he knew about the illegal Union and Employers Court and the Asbestos scandal - which he covered up by not reporting it, they both were astounded.

The details of their own hypocrisy showed that they both knew about the Crime of the Century and did nothing about it. Disgustingly they realised, that in calling MacConghail to account - their own scurrilous behaviour and cherry-picked reputations would be exposed. So naturally, rather than be exposed as outright hypocrites, they both decided to let the matter drop. If O'Toole and Hynds had the principles they claim to possess - and even at this late stage - had he publicised in the Irish Times the Belfast Docks scandal and Hynes given a commitment to stage 'The Judas Goat' - they both could have continued with their

destruction of MacConghail's reputation. However, their own past would not allow them to do so.

As a past Arts Editor on the Irish Times, and a statesman like Author, O'Toole is known and lauded in American and Europe. My Docks play highlights the Truth in that old saying – 'if you put an Irishman on a spit, you'll always another Irishman - or woman - to turn it'. As Shakespeare said, "The Truth will out", but he forgot to add - "It may take some time".

Did the terms, "Poetic Justice" or 'hoisted on their own petards' ever cross the minds of O'Toole and Hynds. They continue in their respective professions - while wallowing in the perversion of Irish Democracy - "and being told what to do" by the Wealthy.

Now that the days of repression have eased for the Peacock and The Abbey, they have a long way to go, if again they wish to be regarded as a 'Powerhouse of Theatre'. After McConghaill, the Arts Council decided to appoint 'two' Artistic Directors instead of one. This got off to a shaky start with two Scotsmen who were condemned by actors which resulted in a Petition of signatures to the Arts Council. I.e that they were not employing Irish Actors.

However, when their tenure ended, the council stuck to the 'dual aspect' and appointed two *Irish People*. And seeing they have a background in Irish Theatre - hopefully they'll not be influenced by the grandiose decisions of the Wealthy. This will go a long way in re-establishing the Abbey as a power house of Theatre?

A deaf, dumb and blind, metaphorically speaking, Irish Historian has joined the ranks of O'Toole's fans. In reviewing O'Toole's book 'We Don't Know Ourselves' in the Irish Times, Deramid Ferreter has shown himself to be - equally as sycophantic and hypocritical as O'Toole. Thus proving that Ferreter was a good choice for the task. Just like O'Toole he dips in and out of Irish History and laughs at the idiosyncrasies [as we all do] of Irish life.

However, like a genuine revisionist he ignores the parts he doesn't like and for a Historian, this is deplorable. Like a nodding dog he sullies the profession he is a Professor of, and must truly believe, that - just like Irish Times readers, the population wants to be fooled with O'Toole's rose-tinted view of Irish History.

In a stunning Review, this cherry-picking obfuscating historian covers up for O'Toole by denying the truth - and he will be eternally grateful for this myopic cover up.
No matter how much this Historian wriggles - he cannot ignore History - as O'Toole does in Irish Times and his latest book. I have also informed this - Historian - about the unholy alliance of Union and Employers Court at Belfast Docks - and that this Court ordered Belfast Dockers and Citizens to their

Asbestos stricken deaths. Why will this Historian not expose this "covering up of Irish history" - and why are O'Toole and Irish Times are complicit in this cover up? At least let them explain why working class people died from Asbestosis.

When the Union Chairman in Belfast betrayed his Union and took up the position of Labour Controller with the Employers - he obviously reinforced his own 'Napoleon' like belief in himself. So has the same mental condition affected Fintan O'Toole and his Historian? Why else would O'Toole not include the Betrayal of the Belfast Dockers by the ITGWU in his book? Surely this was a perfect example of "the way we were", SOLD OUT.

The Union obviously was not representing the working class but was kow-towing to Wealthy Employers. The so-called 'historian' Ferreter and O'Toole are genuine hypocrites who 'run with the hare and hunt with the hounds.' This professor of modern history is as aware of these mind-boggling facts about the Union, as O'Toole is - and ignores them. WHY?

The sacking of its own members was a betrayal of the ITGWU and its founders and is a HISTORICAL FACT. As both Ferreter and O'Toole well know, this once great Trade Union fought in 1916 as the Citizens Army. They marched from Liberty Hall and took part in occupying the GPO. As every Irish person also knows, the leaders of the Rising were executed, and James Connolly founder of the Citizens Army, and a co-founder of the ITGWU was executed tied to a chair - because he'd been shot in the foot and couldn't stand. However, just fifty six years later the Belfast Employers took their revenge and it was corrupted at Belfast Docks.

O'Toole and his so-called Historian well know, that 'The Citizens Army' was formed during the infamous Dublin Lockout to protect Striking Workers from the savage attacks of the Dublin Mounted Police.

This is the Irish History that the Wealthy Dublin Employer Elite, don't want ordinary people to know about and which O'Toole, Ferreter and the like-minded - keep hidden. They don't to inspire modern-day trade unionists with a non-conformist spirit - or to seek a living wage. This is why the ITGWU changed its name to SIPTU - to appease Wealthy Employers.

This begs the question, why are educated Irish People like O'Toole and his 'roped in' Irish Historian' turning the Spit' on Irish History'? To both these intellectuals I say this - which is universally evident but not to these Irish sycophants. "No matter how much you - the Wealthy, the so-called Unions TD's and the unelected Robert Watt and his conies, deny or attempt to water down the Truth - the Truth remains the Truth.

CHAPTER TEN

Below is an letter I sent to Joe Duffy of 'Talk to Joe Fame' but for some reason, Joe won't talk to me. I print the letter in full so anyone reading it can understand - that Joe Duffy for RTE also censors the Truth.

Dear Joe Duffy,

I really enjoyed your programme about inequality in the education system in Ireland. However, you have steadfastly refused to expose my case against Jack O'Connor and SIPTU. I will state here that I went to work at Belfast Docks aged 15 and experienced the worst of the casual system policed by supposed followers of Larkin in ITGWU. However, after 1972 with the advent of Decasualisation when the union chairman joined the employers as labour controller, he also set up a new regulatory system which officially joined the Union with the NI employers.

This new body was officially named "The Northern Ireland Federation of Employers and Irish Transport & General Workers Union, Joint Disciplinary Committee". [See website] This was in fact a Private Court System for getting rid of "undesirables" - who wanted the Union to act like a Trade Union and not the disciplinary arm of the employers. The Union head office in Dublin and the Irish Congress of Trade Union's were fully aware of this amalgamation and must have given their blessing to it - because they did nothing about it.

This disgraceful rejection and overturning of normal trade union principles and practices - whereby a trade union represented its own members had been stood on its head. For a Trade Union to be more concerned with the policies of Employers is an abject betrayal of the people who fought and died to establish Trade Unions in the first place.

Instead of being lauded for 'crossing the line' at Belfast Docks, 'The Judas Goat' of a Union Chairman should have drummed out of the Union in disgrace.
Documentary proof of the marriage between the Employers Federation and the ITGWU can be seen in the information websitewww.siptupresidentjackoconnorexposed.com – which shows the Union and Employers Court at work. To add insult to injury the Union Chairman had no sooner joined the Union with the Belfast Employers, when he astounded everyone by leaving the Union and taking the position of Labour Controller with the employers.
At the time - I objected most strenuously to this behaviour and informed both head office and ICTU of this new development in Trade Unionism.

Particularly enlightening is the letter from Jack O'Connor's Belfast solicitor, one John O'Neill of Thompson McClure's. Jack O'Connor engaged him to "sue the arse of me", after I accused him at a large meeting in the EU rooms in Dublin City centre during the Irish Ferries dispute of being "corrupt and of covering up corruption". This was only in regard to his Union's behaviour at Belfast Docks. To say he was angry would be a gross under- statement and he yelled the above statement at me.

Sadly, he went back on his word, which is perfectly understandable, considering that his own solicitor confirmed in writing to him, that what I said about his Union and Belfast Docks was perfectly true. [Letter on website] I say sadly because I cannot get a solicitor to take on this case – and would have been delighted to have been sued, and thus able to prove in Court my accusations.

While this all happened a long time ago, the cover up continues to the present day, and in a similar fashion. Back then, the Employers Federation and the Union turned the Dockers against me. They did this by the 'New' Union Chairman Bobby Dickey, continually telling the Catholic Dockers that 'I am a Communist', and by the Labour Controller sending me – and the men around me – to the most dirty and worst paid jobs at the Docks.

This resulted in the Dockers getting as far away from me as possible when the ex chairman was allocating work - so as not to be sent to the same terrible job.

Then the Union started malicious rumours to blacken my name before they and the Employers Court sacked me. However, the Dockers did protest and went on strike for 3 days, but were talked back to work by the new chairman, who also stated that I was a communist and that the Union was going to sack me for writing and printing 'The Dockers Voice'.

This blacking of my name continues to this day in the Arts. An Aosdana and Arts Council member has informed me of this but has asked me not to publish his name. After I was sacked by the Union and Employers Court I wrote my first play 'The Judas Goat' which shows how the ex union chairman and the committee dealt with the Dockers, prior to conning them into accepting the unification of Union and Employers.

This acquiescence didn't happen overnight but was accepted because of the indoctrination and persecution of Belfast Dockers over many years by the Union.

The Union is covering this up to this day, however in Dublin it is not as 'in your face' as it was at Belfast Docks. Since the Union changed its name to SIPTU, by a steady process of osmosis from middle class members it's not seen to be 'nice' to object to anything and to allow the Union to settle all disputes. This has given more credence to the AMID and the ATL's. The Arts Mafia In Dublin - and The Above Law's.

These 'powers that be' control every aspect of Irish Life and are able to censor my Docks play and all my writing. The censoring of 'The Judas Goat' by the Arts Council and Dublin City Council can be caustically viewed as simply 'oiling the wheels of industry' so government will look beneficially upon them.

However the passage of over fifty years does nothing to alleviate the injustice of what transpired, especially to the dead and dying Belfast Dockers - ordered by their Union Chairman to discharge Asbestos without protection, to save the employers money.

Anyone with sense knows full well that a Trade Union cannot join with Employers and persecute and sack its own members – but this is exactly what happened. Not only is this against Trade Union Law but is against the law of the land. At Belfast Docks the Union and Employers Court was named, "The Joint Disciplinary Committee" for a reason, thus dispelling any notion that the Union was on the side of the Dockers - and the only time in Trade Union History that a Trade Union disciplined and sacked its own members for and with the Employers. While this deplorable and utterly illegal, the behaviour of two Councils, the Arts Council and the City Council pales into insignificance when compared to the sycophantic behaviour of the "Free Press" - led by such illustrious organs as Irish Times and Sunday Times.

They contradict their 'reason for being' and covered up the corruption and cowardice of Jack O'Connor, the ex president, and the current leadership of SIPTU.

Obviously, these two so-called newspapers [and the rest who follow suit] know exactly what they do. By protecting the reputations of O'Connor and Co - they are denigrating, and making a laughing stock of themselves, as supposed independent purveyors of truth, honour and justice?

After receiving a very good Readers Report which Ray Yeates, Arts Officer of DCC commissioned, he supported my play 'Daddy' [which is about the after effects of child abuse on two adult sisters] and granted me four weeks free rehearsal space in the LAB, DCC's headquarters for the Arts. When I asked for the same consideration for 'The Judas Goat' the censorship from DCC swung into action.

Previous to this, I was expelled from an Artist Group I was in - for wanting to stage 'The Judas Goat'. [details on Historic Censorship from largest Trade Union in Ireland, on linkedin] This happened two weeks before they staged 10 short plays in Liberty Hall, five of which went to New York. Of course, the leaders of the group deny this had anything to do with my expulsion but will not say why I was expelled. In response to their censorship and that of Garry Hynd's of Druid who asked me 'in writing' not to tell anyone she refused to stage 'The Judas Goat', I founded the Heart and Soul Theatre Company. With this I staged 'Daddy' and 'The Grandeur of Delusions. The latter is a two hander and is about an Alcoholic talking to himself through interacting with his delusion.

Hynes took her revenge by withdrawing four nights at the Mick Lally Theatre which my producer had booked for 'Delusions'.

In any other situation, the corruption and abject cronyism would not be tolerated, but in Theatre in Ireland, any criticism of it, no matter how valid 4of4

is stamped out. The similarities with Belfast Docks could not be plainer.

My play 'The Judas Goat' shows the Union Chairman at the time, using his position to sell out the Belfast Dockers and to garner for himself a good position with the employers. He also ordered the Dockers to their deaths by ordering that they discharge Asbestos, without protection to save the employers money.
OBVIOUSLY JOE YOU AND RTE AGREE WITH THIS
Hugh Murphy

As previously stated, my Docks play was originally named One Big Onion, which was a play on the slogan of Jim Larkin, i.e. - ONE BIG UNION. This name also reflected the layers of corruption within the union leadership. However, because of the deliberate dummying down of the Union's illustrious past whereby no union member I spoke to - knew of this slogan or indeed, of the workers solidarity that engendered it - I reluctantly changed the name to - 'The Judas Goat'.

This name and the play show exactly what happened at Belfast Docks.
In what can only be described as a CORRUPT FARCE - the Union Chairman joined the Union with the Employers and persecuted union members. While this was an an unbelievable and disgusting betrayal of everything the Union founders stood for when they founded the ITGWU - it was compounded by the enthusiastic manner in which the ex union chairman went about his new duties for the employers.

No lawyer, journalist or newspaper for the past fifty years will expose this scandal. While ignoring the Truth they self-censor and jump through
'censorship hoops' for Wealthy Employers who owned the deadly Asbestos.

The so-called Newspapers, so-called Lawyers and so-called Human Rights Activists in Ireland know better that expose this or their lives will be ruined. However - why will the 'Left' not bring this Corruption of Trade Unionism and of Irish Life to the Public's attention - and exposé these deplorable acts. I have spoken to the leaders of the two small parties in the Dail, but to no avail? Why are they siding with the moneyed elite against the downtrodden workers by remaining Silent?

When no Journalist in Ireland would expose the Belfast Docks scandal - I went further afield and asked the philosopher who wrote for Sunday Times for his opinion on a Trade Union that sacked its own members.

I supplied him with the proof, and sources where he could check out the veracity of what I claimed.
Not wanting to scare him off, I didn't mention the degree of the Wealthy involvement. He replied by email and agreed to expose and discuss, in the following Sunday's paper the legality and moral issues surrounding the fact - that a Trade Union that sacked its own members. However, he said he would 'not' name the Trade Union -
to which, after some thought, I agreed. I reckoned everyone in Ireland would know the Union involved from the details I'd given.

I spent the week in turmoil believing that the Belfast Docks scandal was about to be printed in the Sunday Times. I can honestly say it was the longest week of my life. The following Sunday I opened the Sunday Times magazine to his page and it wasn't there. I scanned the magazine to see if he'd been moved but found nothing. I then turned to the full paper with the same result. I emailed him, and got the response, 'gone on holiday'. I waited two weeks and emailed again, and again and again, but got no reply. He never has written for Sunday Times again and I cannot contact him. That he was leaned on when he submitted article his article for publication, there can be no doubt, and ultimately sacked for wanting to print the Truth. No doubt he was warned to keep quiet.

Only in a Court of Law will he feel free to impart this information about what occurred.

For the sake of the philosopher's philosophical conscience I hope he can justify his non-action and hypocrisy.
Obviously the 'Right Wing' in Ireland pressurised the Right Wing in London to censor what goes into the Sunday Times 'newspaper'. Now that the Sunday Times editor has been replaced, maybe the new editor - when he learns of this corruption of the supposed Free Press will challenge the status quo and divulge the Truth?

The cover up about the Deaths of Belfast Dockers and Citizens are at the core of this story - and a Pulitzer Prize awaits the first Journalist with Principles 'who has a second string to his bow' and not afraid to expose this blatant right wing dictatorship by denizens of the 'stiff upper lip'.

Some day in the future when Democracy takes precedence over Corruption on these two islands, the ex Sunday Times Editor and all the others who have been silenced will 'under oath' be made divulge who pulled their strings? The similarity between what happened to the Philosopher and the censoring of myself and my writing is glaring and we must go back to the start to show from where it emanates from.

In 1907, Jim Larkin was Union Organiser the NUDL- the National Union of Dock Labourers. He was sent to Belfast from Liverpool to unionise the Dockers and Carters. He was a great organiser and had Unionised the Liverpool Dockers and many other Ports others into his Union. In Belfast He united

Protestant and Catholic Workers under the banner of Workers'.

In 1907 he had his famous strike and even got support from Constable Barret in the hated RIC. They were being used to protect strike-breakers imported by the employers. To combat the new found solidarity between religions. The Orange Order and Belfast Employers pressurised James Sexton, the union president in England, to recall Larkin, but he refused to go and he refused to be silenced.

After several attempts to stoke sectarian tension had failed the Belfast Employers persuaded the British government to station British Soldiers on the Catholic Falls road. They erected checkpoints and stopped and searched anyone going through them. This obviously led to the people protesting and on the near-by Grosvenor Road they opened fire -killing two people and wounded many others. Larkin condemned the troops, stating that 'the strike they were here for was taking place in another part of Belfast'.

The Protestant newsapers attacked Larkin claiming that he wasn't here for the Dockers and Carters but was engaged in a conspiracy against the Protestant Unionist cause in Ireland. Because of the killings Sexton and other Union Leaders in Britain arrived in Belfast to put an end to the strike. They side-lined Larkin and announced that the strike was settled and refused to pay any-more strike pay, so the workers were forced back to work. However, what Sexton agreed to was scandalous.

The Protestant carters and coal fillers got a slight increase in wages but the Catholic Dockers got nothing and the use of non-union labour was to continue. They also had to apologise for causing the strike.

Larkin left Belfast but continued to organise for the NUDL and when in Derry he heard that the Dublin Carters were in trouble he rushed to their aid. The Dublin Carters were already in the NUDL but for some reason the Executive refused to support the Strike. They told Larkin they wanted nothing to do with it. Larkin ignored them and was soon in Dublin organising them. For this Sexton had him sacked.

In the front room of a house in Townsend Street in Dublin, Larkin, James Connolly, William O'Brien and others founded the ITGWU. The Belfast Dockers remained true to Connolly and Larkin and switched from the NUDL to their New Union. From the early days and over the years, especially after Partition the ITGWU was seen as a Rebel Union, and had no backing from the English based Unions. However in the South ITGWU made great progress Unionising every worker under the Sun into 'a general workers union'.

This culminated in William Martin Murphy who owned practicably everything including the Trams ordered that members of Larkins Union would no longer be tolerated or employed.

When workers wouldn't sign a pledge to this effect they were 'Locked Out' from their employment. Soon the Dockers and Carters joined the Tram workers and Dublin came to a standstill.
Eventuality the strike was broken by the Wealthy - with the support of the Catholic Church. They refused to allow starving children to be sent to 'Protestant' England to be looked after and fed. Obviously not caring if they died from hunger, but declaring they would die Catholics. British workers supported the Irish strikers and a series of food ships were sent from Britain.

Eventually the Catholic Church and Employers succeeded in getting support for the strikers stopped. Because the striking workers children were in danger of dying from starvation the strike was eventually broken.

Larkin went to the States to raise money, and was jailed for Trade Union agitation. In his absence, the Union swung to the 'Right'. He missed 1916 which he regretted for all of his life.

Upon Larkin's return in 1918 he was sacked from the Union he founded, for being too militant, and set up a rival Union.

In Belfast without support from the South and antagonism from Northern Unions, ITGWU at Belfast Docks was on its own. Gradually it drifted to the 'Right', where strike action was never even considered. And in fact, strike pay was only paid once, since the Union was founded.

This happened in 1970, during the two weeks of the Twelfth Fortnight, in July. For anyone who doesn't know it, everything stops for the Orangemen's celebrations and nothing went in or out of the Dock Gates. We picketed the gates for two weeks without stopping one lorry.

Over the years the closeness of the Union with Employers culminated with De-casualisation in 1972. This new system was instigated by Head Office in Dublin to abolish the Casual System of employment, and was willingly endorsed by the Belfast Employers. Which I found strange to say the least? Why would they embrace a system that would legitimise the Dockers employment, give us the benefits that workers in factories have, and cost them money? And above all remove from the Dockers the yoke of Dictatorial Discipline which the Union wielded for over the Dockers? E.g. the Union Policed the Docks for the Employers with the minimum punishment being a Ten Pound Fine.

However, unbeknownst to us at the time, with the new way of being employed, the Employers and Union formed a Joint Disciplinary Committee for disciplining and sacking Union Members. This was in fact a Union and Employers Court, with the only thing missing being a Bible.

That this stood Trade Unionism on its head is undeniable - and was unbelievably sanctioned from headquarters in Dublin.

For the enlightened people like Fintan OToole, his Historian - and the 'bought off media', they all claim this was a good thing as it got rid of the Casual System. This is understandable. They don't want to upset the Wealthy in Ireland or their Champagne Socialist friends by telling the Truth. They fear this could of bring retribution upon their own heads as any whistle-blower will attest to - so they claim ignorance.

This works well for O'Toole and the rest of the cover up Journalists, but for Ferriter, a Professor of Modern History, it's a sick joke and beyond the Pale.

I have told him, O'Toole and the supposed "free press" many times about the abject betrayal of the workers by their own Union and they ignore it.

50 years ago, the Union committee men who sat on the JDC not only participated in depriving Union Members of their livelihoods but actually instigated many of the sackings. They did this by making complaints to the ex union chairman. No doubt - by ignoring the truth, the Irish Times and the other 'self censored' Irish media will "not" be exposing a Professor of Modern History, who steadfastly ignores Modern History.

While not wanting him to loose his position in the University, maybe one of his students will ask, who benefits from the denying and cherry-picking of Irish History? A small but pertinent fact for the History Professor, is - that the subject of his glowing book review, O'Toole, has blocked my emails at Irish Times. "There are none so blind as those who will not see".

With my articles on Linkedin, Facebook and Twitter I was

'chomping at the bit' hoping to get myself sued for defamation, as I cannot afford to pay for Justice in Ireland. { *Pun intended*} However it seems the Truth has silenced anyone who normally would be expected to take offence at this injustice.

While the Irish Times and the dumb and Blind Media garners many prizes for "Investigative Journalism and Reporting" how in truth can they accept them - while ignoring this blatant example of a corrupt trade union and stroke politics in Ireland? Granted, the corruption happened 50 years ago. However, the corruption of cover up by all media and the legal profession, North and South is happening right now.

This blindness extends to the highest levels of society. Were possible I name the Corrupt members of the Legal Profession, who side with the Wealthy - but in Ireland this Truth is ignored. Both so-called Law Societies are aware of this scandal but believe its too big to be exposed.

This is simply because of self-preservation and their own involvement.

SIPTU, Journalism, the Arts and all the Professions cover up what took place at the Belfast Docks. James Connolly had a disparaging name for people who behave in such a disgusting fashion – and it was "Lickspittles".

While the legal and journalistic professions In Ireland cover up in the present day, many Historians are also to blame for their betrayal and cover up of History. In particular is the publicity seeking Diramid Ferriter, professor of modern history at UCD. University Collage Dublin. Maybe 50 years is too modern for him? While he can speak eloquently about events of 100 years ago when the British were put out - he ignores the silent 'Counter Revolution' of Corruption.

While no-one in Ireland with any clout will question this scandal, hopefully some American students from Princeton University who recognise O'Toole's grotesque cherry-picking -

will demand Justice for the Belfast Dockers? And in a civil and non aggressive manner question O'Toole, on why he covers up this scandal - and how this equates with his humanitarian principles? This exposé and his answers should be recorded.

With the British gone to stop the country becoming a shambles, the Irish Civil Service had to be kept in place. Over the years they became the new Rulers and gradually learned to control the new Democracy. This is how the unelected back room boys like Robert Watt attained so much power. They used the tactics of the British, 'the few controlling the many' to rule Ireland.

Once the power of successive Secretary Generals was established every Irish government was under their control. To attain this they had to recruit and control the 'Professions' and most importantly the Law. Once established the others all fell into line - and the SILENT counter revolution was established. In the present day Ireland will never be a Democratic Republic while Robert Watt and the other unelected Secretary Generals are above the Law and answer to know one.

For Robert Watt to behave as he did in **not** informing the elected TD's of what he was doing in the Tony Holoahan affair - and claim that he broke no Laws - proves all I have said.
The reason why O'Toole, Irish Times journalists it's editors, the legal people I've mentioned - plus all the so-called Human Rights bodies in Ireland - and the so-called Historians ignore the HUMAN RIGHTS ATROCITY at Belfast Docks - is because the unelected control them. To do otherwise would expose Ireland as a Mickey Mouse Democracy.

Like Hitler's henchmen they follow a well established route to the top of their profession. The wives and children of the three Browne brothers, two of whom have already died from

Asbestosis, will not sleep easily in their beds. They know that their husbands and fathers unnecessarily died, to make Wealthy Employers even richer.

I know it's useless appealing to Politicians, and the sycophants I've mentioned, by asking them to tell the Truth? They will not commit 'Hari Kari' - and see their 'well paid' cushy lives go down the tubes. However, hopefully a foreign Journalist will expose the silence of these 'champions of democracy'. If they decide to investigate, I suggest as a starting point they watch UTV's 'DEATH TRAP ON THE DOCKS' - and Northern Visions - DYING DOCKERS'. In these TV Programmes they will see grief stricken family members, describe the last days of their loved ones, and the terrible deaths they suffered.

Also on the Videos a Doctor describes the terrible prognosis of Asbestos stricken people, while a Solicitor suggests that the employers could be guilty of 'Corporate Manslaughter'. This must also apply to the Union officials in Dublin and Belfast.
A Politician in the video also condemns the Dockers Union for their unfeeling hypocrisy in denying help to the Dockers and their families.

While successive Irish Governments, Trade Unions, Human Rights groups, Historians, Journalists plus many TD's - will *not* expose this Travesty of the Truth - the dictatorial hand of Oliver Cromwell still rules Ireland. I have also complained to the European Parliament about this shocking state of affairs but they have stopped even acknowledging my emails. Obviously they believe the 'stories' from elected members from Ireland. That is - if they even bother to inquire.

To try and expose this scandal I sent a letter by recorded delivery to the President of European Courts of Justice - and the tracking device said it was delivered. So... it looks like I must add the European Court to the long list of cover up bodies.

The reason why I wrote to the European Court is because the President of it is an Irish Woman, Judge Siofra O'Leary. No doubt she will be delighted to hear that the Dean of Law Professor Laurent Pech of Sutherland school of law, which she attended - also doesn't wish to know anything about this Irish Corruption.

Why are these Truth Deniers elected to the European Parliament? Why are they not showing the contempt the Wealthy have for the Law and the lives of Irish Citizens, which they claim to Honour and Respect.

Only when they accept {If only to themselves} that the professions of Ireland, and even the Arts - which are lauded around the world are totality corrupt - will the Truth of Ireland's "Sham Democracy be exposed.

Ireland is a Dictatorship that's controlled by the Wealthy... and any objectors feel the full wrath Silence and Censorship. The Belfast Docks scandal, my play and hopefully an Honest Lawyer...will some day expose the Corruption that rules Ireland. The Truth can be buried but it will never stay buried.

In 2011 after only sleeping in snatches for weeks - and after being up all night with my dying wife, she passed away about 3 O'Clock in the morning at a Hospice in Belfast. The Undertaker was bringing her home in the afternoon and I was driving to her brother's house to fetch him.

However I touched off another car that contained someone of importance - as the glass on the windows was half an inch thick. I noticed this when the driver only moved his window down a fraction. I was all over the place and in a garbled fashion accused the Driver of having ran into me. I stated but that I couldn't stay as I had to get home because the undertaker was bringing my deceased wife home.

The other driver claimed that he was a policeman and that I couldn't leave the scene of an accident. There was a slight scratch on his paintwork and no damage to my car.
However in correspondence with the insurance company he claimed what I said, was "Do you know who I am, and I cant stay here".

Obviously this is what he also told the police when they arrived. As I explained in the insurance papers this was ludicrous. He got out of the car when an ambulance and traffic police arrived. I was breathalysed and when the police checked me out, they obviously found out about the planted bullets and my acquittal and decided to put the boot into me.

The driver claimed and was awarded three thousand pounds for whiplash. In the insurance papers the lawyer for the Insurance noted that he was being economical with the Truth when he denied having received compensation for a similar injury - as he had done so once at least once before.

When I was being breathalysed I noticed a policewomen in my car and she said she was putting the handbrake on as the car had moved. I accepted this but when I got in to drive away I noticed that things had been moved about and that several used tissues were missing. This means that they have illegally taken my DNA and have passed the made up criminal record about me to the Police in the South of Ireland.

This is particularly obvious with today facial recognition and ear-buds.

This false record has followed me and every time I go into a Library,Garage, Shop or supermarket the shop assistants and security staff are alerted through their ear-piece. I don't know what they've being told but its sufficient for them to hover around and watch me. I first noticed this in a McDonalds. When I would go into the gents toilet, after about a minute the manager would quickly enter and at a frantic pace, check every cubicle and lift every toilet seat, and leave. A few times I asked him what he was doing, but he always ignored me.

Surely this is an abuse of my human rights. Several times when a shop assistant has a reaction and stops back, I tell them what they've just heard through their ear-piece is lies. On one occasion in a Library as usual the security person would kept hovering around me, which I always ignored. However, this time it was particularly intrusive. When I was leaving I addressed him, saying, what have you been told about me?

Flustered, he became tongue-tied and pretended he didn't know what I was talking about. I repeated, 'what were you told in your earpiece, will you tell me what was said'. He shook his head and walked away, saying I'm not allowed to talk to you. Another over the top culprit is Lidel. When I go into the local shop a member of staff - drops whatever they are doing to walk quickly past me and then hover around Why? Are the security cameras not working or is this just harassment.

Has Ireland become a police state, whereby the records of criminal behaviour {WHICH IN MY CASE IS FALSE} has being given to shop-holders by the police. How as ordinary citizen do I stop this Travesty happening? In the South of Ireland, solicitors and Human Rights groups don't want to know about this abuse of my Human Rights.

This I believe is why I can get nowhere with my writing - because of the erroneous and falsified criminal record attributed to me by the Belfast Police, which was then, the RUC. Obviously this has been passed to the the shops and public bodies in the Republic. I am being pilloried because a bigoted policeman in Belfast decided to either make up - or attribute to me someone else's criminal record.

Obviously, I'm designated by the 'powers that be' who control society and Theatre as an undesirable violent upstart who needs to be watched.

This was hinted at by the Aosdana Member but he wouldn't tell me the full story. No doubt the Wealthy and their lawyers in both jurisdictions are delighted with these lies and perpetuate them. This also allows them to silence me over the Asbestos cover up and money inspired deaths at Belfast Docks. These lies and the false record originated with the RUC
and continued by the PSNI - and passed on to the police in the Republic.

Another reason for this... is because I was acquitted 40 years ago of having bullets in planted my Taxi. This proves that the N.I. is still a Police State - and that the Police in the Republic believe their lies and have placed me on a "watch list".

About two years ago I asked a Left wing TD for the name of his solicitor, and phone number, which he gave me. This solicitor arranged a meeting and I informed him of the surveillance that I'm experiencing. As a first step he gave me a form to fill in and send to the Chief Constable asking was there any reason for this. A few day later the form came back saying they had no interest in me, which the solicitor photo-copied it and kept a copy.

However shortly after this he lost interest and told me their was nothing more he could do. I protested and wanted him to put my case in front of a Judge which he said he couldn't do without evidence. I told him he could get abundant evidence from the Security cameras from the Shops involved. Which he refused to do.

I protested saying "What can I do"? He replied? "Get a Private Detective" and he left the room and that was the end of the matter. Who or what has silenced this solicitor?

I want to know what is being said about me so that I can challenge this and get this false record expunged. That is - if I can ever get a solicitor to take my case. Which I am supposedly entitled to under European Law This situation still pertains.
Once in Lidel as I approached the back of a queue - four checkout girls turned as one, and looked at me. This surveillance can at times be very annoying - and is petty in the extreme.

If I was a threat to these shops why would they broadcast the fact that they're watching me... but what are they saying?

Over the years I've realised, how we live our lives reflects our childhood realities. I got the good and the evil. Only for the goodness of my Mother I would be deserving of the Criminal Behaviour Label that the RUC invented and have hung around my neck. To smash an eight year old child into a wall for following a Train - and to fingerprint him and take him to court shows just how Corrupt the RUC was.

The Truth of the matter is, any amount of alcohol, and even the smell of it brings about such a reaction in me... that my emotions and rational thinking shuts down. I stop functioning as an adult human being and turn into a child being whipped. Only now seventy years after the beatings have I learned a strategy to circumvent the memories. But it doesn't always work.

I - nor my family can forget the whippings that we got, and I really understand that saying - Violence be-gets Violence - because we live every day with its aftermath. Below is the refusal from Druid to stage my Belfast Docks play.

What lies was Garry Hynds told by the theatre establishment to make her reach this decision - and below that a newspaper article about my child abuse play.

Flood Street
Galway, Ireland

Tel +353 91 568 660
Fax +353 91 563 109
info@druid.ie
www.druid.ie

Artistic Director
Garry Hynes

28.3.11

Hugh Murphy
203 Castle Park
Tallaght
Dublin 24

hughmurphy@eircom.net

Dear Mr. Murphy,

Further to your recent enquiry to this office, I am writing to you to confirm that we are not in a position to produce your play, *One Big Onion*, and that we consider the matter closed. We would ask that you refrain from bringing Druid's name into public statements about the play. We would hope that you would respect our wishes in this matter.

We hope that you will continue to attend Druid productions and to consider Druid as having provided some of your more memorable theatre experiences.

Kind regards,

Thomas Conway
Literary Manager

Cabbie is driven to take up pen and ink

Anne Maguire talks to cabbie turned writer Hugh Murphy who found his art driving through the mean streets of Belfast

For Fifty years Irish Times has managed to keep a lid on the scandalous behaviour of rouge elements in ITGWU at Belfast Docks. 'Rouge', as in the Union sided with the employers against their own members – and the Irish Times effectively 'sent to Coventry' and refused to act or highlight this Human Rights Scandal. Today, Fintan O'Toole boasts in the US about his working class roots and credentials - while he and his paper hypocritically ignore the passive support his paper gave to Union Leaders who persecuted the working class in Belfast.

O'Toole is a high-minded purveyor of Corruption who knows exactly what he's doing - and who to expose and who to leave alone?

As Arts Editor for a long time, his article about sexual abuse in theatre was a tour de force in obfuscation. I.e. "If theatre is not a safe space, what is left"? In one fell swoop 'without saying' so - he declared that he knew nothing about the abuse of women in the entertainment industry, and in particular at The Gate Theatre.

He fooled Irish Times readers into thinking his comments were believable and well intentioned. Nothing could be further from the truth.

He was effectively covering up for his own cowardice and that of the Irish Times. This was another blatant example of his cherry-picking and '*not*' exposing a scandal. As Arts Editor - he was neither deaf, dumb nor blind - so was well aware of the ear splitting klaxon of gossip regarding
'The Gate' - and the behaviour of "its charismatic and highly successful director". O'Toole's words.

Like everyone else I was aware of the goings on at the gate regarding the treatment of women. This was common knowledge, spoken about openly and even joked about. For O'Toole to pretend that every journalist in Dublin including himself was not aware of this behaviour is beyond belief. The awards O'Toole and Irish times have garnered should be for Censorship and support of dictatorship. On occasions when the sexist and uncouth language was spoken about I would ask: "why do the women stand for it".
The answer was always the same, "what can they do about it"? Obviously it would take a freedom loving Journalist and a freedom loving newspaper to expose - the sexist language and the put-down-behaviour that the women had to put up with? However when the abuse was exposed by the women involved O'Toole jumped onto the his cover up band-wagon.

When the Harvey Weinstein's behaviour and abuse of women became public-knowledge, O'Toole could no longer ignore the vulgar sexual uttering at the Gate. As proof of his sham sincerity he cited several other perpetrators and asked, "how has this silence prevailed for so long"?

{The mind boggles} It prevailed in the exact same way he

covered up for the Gate - and keeps the Belfast Docks scandal hidden - by silence.

O'Toole and Irish Times with their Perverted Newspaper refuse to expose corruption and cover it up.

Like a woman-hating worm on the hook, O'Toole wriggles. Why is he blaming the victims? Obviously he and Irish Times editors are singing from the same hymn- and don't want to upset their readers with some nasty truths. This could spoil their next visit to the Gate?

O'Tooles skewed philosophy and that of his editors, i.e. that they are in the newspaper business for their respectable 'wealthy' readers... is so arrogant that they can't see the blatant contradictions? Without a doubt the Irish Times readership agree with these 'holier than thou attitude and observations'. While In the US he plays down the truth and promotes his blue collar background?

Just what world does O'Toole reside in... when he can 'run with the hare and hunt with the hounds', and he does it so brilliantly.

For him to state, that he believes the women who suffered the indignities and foul mouth rants from their employer, are "brilliant, articulate demonstrative women and vulnerable... with no security of employment" is an absolute and ridiculous slur on them? Obviously he was muddying the waters and praising them with his linguistic wordplay - to cover up his own shabby acceptance of what they'd suffered for years. The world and women have moved on from getting a metaphorically pat on the head from him.

O'Tooles, and Irish Times silence over the years about how the women were treated - condoned it. His, articulate brilliance and the Irish Times could've stopped it, years ago. He consciously and deliberately was making excuses for his own silence regarding the treatment of the women at the Gate?

Shame on him for attempting to garner compassion for his own and his newspapers jaundiced and cowardly point of view.

He and Irish Times know all about censorship - and the quashing of unpalatable truths to suit the holier than thou attitudes of their readers.

This is deplorable and disgusting. Their ability to stand the Truth on its head, and is a testament to his and his papers ability to ignore or cover up wrongdoings especially if it has been carried out by the employer class.
O'Tools says "if this behaviour and this silence can take root in the free space of the theatre, this can happen anywhere". Free space what a joke – was 'free thinking' while also being a confounded lie - too much hypocrisy for even him to imply? O'Toole is an expert at talking out of both sides of his mouth. How much longer must the Belfast People and the Dockers wait - before the Asbestos scandal and that of a trade union that sacked its own members, is exposed? Another 50 years?

Before I was sacked from the Docks, besides the Union and ICTU - I posted 'The Dockers Voice every week to the Irish Times. After I was sacked I continually wrote to them, and various union branches but to no avail. No doubt when it eventually happens and O'Toole and Irish Times have to print the truth about the Union Corruption - he will also will jump on the band-wagon and condemn it.

In a free and supposed liberal society for The Wealthy to decide - what a newspaper like Irish Times can report on, is utter Dictatorship. What sort of country is Ireland when its People are not allowed to know the Truth?
I say this in the full knowledge that there are many more 'silent' so-called newspapers - who all follow the Irish Time's lead.

Theatre in Ireland, like the newspapers is controlled by the Wealthy - which O'toole and the Irish Times facilitate. They do all in their power to quell the truth if it doesn't suit their agenda, no matter who suffers?
Many Readers will wonder, why the the Irish Times won't report that the "Champions of the Working Class" ITGWU persecuted and sacked Union Members.

The unpalatable answer is - because it suits them. Why would they 'bite the hand that feeds them'. Indeed they were delighted that Union Leaders both in Belfast and Dublin - betrayed the working class to advance themselves and curry favour with the Employers. However, they don't want today's union members in the Republic to know of this betrayal? If the Irish Times ran this story and exposed the Truth, union members would turn on the Union Leaders - and the special rapport between Unions and Employers would be destroyed. This would lead to the wealthy losing control over the trade union movement.

This is why the Monied People in Irish Theatre censor 'The Judas Goat'.

They know that a play depicting the largest trade union in Ireland betraying and persecuting its own members would cause uproar. So just like Garry Hynds they refuse to stage it.

Proof about the censorship of my play is all over the web, in particular on Linkedin, in 'the corruptoconnor website' which accompanies this book. I name 'some' of the people who censor this story- I know of others - but will only name the people involved when I have the proof.
I believe in Trade Unionism when it supports workers – and not union leaders who pay themselves telephone number salaries from member's contributions.

Fintan O'Toole and the Irish Times wallow in the the silence of Censorship because it suits the rich elite and is an insult to Democracy. This cover up corrupts everything and everyone who practices it. Especially the supposed poster boys and girls in Irish Times who pay lip service to freedom of speech.

With the Heart & Soul Company and after the successful staging of two plays, 'Daddy' and 'The Grandeur of Delusions' I applied to the Arts Council, on-line and filled in the onerous forms for two arts awards. Both forms were rejected several times because they were not filled in properly. I then got a young girl related to a company member to fill them in, and they were accepted - so obviously I believed that they had been completed to The Arts Council's satisfaction.

The first application was for personal funding, as a playwright, but I foolishly stated that if awarded the grant I would take 'The Grandeur of Delusions', to the Edinburgh Fringe Festival. This application was rejected on the grounds - that there was specific funding for this purpose.

The second application was for specific funding, to take 'Delusions' to The Edinburgh Fringe. This was also rejected. This time, because the name, time and dates of the proposed venue at the Fringe Festival was not included.
This could not be done. No Theatre would accept a booking - without a guarantee of funding from the Arts Council being in place. This bureaucratic catch 22 was obviously deliberate and amounted to Censorship from the Arts Council. I thought that by applying for both awards, this would show my sincerity, and if even awarded a grant for personal use, I would still use it to promote my play in Edinburgh.

More to the point and proof of Censorship is - someone is obviously monitoring these onerous forms so why did they reject them - and then accept them? When, by their own criteria they were not filled in to their satisfaction?

Several years ago I asked for a meeting with the Arts Council so I could present my case in person. This was rejected with the curt reply,
"everyone has to fill out the forms". Obviously the Arts Council under orders from the Wealthy were told to censor me - so I had no leverage from which to stage "The Judas Goat".

The moving the goalposts was Censorship had the desired effect I never applied again. On this evidence it's obvious that these forms are used by the Arts Council to deny funding to a project or play they don't approve of? This obviously applies to plays that portray the elite - who control Theatre - in a less than favourable light. The writers in Dublin and Ireland know they must adhere to - this 'Thought Control or Else', if they want any work staged.
Anyone who puts their head above the parapet - as I obviously have done by writing 'The Judas Goat' - is denied funding for any project. For the life of me I cannot understand the schizophrenic thinking of the previous Arts Minister and the women who run The Arts Council. If women are ever to be promoted on the basis of ability and not gender, then they must be able to sack someone who is not doing his or her job.

Whether the Arts Council admit it or not, the Wealthy, through SIPTU, and its cronies in the Arts, are undemocratically deciding which plays are staged in Dublin. In so doing they are not being hypocritical, but are steadfastly sticking to the Right Wing Beliefs of those who control the purse strings.

These beliefs are what ordered the Belfast Dockers and People to their deaths. The Wealthy obviously believe that money creates good people and good Theatre. The Bankers proved the fallacy of that.

My poem, the long version of 'The Judas Goats', sums up the Union's behaviour over the past one hundred years - and my play of the same name shows the union and employers sacking union members.

Obviously this is in direct contradiction of the fundamental beliefs of James Connolly and Jim Larkin. At Belfast Docks this corruption took on a life of its own - when the Union Committee took on the mantle of the Employers and sacked Union Members.

And lest we forget, the forerunners of the present day Dublin leadership sacked Jim Larkin.

He saw what they had become, "an employers plaything" who were more dedicated to their own importance and lifestyle than Unionising unskilled workers.

What has changed? The salaries that union leaders receive are an absolute disgrace - and when Patricia King was leader of ICTU to put her arm around my shoulders - after I'd pulled the mike from Jack O'Connor's hand - and and say "you've made your point" and do nothing about it... shows the state that ICTU is in.

My Belfast Docks play was originally named 'One Big Onion', but The Judas Goat' is obviously more to the point. No-one in Dublin - or indeed elsewhere, seems to know about Jim Larkin's famous slogan, 'One Big Union', hence the double meaning about the layers of corruption was being missed.

The Union hierarchy while paying 'lip service' to the founders of the Union are betraying Connolly and Larkin's principles. By covering up the

"Union and Employers Court". that persecuted Union Members.

Capitalism makes the world go around and will never be, eradicated - so ICTU and the Unions should start injecting some Socialism into it. This can easily be achieved - by using the Union Millions to buy up ailing businesses thus guaranteeing the jobs of workers.
Once started this will snowball with workers only shopping in, and using, Worker Owned Shops Services and Businesses. This is not airy-fairy talk but will be ridiculed, by the well salaried, well pensioned, Union Leaders.

In this scenario which shop or businesses will be successful? The Wealthy claim that they want Competition - so should be glad to have it from a workers owned enterprise. If workers don't take control now and buy out their places of work - their jobs will vanish, taken over by automation. They must stop being reliant upon fat bellied so-called Union Leaders who pay themselves a fortune in salaries and pensions and whose only loyalty is to Wealthy Employers.

The best way in the short term to protect workers is to encourage them to join Trade Unions, and for the leaders of these Unions to be genuine in their dealings with union members. Employers are only employers because they want to make money. If Union's were Employers with a working class board of directors, there would be honesty and fairness in the workplace and the well-being of workers would be paramount.

This situation can be easily achieved but first, workers must stop allowing the present day Trade Union Leaders to betray them?

Why should the likes of Michael O'Leary who depends on the masses to make him Billions - in the future, not have competition from a Worker owned Airline?

When my strategy to buy up business's is adopted and applied to every industry in the country, this will give the workers guaranteed security of employment and a happy life. The Union Millions can easily start this ball rolling. When Employment is used for the benefit of workers and the profit earned – used to buy up - more and more work-places - this system will spread around the world.

And when it does it will enhance the lives of people in underdeveloped countries by creating opportunities and work in their own countries. When Human Beings help other Human Beings to flourish the terrible examples of starving immigrants drowning at sea will be obliterated.

This strategy will work in every sphere of human endeavour - and particularly in the Arts. Struggling artists would no longer have to starve or put up with living in hovels to participate in their vocation. Anyone who wishes will be able to avail of the well subsidised training schemes for them to achieve their potential. And if their talents are on the academic side this will also be encouraged? How many more Oscar winning writers will there be - when they graduate from the Workers - Arts Colleges and Academies?

At Belfast Docks in 1971, due to the help and good work of John McGee of the Young Socialists, I continued to publish The Dockers Voice. In this I exposed sell-out and capitulation of the Union. A few copies have survived the years.

These show how the Union and Employers Court gave credence and a semblance of legality to their corrupt anti-union and anti worker activities. And just like a Court of Law, they attempted to put legitimacy to it - by putting everything in writing.

I have included samples of this corruption at the end of this book – copies of which I sent at the time to Union HQ and ICTU, but as usual they were ignored.

No doubt, today's Union Leaders are thankful that neither James Connolly nor Jim Larkin are around to see… how the Union they founded became corrupted by Employers. Needless to say, they would never sanction this betrayal of workers - yet at every turn SIPTU and Labour TD's scandalously invoke their names - in a vain attempt to cover up their own wrongdoing.

My play 'The Judas Goat', shows these illegal and anti worker Trade Union activities as they took place. This continues to this day through SIPTU - who insist that Union Leaders are paid exorbitant salaries from union dues. The present day Union leadership in covering up the corrupt past, actually prove this mindset is still in vogue. This raises another question - why will the legal profession not champion my case against SIPTU's perversion of Trade Unionism?

What's even more perplexing is the non-action of the Legal Aid Board in Dublin. Shortly after they refused me Legal Aid, I received the letter from John O'Neill, a solicitor with Thompson McClures, Belfast he was Jack O'Connor's own solicitor. This proved all I maintain. He categorically states that "the union in Belfast "*did*" sack its own members", {See his letter} but unbelievably states - "that this "is not corruption". I promptly appealed the Legal Aid Board's decision but to no avail. Even in view of O'Neills letter I was still refused legal aid. This is absolute proof that corruption and wealth rules Ireland.

The Legal Aid Board scandal proves that the institutions, supposedly in place to help ordinary people who can't afford to pay for justice is an pathetic joke. This raises an interesting point, just where are my rights to freedom of speech and expression… and able to secure the services of a lawyer. Which I'm supposedly entitled to under European Law?

Obviously the European Court don't care about the Irish Corruption, which they should be - because it also corrupts the European Law… and makes a laughing stock of the European Court of Justice.

My play, 'The Judas Goat', is proof positive that the Human Rights of Belfast Dockers were trampled underfoot. And because it shows these events as they took place - it is censored - as is all my writing. This is to stop me getting a voice in Theatre and obviously able to demand that
'The Judas Goat' is staged.

Also, why will no fair-minded person in the legal profession intervene in this matter? Is it because they know if they do - that their career in Ireland is finished? I don't want an inquiry. God knows there's been enough to sicken any right thinking person, and nothing of any substance will be achieved. All I'm asking for is a solicitor to take action, which I'm supposed to have access to under the European Convention of Human Rights.

When and 'if'… I ever get my case in front of a Judge the documents from the Union and Employers Court will speak for themselves. I ask this – how can a small insignificant Country like Ireland ignore the ideals of the European Union? I have complained to the European Court several times about this matter but have been ignored. I don't mean to be cynical but must ask this question. Why 'through silence' has so much evil and corruption been allowed to prevail in Ireland?

Why is the enlightened "Free Press" so adverse to exposing the truth in their own back-yard - while in other matters are not so reticent. E.g, Fintan O'Toole had an excellent article on Bankers and asked this question – "Why has nobody been prosecuted for the enormous tracker mortgages scam?" A fair question, but I ask O'Toole and the Irish Times Editors - "why do you ignore Belfast People and ex Dockers dying from Asbestosis"? Why does your illustrious newspaper not ask, "why has no Employer or Union Official at Belfast Docks been prosecuted"?

Is this Union's diabolical behaviour in siding with the Belfast Employers against its own members - not news - and not a world-wide scoop?
A while back Irish Times reported that a business woman faced charges arising from collective redundancies - thereby - giving the impression that they supports workers rights? At the same time it keeps from public scrutiny the wholly preventable Asbestos Deaths and the fact, that this deadly dust was blown all over Belfast. How many people have died from Asbestos related Cancers and didn't know what caused them?

What happened in Belfast is not only against Trade Union Law but against the law of the land - in whatever country it takes place? Surely this is of special and general importance – and has a lot of novelty. What protection were the Belfast Dockers and citizens given - under the law - any law, when they were ordered to their deaths? The TV media is also not without blame. I have emailed the previous Director of RTE many times plus RTE investigates and Prime Time but have been repeatedly ignored. The new director does the exact same thing.

A country-wide conspiracy of silence is in place to stop all knowledge of this degenerate behaviour from becoming Public Knowledge. Obviously, RTE and its "Investigative Programs"- don't want to upset the luxurious lifestyles of the Rich and Powerful. These Humanitarian and wonderful people have more regard for their money and reputations than the lives of Belfast people who lived in areas surrounding the Docks. Obviously RTE and Primetime hypocritically deny this fact, and like the Wealthy consider the lives of the Belfast People mere statistics on a profit and loss sheet.

Actually Miriam O'Callaghan confirmed this when she told me on twitter to take this matter to BBC or UTV. This disgraceful and deplorable action, can only be described as the death of decency? Her statement on twitter came the same week that O'Callaghan received a human rights award for Investigative Reporting from University of Ulster. See my old account on Twitter. {sackedbymyunion}

When I saw in the media that she was holding one of her 'information nights' in Dublin, which were to empower women, I attended and questioned her, asking why she wouldn't expose the Belfast Docks scandal. However, she fobbed me off - by saying there was a lot to get through but that she'd speak to me at the end of the night. However, this never materialised. At the end when I tried to approach her, a very forceful American woman who said she was Miriam's PA would not let me approach her saying, "she didn't want to speak to me". She stood in my way, with arms outstretched and would not let me past.

She insisted I could not speak to Miriam. I protested and was creating a scene, and could see Miriam looking at me. I shouted to Miriam, "Why will you not talk to me, but she ignored me. I would have had to physically remove the PA from in front of me, and had I done so I would have been arrested.

Many women in the audience saw what happened, and obviously heard her say 'that she would speak to me later'. This begs the question - why did she receive the human rights award?

Obviously Miriam knows how to 'play to the gallery' while not upsetting the Wealthy who rule Ireland, and upon whom she relies for her comfortable living.

However, she told her audience a different story. The assembled women were delighted at her stories about how she 'bit her lip and made "their coffee" while she climbed the ladder in RTE until she could take her revenge. Like many other so-called investigative Reporters and interviewers, she and they know who not to upset.

When I left her meeting in disgust I drank a half bottle of vodka I had in my pocket then entered a pub and in quick succession drank three pints of Guinness. I had just started on my fourth when two men entered.
They were wearing suits and ties and looked like policemen. After they ordered a drink and we got into Conversation.

I asked were they Solicitors and they replied and they replied no, they were accountants and asked what I did. In my drink addled brain I quickly devised a plan to get attention for 'The Judas Goat'. This was to get myself arrested and charged with a fictitious crime which I would reveal in Court was made up. When the Judge asked why I did this I would tell the truth about the Docks.

So I stated to the 'Policemen' that I was a writer and that I defrauded the Arts Council every year by using different names to get grants, at least five or six every year. One of them asked my name and I willingly told him. When I turned around the other one took my photo and I thought my drunken plan had worked.
These events transpired shortly after my wife had died when I was all over the place, no matter how much I drank I couldn't get drunk.

However, I was never charged with defrauding the Irish Arts Council and have in fact never received an award from them.

Coming from the Falls Road in Belfast I was well aware of the listening methods of the British Army. Everyone with a phone in the house was aware, that even with the phone 'hung up' they could still listen to conversations going on in the room. In the last number of years 'when drunk' because of the advent cell phones when one was prominently displayed I would hint at various nefarious activities by myself. Again in the hope of being arrested so I could relate to a Judge the Asbestos Deaths at Belfast Docks - but nothing ever materialised. Obviously my stories were made up and the listeners weren't fooled.

CHAPTER ELEVEN

Determined to bring attention to the Belfast Docks Scandal I started a book - and every time I was drunk would add to it. This was to expose the cover up of ICTU and SIPTU and it contained the documentary from the 'Joint Disciplinary Committee' which was in fact a 'Union and Employers Court'. This contained details of my Trial and appeal. In 2019

I self-published it with the title 'The Judas Goats' and hand delivered 40 copies to TD's chosen at random, to the Dail. Plus to the Irish Times for Fintan O'Toole. I also delivered it to the Phoenix magazine and two copies to RTE for Joe Duffy and Miriam O'Callaghan. Finally I tried to hand deliver a copy to the President Michael D Higgins but the policeman at the gate refused to accept it. He said for security reasons it would have to be posted in. This I did at a cost of 9 Euros.

The reason I went to these lengths is because - *'while I knew'* I wouldn't be sued for defamation - the fact that I wasn't - would be reported in the media and cause Investigative Reporters to ask why not?

I hoped this would achieve the desired result of exposing the cover up - but this was not to be. To their eternal shame the people in all media continued with their "Blanket Censorship" and for self-preservation will not speak out and do their job.

To this end - those in the Law, Trade Unions and Human Rights will expose abuse thousand of miles away and ignore it on their own doorstep.

I was particularly upset at President Michael D Higgins avoiding of the Truth, seeing he is a man of Principle. I informed Michael D of this betrayal, at his first garden party. Because I'd been emailing Michael D' on a regular basis about the corruption at Belfast Docks, and just received the standard reply… Obviously they had my email address and I was mistakenly invited to his first Garden Party and I could also bring along eight others. So I invited the Dockers who appeared in the Utv Asbestos documentary. Only one Arthur Rafferty was able to attend, .
We duly arrived, queued up and were greeted by Michael D and his wife.
I immediately launched into who we were and stated "that the Union in Belfast along with Employers had formed, a Union and Employers Court.

This ordered union members to discharge Asbestos without protection and sacked those who didn't comply.
I pointed out that so far I was clear, but that Arthur and others had full blown Asbestosis".

Michael D took my arm and moved me to one side, I thought he wanted to talk to Arthur, but no - it was to facilitate the photographer who took a photo of us and we were moved on. "Well that was a waste of time" I declared.

Outside it was a fine day and the Saw Doctors were playing. The best of food and drink was in abundance. My only quibble was - that a party of young people with learning difficulties were availing too readily of the free drink, and obviously were the worse for wear. I enquired of a barman should he continue to serve them drink. He shrugged and said: "I'm only here to serve it". A lady beside me commented, "And why should he not serve them, do you want him to discriminate against them".

Not at all, I assured her, 'It is their 'well being' I'm concerned about'.

"You're all the same" she said and flounced off. Whatever that meant.
Myself and Arthur availed of the lavish food and I had a several pints of 'Free Guinness'. After about two hours we decided to leave. When we re-entered house Michael D and his wife were still greeting new arrivals.

They were in fact posing with a couple getting their picture taken. I stopped to allow the photographer to take the shot - but Arthur walked on and spoiled it.
After another photo was taken I proceeded. I never received my photo with Michel D and his wife, and often wondered was it because of Arthur's actions - or - what I related to Michael 'D' about the Belfast Docks.

Over the years because of childhood beating and my futile quest for Justice and my illegal sacking, I buried myself in drink for a long time After being shown the reason for this I straightened myself out. However, with the death of my wife who always supported me in my fight with the Union at Belfast Docks, the drink returned. Her death and the continuous denial of the media to accept the Truth in what I was saying - sent me into a tail-spin.

While I accepted that no-one who relies on the media for their living, {for self- preservation} would expose this scandal. However, I believed that that the cantankerous old reprobate Vincent Browne would not baulk from the challenge. {I was wrong} For several years before he retired I had been contacting him. Only once did he reply, and all he said was, "show me the proof"? Which I did - which he also ignored and never heard from him again.

Years back, when I heard that Jack O'Connor, then still SIPTU president, was to appear on his show I fully expected him to lambaste O'Connor about his Union's diabolical behaviour at Belfast Docks. Naturally he questioned O'Connor in a provocative manner, but what else did he expect? Then in a well rehearsed hissy fit O'Connor took umbrage over some inconsequential thing, stood up fumbled to take off his mike and staged a walk out.

I fully expected Browne to say, "The real reason for his walk out and non-participation is - because I was going to ask him, 'why do you cover up the fact your own Union sacked its own members for and with the Belfast Employers at Belfast Docks'? And... do you know or care how many Dockers and housewives have contracted Asbestosis seeing your union ordered the Dockers to discharge it - and it was blown all over Belfast?

Sadly Vincent Browne said no such thing. Had he of done so he would've retired in a blaze of glory, having cemented his reputation and went down in TV history as a hard nosed interviewer. Instead cowardice set in and he said nothing. Had he done as I expected and what the Truth demanded - when O'Connor denied it, he could have thrown the Documentary Proof in his face. Instead, Browne retired a damp squib, who at the end of his TV life couldn't and wouldn't ask a truthful question.

No doubt his journalist friends from Belfast had a lot to do with Browne's decision. I believe they misled Vincent Browne and I must ask, why?

See - www.siptupredidentjackoconnorexposed.com for the documentary proof. This file shows the Union and Employers

Court in action.

Another Belfast media person similarly stricken with cowardice is David McWilliams. At a meeting in 'Crawdaddy' a now defunct nightclub in Dublin city centre at which Jack O'Connor was speaking, I accused O'Connor {for the second time} of 'being corrupt and of covering up corruption'.

While he was stunned and searching for words, I launched into the anti worker behaviour that his union engaged in at Belfast Docks. McWilliams interrupted me saying "let him answer". O'Connor then lied through his teeth and said, "Just this morning I received a letter from my Belfast Solicitor and he can find nothing to substantiate your allegations".

I replied: "Either you are a liar or your solicitor is a liar". - As it subsequently turned out, is was O'Connor who was the liar. His solicitor, John O'Neill of Thompson McClures, Belfast, confirmed everything I had said. See the letter dated 31st January 2006, although O'Neill tries to spin it so O'Connor is blameless - by saying, "while not an ideal situation for a trade union to be in, i.e. 'sacking its own members' this is not evidence of corruption".

What else could it be? Obviously this was before O'Connor retired. However, leading up to retirement he continually boasted, that he was standing for election in Bray, for the Labour Party. However, I must take the credit for him ' not' doing so. No doubt the labour Party saw I had already accused him at large Public gatherings of being corrupt and of covering up corruption - and would not desist. So they deselected him. Actually I accused him once more at a large meeting.

While this robbed O'Connor of the opportunity to continue his posturing to Wealth, in the Dail - it also stopped me from bringing to the attention of Labour Party supporters the scandal of the cover up by the Labour Party and SIPTU.
The last thing the Labour Party needed was attention being

drawn, to their own, and Pat Rabittes inaction in the matter. *{See Rabbitte's despicable letters}* So O'Connor was unceremoniously dumped.

When I received solicitor John O'Neill's letter from Martin Naughton of SIPTU I contacted David McWilliams on twitter and asked him to denounce O'Connor. He waffled and said "I remember that night Hugh but have not set eyes on him since". Whatever that is supposed to mean?
See his tweet in the the letter. A while back David McWilliams rightly complained that: "The Irish State is going to pay the lion's share of rolling out broadband around the country and then is going to gift this infrastructure to a private investment company". What a turnaround. Has he joined the hard Left in exposing the contradictions of Capitalism?

Quite recently he was 'singing the praises' of the rise of the middle class in Ireland, which I have no problem with as long as the don't do it on the backs of workers. I can honestly say without contradiction, that no working class person had an input into the nonsensical decision to give broadband away. No doubt the 'unelected who run the country decided this'.

David states, "The private company has the potential to sell off these assets at a profit - even if the State allows itself some claw-back of such funds. That is what private companies tend to do.
As a result over the next 15 years or so the average citizen will end up transferring billions to a small number of people. And we still won't own the infrastructure".
While he is entirely right in what he says - what is he complaining about?

This is the tried and tested Capitalist and Wealthy way of doing things in Ireland - to screw the ordinary tax-paying people. His excellent article would be more suited in a left wing publication instead of the Irish Times.

It points out the benefits of the PPP's Public Private Partnerships - "whereby in motorway building the infrastructure is eventually owned by the Irish People" - and he ends with: "And now the coup de grace. The department of Finance estimates that "Granahan' will have paid back all its borrowings by 2028. At which stage it will own the Irish broadband network. And we will be in its pocket. How does that make you feel"?

Again I ask what he is complaining about. This is the System that he supports - and that supports him. If David McWilliams is to be believed with his 'about turn', seeing there was only one bidder left for the broadband installation - why is he not calling for the setting up of a government controlled building firm to build the system - or a PPP?

Once established, this could continue on and build social housing for the Plebs. While this would get up the noses of developers and house builders by guaranteeing accountability - so no more sub-standard houses or apartments would be being built.

Why is the Mickey Mouse "unelected government" led by Robert Watt - allowing the people who supplied sub-standard materials which led to housed literally falling - down not to pay redress? Why is the taxpayer again footing the bill for Billions of euros - just like they did with the apartment blocks that people bought - and can't live in?

Ireland has stood one of the fundamentals of capitalism on its head, i.e. 'you get what you pay for'. Instead of wasting money for remedial work - a government owned Building Firm would have building inspectors on every site to oversee and guarantee each and every Build. And more importantly this would also guarantee that the children's hospital would be built to a world class standard without the overrun of countless millions, to date. These common sense practices would stop the ripping off of the tax payer.

Maybe this is a step too far for David and smacks too much of the dreaded Socialism, although he could put a spin on it and call it 'fair play' for the Irish People. While he rightly moans about the Broadband fiasco - the setting up of a Public Building Company would entail, him admitting, that Capitalism doesn't work - especially in such a small country like Ireland.

More importantly if there was a government department specifically for building houses and apartments there would be no more homeless people. And just like in past years, there would be a steady stream of public housing becoming available every year.
While this would upset the Landlords in the Dail - and keep house prices low, David is in the perfect position {with his about turn} to run for the Dail and to implement my proposal of... injecting some Fair Play into Capitalism.

David mentioned "Claw-back" which I agree with. In a different though similar financial context, I believe - if a Theatre Company which receives public funding at the outset and makes substantial remuneration, there should be a claw-back. I don't necessarily mean taking money off them - but their next grant should be reduced by the amount of profit they have in the Bank. After all, it's the taxpayer who funds their enterprise in the first place.

If David McWilliams with his expertise in financial matters and his undoubted social conscience, choose to do so, ' he' could change Ireland for the better. If he set up a new party and named it The Fair Play Party which as the name suggests wanted fair play for everyone, he and his new party along with Sinn Fein would run the country for the benefit of the Irish People.

With McWilliams expertise in Finance - he could insist that Vulture Funds have no place in Ireland and in a Revolutionary Move could persuade Trade Union's to use their millions to compete with the Multi-Nationals.

They could buy up businesses, ailing and otherwise and pay everyone a fair wage.

The eventual aim of the FPP would be to unite every Union in Ireland into One Big Union, which was Larkn's original idea. The combined wealth of the 'Union Owning Businesses would be used to compete with the Employers, and to pay a substantial fair play wage.

When ordinary union members in Britain and further afield see the benefits, they would clamour for their own union to join up.

A workers utopia would be the result, with workers owning their own factories and businesses. David could take the principles of 'The Fair Play Party' World-Wide and use his financial knowledge to alleviate poverty in developing countries. The fair play movement would upset no-one because it's adhering to the financial rules of acquisition and competition - but with one big difference. It is for the benefit of all and not for the few.

When personal greed is taken out of the equation and everyone treated with respect - then the good people with money will come to the fore and embrace the fact - that no-one deserves to be poor and without hope.

The ideals of the Fair Play Party "if embraced", will one day be the standard practice of Humanitarian Behaviour all over the world.

To achieve the ideals of the FFP David will have to confront is fellow Journalists and the supposed upholders of Democracy in Ireland.

At least two of the "cover up journalists" live in Dublin, and have been honoured as Eisenhower Fellows - this is awarded to Journalists for their courage in exposing wrongdoing. I don't believe Fintan O'Toole, is an Eisenhower Fellow, but I could be wrong.

He holds the right cover up credentials and has many other honours and awards. As Arts Editor of Irish times for a number of years, he is supposedly a champion of Theatre and free speech. He has shown however, that by ignoring SIPTU's corruption, he has a deliberate blind spot where the Union and ICTU are concerned. This is manifest in his refusal to support my play 'The Judas Goat' which shows the Union's behaviour and betrayal of workers at Belfast Docks. How can anyone dispute that the Wealthy are not influencing his decisions?

An interesting example of O'Toole's cherry-picking of the Truth happened several years ago. O'Toole chaired a conference for the launching of an information book by Transparency International. This took place in Buswells Hotel, Dublin. The book gave names addresses and contact numbers where whistle-blowers could register their complaints. After a few whistle -blowers told their stories, I was allowed to speak. I immediately launched into the cover up by SIPTU, of the corruption at Belfast Docks, whereby when still ITGWU the Union persecuted and sacked its own members and ordered them to work at Asbestos without protection.

There was absolute SILENCE in the room so I continued, stating: the Union Chairman, Jim Austin, negotiated a Decasualisation Scheme then betrayed the Dockers by joining the employers as Labour Controller.

O'Toole quickly interupted me stating, "You cannot name names" and called for the next speaker.

I persisted and got support from many people including several who declared they were ex Dublin Dockers. A shouting match ensued as they demanded that I be allowed to speak. This was calmed, by the intervention of Transparency Internationals Director in Ireland - John Devitt. He said: that "What I had to say was most interesting but this was not the place to discuss it, and that he would have a coffee with me later and discuss it".

Again I persisted and asked "where better a place to discuss, a Trade Union joining with employers and sacking its own members, than at a whistle-blowers conference"?
Devitt replied: "We are pushed for time and I will speak to me afterwards and take notes about your case".

This caused uproar from the ex Dublin Dockers, and Devitt appealed to them to moderate their language as the event was been recorded and would be posted on their website. However, not posted was my questioning of O'Toole and himself? Some transparency? Because of my intervention and refusal to be silent, dissent had stirred among the whistle blowers, who began to see that their situations were being used for ulterior motives.

O'Toole continually called for the next speaker as Davitt appealed for calm.
They were both shouted down by Genuine People. They were in danger of losing control of the meeting as the ex Dockers were demanding I be allowed to speak. O'Toole then delivered his well-planned master-stroke. This silenced the ex Dublin Dockers and got everyone present back on board, i.e. supporting the Irish Times led protest.

With a flourish O'Toole introduced an Army officer {Can't remember his name} who had to resign his commission because he objected to and reported sexist wrong-doing in the armed forces. Everyone in the room applauded the ex army officer who was present - now jobless and facing a bleak future. Then, grinning like a Cheshire cat, O'Toole delivered his 'master stroke'. He revealed that the Irish Times had stepped into the breach and saved the day, by appointing the officer as Chief Security Officer at Irish Times.

This led to loud applause and much congratulation of the Irish Times, mostly from the media. O'Toole almost floated to the ceiling on the wave of adulation.
This orchestration between O'Toole, Transparency International and Irish Times is a devastating example of how the people who supposedly represent the Underdog - are able to direct and control decent.

Obviously this suits and benefits the Employer class, whose main aim it to stop the knowledge of the Asbestos deaths and Union involvement from becoming public knowledge. They ultimately use genuine workers protest for their own ruthless ends.
Needless to say, the ex Belfast Dockers who were sacked for refusing to discharge Asbestos by own Union and their wives and families didn't get another mention.

That same day I complained to Transparency International office in London but was ignored. Only in Ireland could we have this upside down farce. I had just informed a whistle-blowers champion, 'Devitt' of a monstrous denial of Human Rights, i.e the right to life of Irish Citizens, and it was ignored. This fact plus the deaths of workers and women washing their clothes did not cost John David a thought.

This in entirely in keeping with O'Toole's and Irish Times

ethos which is to control and ultimately side-line legitimate protest for the benefit of the Wealthy. As usual in Ireland the Truth comes far down the list when vested interests are concerned. I admit I'm flummoxed. Why did the Transparency International office in London not investigate what I'd said, sack John Davitt - and hold an investigation into the Asbestos Scandal themselves. Surely, they're not as corrupt as O'Toole, Diramid Feriter and the Irish Times?

That this happened at a WHISTLEBLOWERS conference specifically held to give them a voice is beyond belief and - shows just how powerful they wealthy in Ireland are. Obviously Davitt told his head office in London, that I was some sort of nut-case and there's no-way that the world famous ITGWU would behave in such a disgraceful fashion. Obviously John Davitt, is ' *not*' representing Transparency International - and therefore has been corrupted by the Wealthy in Ireland.

Not only has he been corrupted - but by association he has also corrupted Transparency International. Whistle-blowers who suffer the full force of the Right Wing impositions for speaking out about Injustice - need to take control of their own protests. At present they are led by Devitt, O'Toole, Irish Times and the so-called "Free Press" who were present in their droves at the Whistle-blowers Conference. Not a word about what I said was printed the next day - but full coverage was given to the Irish Times humanitarian gesture.

The corruption of John Davitt cannot be ignored. If Transparency International is to live up to its name it must sack Davitt for selling out.

Likewise - David McWilliams cannot ride two horses. If he is going to confront the Wealthy in Ireland he must run for the Dail. Unlike myself he is educated will threaten their privileged position with his fair-minded proposals. The Dail - is the only way he place where he can resist the obvious censorship that is controlling Whistle-blowers in Ireland.

Ultimately, the screws will be turned on him to support them This is why - O'Toole, Irish Time's and Davitt were involved in launching the Whistle - blowers book - to hijack protest - and to sideline it.
Which they have effectively done. However, for them to have 'Turned' John Davitt must have them wallowing in self praise? No doubt if and when he's exposed
- a well paid position with the Wealthy will be guaranteed.

They Irish Elite naturally will have a frantic desire to silence David McWilliams... They've already started - by launching a charm offence by having him write a column for the Irish Times. Naturally, David will deny this, but stranger things have happened. E.g. The Union Chairman at Belfast Docks, Jim Austin, before and after he sold out to the Employers and took the job of Labour Controller... maintained that he did so for the benefit of the Dockers.

Even when he was prosecutor in the Union and Employers Court and a Docker was sacked, he would maintain that he'd done everything possible for them, but that they'd brought it on themselves. Unlike John Davitt he made no bones about his changing sides. David should be made aware of how cunning and manipulative the wealthy can be. If circumstances don't present themselves naturally through greed, they can create circumstances that will.

To fool workers, SIPTU and ICTU keep their support for the Wealthy completely hidden. This contradiction and cover up is what keeps the 'Right' in power. While Union Leaders will be completely opposed to Union's owning factories and business, McWilliam's with his undoubted social conscience could bypass them.

He can point out to workers - If they don't support the Fair Play Party - in future there will be only be the Wealthy in the world - and hordes of Robots working 24 hours a day seven days a week, while the poor exist in squalor.

In her excellent book, WHISTLEBLOWING TOWARD A NEW THEORY, Author Kate Kenny acknowledged John Devitt as one of her sources for meeting Whistle-blowers.

If Davitt had a fraction of the principles that Transparency International believe he has - he would've told her about the Union at Belfast Docks that sacked its own members. While she was in shock he could've shown her the documentation form the Union and Employers Court, to convince her - and my attempts to bring this to the Public's attention?

However, Davitt, with his 'employers hat on' while not able to stop Kate Kenny's book was able to control what went into it. These facts are without doubt and if disclosed will prove that 'Davitt' has sold out and is corrupting the 'Left' who believe in him.

Kate Kenny, besides crediting Davitt, also credits Shane Ross, an ex stock-broker and ex TD who was a Irish Senator at the time of his disclosures. She writes, that Ross brought attention to a whistle-blower, who was being snubbed, and raised the matter in the Senate. He got much needed publicity for the case which was even reported in the Irish Times.

However, either Kate Kenny's sources were being 'very' economical with the truth or maybe they just 'forgot' about another fascinating and very interesting story regarding Shane Ross. This also took place in the Senate and was "very worthy" of inclusion in Kate Kenny's book.

What transpired was: Shane Ross, filled with righteous indignation trumpeted on the floor of the Senate that millions of Euro were being siphoned off from training schemes for the unskilled, into secret SIPTU bank accounts. He labelled this conspiracy A SLUSH FUND. A media frenzy descended upon this controversy and SIPTU leaders denied any knowledge of these bank accounts. This focused attention onto the named holders of the secret accounts, who were SIPTU members. After much prevarication and when their names were eventually disclosed, they refused to attend the Public Accounts Committee to be questioned on the matter.

Why did John Davitt nor Shane Ross inform Kate Kenny about this Slush Fund? An interesting point is, the missing millions were used to pay for drink fuelled junkets to New York for St Patrick's Day - and other holidays for those in the know. The beneficiaries of this largesse were both employers and trade union officials? In any other situation, the Wealthy would've been calling for a police investigation, which proves that Money Talks. There never was an investigation and the matter fizzled out. Why? This was taxpayers money that was being used to bribe both employers and union officials and nothing was done about it.
No doubt Kate Kenny will be disgusted that she was kept in the dark about this corruption, as no doubt they'd have been included in her book. But will she challenge these champions of Democracy over their deceit.

Not, unless she wants a whispering campaign of lies and slander to blacken her name? While Kenny's sources can brush the Belfast Docks scandal aside by claiming that 'it is not related to Finance', this hardly applies to Shane Ross's - NON exposure of the Slush Funds. Another interesting point is - the ignoring by the Public Accounts Committee of the men in whose names the secret accounts were held. Why were they allowed to thumb their noses at this powerful committee?

Why were they not arrested and held in contempt until they confessed just who had told the to set up the secret accounts.

Don't get me wrong - I don't want to see ordinary people arrested - but these 'Cat's Paws' knew who was paying the "Bribes" and after a few nights in the cells they've have told all. Why did Shane Ross not report in the Sunday Independent about the 'cherry-picking' of his statements which are on the Records of the Senate.

While the misappropriated money siphoned off from training schemes for the unskilled was a dastardly act, for it to involve the trade union founded by Connolly and Larkin is beyond belief. The fact that the Wealthy were not calling for the heads of those involved, proves that they were up to their necks in it.

What better way to control trade union leaders than to blackmail them with the fact - that they were robbing the unemployed in such a dastardly fashion. This scandal and the even worse one, that Belfast Dockers were ordered discharge Asbestos without protection to save the Employers Money were - ignored?

Had Kate Kenny known of these corruptions and included them in her book - it wouldn't been a best seller? Actually - now that she knows will she admonish these deniers of the Truth and reissue her book to include these facts? Highlighting of course Ross and Davitt' cover up of the cover ups.

No doubt Kenny knew nothing about the whistle blowers conference in Boswell's Hotel - and - a more important conference held two days later in the College of Surgeons. This one had Judge Peter Kelly chairing the Q&A session. Geraldine Kennedy was still Irish Times Editor at the time and on the panel.

She proved all I maintain about the Irish Times and the Wealthy. This conference was to discuss the changes in the Defamation Laws. After some legal debate from the panel, about the pros and cons of silencing honest opinion in a Democracy - with various opinions on the Draconian new laws, expressed - Judge Kelly called for the first speaker.

As is usual in these circumstances things were slow to kick off, so I raised my hand and Judge Kelly directed a young lady to bring me the mike.
I shocked the assembled Lawyers by announcing: that, "I tried to get myself sued for defamation by telling the truth" , The large audience gasped as one. I elaborated, that "three times I accused Jack O'Connor, SIPTU President, at large public meetings of being corrupt and of covering up corruption".

The assembled Lawyers did not know where to look or what to do. You could have heard a pin drop, so I continued saying, "The first time I accused him was during the Irish Ferries dispute at a conference in Dublin - and O'Connor was so offended they he yelled 'he would sue the arse of me'. I was delighted".

There was another audible gasp from the assembled barristers and solicitors. I continued. "However, when the Belfast solicitor he engaged, one John O'Neill of Thompson McClures, Belfast advised him by letter, that I Spoke the truth about the Belfast Branch - and what I said was entirely true, he regretfully dropped his action". Judge Kelly allowed me five minutes to outline the corruption of the Union at Belfast Docks, then asked, "did I have a question".

I replied I did and it was for Geraldine Kennedy. Pointing at her, I asked: "Why do you, Fintan O'Toole and Irish Times censor the Belfast Docks scandal? As you well know this trade union collaborated with employers to form a Union and Employers

Court that ordered the Belfast Dockers to discharge Asbestos without protection - and sacked anyone who refused to do so"? While the legal establishment looked on, in shock, Geraldine Kennedy sat with her mouth hanging open. Foolishly I cut short her embarrassment by stating: "You are not alone in covering up. At a whistle-blowers conference two days ago, Fintan O'Toole would not answer that question either". Like a drowning woman the Irish Times editor latched onto what I had said - and gave an answer which will go down in the annals of the Irish Times and 'Free Press' history: She said: and I quote "I cannot answer your question until I've spoken to Fintan 'OToole".

A collective gasp was uttered from the assembled Lawyers - then following her statement complete silence prevailed. While Geraldine Kennedy thought she was getting herself 'off the hook' - she didn't realise the significance and implication of her refusal to answer a simple question. Or - even to be offended at the slight on her newspaper? The editor of the Irish Times had just denigrated and held to ridicule, the self-professed and pompous leading organ of 'supposed' free speech and democracy in Ireland. This refusal to answer proved everything that I accused the Irish Times of.

While Geraldine Kennedy was blissfully unaware of this - at the time, the assembled legal eagles knew full well of the implications. I also had just defamed herself - Fintan O'Toole and the Irish Times, and did so in front of the finest legal minds in the country - IF IT WAS NOT TRUE.

Worst of all, { *from her perspective*} she had 'jumped in with both feet' and refused to answer - at a conference which was called to discuss the denial of 'Free Speech' in Ireland. The deceased comedian from Belfast Frank Carson had a saying, "You couldn't make it up".

Kennedy's ignorance on the matter shocked the assembled lawyers.

From an non journalistic person this would be deplorable - from the editor of the Irish Times it was revealing and disgusting. Obviously, not as quick witted as Jack O'Connor who in similar circumstances denied complicity to the high heaven - and threatened to sue me if I did not apologise - then quietly forgot about it. No doubt this was the beginning of the end for her Journalistic Career.

Faced with the non legal action of Jack O'Connor, and the bumbling of Geraldine Kennedy, the finest Legal Minds in the country knew full well what they had just witnessed. They knew, because of the circumstances that. by no stretch of the imagination was I guilty of Defamation - and they were also aware - I didn't have the money to get this matter into a Courtroom or I would already have done so.

That said, no doubt every Barrister, Solicitor and Judge, in attendance at this conference squirmed a little in their seat. They knew they were identifiable through, having signed in on the on the web and could see - what could transpire from this situation. I.e. 'That they all had just been given knowledge of a cover up of corruption by SIPTU the Irish Times and the Wealthy.
And by their subsequent non action, which was apparent, and foreshadowed by their silence - the finest legal minds in the country were guilty of a conspiracy... comparable to Malice of Forethought.

If some ambulance chaser of a solicitor got wind of this conference they all could possibly be called, as material witnesses. However, the unbelievable assertion that several hundred highly intelligent Barristers and Lawyers were all struck with amnesia at the same instant, could even see them charged with perverting the course of Justice. Of course this was just theoretical - the legal eagles and members of the Judiciary knew full well that this would never happen.

After the conference, when wine was served, I was disappointed that neither Geraldine Kennedy, the panel nor Judge Kelly were present as I had wanted to question them further. Foolishly, with so many high ranking lawyers present I thought that I would be deluged with offers to take up my case – but received not even one. Geraldine Kennedy has long since departed the Irish Times and is teaching Journalism [sic] at the University of Limerick.
Although... the legacy of censorship the new editor of Irish Times inherited, is still promoted. This begs the question, just what sort of Journalism is Geraldine Kennedy teaching?

If proof of the power of the Wealthy is doubted - the back two rows at the Defamation Conference which Judge Kelly chaired were filled with print and Television media, who recorded everything that transpired.
Yet save for a few lines in Irish Times the following day, { *and nothing about my contribution*} or Geraldine Kennedy's avoidance of the Truth - a news blackout descended upon the Defamation Conference. If Kate Kenny 'is' to reissue her book - and seeing that nothing is every 'forgotten regarding digital recordings, she could track down and print my disclosures... and the Irish Times cover up at this conference Likewise, my contribution to the Transparency International Conference was not reported either, and my contribution was deleted from the video they posted on the web.

Regarding Judge Kelly, he had a successful career in the Law and attained the position of president of the High Court before being compelled to retire when he reached the age of 70. This was 12 years after being told by myself of of the Union and Employers Court and the deplorable Trade Union behaviour at

Belfast Docks. However the reason for his silence has become absolutely clear - its in his DNA and that of the wealthy. Obviously the Union leaders were just doing as they were told. What possible good could come from highly respectable employers, his neighbours, being dragged into a Courtroom and charged with God knows what?

After he retired, himself and and another former Judge, Frank Clarke who was chief justice when he retired - unbelievably... were both sworn in as Judges to the DIFC - the Dubai International Financial Centre.

Needless to say, Dubai has no Trade Unions, Freedom of Speech, or Democracy and has been condemned by the UN's International Labour Organisation... Amnesty International and every Human Rights groups around the world. While the good Judges were able to ignore these
"inconsequential matters" it gives an insight into the thinking of Judge Kelly.

The unfree Press for once got their principles our of the pocket of the Rich. They had a field day reporting that the Dubai ruler Sheik Mohammed Al Maktoum who owns a 1,500 acre stud farm in Co Kildare, had harassed one of his four wives who fled to Britain fearing for her safety.

He found out where she was living, bought up land surrounding her house and hacked her phone. A British family court found that she had been coerced and was entitled to sole custody of their children. Ex President Mary Robinson had to admit that the Sheikh had fooled her.
After his daughter Sheikha Latifa tried to cross the Indian Ocean in a yacht to escape from him - Robinson claimed that the young woman was suffering from a "bipolar disorder. She compounded this by claiming that the young woman "was clearly a troubled and was in the care of her family". When

presented with the facts our ex president admitted that she was wrong and had been used. I wonder why she was silent when I told her about the Union's Corruption?

When these facts were splashed all over the papers - one of the two Judges - Frank Clarke resigned, stating that he "was concerned that the controversy could affect the important work of the law commission" to which he had been appointed. A few days later Judge Kelly also resigned. He told the Irish Times "I have decided to resign from the Court of Appeal of the DIFC since, as a private citizen, I do not want this controversy to disrupt my future time in retirement".

What gobbledegook. It was not his status as a private citizen that the democratic institutions in Ireland and several Professor of Law objected to - but what his actions were saying about the law itself. "That it was for sale". I will simply say to Judge Kelly, there are Belfast Dockers and many Belfast People who will never get to enjoy their retirement. This scandal cannot be allowed to rest here because it obviously gives an insight into the thinking of the Rich- and the subsequent silence on the Belfast Asbestos Scandal.

This also exposes the sycophantic actions of Fintan O'Toole and Geraldine Kennedy, who at the time were the leading reporter and editor of the Irish Times. Not to mention the multitude of high ranking Barristers and Solicitors who attended the defamation conference? Judge Kelly is Professor of Law at the National Union of Ireland at Maynooth and obviously saw no contradiction in his and Judge Clarke's actions.
However another Professor of Law, Donncha O'Connell of NUI Galway condemned their actions.

He said: "retired Judges should not be lending credibility to one part of the Judicial System of a highly oppressive regime".

He added: "the Judicial Council should pro actively develop rules for retired Irish Judges that are mindful of the need to protect the rule of law globally, not just in Ireland".

Seeing Donncha O'Connell obviously has Principles - I have sent him details of the cover up by named Solicitors - of Asbestos Deaths at Belfast Docks. I want him to present this evidence to Judge Frank Clarke and the Law Reform Commission - with the intention of having it Written into Law: I.e 'that if a lawyer refuses to act in a case involving another lawyer - that he be named, shamed and struck off. Because of the closeness of Frank Clarke to Peter Kelly - and their obvious wiliness to be in the pay of repressive regimes - is Frank Clarke the right person to chair the Law Reform Commission? Would not the likes of Donncha O'Connell not be more suited to lead the Commission?

While I was conned and fooled by Solicitor Norman Shannon in Belfast, who sat on my case until it became Statute Barred - after I moved to Dublin I applied for legal aid to sue SIPTU. This was refused so I appealed and presented new evidence - which was the letter from Jack O'Connor's own solicitor. O'Neill stated categorically, that the Union in Belfast did sack its own members at Belfast Docks, but to no avail - I was still refused help legal aid.

After waiting for seven years I put the first open letter to Judge Kelly on linkedin. This was to try and counteract the censoring of my writing.
In particular, of my play 'The Judas Goat' - which shows the Union Corruption and the pandering to the Employers at Belfast Docks? Also shown in the play, is the Union ordering Dockers to discharge Asbestos without protection - when they should have been doing the opposite. I felt compelled although reticent to expose the Docks Corruption in this, manner because of the power of the Wealthy.

I was blocked at every turn. With the quashing and non-reporting of the Belfast Docks scandal, I had no other options.The combined power and whispering campaign had already turned the so-called 'Open Theatre'
against me.

Foolishly I thought having the scandal exposed on linkedin would 'persuade' the media to expose the Asbestos Scandal and the Union sacking its own members - but I was wrong. The Truth was and still is ignored by the supposed Left thinking people.

To be honest I thought 'Theatre in Ireland would expose the censorship of the Arts and all media who censor the Truth, but I was wrong. Why… in this Democratic Republic is this allowed to happen? I should have said - so-called. Even Shane Ross is afraid of them. When he was elected Transport Minister, instead of demanding answers about the Slush Fund and paying off of Union Officials with free holidays with Taxpayers money - he went deadly silent on the matter. Shane Ross knows what not to expose.
What astounds me in Ireland is: some of the people who suppress the Truth are those employed to expose the wrong-dong. This is proven by RTE with its state of the art investigating program that refused to expose the Corruption at Belfast Docks? Especially when it trumpets at every opportunity their slogan "The Truth Matters"? The reporters on their flagship RTE INVESTIGATES are fully aware of this scandal as I have emailed them many times about it. Do they not feel ashamed that their employer is making a mockery of them? Obviously democracy, freedom of speech and freedom of the press in Ireland is an unfunny joke.

The "Free Press and media" and the so-called "champions of Democracy" claim they can't tell the Truth because they will be sued for Defamation - which is nonsense. The Truth defames no-one. This is why I tell the Truth about SIPTU who cover up. I want them to sue me, but they won't. This is the only way I can get Justice in Ireland because - I can't afford to pay for it. I know what I just said is a contradiction in terms but it shows the state of the Legal System here.

A defence the apologists for the wealthy use, is the fact that I have no money, and it would be useless to sue me. While this is perfectly true, I point out, that: face-book, twitter and linkedin have plenty and they refuse to be dictated to by the wealthy Irish elite. This fact shames them up and they slink away. While the Wealthy control Ireland through The Press, Trade Unions and the cover up by Human Rights groups, Justice will never prevail?
Money controls Democracy in Ireland and the dead and dying in Belfast from Asbestos don't even cost them a thought.

Several years ago in correspondence with Andrew O'Rourke, of O'Hayes solicitors, who is the solicitor of Fintan O'Toole and his then editor Geraldine Kennedy - I raised the matter of their cherry-picking of the Truth. And as anticipated O'Rourke responded like their solicitor. He stated that: "I had made defamatory comments about two of his clients and that our correspondence was not privileged."

By return, I advised him to sue me, but that his clients would not allow it. And furthermore stated: that "I hoped I was wrong as I looked forward to the opportunity of proving in court that everything I said about their cherry- picking and adherence to censorship was and is the truth. It also is an affront to democracy, and is nothing but fair comment". Needless to say, I never heard from Andrew O'Rorke again.

CHAPTER TWELVE

In the Irish Times Fintan O'Toole nails his right wing principles to the mast. In an article entitled: DON'T NORMALISE DONALD TRUMP, O'Toole, castigates Trump. In the opening paragraph, he states: "Diplomacy is sometimes just a polite word for shaking hands with the Devil. Its practitioners need strong stomachs and a poor sense of smell.

Ireland like every other Democracy, maintains diplomatic relationships with repressive and even murderous regimes". This sets the tone for the rest of the article. Obviously O'Toole is diverting attention from his own corruption. He and Donald Trump are two sides of the same coin and if anything, Trump whom he eviscerates is the more honest. For O'Toole to claim that Ireland is a Democracy is a sick joke - and he knows it.

The electorate, people here, are fooled into voting for people with similar cover up perspectives as himself - who allow unelected faceless bureaucrats to run the country like their own Fiefdom. Hopefully this will soon change. Well 'Faceless' until quite recently when Robert Watt, came out of the shadows. He changed departments and as the new head of the Department of Health he awarded himself Eighty One Thousand Euros of a pay rise.

The ink had barely dried on this 'snout in the trough' decision when the words of John McGuiness were proved true in dramatic fashion. He had previously stated that himself and other elected TD's were simply 'Sock Puppets' used to rubber stamp the undemocratic decisions of the 'Faceless' who run the country.

McGuiness claimed 'rightly' that they have all the power, pay themselves what they want which in some cases more than the elected leaders of the country.
Obviously Robert Watt decided that he had been in the shadows for too long and it was time that the Irish People knew of his brilliancy. Knowing full well 'that self praise is no recommendation' he embarked on a strategy whereby the Public would become aware of him and his undoubted power. While his massive salary increase was despicable, it was a 'flash in the pan' and would be soon forgotten about. However, to make sure this didn't happen he announced that he wouldn't take his self-appointed salary increase until the country was back on its feet.

Leeks to the Press kept this in the public's mind and questions asked - if and when - if ever did he forgo his pay rise?
Every day this was the talking point in the papers and when it began to slip, a crafty stage-managed altercation in a Public House helped keep it to the fore.Then in a master stroke, to prove that he really runs the country he appointed Tony Holouhan - the Public Face of the Covid Crisis to a new position in Trinity College. This carried with it an increase in salary of thirty thousand Euros - and as it later transpired would also cost the dep't of health 20 million over the next ten years.

Holohan's appointment came as a surprise to many – including everyone in "the Elected Government" including the Taioseach himself.

When this became public knowledge there was an outcry from

the 'Sock Puppets' which Robert Watt couldn't understand. What were they objecting to - and why were they objecting - he was just doing his job running the country as he sees fit?

However, because of the suggestion of sleaze attached to his new appointment and because no-one else knew of it - Tony Holohan withdrew from the fray and announced he wouldn't take up the position.

And who could blame him. The attitude of privilege that Robert Watt epitomises is that of Fintan O'Toole - the Irish Times and the Wealthy who run Ireland. No-matter how much these people claim this is 'Leftist nonsense', it's the Truth.

To take their smokescreen of Democracy to its logical conclusion, if Ireland is a Democracy how can unelected people like Robert Watt disregard the Dail and run the government and the country? Who... is allowing this?

Another point regarding so-called Democratic Ireland, is - on the surface no one agrees with censorship in Theatre, yet it exists and everyone in the Arts including O'Toole is aware of it. Yet to survive in Theatre you must keep quiet. Obviously, every Arts Minister knows this - because as proven by Josepha Madagins behaviour... they are told operate it. No doubt they call it 'Constructive Censorship' and for the Wealthy it is... as it keeps the Truth of an Irish Stage. These censors are is not just puppets, but like Robert Watt, willing pawns of the wealthy.

No doubt over the years, O'Toole has spoken to, and shaken hands with many SIPTU officials. He also has refused to report in Irish Times about the Union and Employers Court and Belfast Dockers ordered to discharge Asbestos without protection, knowing that it would condemn them to a terrible death. Why is O'Toole not and condemning the Union and Employers Court that operated at Belfast Docks - as a murderous regime? The reason is - because it would upset the Wealthy and draw attention to their involvement. O'Toole, just like them and the supporters of every Dictatorship keep quiet - because they profit from it.

Many Americans agree with Donald Trump, like it or not that is called Democracy? When he said he would do something he did it or attempted to.
Had his "long withdrawal" from Afghanistan been followed American would not have become a laughing stock and leaving behind 80 Billion of munitions and infrastructure. Has President Bidden forgotten about the disaster of Vietnam?

Besides Fintan O'Toole's often very good Journalism - behind the scenes he does what the Wealthy want and knows not to upset them?
Just another proponent of the false Democratic image of Ireland.

However, now that Robert Watt has thrown off his 'cloak of invisibility', will O'Toole upset his wealthy masters and condemn him for his dictatorship? Another fact about the hypocrite, O'Toole, is - he will not reply to any of my correspondence, yet the "champion of unfree speech", when I tweeted to him "you refused to review my play 'Daddy' will you now review 'The Grandeur of Delusions'"? He mockingly re-tweeted my comments to his followers.

This proves that the censoring of my writing - or any writing that doesn't conform to the sanctimoniousness of himself - Irish Times, Sunday Times, and the wealthy, is to be ignored. The Sunday Times, this is an entirely different paper from Irish Times, however both have in common – a sycophantic deference to the Wealthy. Both show that all I maintain about Ireland and its so-called Newspapers is absolutely true.

Although at times they scratch each others back to cover up their wealthy champagne beliefs and support the silence about SIPTU on their despicable behaviour at Belfast Docks. A Trade Union cannot sack its own members, no matter what the reason.

As a perfect example of O'Toole's cherry-picking, a few years back he had an article in Irish Times regarding 'silence', at which he is an expert. He questioned why... Ryan Tubridy didn't ask, Billionaire Richard Branson, "so do you regret the way you've made such a public point of grabbing beautiful young women, lifting them off their feet, and in some cases turning them upside down". Yet The news blackout on the corruption of Jack O'Connor – now retired, led by O'Toole and Irish Times is complete, as no newspaper will expose how the largest trade union in Ireland joined with Belfast Employers to persecute and sack its own members.

Also Mark Hennessey, the editor has joined with O'Toole in the censoring of this 'story of the century'. The documentary proof of the Union and Employers Court at Belfast Docks, can be viewed on www.siptupresidentjackoconnorexposed.com – This Court persecuted, fined, suspended without pay and sacked Union Members. However, these were the lucky ones – the unlucky ones were ordered by the Union to discharge Asbestos without protection to save the employers money. What about my free speech and the censoring of my play by the Arts – on the orders of SIPTU and the Wealthy, which O'Toole agrees with?

For proof of Arts involvement in censorship, see, 'Historic Censorship from Largest Trade Union in Ireland', on Linkedin, plus many other articles. This shows the Hypocrisy which the Irish Times and Sunday Times promotes to the Irish People.

Just after Covid, in a timely article in Sunday Independent, Shane Ross, stated: "Mandarins Lording it over Ministers and controversy over Tony Holohan's – now abandoned appointment to a role at - Trinity shed more light on the influence of those who really wield power". Ross has not always been so willing to divulge explosive information, although in this instance, it smacks of jumping on the bandwagon and gleefully taking revenge.

In an article which can only be described as 'brilliant' {I wish he'd applied a modicum of this to SIPTU and the slush fund} Ross gives a rare 4of4

window into the thinking of Robert Watt and his "outrageous"

81

25/05/2019,14:04

p 249

thousand Euro pay rise. "When I was the Sports Minister, Watt asked for my approval to be a director of the FAI. I was stunned. When I said it would not be forth -coming because it would have resulted in a conflict, he was far from pleased. As a director of FAI, he would be seeking huge funds from himself - in his position as 'then' general secretary of the Department of Public Expenditure and Reform. He had guile. He simply plotted a cunning course, agreeing with FAI to reserve a vacant seat until I was put out of office". "Today he is **'on'** the FAI board. No longer in the Department of Public Expenditure and Economic Reform, but in Health"

For Shane Ross to write this after being 'Silenced' over the Slush Fund' shows he is a bought off mouthpiece with an axe to grind. He continues,"Watts weird reign at the top is not the only example of mandarins running the show. Appointments at the highest level of the civil service are an insider's paradise. Last week, under the radar, while the Holohan row was raging, the most powerful post in the entire civil service was filled. There was no open process. A new secretary-general to the Taoiseach himself was quietly appointed. A few weeks ago "expressions of interest" were sought from civil servants.

Whatever number were sent, all disappeared into the Merrion Street ether. Were there any interviews, or public advertisements for the job, which also carries the title of general-secretary to the government itself"?

Ross continues in this vein and rightly lambastes the Taoiseach for his lack of transparency – and likens the government to an episode of 'Yes Minister'. I cannot praise Ross enough for this article and his 'sour grapes', I just wish he'd had these principles when he was an "Elected Minister" I shall cut out Ross's article and put it on my wall – although I doubt the ex Belfast Dockers and the forgotten Belfast People dying from Asbestosis will be pleased at his hypocrisy?.

If the unelected who run Ireland are ousted - hopefully, Ross's article will inspire any TD's sitting on information about powerful figures and too afraid - for self-preservation - to reveal it - will have a change of heart.
{Or like Ross - to speak out when they're ignored in the Polls?}
Those who chose to keep quiet must suffer the consequences.

Only when elected TD's, have the courage to demand change and to face up to Watt and Co, will the the culture of cronyism that's rampant in Irish Life and Politics be eliminated. This 'change of heart' must originate in the Dail. If it's discovered that a TD or Minister remained silent to curry favour, or for whatever reason - then they must be exposed and driven out in disgrace.

The above denigrates our supposed Democracy and it translates into Corruption. Every person in Ireland is thoroughly opposed to home - lessness, yet thousands of people and their children are homeless? This is because the the "Unelected State" that control the elected government has been more concerned about their own careers and financial well-being than the Irish People they treat with contempt. To this end they've allowed Vulture Funds to take over housing and to make millions from People who must pay an exorbitant

Rent.

The Editorial policy of the Free Press is dictated by the Wealthy, whose first line of defence is Watt and his cronies. This is why the Truth about Belfast Docks is never disclosed? If it was and the People became fully aware of the Corruption of the Wealthy - they would not only question - but would have the answers - as to why Watt and the other Secretary Generals slavishly carry out their orders.

Dead Belfast People cannot be ignored any longer. The so called free press know full well that the Defamation Act {which they hide behind} does not apply in the Belfast Docks Case - because they will be printing the absolute truth about the cover up.

Another defender of the 'keep quiet' Irish Democracy is Ray Yeates Arts Officer of Dublin City Council. Yeates, on the basis of a good Readers Report, supported my play 'Daddy'. {which O'Toole refused to review}

Even though I hand delivered a copy it to Irish Times, with his name on it.

Obviously O'Toole, wasn't aware of this. Here is the readers report for my play which Yeates commissioned.

TITLE: Daddy

AUTHOR: Hugh Murphy

READ BY: Joseph

ACTS: 2 (1st act 7 scene, 2nd act 5 scenes) CHARACTERS: 5, 3 female, two male. Mother and two daughters.

SETTING: A home with a coffin set in the middle of the stage on two metal stands

OVERVIEW

'Daddy' is a deeply felt, emotionally intense and ferocious dramatization of one family torn apart by the abuse by a father of his daughters with a focus on the self-harming, self-destructive consequences. Structured in a sequence of scenes over two acts, the play starts after the death of the father and goes back to the period leading up to his death – though he never appears on stage. The core of the play is Carol, who has four children by James, with whom she has broken up in contested circumstances.

Carol is both self-destructive and an emotional truth-teller who forces her mother and sister to at least recognize the damage done to them by their father whilst generating a new cycle of an abusive relationship with new lover, Mark. The play is written in direct, colloquial dialogue with plenty of drink fuelling the outbursts, a few scenes are drunken monologues to the father via the coffin. The play concludes with sister, Sharon, who has been seeing a counselor, forcing Carol to accept that the cycle of abuse cannot go on into her own children, whom she loves but to whom she cannot express that love, and try to at least pretend to forgive her own father so that he can be left behind.

STRENGTHS:

The power of this play is in the intensity with which the play stays focused on the subject of the damage of abuse and keeps scenes intense and vivid. Some scenes, as stand-alones, (such as act 2, scene 3) are disturbing, visceral and dramatically convincing. There is no doubting the integrity and passion of the writing and the feel of the play is one that a traumatic subject is being dealt with from the inside: experientially as it lived rather than from a detached perspective. Whilst the characters are written inside the limited range required by the play, they are individuals and seem alive and capable of surprising themselves and an audience.

AREAS FOR IMPROVEMENT:

The play opens at a very heightened moment and puts all its cards on the table from the start. There is very little sub-text and an audience might feel confronted and not wish to go on this journey. This is artistically fine but might cause difficulties as people are distanced, rather than drawn in by the drama. Whilst the four younger characters are individuals, the mother (who does not get a name), is a touch generic both in her presence and in her reaction to being told of the abuse. It might be good to look at her journey again.

Whilst each scene does have something going on and often a lot, the stop-start structure, might make them frustrating over time. It might be worth considering looking to create a fewer number of longer scenes so that the drama can really ebb and flow. At times the 'on the money' dialogue, particularly from Carol, is very powerful but the characters nearly always saying exactly what they think may become wearing, also some of it at times sounds like authorial comment and this should be looked at. A combination of editing and looking to keep the powerful emotions but expressed in different ways might help.

The ending moves towards a dramatic satisfaction, but may be at the expense of credibility. I get why Carol may have to try to come to terms with her past, and her emotional relationship with the past, but the need to pretend about her father to her children is not clear and sounds damaging in herself. It may be worth looking at the end again to reduce the extreme change in character and/or consider a different ask in terms of her breaking from the past to create a better future for her children. Like the mother, the (non-appearing) children feel a little generic and perhaps this can be looked at in terms of making them generically real.

THOUGHTS:

This is a powerful play which has real heart and insight into a subject which has been much investigated, but which is still sadly current and of ongoing importance. It feels as if the author has put a great deal passion into the play, but some of that comes across as anger at the reader/audience rather than an anger that might move people. If the playwright could be encouraged to look more objectively at their and work to use a richer sense of dramatic structure with dialogue that was more deeply originating from the characters might make this a stronger work.

On the basis of this Readers Report Ray Yeates, DCC Arts Officer granted me four weeks free rehearsal space in the Lab, DCC's Arts headquarters in Dublin. We then staged this for a week at the Teachers Club in Dublin. This stopped Fintan O'Toole's sly tweeting and left him with Artistic egg on his face.

This is a good example of The Conspiracy of Silence from the Wealthy, regarding my writing. At the time Yeates was not in the Loop regarding the Censoring of me and the Docks play, however, this soon changed.

When I asked for the same support for 'The Judas Goat, i.e. 'rehearsal space', Yeats replied and made a mockery of his position as DCC's Arts Officer. He stated that "he had moved on and was supporting other writers". See his emails. In effect I was censored by Yeates and Dublin City Council.

Where is the Arts Plan, here? Can Yeates at the whims of SIPTU and the Irish Wealthy Elite, disregard a well-publicised Arts Plan designed to support the Arts and Writers. The answer is obviously, yes. When I complained to DCC about the censorship and filled out a complaints form, they denied ever having received it.

This was rather silly because I'd sent it recorded delivery and was able to cite the person who'd signed for the letter.

It mattered not as my complaint was dismissed. I then complained to Owen Keegan but got the same result, who in fact praised the work of Yeates. Obviously the Wealthy have taken over every aspect of Irish life, including Dublin City Council.

When I complained to the Dublin Lord Mayor, 'then Christy Burke', about the censoring of my Docks play by DCC he appointed Josephine Feehily to investigate the matter. I informed him that she was not the right person because she and DCC director Owen Keegan found nothing amiss about this situation. No Wonder. My play shows Belfast Dockers being ordered discharge Asbestos without Protection by the Union.

It also has a scene {which is true} showing The Union and Employers Court sacking me because I wouldn't work at Asbestos. No doubt, Feehily as chairwoman of the Policing Authority will use her investigative powers in the best way possible - and cover up any unpalatable truths that could upset the Wealthy. This state of affairs must end.

While its expected that the establishment Puppets would behave as they do - I'm particularly disgusted at those in the Theatre World - the supposed nonconformists? They've allowed the Arts to be denigrated and to become a Tool of the Wealthy.
A multitude of Theatres and directors, plus many in the legal profession, or at least the ones who attended The Defamation Conference - have been willingly silenced.
In covering up for the Wealthy who control SIPTU and ICTU - they not only agree with, but actively promote the unjust objectives of Dictatorship.

This is an absolute disgrace yet completely understandable as the 'nod and wink attitude' which dictates the morals of those in public life, has been ingrained for years. Journalists in all media led by the Irish Times, and Sunday Times won't 'rock the boat'. They fool themselves into believing that the Wealthy are right in censoring the truth - and that it's necessary for the protection of society. Instead of exposing the real perpetrators and destroyers of society who - by their Wealthy status are above reproach. Disgustingly the Arts - and its practitioner's take the easy way out. and do and say nothing.

The un-free press ridicule any suggestion that the public school educated don't live up to their own standards. When the Wealthy trip up and the veil is lifted e.g. with the insider trading scandal from 'Davies' stockbrokers, Queen Victories edict about women rules the day - and they are allowed to resign with not even a legal slap on the wrist.

Undoubtedly the 'Nelson's eye' type of Investigative Reporting suits the perpetrators and gains 'benefits' for the supposed investigators. The corruption in the system is well known - but all concerned know to ignore it. A classic example is RTE Investigates.
These reporters know they cannot object to the dictatorship of Wealth or the full force of 'Silent Repression' will be applied and they will be forced to emigrate. This proves if proof were needed, that in Ireland there is no such thing as Free Speech. Instead Truth, Justice, and the Beauty of the Arts are controlled by the evil politics of the Wealthy.

A case in point is the article below which I posted on linkedin. I thought the title would provoke a response but sadly the champions of democracy on the Public Accounts Committee thought it better to adopt the tactics of the Deaf, Dumb, and Blind. I reprint the article here so ordinary people can ascertain the degree of skulduggery and knowledge of wrongdoing that both the elected and the unelected working together, engage in.
THE PUBLIC ACCOUNTS COMMITTEE IS A JOKE AND AN INSULT TO THE DEMOCRATIC PROCESS?

Next week, by a majority vote, the PAC has decided to discuss Presidential Expenditure and Martin Fraser, Secretary General of the department of the Taoiseach - will be required to be in attendance.

Lucky him, this matter grave as it is – just about money. When I wanted to go in front of the PAC it was to expose [to put it nicely] a Chairman of a Trade Union who fooled his union committee into acting for the Employers instead of union members. I hoped this opening statement spark a controversial debate on the matter? Plus I also wanted the Committee to investigate why ex Belfast Dockers were dying from Asbestosis?

However – I was told that only the C&AG Seamus McCarthy could decide what matter went before the committee. And in his wisdom {or the wisdom of the Wealthy} he decided this was not an appropriate subject for the PAC to discuss.

As I have just learned, this was blatant lies from Seamus McCarthy and the - oh so honourable Public Accounts Committee - as the committee can decide for themselves who or what they investigate. I respectfully suggest to Mr Fraser, there are several ways to avoid appearing before the PAC - either tell the Truth... or join SIPTU. On this evidence it is obvious that Seamus McCarthy has been recruited and bought off by the Wealthy, but the question must be asked - why is the PAC agreeing to this cover up?

Have they not accessed Documentary proof of this is on – www.siptupresidentjackoconnorexposed.com -
The Belfast Chairman's worst crime was to order Dockers to discharge Asbestos without protection to save the employers money. I will never forget his comment, "how can dust kill anyone". Shortly after establishing the 'Union and Employers Court' the Chairman left the Union and took the position of Labour Controller with the employers, and unbelievably, was allowed to remain a Union Member.

This was the first time in Trade Union History, anywhere in the world that an Employer was a Union Member and allowed to attend the only union meeting ever allowed at Belfast Docks, which was the AGM.

To add insult to injury over ten years ago the ex Union Chairman turned employer was awarded his fifty year long service badge by Jack O'Connor.

Not only is the PAC as a body covering this up but many individual TD's do as well, including such distinguished figures as Alan Kelly, Sean Fleming and Micheal Martin, who promised me 'to my face' in the Square shopping centre, that he'd contact Jack O'Connor {whom he knows personally and will get back to me} Jack O'Connor was still union president then. I am still waiting.

I will state here again, Larkin's Union through the greed of an individual Chairman, betrayed every Trade Union Principle devised by Connolly and Larkin for the protection of workers – and behaved worse than William Martin Murphy did during the Dublin Lockout. Anyone watching Sean Browne's grieving widow on UTV's programme 'Death Trap on the Docks', will be as flummoxed as myself as to why this has not been exposed before now.

Exactly how and why this Cover Up has infested successive Irish Governments, 'the free press', present day Union Leaders, Politicians, every Human Rights Group in Ireland - and now THE PUBLIC ACCOUNTS COMMITTEE - must be Publicly Explained. At least John McGuinness did pass on my complains to the Law and Art Ministers at the time - who as usual did nothing about them. I make no apologies for quoting Alan Kelly in this matter - "we are called the public accounts committee for a reason?
Hugh Murphy

While the PAC tore strips of Angela Kerins why will it not investigate and expose these despicable actions by the Unions and the Wealthy?

Alan Kelly has been replaced as Labour Leader by Ivana Bacik. She is another Hypocritical Labour Leader who sends her children to fee paying schools. This is a direct contradiction of the Labour Party's stated policies - so who can accept anything this hypocrite says. No doubt Ivana will agree with this obfuscation about Belfast Docks and will keep as quiet as her predecessors on the Wealthy cover up scandal.

To hide her duplicity she'll create a smoke-screen by declaring how 'Left' she is, then make a 'Liar' out of herself. But what else can you expect from Labour Politicians? They will not investigate the cover up by SIPTU, and ICTU at Belfast Docks because it would expose their cover up hypocrisy and posturing to Wealth?

Ireland is ruled by those with the most money and any investigation will expose to public ridicule, the "Yes Sir" Politicians. Until the Truth is told and exposed Ireland will remain a third world {Re Principles} very Wealthy Country. I have noticed that many TD's - when the electorate get sick listening to their empty promises, don't elect them again.
However, after a suitable period many are often offered plum jobs. This brings me nicely to Pat Rabbitte, ex Labour Leader. He also refused to confront SIPTU about the Union's betrayal and the Asbestos Deaths.

In 1999, Rabbitte while pretending to be on the side of workers - attempted to introduce a Whistleblowers Bill in the Dail. This was not accepted and fell by the wayside. Had this of been implemented a lot of misery enacted upon many innocent people could have been avoided.
No doubt he was pleased when the "Protected Disclosures Act was introduced in 2014. This is well and good. However why did Rabbitte not re-introduce his bill when I contacted him in 2003? {See his eye opening correspondence}

The documentation I provided him with, proved beyond a shadow of a doubt that his own Union in Belfast had joined

with Employers against Union Members - and this was covered up by SIPTU and ICTU. My point
being - had he disclosed this to the Dail and re-introduced his Whistle blowers bill, he would have guaranteed his bill would be passed into Law.

This was almost 15 years before 'The Protected Disclosures Act' was passed. But of course doing so would have made him Persona Non Grata to his erstwhile Labour Friends.

They would have to admit to ITGWU and ICTU's part in Asbestos Deaths, the cover up by SIPTU and the persecution of Belfast Dockers by the Union. *{see Rabbitte's letters below}* To cut a long story short, my first letter to Rabbitte was sent just three years after his Whistleblowers Bill was thrown out. Why did he not demand a special sitting in the Dail and get his bill reinstated? The facts I presented him with proved absolutely the need for his bill. However, they also proved collusion between ITGWU, ICTU. SIPTU and the Wealthy - so they coerced Rabittee to cover up this scandal.

In one letter he amazingly states: "If a fraction of what I allege is true then the situation at Belfast Docks, to put it mildly, was far from satisfactorily". Did he think I made it up and forged the letters from the "The Joint Disciplinary Committee" in Belfast. This, to all intents and purposes was a "Union and Employers Court". Obviously Liberty Hall and ICTU were told by the Wealthy to brush the Belfast Deaths under the carpet - and to his eternal shame Pat Rabittee acquiesced.

Was he told on the 'quiet' that he'd be "looked after" if he dropped the matter? Why else would the leader of the Labour Party KEEP QUIET.

Obviously the lives of Belfast People and the Dockers were of no consequence when compared to embarrassment caused to the Wealthy and the Irish Trade Union Movement. Proof of this is given in UTV's Video - by Sean Browne's Widow. If this scandal had been exposed by Rabittee in the Dail, the 'elected' government was duty bound to act.

While its obviously is to late to take action against the Union Puppets - at least the Truth should be told about them, the Wealthy and the Deaths that they allowed to occur?

That said it's not too late. Alan Kelly could use this scandal to usurp Ivana Bacik and re-take the leadership - and thus get the Irish People once again to support the party of James Connolly and Jim Larkin.

This brings me back to my original point. Rabbitte was well rewarded for keeping quiet and not embarrassing - SIPTU, ICTU, the unelected and the Wealthy who control Ireland. After being rejected by the electorate, and after suitable period in oblivion, he was made Chairman of Tusla - The Child and Family Agency. In its most recent annual report - among other things - Rabittee said: "Continuous change is our defining feature and this is reflected in many positive improvements. We recognise as a public service organisation that we have many more challenges to address and there is no shortage of effort on our part in facing those".
WHO CAN BELIEVE THIS HYPOCRITE?

He had in his grasp the opportunity to make Labour great again - and in so doing would have exposed the Wealthy manipulators and the 'Bribed' in the Union and ICTU. But no - he kept quiet and was well rewarded. At least in Tusla there are many more people working for the safeguard of children - who will ensure that his words are carried out. This cherry-picking "Stroke" pulled by Pat Rabbitte must be exposed.
While this will not sit well with the hierarchy of SIPTU and ICTU - and past and present TD's - who won't act in the best

interests of the electorate - but instead act for the Wealthy - ' *must be exposed'.*

In Pat Rabittee's case there should be no ambiguity about his punishment. For cowardice and corruption and for mis-leading the Dail by the omission of relevant facts, he should be sacked from Tusla stripped of his Dail Pension rights and disgraced. Why should a man, who ignored the Deaths of Belfast Dockers -and God know how many Belfast People, be allowed to profit from his silence? I watched as clouds of Asbestos were blown from Sinclair Wharf and over the houses in North Belfast.

This Corruption is an example of how the Wealthy bring pressure on Newspapers and Journalists - not to report news that would cause them embarrassment. A case in point is the above. However, given that Rabittee has shown that he's open to 'financial inducements' maybe he should be given the option to resign - and to keep his Dail pension - if he comes clean admits the truth and spills the bean on the others involved.

A proviso for this would obviously be that he names names. Whatever his course of action is, hopefully it will happen soon and give the dead and dying some semblance of Justice. This will hopefully send a message to other TD's who hope to get cosy jobs, for keeping quiet.

On top of the Irish cover up's why, as a European Citizen am I not guaranteed protection under the European Convention of Human Rights?

Where is my freedom of speech and my right to a speedy resolve of my disputes, under European Law? I have emailed the EU Justice Minister many times and for 50 years I have been trying to expose the Belfast Docks Corruption? Under EU law, the fact that I cannot afford to pay for Justice is 'not' supposed to be an impediment to me receiving Justice?

To the Wealthy and their Puppets in the Dail, I'm a non-entity. TD's and the supposed "great and the good" don't even bother lying through their teeth - they just ignore me - knowing full well that while they control Democracy and the Law, there is absolutely nothing I can do about it. All I want is Justice - which is supposed to be my right as a European Citizen - and I am not even getting a hearing in Ireland.

The Wealthy dominate with their money every aspect of Irish Life. In this EU country I'm supposed to have "Free Speech", but cannot get a lawyer or human rights activist to investigate this corruption? This is an obvious aspect of the power of Wealth and the fact that my writing is being censored proves it.

My first play 'JUSTICE' was very well received and financed by ACNI. It toured The Northern Six Counties for three weeks and was in the Dublin, Belfast Theatre Festivals - plus a week at The Tron in Glasgow. This was in 1992.

However, when I tried to get my second play, One Big Onion renamed 'The Judas Goat' which is about the Belfast Docks, staged, I was blanked by every Theatre I submitted it to. My Drama about the insidious behaviour at the Docks was written off by the powers that be in Theatre.

I was Baffled and it took a while for the penny to drop. It was the Wealthy who control the Unions who don't want this play staged as it will expose their manipulation and cause People to ask questions. Garry Hynds knew who not to upset. As previously stated their puppets in the media and the supposed free press censor my plays so I don't have a platform from which to demand 'The Judas Goat' is staged. I have been excluded from both the Dublin Fringe and the Dublin Festival.

I have a limited profile on Facebook and Twitter, but many of my articles which were originally posted on Linkedin are on them. One article "Historic Censorship from Largest Trade Union in Ireland" shows how the 'breast beaters' who proclaim how liberal they are, and that freedom of speech and European Law is paramount here - are absolute Liars. My articles expose the vile censorship I'm experiencing - and names some of the people responsible.

I know of others - but will only name them, when I can prove what I say. E.g Patricia King, Fintan O'Toole, Geraldine Kennedy, Miriam O'Callaghan, RTE, David McWilliams, plus others in the 'free press' and TV media. All proud Europeans who laud the Democracy of Europe - yet jump through hoops for the Wealthy in Ireland.

As a one time leader of ICTU - if Patricia King would use her mandate to persuade our Leftist MEP's, Mick Wallace and Clare Daly - to expose in the European Parliament the deplorable treatment of Belfast Dockers with Asbestos, action would be taken? However, while Patricia obviously believes this would be like cutting her own throat - the opposite would be the case. She would be lauded as a true champion of workers and in a position to demand that well paid Puppets who play fast and loose with the law- are answerable to the Law.

As a 'True' workers representative she could get elected to the Dail and rally the Workers behind the beliefs of James Connolly and Jim Larkin. Using this as a stepping stone she could get elected to the European Parliament and give Workers a voice in Europe. As her rallying cry she could demand that the fourteen billion from Google, is paid and accepted.

But obviously she prefers a quiet life?
On the world stage, other countries are not as tolerant of

White collar crime as Ireland. In Spain, the former Spanish IMF Member Rodrigo Ratto, was jailed for defrauding his own bank. Why has this not happened on a large scale in Ireland? Here, the Wealthy cherry-pick which European Laws they allow to be implemented.

Mr Ratto got four and a half years and another banker, Miguel Blesa got six, while another, sixty-five bank executives were convicted and received lesser sentences.

It's good to see that another EU country is taking seriously, the crimes of the Wealthy, hopefully Ireland will follow suit. Mr Rato and others employed in the bank, saw it... and its funds as a cash-cow to which they helped themselves. In two years Mr Rato misappropriated almost one hundred thousand Euros, and the others, twelve and a half million.

This happened while the Bank was bailed out for twenty two billion by the Spanish taxpayer. Mr Ratto and his associates treated Spanish Citizens like the Irish Wealthy treat ordinary people - with contempt. Mr Ratto and his bankers invented an ingenious and fraudulent system whereby money spent on personal credit cards issued to them, was not registered on the books. But the Spanish government wasn't afraid of them and made them pay the price for their grandiose lives.

Mr Ratto's bank also had to pay back one and a half billion Euros to duped small time investors. Ratto and his associates would definitely have been in favour of the corrupt Union and Employers Court in Belfast.

During the Spanish property boom, Mr Ratto was Minister for the Economy and funded out of control house building, with disastrous results. This necessitated a forty billion Euro bailout and may well have been why they had an investigation... and went after him.

However, the Wealthy in Belfast and Dublin used their influence and money - to prevent themselves from being investigated for more serious offences.

The Wealthy and their Lackeys in the Union and ICTU are not only guilty of Corporate Manslaughter - they are guilty of Corporate Murder. At this late stage, this is a moot point because all those involved are now deceased, but at the very least the families of the dead, and the still dying ex Dockers and Belfast citizens - should at least know who is responsible for their deaths.

What we need in Ireland is a Spanish Prosecutor, someone not in thrall to money. It's too late for the Belfast Dockers to get Justice, because Jim Austin, the Union Chairman who sold out the Union and joined the Employers is also now dead - however, Jack O'Connor is still alive. He must be questioned on the facts? Why did he PERSONALY give the ex union chairman who betrayed the Belfast Dockers and who formed the 4of4 Union and Employers Court - his fifty year - long service Union Badge?

This is ludicrous. An Employer cannot be a Union member and especially one who betrayed the Union and its Members in such a notorious fashion. This scandal is a perfect example of the hold the Wealthy Elite have over the Union Leadership.

What I believe happened is - that, Jim Austin threatened to 'spill the beans' and get the Wealthy and Union Elite Jailed, unless his reputation was restored.
Jack O'Connor was then ordered to comply. Why else would the 'then' President of SIPTU to behave in such scandalous fashion and honour this "Employer". I also must ask, where are the numerous human rights bodies in this scandal? In Spain the corrupt Union leaders who align themselves with employers would feel the full wrath of the law.

The above is a perfect example of the so-called elite who run this country. With their money the Wealthy have corrupted the Trade Union Movement and bribed and blackmailed the media into silence. At the same time they believe they are entitled ' *not*' to pay tax to support hospitals, schools and essential services. From the treatment the Workers receive, I have come to the conclusion that the Wealthy {*including those who run the Unions*} despise ordinary people who must work for a living. And it's not just for being workers, it's for being so stupid.

It's not just one or two Rich Individuals who think like this but the entire spectrum from which they spring. Obviously the workers must be stupid if they to allow the government to pay over one hundred and twenty million Euros a year to private schools, from the taxes of PAYE workers.

This shocking situation takes place while parents of children at state schools have to pay a 'voluntary' contribution for school books. And if they don't cough up their children are penalised by being refused a locker or not allowed on school trips.
If the shoe was on the other foot, the Wealthy would be incensed and would refuse to allow money to be taken from their school fees, and given to workers children. To add insult to injury the Wealthy school principles insist this money is only used for sporting facilities. This is treating ordinary people with contempt and rubbing salt into the wound.

No wonder these privileged children "future TD's bankers and busines people who will run the country, grow up believing they can tell obvious lies with impunity - and are entitled to everything.

While pretending to be impartial, the Propaganda of the Wealthy in newspapers like Irish Times and Sunday Times does a fine job of serving their bigoted and educated readership. Their only worry is that sometime in future an "elected government" will decide to withhold the 120 million that workers pay to Wealthy Schools. It's not to say that they aren't capable of paying for their own children's school - but for the Wealthy its a matter of Principle.

Without them having to do a thing- Workers are told by the Unelected Government 'pay up and shut up'. Obviously this reinforces the 'touch the forelock' mentality of old and gives the Wealthy children an inbuilt snobbery which they have for life.

Alongside this 'Robbery of Workers, the State Broadcaster RTE does all in its power to keep the truth hidden.

On several occasions its directors - to justify their large salaries - have Slandered totally innocent people. In trying to be relevant. To much Trumpeting of lurid stories they have had to pay large sums in compensation to maligned individuals. But so what?

Like the 'sports facilities' it's the taxpayers who pay for the Defamation of the Innocent. This gives them credence and shows they'll report what they believe is the Truth... even when they're wrong. This keeps everyone happy and they avoid the Cesspit of the Union's and the Wealthy cover up.

A recent documentary by RTE showed Brendan O'Beaglaich [Begley] in his fight with County Council Council to be allowed to build a house on his own land. While this was an important victory for Mr Begley and showed the ridiculousness of County Kerry's planning laws - why was a program not made about the Belfast Docks Scandal?

In Ireland the Wealthy control every aspect of Irish life, including the Legal Aid Board. When I applied for legal aid to sue SIPTU and Jack O'Connor, I was turned down. I appealed this decision and presented them with 'new evidence', i.e.the letter from Jack O'Connor's own solicitor, John O'Neill of Thompson Mc'Clures, Belfast - { *See letter*} confirming that everything I said about the Belfast Docks branch sacking its own members, is true.

No doubt the board of the legal aid department, who made this scandalous sycophantic decision, have progressed well in their chosen field of human endeavours. Evidence abounds of a conspiracy of silence from all media and professional people on the orders of the Wealthy. An exposure of this magnitude about the Belfast Docks cover up and the inaction of ICTU and SIPTU would cause great dissension among workers.

This would seriously affect the 'crafted' tongue in cheek respect that the Employers bestow on the Unions - and seriously question those of the Left { *in the present day*} who know about this Betrayal. I have personally told the leaders of the two smallest parties in the Dail about this cover up but to now avail.

All and sundry in Irish Politics, Human Rights, Print and TV media aided and abetted by the Irish Congress of Trade Union's - regard the lives and Deaths of Belfast Dockers and Citizens to be worthless, and mere statistics on a profit and loss sheet. This is 'the death of decency' in Ireland. Yet entirely in keeping with their skewed moral compass - the Wealthy ignore the scandal of dying Irish People which they have caused. At all costs they keep this past degenerate behaviour from becoming public knowledge.

Surely to the higher echelons Law, this is of special and general importance and has a lot of novelty. If any of the Democratic Institutions in Ireland were free and unfettered, they would use this as a stepping stone to get into the High Court challenging this corruption of Irish Society. This exposure is exactly what needs to be done.

If Ireland continues to cover up the illegal deaths of Irish and EU Citizens then the European Court must do it. Why else are we in Europe if not to achieve freedom of speech, thoughts and actions?

Belfast Dockers - under the law - any law, were ordered to their deaths by a Union Chairman who joined the Employers. I have asked many times at Human Rights Conferences - where was the Dockers and Belfast Citizens 'Right to life'? Does the exposure of this scandal not supersede the right of the Wealthy to make a profit at all costs?

No-one at any of these conferences wanted to listen to me. So I ask - would someone in authority in this supposed free and Democratic Country tell me - why am I and the Truth censored - and why is my Belfast Docks play censored? The answer to these questions is simple -

"Money". I ask O'Toole and the Irish Times Editor - "why has nobody been prosecuted for what happened at Belfast Docks"?

I am going to make a shocking statement. Something stinks in The Dail and in so-called Irish Democracy. The corrupt Union Chairman at Belfast Docks who sold out, and the corrupt committee who sacked their own members, were in fact more honest than many TD's in the Dail. These TD's know the Truth but won't tell it. At Belfast Docks the Corrupt didn't attempt to hide their corruption, and were actually proud of it.

These were Rabid Catholics and led by the ex Union Chairman Jim Austin and aided and abetted by the "good living" Union Leadership. To turn the Dockers against me, the "good Catholics" named me an Evil Communist.

CHAPTER THIRTEEN

In Dublin in recent years - the 'puppets' and others in the intellectual strata of government and the Arts, use the same tactics to do the bidding of the Wealthy. Only - this time they use a false criminal record of assaults and brutality to maliciously slander me - and thus justify their non-action.

These Lies were invented by Corrupt RUC men to persecute a child who answered back. This false information spreads like a cancer through the arts and and can be backtracked to a policeman slamming an eight year old child into a wall. This shows how Corrupt the the free press the arts and so-called Irish Democracy has become - they believe these Lies because it suits them to do so. This gives Theatre Directors and Arts practitioners a supposed reason to censor my writing.

Druid's letter and thinking is a prime example. With whispered gossip - under the radar they convince theatre companies that... this is not censorship but is keeping the 'wrong sort' out of Theatre. Anyone who objects is persuaded with the argument: 'Why should they stage and facilitate the writing of an violent Thug - with his anti-trade union stage-play' which lambastes the great ITGWU, which fought in 1916 to free Ireland?

With this rhetoric, they know, 'not to censor' would jeopardise their own funding and put them in the 'bad books' with the government. I believe the main culprits for this are the Arts Council, who are a conduit for the Arts Minister. This has been verified by the previous Arts Minister, Josepha Madigan, in her email to me - and - when she censored and deleted me from her account on linkedin.

Obviously she was following orders from the 'unelected'. Without the financial stranglehold Theatre People would not only stage plays that show dramatic reality but would relish in the novelty. If and when this happens Ireland will once again become a leader in the Dramatic Arts - however, today, Cancel Culture flourishes. Like Nodding Dogs or Lemmings rushing to a cliff top, for self-preservation they acquiesce - not needing to be overtly told anything, a nod and wink does it - as they 'do the Right Thing for the Wealthy.

Theatre is supposed to be rebellious and against the Status Quo, but today, anyone who sides with a writer not willing to accept their odious dictatorship is putting their head on the chopping block and it's a career
ending move. Because the unelected people in government, like Robert Watt control the purse-strings and pay themselves a fortune - there's no way Willie White, or his cohorts like Garry Hynds and Cian O'Brian- will upset their financial apple-cart and stage 'The Judas Goat'.

The Wealthy down the years are terrified, that if... the Public became aware of the Union's corruption in Belfast - the deaths they caused and how they manipulated the Truth about ITGWU, SIPTU and ICTU, they'd protest in droves. Only when this happens will Ireland once again become a leader in the Dramatic Arts, The enlightened people will demand 'the truth' - that every government, including the present one, plus a a string of eminent Historians have kept secret from for the past 50 years.

When the used and disgusted People of Ireland finally are aware of what was kept from them, they'll also want to know... how many Asbestos Deaths occurred in the Republic? Because if they happened in Belfast they also happened in Dublin? At long last the Dictatorship and code of silence that exists and is operated by the Wealthy would be exposed. At the same time the stranglehold that manipulating theatre companies have on Drama would come to an end. Once again, Ireland would welcome enlightened Theatre People from around the world, and not be ashamed of the Stazi like conditions.

When this happens, especially on Broadway - where Theatre People are genuine... they'll question the award winning Garry Hynds as to why she wouldn't stage 'The Judas Goat'?
And the other modern day pundits who praise Irish Society and the Arts for its openness - and hold them to ridicule. The Wealthy 'rightly' believe, it won't auger well for them when this happens, and is why for 50 years they've corruptly kept a lid on this corruption.

When it's shown that they corrupted the Trade Union that fought on the streets of Dublin as the Citizens Army - the Army that was formed to protect strikers from the Dublin Mounted Police - when William Martin Murphy, the Dublin millionaire Locked them out from their employment. They will not be forgiven.

And then just three years later the Citizens Army marched from Liberty Hall to join the Rebels who had occupied the GPO - at the start of the Easter Rising. How... with this glorious history, 50 years ago... just what did it corrupt the 'then' leaders of this magnificent Trade Union, with? To my way of thinking there is nothing in this world that would compel the union leaders at the time to take part in a conspiracy of this magnitude -

therefore, Blackmail must have been used. When this happened ordinary trade union members could not object - because no-one, would or could object to the Union that fought to free Ireland from British Rule.

Also it must be noted that the Catholic Church was the main instigator in these underhand dealings. Before 1916 the church with a few notable exceptions supported British Rule. And after 1916 was determined to keep control of Civil Society.

Therefore, with the Champion of the underdog, ITGWU, corrupted, the ruling elite kept their stranglehold on democracy and their involvement well hidden. The Church infiltrated the fledging State and kept hidden their manipulations. Besides the corrupting of the Union Leaders the corruption of the Arts was the next target. They were a bastion of Free Speech that had to be controlled.

This policy is obvious today - when the leading Historians have blacked out - the Union and Employers Court in Belfast - which was first tried out north of the border, to get it established... and to get rid of the Belfast Dockers. Who can doubt this when down the years, their puppets in the back rooms of government - pay themselves a fortune and make blatant undemocratic decisions.

The unelected, like Robert Watt {who pays himself what he thinks he's worth} and the other secretary generals, run Ireland for the benefit of the wealthy, who control them. In recent years the Arts have become nodding dogs to their Wealthy Masters. Theatre Company's know what to stage if they want to be funded. This Censorship has been achieved by the tactic of 'divide and conquer'. Independent thought and plays they don't 'bend the knee' are ignored.

The Arts Council is supposedly in place to ensure that

corruption and censorship doesn't happen and are seriously deluded. Hopefully the new payment of 350 Euros will give some security to struggling artists and encourage them to speak up - but will they? If they do - just how will this affect their payment? Will the most outspoken be consigned to a lifetime on the Artists Dole? Or after a period of 'not getting any acting roles' will they be deemed to be "not" an actor and be pushed onto the real Dole?

By its very nature censorship cannot remain static but must grow to protect the perpetrators, and thus consume all that's decent in the Arts and society. This cancerous growth has been visited upon my plays by the Wealthy and their puppets on the Arts Council. They do all in their power to prevent me from having any plays staged in Arts Council funded Theatres. They { *rightly*} believe this will ultimately lead to the staging of 'The Judas Goat' and thus expose the betrayal of workers by their own Trade Union - who in turn were manipulated by the Wealthy.

To ease their conscience the likes of Willie White and Garry Hynds pretend that it's for "the greater good", but know full well that the Elite are using the Arts as a weapon is to deny the Truth. Dictatorship just leads to more Dictatorship.

UTV's insight programme, DEATH TRAP ON THE DOCKS, {available on youtube} - and Northern Visions DYING DOCKERS, made videos about the Asbestos scandal. The Belfast Union Chairman- both before and after he joined the Employers ordered the Dockers to discharge Asbestos without protection to save the Employers money. While 1 believe in Trade Unionism, I just wish the Leaders of SIPTU, did. A strange thing happened.
After UTV broadcast the Insight programme, this highly popular and successful programme was shut down.
Regarding 'The Judas Goat'. Every Actor, Producer and Director

could see the 'writing on the wall' and knew not to touch it with a barge-pole. If they produced it.. their career in Theatre was over - and they only spoke about it in whispers, to trusted friends.

At Belfast Docks the Union and Employers were not so subtle. The illegal Union and Employers Court sacked any objectors to their dictatorial rule. This kept hidden the Asbestos Scandal and its life ending possibilities.
This is the reason why "Controlled Theatre" in Ireland will not stage 'The Judas Goat'.

Because I continually harangued Jack O'Connor { *see letters*} about the Asbestos scandal - he and SIPTU leaders established a sub-committee, { *supposedly*} to look into the take over of the Belfast Branch by the Employers.

However, as the date for the sub-committeed meeting approached, tje SIPTU Finance Director, Martin Naughton, ensured that I could not participate in it. He told me on the phone and confirmed it by letter, dated 3/5/06 that "the sub-committee was **'not'** to investigate corruption and collaboration which I stated took place in Belfast but to listen to what I had to say,". Etc etc. Why then was the Sub-Committee established?

In view of this statement I could see no reason for attending the sub-committee meeting, which was to be a whitewash, with the outcome clearly pre-determined.
Another thing that annoyed me was the fact - I was corresponding with Jack O'Connor - **[not]** the Finance Director and wondered what it had to do with him. Clearly he was not a policy-making union official - so this suggested to me that they were sending me a non to subtle message that they were prepared to buy my silence. Because of Naughton's his involvement I refused to attend the many meetings they set

up. *[See letters]*

With documentation I can prove that the Union at Belfast Docks was not a Workers Union but instead an Employers Union. I had photo-copied this information so O'Connor, the Union hierarchy and Martin Naughton knew exactly what they were dealing with. I.e. the Union and Employer Corruption through an illegal Union and Employers Court.

That the Union ordered Belfast Dockers to discharge Asbestos without protection - there is no doubt. O'Connor and Naughton knew what would happen it this information became Public Knowledge? They would be scandalised. The fact that their Union had formed a Court with the Employers, and called it a "JOINT DISCIPLINARY COMMITTEE for suspending and sacking Dockers would sound the death knell for the Union.

This would also make them a laughing stock around the world. No doubt the Wealthy told them to 'get a grip on themselves'. And that they'd keep censoring me, so no newspaper in Ireland or indeed the world would report this obviously ridiculous story.
If the Union Leaders still showed concern, the Employers would quieten their worries by saying, a lible writ works wonders and this also applies to his play.

This is not supposition. None of the award winning so-called news - papers in Ireland, {including 'The Sunday Times', will report on this Scandal, despite being in possession of the facts. They all censor the Truth. Likewise, the the threat of a Libel Writ also guarantees that my play will never grace a stage.

Because I refused to be 'silenced' when I contacted the supposed supporters of freedom of speech and Human Rights in Ireland, plus Flac and the IHRC, not one was interested in this denial of democracy. Just what were they told to silence them? Hopefully, some day when there's a change of government in Ireland, things will change. The Puppet Masters who control the purse strings don't want the 'Points of Law' raised at Belfast Docks to be aired in a Court of Law. The most serious point being: "can a Trade Union, acting in concert with Employers, Lawfully sack Trade Union members who refuse to work at a deadly cargo"?

The answer to this is blatantly obvious, especially when the sacked members are fully paid up union members and therefore entitled to be protected by their Union – not the opposite? Solicitor Norman Shannon was well aware of the "Ultra Vires Law". Had he acted in the best interest of the Belfast Dockers, his name would be written proudly it the Law Books, but he was bought off and did the opposite.

This Law states: that anyone acting outside their jurisdiction or assuming "powers that they don't have" is guilty of a Crime. This is especially relevant when these powers cause the Deaths of Dockers and Belfast Citizens. This is why 40 years ago Shannon was bought off in Belfast and why today the Human Rights People in Belfast and Dublin will not investigate this "crime against humanity". Obviously, the Union's participation Sacking Dockers from the Docks when they didn't employ them was a blatant example of the Ultra Vires Law.

This is why Norman Shannon corrupted my case and sat on it for seven years until it became Statute Barred - and why other solicitors refused to take on this case. An investigation into the Union would also draw attention to their Policy at the time, which was to fine Dockers, {but only union members, £10.This transpired if the Dockers offended the employers in any way - or fell behind with their union dues.

When I asked this question of Human Rights People and

showed them the proof, they panicked and waffled - and insisted that trade unions are there to protect the Rights of Workers from Employers. It seems someone forgot to tell the Union and Employers in Belfast this.

For a time Fintan O'Toole and Irish Times seemed to have changed sides and led the bandwagon of protest in Dublin - but it was all part of the Right Wing plan. When O'Toole moved - on the organised protests fell apart. At that time in Dublin, SIPTU and ICTU were afraid - that if the lid on their behind the scenes manipulation was exposed - other Unions would want their heads. At the same time the Wealthy didn't want their manipulations exposed to the lower orders. To this end the Rich and well connected have ensured that I cannot get a solicitor to take on my case.

This, despite appealing to the Law Society - and even publishing an open letter to them on linkedin, I still cannot get Legal Representation. No solicitor in Ireland will expose this corrupt edifice - for fear of the repercussions it will engender.

The most disgusting example of the Ivory Tower values of the wealthy, so far, is the refusing to take the fourteen Billion from Google? These are the honourable people who claim 'that this is a great country for doing business'. Provided of course that their parents, and their parents come from an abundance of money - so the Laws of the Land do not apply to them.

The fourteen billion would pay for the Children's Hospital many times over, and whatever money left over could be used to build public housing for the homeless. This decison should have been decided by TD's in the Dail and not the Unelected People who call themselves "The Government". They've spent over five million Euro's in lawyer's fees so far, to appeal the EU's decision - however the EU have repeated their decision - "That Ireland is entitled to the money" so. three cheers for the EU.

That the "unelected" are a law onto themselves was proven by the Covid Restrictions, which they flouted with impunity.This contamination of Public Life needs to be investigated by Truly Democratic People. The so-called, great and the good - live a life of luxury paid for by the devastation of services for the people they despise.

The Wealthy claim, its our liberal tax system for 'outsiders' is that attracts foreign companies and provides work for the Plebs? However, when workers provided for their families by buying a house, the Wealthy in government allow their mortgages to be sold on to vulture funds who vastly increase they repayments.

If the government had a modicum of the care they claim to have, then they'd pass legislation - stating, that any mortgage sold on to a vulture fund, or indeed to anyone the householder did not borrow from - does not need to be paid at all. This would stop vulture funds and speculators in their tracks and guarantee the person who bought the house as family home, can continue living there. By forcing Irish Citizens to pay their mortgage to a fund they did not borrow from, and by no stretch of the imagination could agree with, the "Unelected Government" have aligned themselves with the policies of Trevellan.

The Wealthy, plus a host of multi-national businesses refuse to pay tax in Ireland, and are actively encouraged not to do so. The financial burden of this evasion is why the our hospitals and essential services are in such a bad state. The rich non-payers have reduced PAYE workers to financial slavery. To the children of the Wealthy snobbery is inherited from their parents - with their holier than thou attitude.
This is juxtaposed by the blatant lies told by their headmasters - which sees them through private schools and University to

emerge as a fully fledged unscrupulous elite.

The thing that baffles me most, is: the people in positions of power, in the Dail, media and especially in Trade Unions - rather than object to the perversion of Irish Life, pretend - 'to further their own individual careers', that it's not happening. Fintan O'Toole in Irish Times has once again shown the inner working of his devious mind. In an article with the heading:
'FOR PUTIN TO PAY FOR WAR CRIMES THE WEST HAS TO UPHOLD THE SAME STANDARDS'.
Anyone reading this article must be impressed by his Democratic principles and his undoubted bravery in exposing the duplicity of the U.S.

When he works there for half the year? The by-line is even more impressive. It states: "US refusal to join the International Court undermines the only system that could prosecute Russia over atrocities in Ukraine".

In his usual forensic fashion he eviscerates the double standards of the US with some shocking facts. For this article alone he should be awarded the Pulitzer Prize. I reprint below a portion of this truly remarkable example of Humanitarian Journalism. In doing so I am utterly baffled. Fintan O'Toole is obviously not lacking in Moral Courage. This is a fact. He is now living and working in the US for part of the year and is obviously not afraid of Official Censorship?
So this raises the damning question - WHY will he not write about, or include in his damning analysis of Corruption - the Irish Employers or the Irish Trade Union Movement? This evasion must pose the question: did he - or a member of his family profit from the Asbestos Deaths - or, is he - or a member of his family connected in some way to the scandalous Union behaviour?

O'Toole knows full well that who owned the Asbestos - and

that Belfast Dockers through a corrupt and "bought off" Union Chairman were ordered by their Union to discharge it? He also knows who pulled the strings in the Union and the government of the day to stop this scandal becoming exposed. His brilliant article proves that he's not afraid to write the Truth - so obviously he must agree with the Irish betrayal of Trade Unionism and does not see his own Hypocrisy as Human Rights issue?

THE ARTICLE BY FINTAN O'TOOLE
"On September 2nd, 2020 the US imposed sweeping sanctions against Fatou Bensouda and Phakiso Mochochoko. Who are these people? International terrorists? Drug lords? Human rights abusers?
War Criminals?

The very opposite. Bensouda, a former minister for justice in Ghana was the chief justice prosecutor of the International Criminal Court [ICC] that seeks to bring the perpetrators of war crimes to justice. Mochochoko, a lawyer and diplomat from Lesotho, was instrumental in the creation of the ICC in 2002 and heads one of it dvisions.
The US sanctioned them, and two other unnamed ICC officials, under an executive order that declared their activities a "national emergency". The emergency was the possibility that they might become "involved in the ICC's efforts to investigate US personnel".

The fear, in particular, was that Bensouda might launch investigations into the possibility of direct and indirect US involvement in war crimes in Afghanistan and possible war crimes committed by Israel in Palestine.

A year ago, Joe Biden's administration quietly lifted the sanctions against Bensouda and Mochochoko saying they were "inappropriate and ineffective". But it did not soften its underlying stand, which is that, as Biden's secretary of state Anthony Blinken put it, "we continue to disagree strongly with the ICC'S actions relating to the Afghanistan and Palestinian situations".

A year on even before the emergence of direct evidence of the murder, rape and torture of Ukrainian civilians by Russian soldiers, Biden was calling Putin a "war criminal". It is an immensely serious charge and almost a certainly an accurate one. But it is undercut by the continuing refusal of the US to join the 123 states that are members of the ICC. The US is equally fierce in its insistence that the ICC cannot investigate any crimes committed by its citizens in countries [like Afghanistan] that do not accept the ICC'S
jurisdiction.

At the end of last month, 39 of those member states, Ireland among them, formally asked the ICC "to investigate any acts of war crimes, crimes against humanity and genocide alleged to have occurred on the territory of Ukraine from November 21st, 2013 onwards". ICC prosecutor has indeed begun to do so". ETC.

I urge everyone to read O'Toole's great article and marvel at his schizophrenic duplicity and contradiction of - himself. He rightly condemns the silence and inaction of the US regarding crimes against innocent people - but not his own - by covering up for the Belfast Asbestos Deaths.

Who in Ireland today can deny that the Wealthy through their faceless bureaucrats rule Ireland? Although they are no longer as faceless as they used to be. This is entirely due to the arrogance of Robert Watt, the general secretary of the Department of Health. He gave himself this job after moving from the department of public expenditure where he was also general secretary – and pays himself whatever he likes. I.e an unprecedented Euro rise in his salary? He has omnipotent power over the elected people who supposedly rule Ireland. This was shown in the way he created a job for the 'National Hero' Dr Tony Holohan in Trinity College.

Watt, with his usual bombastic method of ordering people to do as he wants, controls people like pieces on a chess board and in a master-stroke catapulted the good doctor into Trinity College.

To ensure Tony was not at a loss financially, he manipulated this move by making it a secondment - which was not tempory but Permanent. However, when people in the department of health learned of the secret undemocratic nature, of this "stroke", they leaked it to the Press and to the public's gaze. Because of the arrogant way that Watt runs his department, plus all the previous 'bad press' attached to him, the three leaders of the coalition who purport to run Ireland - had to state Publicly that they knew absolutely nothing about his undemocratic decisions.

In view of the feeding frenzy from the 'unfree press' - the Leaders expressed 'shock horror' that this had taken place. Although the Taoiseach in a more moderate statement said "it could have been handled better". Wow? He asked Watt for a written report on the matter.

This was to address the fact that - the "Elected Government" nor himself had known anything about this matter? More importantly, why didn't he just verbally ask him? Was he afraid to confront him? The obvious delay in 'Watt' writing the 'report' would take the heat out of the situation?

Normally the elected people who supposedly run the country are happy to know nothing. This always gives them and 'out' when the 'proverbial' hits the fan. However on this occasion the good doctor was being put under a cloud 'not of his making' and he walked away from the stinking mire.

This loss - for the people of Ireland is entirely due to machinations of General Secretary of the Department of Health, Robert Watt. As usual, this unelected man who runs the country claims that he has done nothing wrong - and that he is "legally entitled [not] to tell the leaders of Ireland what he is doing when he takes decisions that affect the People".

It seems he was right as nothing whatsoever was done about his Ultra Vires posturing. His Dictatorial manoeuvring didn't even get him a slap on the wrist. This despite the fact that the position he envisaged for Tony Holohan would have cost the Department of Health 20 million for the next ten years. This obviously shows who runs Ireland.

The power of this Robert Watt must be curtailed - and he should be compelled to disclose "when he stopped taking his pay rise" if indeed he ever did - after stating he wouldn't take it until the economy recovered.

At the moment he is paid 300,000 Euros - but his tax and pension details are private. Why! Does he not pay tax and just what enhanced pension rights has he got? The very secrecy of this raises massive questions?

Just what is this Dictator and the other Dictators within government receiving from the Public Purse? Every elected or non elected person working for the government must be accountable to the Oireachtas and their salaries and benefits known to everyone in Ireland. This is because the Public is paying them? That this is not happening is mind boggling.

Bureaucracy in Ireland is the norm and a Tsunami of Silence rules the country. This is apparent in every sphere of government where unpalatable facts are buried. A new 'openness' would enhance and clarify every situation and give

Democracy and the running of Ireland back to the TD's elected to rule the country. The exposure of the Asbestos Scandal would be a perfect vehicle to expose to public scrutiny the depth and scale of the Silent Dictatorship.

Several years ago when Heart & Soul Theatre Company was staging my play 'Daddy', which is about the after effects of child abuse on two adult sisters, the producer rang the Rape Crisis Centre and gave a synopsis of the play. She invited them to send along observers but no one ever turned up. When she rang other women's organisations she got the same frosty response. It was only when we learned later - about Noeline Blackwell's involvement with The Rape Crisis Centre that the penny dropped. No doubt Noeline Blackwell will bring her fine sense of Justice to the Policing Commission, to which she has been appointed.

No journalist or Politician in Ireland will expose the cover up at Belfast Docks or the collaboration by the government, the Wealthy and the Unions, for fear of bringing retribution upon their own heads. I have also mentioned two ex TD's Mick Wallace and Clare Daly who are now MEP's, to whom I have on several occasions, emailed the information and proof of all I maintain. Even now, they ignore this fact. Why ? Have they not got the courage of their convictions?
As champions of the Left they'd cement their reputations if they exposed the Belfast Docks scandal in the European Parliament. They could start the ball rolling by exposing the so-called Left in SIPTU - which isn't 'Left' any-more but the 'Right' in disguise - albeit, still the largest trade union in Ireland. This is because the membership is being fooled.

To Mick and Clare I say this: **A CORRUPT TRADE UNION IS NOT BETTER THAN ANY TRADE UNION**. If these Irish European MEP's can expose other corruptions in the North of Ireland, why will they not expose the cover up of the

Belfast Docks scandal? If Mick and Clare exposed this scandal in Europe - it would pave the way for TD's in Ireland to take action.

The Oireachtas could have a 'special sitting' to debate on the 'Amalgamation of Corruption' that took place between the Union and Employers at Belfast Docks. This would guarantee Clare and MIck's place in History - by showing - that while they are of the 'Left' they will expose corruption from whichever quarter it comes.

The undeniable documentary proof of the Union and Employers Court is on the web at - www.siptupresidentjackoconnorexposed.com If Mick and Clare and the many TD's to whom I've written are still in doubt, they should watch the Docks Video I mentioned earlier - and have their eyes opened. Surely the Wealthy in Europe are not stopping 'Mick and Clare from exposing the facts and the Truth - about what the right wing monolith named SIPTU has become.

While Dockers at Belfast Docks no longer exist the corruption that led to their demise has continued until the present-day. This is just part and parcel of the sanctimonious control of Society by the Wealthy - which most TD's accept as normal. Why will the 'so-called' free press, led by Fintan O'Toole and the Irish Times not print these facts? This is an affront to Journalists the world over. O'Toole's life nor those of the 'silent media' are in danger - so, by remaining silent they insult the genuine journalists who put their lives on the line every day to report True Stories.

Irish journalists gleefully hide behind the Defamation Act as justification for not being a 'free press'. Even the most junior student of journalism - whom Geraldine Kennedy is 'brain-washing' - in the University of Limerick, must be told - and taught - that the 'truth' is not defamatory.

Because of her past behaviour in covering up for SIPTU, this establishment hypocrite should not be teaching journalism. Instead she should be called to account for her cover up - and for the mocking of Democracy. Even the most cursory examination of the facts and documentation from the Union and Employers Court - which named itself "The Joint Disciplinary Committee" proves their collaboration and Geraldine Kennedy's corruption. And... for the 'slow' well-paid Journalists – Joint – means the Union and Employers working together.

To genuine Investigative Journalists this documentation would be 'mana from heaven' and have them chomping at the bit to report on this story and expose the Wealthy and SIPTU. So the question must be asked: why are O'Toole and the Irish Times [not] leading all other newspapers In covering this story? I can't believe that they simply are feathering their own nest by censoring the Truth. To behave in such a frightened and cowardly manner, they must have been Leaned on and threatened in a most diabolical fashion by the Wealthy. As an old Docker used to say, "This scandal is crying out to Heaven for vengeance".

O'Toole has shown that he's not afraid of the US Government so what is he afraid of in Ireland. Someone must ask him this question. Setting aside heaven and vengeance, the fact that three presidents of Ireland, including the current one, Michael 'D' - refused to help the ex Belfast Dockers, "Irish Citizens". Many of whom are now suffering from Asbestosis - 'or' to bring to the attention of the High Court a very important Point of Law. Which is: In the 60's and 70's - how could a Trade Union, especially one with the antecedence of SIPTU, form a Union and Employers Court and sack Union Members?

The main sacking offence was to refuse to discharge Asbestos without protection.

While Ireland is obviously a Dictatorship that's controlled by the Wealthy and the Secretary Generals, it won't sit well with Journalists I've mentioned - who don't wish it to be known... that they've either been blackmailed or willingly censored.
How can Fintan O'Toole or any Journalist, knowing the truth - not feel duty bound to write about it? That aside, however - they are not alone in covering up this shocking fact and denial of human rights.

The Irish Human Rights Commission, { *as it was then*} contradicted it's own 'reason for being' when it refused to take up my case and hold an inquiry into the Belfast Docks and Asbestos scandal. Not one of their documented reasons was valid because they are based on a corrupt premise. The very fact that IHRC could see no wrong in a trade union persecuting and sacking its own members and ordering them to their deaths, must give grave reason for concern.

How could they think that the Belfast Employers and a trade union behaving in this fashion was not a denial of Human Rights - and of public importance, never mind of constitutional importance?

Also the fact that the IHRC has added an 'E' to its name and is now known as the Irish Human Rights and Equality Commission - begs the question - just what are they equal to - Holocaust or Famine deniers?

There's no doubt Mary Robinson, with her knowledge of 'Human Rights' was well aware of this - when she decided to remain silent? To do otherwise would upset the devious, dictatorial hypocritical apple-cart of the Wealthy in Ireland.

This was before she was conned by Wealthy Arabs. No doubt ex President Mary lives in the upper stratosphere of Irish society and feels duty bound to save the suffering of the world, excluding the Irish, stricken with Asbestos Poisoning.

Ray Yeates was the Dublin City Council Arts Officer, to whom I sent my play, 'Daddy'. This is about the after effects of child abuse on two adult sisters - and how it affects their adult life and subsequent relationships with men. Yeates lived up to his Title and commissioned a Readers Report for my play. Thus, after receiving a good Report [below] granted me four weeks free rehearsal space in the LAB, DCC's headquarters for the Arts. For this we were grateful and subsequently staged the Play at the Teachers Club - in Dublin City Centre for a week. We then took it on a short tour ending up in Mayo, where it got a standing ovation on the last night.

The following year I approached Ray Yeates again, this time seeking the same consideration for 'The Judas Goat'. Upon reading a synopsis Yeates attitude changed, he became belligerent and I got a very frosty reception from him. He refused point blank to consider my play, or send it to a Reader. And when I asked, how does this fit with the DCC Arts Plan for new writers and new writing, he refused to answer. Yeates, along with many others is just the latest in a long line of Arts Officials, and arts workers who censor 'The Judas Goat'.

Because of Ray Yeates blatant censorship I complained to Owen Keegan and Mary Freehill of the DCC.
I informed them both, that I'd lodged a letter of complaint with Dublin City Council – and that this is about the censorship by Ray Yeates. There's no doubt the DCC Arts manager was leaned on by SIPTU and the Wealthy. By his actions Yeates is acting against the very ethos of the Arts Plan and therefore has another agenda. This is to protect from public exposure SIPTU, and the interference of wealth in the Arts.

Below is an email that I sent to Mary Freehill and Owen Keegan of DCC

COVER UP OF CORRUPTION
Dear Mary Freehill, Owen Keegan.
For your information,

I have lodged a letter of complaint with Dublin City Council about the censorship by Ray Yeates, the DCC Arts manager, of my play, The Judas Goat . By his actions there is no doubt that Yeates is acting against the very ethos of the Arts Plan and therefore has another agenda – which is to protect from vilification the Right Wing in the Arts, and in SIPTU.

You both are covering up the scurrilous behaviour of Ray Yeates, who in turn is covering up for Jack O'Connor, who is trying to keep the lid on the fact – that the Belfast Branch Chairman of ITGWU was corrupted by the employers – and persecuted his own members. The documentary proof of this is on www.siptupresidentjackoconnorexposed.com but please read the first five pages – and let what I say there sink in. Or better still, go to my profile page on linkedin and read the play - so you will know exactly what you are covering up.

Mary, Owen, because you both - and Ray Yeates, have embraced the cover up of corruption that prevails in Ireland, regarding this matter, and the censorship of my play, The Judas Goat – I take no pleasure in labelling both of you, and Ray Yeates thoroughly corrupt.

Mary, Owen, please feel free to take any Legal Action you wish to take – because I will plead guilty and prove that everything I say is Fair Comment. Incidentally, Jack O'Connor threatened to sue me for telling him to his face, at three large public meetings, that he is corrupt and is covering up corruption.

Incensed, after the first occasion – he shouted that he would "sue the arse of me".

However, when the Belfast solicitor he engaged, one John O'Neill of Thompson McClures, Belfast, informed him that I spoke the Truth, he swallowed his hurt pride – as will you two – but I live in hope that I am wrong. A similar situation occurred with the solicitor who represents, Fintan O'Toole and Geraldine Kennedy, one Andrew O'Rourke of O'Hayes solicitors. He inferred in a letter that I had liabled his clients.

Delighted – I told him to go ahead and sue, as I wanted to prove in Court that everything I said about their cherry-picking was correct. I also told him that his said clients – much to my disappointment - would not allow him to sue me. I was right.
Mary, Owen, this matter is too serious for me to wait for my complaint against Ray Yeates to be investigated. By supporting Ray Yeates and his censorship, you have brought the entire Dublin City Council into Disrepute – and I am calling for a meeting of the entire City Council to discuss this matter. Action must be taken against Ray Yeates and both of you – and anyone else in the Arts Office or the entire DCC organisation who supports Censorship.

This must be done, if DCC is to retain any credibility whatsoever.
Hugh Murphy

Seeing I was getting nowhere in Theatre, to get some traction for 'The Judas Goat' I wrote a screenplay version and applied to BCI, now the Irish Broadcasting Commission who agreed to fund the screenplay, but stated, "I would need reputable film company on board" before they could release any funding. And guess what - no reputable company or director from the Artists Group I was in would come on board.

I showed them Documentary proof of Union and Employers Court and the sell-out by the Union Chairman, but to no avail. I believed that the letter from Jack O'Connor's Belfast solicitor would convince film companies of the Truth about the Union's betrayal of the Belfast Dockers. Instead it frightened them. None wanted to become involved with solicitors even though John O'Neill confirmed what I was saying about the Union sacking its own members. This frightened them.

Sadly, the Truth - as usual in Ireland - must pay second fiddle to Corruption. I say sadly because I cannot get a solicitor to take on this case – and would have been delighted to have been sued, and thus able to prove in Court my accusations. While the Docks corruption happened 50 years ago, the cover up of corruption continues to the present day.

Away back in 1972, soon after Decasualisation, the ex Union chairman, Labour Controller would send me – and the men around me – to the most dirty and worst paid jobs at the Docks. This resulted in everyone, my friends included… getting as far away from me as possible when the ex union chairman was allocating work. Then, the Union at the time started malicious rumours to blacken my name before they and the Employers Court sacked me. However, the Dockers did protest and went on strike for 3 days, but were talked back to work by the new chairman who stated that I was a communist and that the Union was going to sack me for writing and printing 'The Dockers Voice'.

Even 50 years later No lawyer, journalist or newspaper will expose this scandal. In particular, Miriam O'Callaghan and a host of others at RTE, the supposed 'Voice of the People' will say nothing about it. **THIS IS IRISH DEMOCRACY.** Vincent Browne when he was on TV was another serious let down? All these well paid and sanctimonious so called - 'Purveyors of the Truth' and so-called Human Rights bodies on this Island, who champion human rights around the world, ignore this

atrocity, on their doorstep.
Both UTV and Northern Visions from Belfast made TV
programmes about this – but the investigation has stopped
dead.

Why...?

I also raised the matter of the diabolical behaviour of the
Union with parliamentary adviser Mellissa English. This was
in regard to Denis O'Brien and Angela Kerins having their legal
fees paid by the state, even though O'Brien had lost his case - he
claimed the Oireachtas had acted outside their remit - and he
was right.

Lawyers led by English who is head of the parliamentary
legal advisers office, told TD's and senators that the superior
courts have frequently awarded costs to unsuccessful litigants
against the state - if the point they raised was considered
"constitutionally important". In view of this point I asked
Mellissa English {by email} would she consider providing me
with funds - or a lawyer to take my case into a Court - as a blind
man can see that a trade union cannot sack its own members. I
never got a reply from her.

Why...? Was the scandal of Connolly and Larkin's Union
jumping through hoops for the Wealthy and forcing
Belfast People to literally eat Asbestos, not 'constitutionally
important'.

Well not from the Wealthy's point of view? The Union
and the Employers were obviously acting in 'consort' having
abused their power - and obviously had acted unlawfully.
I received neither an answer nor acknowledgement from
Mellissa English. So, not only does SIPTU, the Law, Journalism,
the Media and the Arts bow to corruption - but the "Legal
Advisers" in the Civil Service and the government does so as

well.

I don't wish to see Mellissa English condemned for the behaviour of Union Officials but as a "Legal Advisers" I want her to act legally and within the Law and not cover up. Why did she not grant immunity to union officials and thus encourage one of them to become a Whistleblower?

The leaders of SIPTU past and present would have got what they deserved - and to avoid Jail, would have implicated the Wealthy manipulators. One day I got on a bus in Dublin, and much to my surprise, an old school friend and ex Belfast Docker Mickey Quinn, was driving it.

Delighted to see him we shook hands and on the way into town we reminisced about the Docks. He told me it got worse after I was sacked. I commiserated with him and said "what sort of union men would sit with Employers and sack their own members"?

He looked at me and said, "I did, the whole committee and the chairman did as well, it was to stop them being sacked". Weaving his bus through he Dublin traffic he continued. "The night before I'd go to their house and tell them what to say so they wouldn't be sacked". In disbelief I looked at him."You went onto the Docks Committee and sat with employers"?
"Had we not done so they were like lambs to the slaughter, cursing and swearing and getting themselves sacked". Shocked, I looked at him. I couldn't believe what I was hearing. "Why didn't you refuse to sit with employers and discipline Dockers, and what give you the right to do so".

He laughed. And said "You tried that". Shocked I looked at him and said: "Had they stayed on strike and not went back after three days, that scheme would've been thrown out".

"Look" he said, "Me and the chairman stopped plenty from being sacked and I never sacked anybody, but in the end it was useless cause they sacked us all'. Yeah, I retorted," Because you had no contract of employment". Disgusted I got off the bus. A few weeks later my brother gave me a copy of North Belfast News which highlighted a disgusting story about the Union Chairman {not the Judas Goat} the one who came after him. He was in a Belfast Court for abusing a young girl.

I brought the paper into Dublin with me. Outside Trinity College I asked a bus inspector did he know my old friend, he did, so I gave him the North Belfast News and asked him to give to Mickey. This was to show him the calibre of the man who was leading the Dockers and who allowed Jim Austin, the ex chairman to sell out and join the employers.

In1973 in the days before my sacking by the Union and Employers Court, by letter and phone calls I pleaded with the Union and ICTU to send someone to observe The Union and Employers Court in action - but no-one ever came. Obviously they knew all about it - and agreed with it.

After I was sacked I lambasted the Union and ICTU about the betrayal of trade unionism at Belfast Docks. I also wrote to every newspaper in Ireland asking how the most famous trade union in the world could betray its founders and align itself with the Belfast Employers. While I was treated with scorn by the Union {see letters} and ignored by ICTU, somewhere my barbs were hitting home. In an attempt to regain some credibility the Union leadership {after I was sacked} appointed Paddy Devlin, ex politician from the first Stormont Assembly - to oversee the Belfast Docks.

Normally this would have been a good choice as the Stormont Assembly was closed down by 'Paisley' and Sectarian Religious Hatred prevailed.

While Paddy Devlin never agreed with the JDC and questioned its diabolical existence, he tried to get the Docks Committee to boycott it. *{without success}* He did do some good. One of his major successes was to picket the gates of Stormont Buildings demanding fair play for Dockers. Looking back 50 odd years, to be truthful Paddy Devlin tried his best but was parachuted in when the Docks, largely due to containers was on its knees.

my first play 'JUSTICE' which was directed by Paddy Devlin's son, Joe, was a success.
It was Funded by ACNI - toured NI and was in the Dublin and Belfast Theatre Festivals 1992, plus a week at the Tron in Glasgow.

Because of this I wanted my play about The Union at Belfast Docks, staged and was shocked at the hostility and brick walls I kept running up against. Not least from Joe Devlin who thought the villain in the play was his father. Nothing I said would convince him otherwise. This could be ascertained from the time-line, as his father didn't arrive at the Docks until after I was sacked by the Union and Employers Court.

Joe was adamant that his Dad's detractors would ignore this fact and destroy his good name. Although I often wonder if Joe had an ulterior motive - and the real reason is: - because he was trying to keep under wraps the fact - that he was Artistic Director of a theatre company that was closed down for corruption. As stated in their letter to me from DENI, {see letter} they fund the Northern Ireland Arts Council emphatically say , **"They ceased to fund Point Fields Theatre Company and have had no more dealings with the directors of the company"**.

The above, coupled with Joe Devlin protecting his father's good name led to the Director of the Civic Theatre in

Tallaght, Michael Barker Caven going silent? I had written to him regarding the censorship I'm encountering. He replied and gave a thorough analysis of why he thought I was encountering difficulty getting work staged, I.e the Far Right's influence. { *See his letter*}

However, to cut a long story short I met him for a coffee in Tallaght Theatre and we discussed my writing.

The only reference to Joe Devlin, whom he knew, was when he suggested The Tron Theatre in Glasgow as an outlet for my writing, as The Judas Goat would be right up their street. I mentioned that Joe had directed my play 'Justice' there. We parted on good terms and I promised to email him my play. Then - obviously after he had spoken to Joe he went incommunicado, both to my email's and phone calls, which to be honest I had been expecting.

A similar situation had occurred some years previous in Dublin. I was on a course with six others given by an American Professor - can't remember his name.

The aim of the course was to turn a previous work of art into a screenplay. At the first meeting we exchanged our work and were expected to give feedback at the second meeting. One of the woman I exchanged with had written a piece which to me was shocking. She had depicted a young girl of 14 falling in love with an older woman and them having an affair. This was told in glowing sensuous romantic terms.

I told her in no uncertain terms that this was child abuse and she couldn't expect this to be tuned into a film. The term used today is grooming. We had heated words and I told her it was crap. Highly indignant she shouted "my writing is not crap".
I agreed, but said "what you are depicting is crap and illegal". In the language of today this behaviour is called 'grooming'.

She reported me to the Tutor claiming that I was homophobic and wanted me put off the course. He disagreed and suggested that she change the subject matter of her screenplay - which she did. I had no idea that she was gay. I'm not anti-gay or anti anything - except child abuse. This woman has since had several screenplays made into films - but not the 'Crap' one. No doubt our confrontation has done the rounds with her friends - with her own 'twist' on it.

A few years back I was blanked by an Artist who was an Aosdana member. I can't recall how I heard of him, but I contacted him and we met for a coffee. He was astounded at the censorship I'm experiencing - and he promised to do something about it. He asked me, had I tried the oldest Theatre in Dublin, Smock Alley and its director. I replied that I had and related how that director had offered me four dates for 'The Grandeur of Delusions' and after I accepted them he went silent.

He was astounded at this because this Director 'is a personal friend of his', and in fact he was meeting him that very night. Delighted, I asked him to ascertain why the silence happened, and to relate this information to me so - at the very least I would know what the worst of the gossip about me was. He assured me this was the least he would do.

We got on so well that we went to his house where he gave me some videos of his work. I was amazed at his latest project. He had travelled to Mexico and contacted the parents of numerous young women who had been kidnapped and murdered in the Desert. From a photo of the young person he would paint a portrait of them and present it to her parents. I was blown away with this. Anyway, We shook hands and as we parted he said, and I quote: "You've made a friend".

I smiled and said: "You will be like all the rest when the gossip gets to you - you will not speak to me again". Which he denied would ever happen. I pointed out to him, that "The Arts since the Bard's time went against the status quo - but now the status quo rules the Arts. When I again spoke to him he refused to relate what the director of Smock Alley, but hinted at some things.

Below are two letters, just a sample of the many open letters that I've posted on linkedin in a [so far] vain attempt to get the powers that be, and the silent Free Press to behave Democratically... in this so called Democracy. Obviously they do their masters bidding and keep secret the dictatorship of the Wealthy, in the Arts. The Irish are lauded around the world for their tenacity to endure whatever is thrown at them. However, it's a terrible indictment of successive Irish Governments - that Ireland is 'stage-management' by Wealthy Corruption.

This allows... in the present day the corruption of Connolly and Larkin's Union and the censoring of the hardships and deaths suffered by Asbestos stricken Irish People. That the Powers that be have also taken over every aspect of the Arts and Irish Life, is testimony to how much they've been Corrupted. Our rulers have managed within Ireland to create a superstructure of two separate but indigenous Irish Peoples, the very wealthy and the very poor.

The struggling people, in the squeezed middle between these two extremes, who get up early and pay their taxes, are penalised from every direction. While paying thousands in PAYE and child care - are forced to emigrate so they can afford to have a family and a home of their own. For years successive Irish governments, to create demand in the 'free market' stopped building Social Housing.

This was to create a Utopia for house building where the large building firms, whose owners, inhabitants of the 'Dublin 4'... who build everything and charge what they like for houses.

With their money-mad ethos many used the worst and cheapest of materials - and all they did was create sub-standard houses and apartment buildings. These were bought by desperate people - who after a few years were put out of them because of dangerous defects. The evicted people have no-where to live but they must still pay the mortgage on their falling down house or apartment?

Homelessness is a scourge in Ireland and Vulture Funds hoover up whole newly built estates and charge what they like in rent.

AN OPEN LETTER TO THE TAOISEACH AND HYPOCRITE LEO VARADKAR

Hello leo,
You were quite right to raise the wrongdoings and cover ups of the Catholic Church with the Pope, but did the old saying, 'people in glass houses shouldn't throw stones' - not occur to you.

You know, you're as guilty as the Pope in covering up what you don't want exposed. Do you and Arts Minister Josepha Madigan actually believe the gossip that is circulating about me, or was it just expedient to censor my play for your friends and backers? Either way, you both obviously collude in the cover up because I've written to you both many times but have gotten nowhere.

This letter will send the gossip-mongers and Arts Minister into overdrive - in exactly the same manner which caused her to censor and delete her [short lived] helpful post on Linkedin.

[See my earlier post] Did a wealthy member of the elite or a Siptu Official, whose salary reads like a telephone number, whisper, that I'd written a play about the Belfast Docks entitled 'The Judas Goat' and it had to be censored at all cost.

An early draft is on my profile page.
Leo, at the Docks I never considered myself anything other than an ordinary worker who wanted a fair day's pay for a fair day's work, but due to the dictates of corruption from head office in Dublin and ICTU, this could never be the case.

When I objected to the abject Cronyism and sell out behaviour of the Union, I suffered for it. The working conditions were terrible with no washing facilities whatsoever - and a filthy canteen left over from the War which was often miles from where we worked. I never considered myself a whistle-blower and just wanted the union ran like a trade union and not like the Union in 'On the Waterfront'. You can see the proof of this from my 1970's letters to the Union and ICTU.

Leo For fifty years I've been trying to tell Truth about the Union at Belfast Docks. At the start I tried to get the Union to behave like Larkin's union - but it persisted with corruption and persecuted its own members with heavy monetary fines and ordered them to discharge Asbestos without protection to save the employers money. They railroaded and sacked anyone, like myself who refused to comply with the illegal Union and Employers Court. The Court's official title was 'The Joint Disciplinary Committee'. As you well know Leo, Documentary proof of this 'Court' is on www.siptupresidentjackoconnorexposed.com - along with many letters from O'Connor and Siptu.

One in particular stands out, which you choose to ignore, it's a letter from O'Connor's own solicitor John O'Neill of Thompson McClures, telling him that what I said about the Belfast Branch was indeed true.

However, he unbelievably insists that 'a trade union sacking its own members, while not being an ideal situation, is not corruption'. Siptu for their part and for self-preservation have successfully covered up this travesty of trade unionism.

Now aged Seventy One - this is my final attempt to get someone, albeit a hypocrite like yourself to live up to your own Truthful and Insightful words to the Pope. Did I see a tinge of redness appear on your face?

When I joined the Union at fifteen years of age the cronyism and sycophantism of the Union towards the employers was apparent, and I objected to it. I see the same cronyism and sycophantic behaviour from your government towards the Homeless. Actually, the play I've recently finished is set in a hostel for the homeless and shows the Truth about the modern day Living in Ireland.

Leo, you boast about transparency and openness in your government – yet not only refuse to expose corruption but by silence actively collude in covering it up. Please watch the UTV video 'Death Trap on the Docks' which highlighted the Asbestos Scandal.

Enough material was recorded for another two programmes. However, shortly afterwards 'Insight' and the investigative reporters were shut down.

Leo, one of the main gossip spreaders is a theatre director who directed my first play – and I publicly sacked him for changing my words and the direction of the play. However, I relented when 'in tears' he said his career would be finished even before it got started and promised to stick to the script. Which he did not do.

My reason for bringing this up is, this director, like the gossip-mongers has an ulterior motive. His father for a time was the leading trade unionist at Belfast Docks and the director thinks 'The Judas Goat' is about his father. This is not the case and I told him so, but to no avail.

However, his father wrote an autobiography, which he typed for him and the Belfast Docks is never mentioned.
This is surprising, because at the time of sectarian tension he led the Dockers on a march and picketed Stormont. Obviously, his father was catapulted in as the Union Organiser when the Docks was on its last legs to try and sort it out. No doubt this was because of my letters to head office and ICTU - about the betrayal of the union chairman changing sides... and were as scandalised as I was at the behaviour of the Union.

I was wrong. While this was the first time in Labour History anywhere in the world that an employer was a member of a trade Union, it was just to keep a lid on this scandal.

If I am the vile and disgusting person that the gossips say I am why will they not prove it?
Leo, you boast of 'our free press and investigative journalists', yet the supposed free press will not report on this scandal. Just who are they covering up for?

A local Artistic director send me a long letter, he understood everything I said, what I was enduring - and the uphill struggle to get new work staged. We eventually met had a coffee and a pleasant chat. I'd previously send him a play, and had a play staged at his theatre before he was appointed. We spoke of Joe Devlin and he didn't know he'd been to the Tron, Glasgow with my play 'Justice'. I said I'd like to make contact with him again. To this end I sent him a play and asked him to forward it to him. Usually I received a reply by return but have got only silence. What is being said about me?

Leo, you know what the gossip about me is, because Josepha Madigan has told you. Will you please tell me so I can repudiate it. Or alternatively ask the 'Free Press' why they won't report on the scandal of a Trade Union persecuting and sacking its own members… and ordering them to a terrible death with Asbestos. If you watch the Utv Asbestos video you'll see Billy Browne who has been diagnosed with it in his left lung. Fighting back tears he tells how he watched his two brothers die from it. You will also see the widow of a brother heartbroken, tell how she watched her husband lose his dignity and die an agonising death.

Leo, you are a medical doctor! Will you for God's sake stop covering up and put into practice what you condemned the Pope for.
Why will you not expose the cover up by Siptu and the Arts - and invite Billy Brown to the Oireachtas and record his recollections! This man knows a lot more about the corruption of the Union at Belfast Docks that I do. Leo, unlike the scandal givers I put my name to everything I say.

TELL JOSEPHA MADIGAN, A SILENT GOVERNMENT IS A CORRUPT GOVERNMENT.

This most diabolical aspect of Dictatorship is when the powers that be {the Wealthy} censor the free press. In countries around the world Journalists have been murdered for reporting undemocratic practices in their own countries. In Ireland however censorship is gleefully applied by the leaders of the 'free press'. This is personified by Fintan O'Toole and past and present editors of Irish Times.

All other so-called newspapers do the same thing. While the deniers of the Truth who refuse to report on the Belfast Docks scandal are not in danger of losing their lives - they ignore the fact that ex Belfast Dockers and an unknown number of Belfast Citizens are dying because of Asbestos? The Cowards refuse to print the Truth and put in jeopardy their own jobs. They know who to expose and who to leave alone.

If the refusal by SIPTU and ICTU {on the orders of the Wealthy} to take action over the Belfast Docks Scandal is exposed - workers in the Republic will see that they are just tools of the Wealthy.
Patricia King knows about this since at least 2007, when she put her arm around my shoulders and said "You have made your point". What hypocrisy from the 'then' leader of the Trade Union movement in Ireland.

As usual Irish newspapers will report on events many thousands of miles away and refuse to report on local events. That said an important matter which involved two retired Judges - Frank Clarke and Peter Kelly and their appointment to the 'Dubai International Financial Centre' raised some consternation. Several of the normally silent censoring newspapers ran articles about these appointments, which had caused consternation with several Law Professors. They claimed that these appointments could bring Irish Law into disrepute - which it obviously did.

The professors of law questioned whether they should have taken these positions, because of the repressive regimes in vogue in Dubai - and one commenter actually said: "It is a little bit unethical." *How observant of him.* To cut to the chase, both the ex Judges saw the folly of their ways and did indeed resign.

My reason for raising this matter is because Judge Kelly has form in this regard. As related earlier, I told him to his face in 2010 at a conference called to discuss the changes in the Defamation Laws - that the Union, when still ITGWU in Belfast ordered Dockers to discharge Asbestos without protection.

And I was sacked by the Union and Employers Court because I would not do so.

My point in relating this - is not just to show the Hypocrisy of Judge Kelly who refused to come to the aid of Belfast Dockers - but to show the Hypocrisy of the "Free Press". They steadfastly refused to report on the Belfast Dockers and Citizens breathing in this Deadly Dust... to protect the Wealthy Dublin Importers. However, there's a more important note which should be noted.

The Professors of Law who {rightly} condemned the Judges appointments - refused to acknowledge or act on the Belfast Docks Scandal. Would some fair-minded person, please comment upon this cover up?

Obviously, by their actions these Law Professors believe in the Rule of Law - so the diabolical Union and Employers Court that sacked Belfast Dockers should have been the next legal corruption they exposed. The facts of the Union and Employers Court are on the web which no doubt these Law Lecturers checked out, so why do they remain silent?

Why do they not expose the wealthy Employers who sent Belfast Dockers and people to a terrible and avoidable Asbestos Death? Surely they haven't been bought by so-called Free Press who exposed the two Judges... or the Wealthy with an axe to grind. I specifically ask this question of Professor, Donncha OConnell NUI- but he must still be away on holiday.

I have also named several solicitors, newspapers and journalists and accused them of covering up corruption, so why will they not sue me for defaming them?

The reason they'll say is because I have no money, which is true, however, facebook, twitter and linkedin have plenty. As proven by Miriam O'Callaghan when she sued facebook. Setting aside money for a moment - if what I'm saying is 'not true' they would have me hauled through the Courts and Jailed. The active word here is 'Courts'.

They know in a Court of Law I will claim "Justification and fair comment" this is what stops them. In an attempt to get them to take action I put an open letter to Fintan O'Toole and Irish Times, on linkedin but to no avail.

CHAPTER FOURTEEN

I think I was expecting too much in the form of Artistic Expression from the 'led by the nose' Theatre People in Dublin. Corruption rules the performing arts and silence about wrong-doing is not only tolerated but is buried deep. No doubt, because of hardship in trying to make a living from the arts - speaking out is the last thing anyone will do. Silence rules everything and everyone who practices it.

While this behaviour is an aberration to the way Theatre People, {going back as far as Shakespeare} are supposed to behave. I.e. gutsy, feisty and free-thinking? In the 'Bards' day, lampooning the foibles and misbehaviour of the aristocracy was 'grist to the mill' of Theatre People.

How things have changed in 400 years. Today no-one dares criticize the Theatre elite - and while they won't lose their heads they will definitely lose their work.
In a modern-day Irish context the deniers of Drama and Truth self-censor on the whispered demands of the Wealthy. By a process of osmosis this infects every Theatre Company. If they want 'grants' theatre people must avoid controversy's and stage wort that won't rock the censorship boat.

Genuine Theatre People with an opinion keep their heads down, knowing, that while Dictatorship is in vogue there's nothing they can do about it. Not only does this undermine Theatre it makes a mockery of Irish Democracy. While the adherents to 'The Truth' keep quiet and try to scratch a living from their Art, not all succeed and leave. They're sickened by the pretence.

What's needed in Ireland is a genuine Trade Union to represent the Arts, based on the teachings of James Connolly and Jim Larkin, where Artists don't feel the need to 'silence themselves' to get work. Instead their Democratic Trade Union… if ever established, will ensure that speaking out benefits everyone and that doing so will enhance their profession - by making it free and equal. However, if this ever came near fruition the Wealthy and the arts council would soon put a stop to it.

The founding of Connolly and Larkin's Union - ITGWU, pre-dates the founding of the Republic. It was established to protect uneducated Dockers and Carters from the inhuman slave conditions they had to labour under.

Not for one minute am I suggesting that Artists are unskilled, actually it's the opposite, but they are working under the exact same conditions as Workers endured a hundred years ago. Today the Wealthy manage and control Artists who are without a genuine workers union to support them… and these conditions are what inspired Connolly and Larkin to found the ITGWU.

The fact that the a previous Arts Minister, Josepha Madagian, censored me on linkedin - proves all I maintain. Maybe Josepha will now come clean and disclose who told her to censor me? Actually if she did this she would doing the job she was elected to do. And furthermore - she would guarantee herself a life-long seat in the Dail - but will she have moral fibre and principles to break ranks and speak out?

I have asked many times of legal people and in particular Charlie Flanagan when he was Justice Minister "is censorship against the law"?

Needless to say I never received an answer. He knows as well as I do that any civilised society and free society access to a solicitor is a paramount obligation. The fact that I can't get a solicitor to represent me show and proves that this is not a Democracy. I have exposed this on linkedin, in an open letter to both law societies - and have been ignored.

This is how else can the Wealthy control legitimate dissent. Why are the Professors of Law not challeging this abject corruption in a Court of Law?
The wealthy and the "unelected" in the Dail and the Arts Council control Theatre asnd ensure that nothing is staged that would upset their contrived Status Quo. Artistic Directors, the law and media all censor the shocking revelations in my play 'The Judas Goat'? Obviously the wealthy believe that their skulduggery will never be discovered. I'm sure this gladdens the heart the nodding dogs, in Dublin City Council, the Arts Council who jump through hoops and maintain the cover up.

Artistic Directors keep quiet... and even if they become famous know to keep quiet and not rock the boat. However, maybe I'm being too hard on them? While they may get to the pinnacle of success by remaining 'silent' on 'Theatre Practices' - had they known that Belfast Dockers and People endured an agonising deaths from Asbestos poisoning, I'm sure they'd have spoken up. Likewise, hopefully the Belfast members of Aosdana will now demand action on this scandal.

With the so called openness on the web, for the past number of years I have *not* been on-line at home. Instead I use one of the many Libraries that proliferate in Dublin. The reason for denying myself this most normal and most basic of functions - is - because I was hacked. Several postings on so-called freedom of speech web-sites were attributed to myself.

These held contradictory opinions to my to own. I've also received emails acknowledging complaints I've supposedly made to several bodies - when I have never made such a complaint to them.
So for many years I have not been on line at home. This is so no-one can accuse me of saying something when I have no access to the web - and only being on-line in a Public Library gives me deny- ability, as they are festooned with cameras and prowling security men. When I wish to say something or complain about the corruption and Censorship by government I say it publicly and put my name to it – on linkedin and facebook and twitter.

Several years ago twitter closed down my account @sackedbymyunion because someone abroad interfered with it and I lost my followers. Why they did this I have no idea but they gave me a number for a new account which I sparingly use, although many of my linkedin articles are on it.

A while back I was annoyed for a short time when I heard that Fintan O'Toole has been awarded an honorary doctorate in Law, by the University of Galway. By them doing so, I believed the University had denigrated the Law by honouring a dyed in the wool hypocrite - who uses the media and the Arts to uphold censorship. To this end O'Toole, along with Irish Times has for a long time has made a mockery of investigative journalism and wielded unlimited power over the Irish 'newspapers'.

It seemed, to add insult to injury - NUIG professor of theatre and drama studies Patrick Lonergan had credited O'Toole with undeserved praise.

He stated in his address, that O'Toole was "preparing the reader for a Global Present - where all political journalists require the skill of an astute theatre critic.

And that this journalist has demonstrated - how power functioned through the creation of 'alternative facts' and how art and life illuminate' each other".

What gobbledygook! I thought this professor had inhaled too much of his students 'wacky tabacky', then I studied what he had really said, and the penny dropped. This 'over the top' fawning over O'Toole was utter nonsense - reminiscent of the King and his 'magical suit of clothes' It became obvious that this was an absolute set up. Lonergan also claimed that O'Toole has shown how "Politics is inherently Theatrical with alternative facts". I near choked laughing at this.

He really put the boot into O'Toole by equating him with the "Theatrical" and ALTERNATIVE FACTS? A blind man can see that there is no such thing - Facts are Facts. The brave professor had just accused O'Toole of telling Blatant Lies - and he... had to grin and bear it. Obviously the professor was referring to O'Toole's silence on the government and Theatre's behind the scenes Censorship.

By his choice of words the professor really exposed O'Toole's Right Wing Politics. Tongue in cheek he was giving OToole, 'Mother Theresa like praise'. I thought to myself this Professor of Theatre is clued in to what O'Toole is really doing? So... that by the unwarranted 'Praise' when he falls, it will be from a great height.
That famous quote attributed to US president Abraham Lincoln who came from a log cabin - comes to mind. "You can fool all of the People some of the time - and some of the People all of the time - but you cannot fool all of the People all of the

time".

Obviously Professor Lonergan realised, that while O'Toole was also awarded the European Press Prize and is the Leonard L Millberg visiting lecturer at Princeton University, in the US - he is an outright phoney. His obvious intelligence has become severally corrupted by a Right-Wing Wealthy viewpoint - and must be exposed and stopped. Thus, I believe, Professor lonergan and NUIG, devised a strategy to draw attention to the real person behind O'Toole's mask of Liberalism?

By giving him an honorary 'Law degree' in such a fawning manner and over the top language, they 'set him up and 'suckered him in'.

By accepting the award, O'Toole has proven he's no man of conviction and obviously wallows in the glory of believing - he has really fooled these silly democratic fools.
O'Toole, by ignoring the corruption of Connolly and Larkin's Union by the Wealthy, copper fastens his Right Wing attitudes and shows his true colours.

He's a past master at manipulating the truth to suit those of Irish Times readers. He and John Devitt did exactly this when they fooled the audience at the Transparency International Conference.
This was just after I had just exposed the scandal of the Asbestos Deaths and the Dictatorial behaviour of the Union and Employers Court at Belfast Docks.

His exposure at NUIG was badly needed and was indeed Poetic Justice in Action.

If and when the Truth dawns upon those who awarded him the European Prize - and the Princeton Residency - under false pretences-they will have to withdraw them. Then - NUIG can then make a meal of rescinding his undeserved honours. I fully intend to send Professor Lonergan the proof of O'Tooles cover up of the Belfast Docks scandal, i.e my play - 'The Judas Goat' - and the Book, The Judas Goats.

However, he can see the documentary proof of the Union and Employers Court on www.siptupresidentjackoconnorexposed.com I wish to personally thank him for doing the Dying and dead Belfast Dockers and people, plus Democracy a great and genuine service.

If I may be so bold, as to offer advice to the Professor and the excellent plans of NUIG. To speed up the exposure of this hypocrite - they could make a video on his life and achievements invite him to a Public Screening in the University. Then, at the end before the applause dies down show the Belfast Docks video, Death Trap On the Docks, which is available on youtube - and ask him to comment.

How would he get out of that? He could not deny the Truth about what he and the Irish Times, cover up? When O'Toole is shamed and his scurrilous activities exposed, the Domino Effect will take place and all his other undeserved awards will be withdrawn. Also, his one time editor at Irish Times, and partner in censorship, Geraldine Kennedy, should not escape unscathed. She Lectures at University of Limerick, { *on journalism of all things*} and must also fall on her sword. Actually, she could also be invited to the O'Toole screening.

I congratulate NUIG and academia for taking matters into their own hands. The honourable Professor of Theatre and his University could not ignore the hypocrisy any longer. In awarding the Law Degree to O'Toole - they obviously got fed up waiting for his, and Kennedy's fellow journalists to break ranks and expose their cover up of corruption. This is an indictment and example of how afraid the Unfree Press in Ireland really is. For this exposure the Belfast Dead - plus the descendants of the men and women who founded the Union and fought for Irish Freedom, will be eternally grateful.

Actually come to think of it, every university in Ireland should grant O'Toole and Geraldine Kennedy, Mock honorary degrees. They could have in their university campus, Statues of them and John Devitt - and name them 'The three Liars'. Then on Rag Days make life-size puppets of them and parade them around their towns - with signs hanging from their long noses, saying "I can't answer that"?

What... if every University in the country made a clay statute, named, 'The Hypocrite of the Year', and it was awarded to the worst example of a journalist, lawyer, public figure or TD who had sold out their supposed principles. The first joint winners could well be, these three sycophants, although they would have a lot of competition from the Human Rights People.

Small plastic replicas of the 'honoured hypocrites' could be sold on Rag Day to raise money for charities. To be completely fair, the person "so honoured" should be allowed to repudiate the shaming of themselves and allowed to take questions on their hypocrisy.

Obviously Patrick Lonergan, NUIG professor of theatre and drama studies, is the beating heart of theatre and protest at Galway University. His devising of a new take on an old strategy i.e. 'give them enough rope and they'll hang themselves' is valid now as when Shakespeare said it?

In fact, every debating society could have a competition on who was the biggest hypocrite of the year? Who knows, a miniature of the Trilogy of Hypocrites statute could even up on University Challenge.

Below is a letter which I sent to Joe Duffy - he, of the famous 'Talk to Joe Radio programme - and what a surprise, he won't talk to me. Has the great Joe Duffy also being bought off as well? The answer must be yes. I await with bated breath for an invitation to speak on his radio program.

However, even if he agreed to a debate with me, will his, hypocrisy and that of the Three Liars, stop RTE from allowing it to happen. See below a letter I sent to him.

Dear Joe Duffy, I really enjoyed your programme about inequality in the education system in Ireland. However, you have steadfastly refused to expose my case against Jack O'Connor and SIPTU. And not a word about the book I left into RTE for you. I will state here that I went to work at Belfast Docks aged 16 and experienced the worst of the casual system policed by supposed followers of Larkin in ITGWU. Because of their dictatorial attitude in fining Belfast Dockers large sums of money, the Union Committee were easily persuaded to join the Belfast Branch with the employers.

To cut a long story short, after I was sacked by the Union and Employers Court I wrote my first play 'The Judas Goat'. This is about the Union and Employers joining forces against the Belfast Dockers. I also included a scene showing the Union Chairman ordering the Dockers to discharge Asbestos, which SIPTU is covering up to this day. The so called 'free press, are using the defamation laws as an excuse so 'not' to report on this scandal and thus are able to censor my Docks play and all my writing.

Also censoring 'The Judas Goat' is the Arts Council and Dublin City Council, This can be caustically viewed as simply 'oiling the wheels of industry' so the Right Wing government will look beneficially upon them for not rocking the Asbestos Boat. However the passage of Fifty years does nothing to alleviate the injustice of what transpired, especially to the dead and dying Belfast Dockers, and People. The Union Chairman ordered the Dockers to discharge Asbestos without protection, to save the employers money.

However, it goes much deeper that that? Anyone with sense knows full well that a Trade Union cannot join with Employers and persecute and sack its own members – but this is exactly what happened.

Not only is this against Trade Union Law but is against the law of the land. This Union and Employers Court was named, "The Joint Disciplinary Committee", thus dispelling any notion that the Union was on the side of the Dockers, and the only time in Trade Union History that a Trade Union disciplined and sacked its own members for and with the Employers.

However, while being utterly deplorable the sycophantic behaviour of the Union pales into insignificance when compared to the "Free Press" - led by such illustrious organs as Irish Times and Sunday Times. They contradict their 'reason for being' and cover up the corruption and cowardice of Jack O'Connor... and the leadership of SIPTU. Obviously, these two so-called newspapers [and the rest who follow suit] know exactly what they do. By protecting the reputations of SIPTU they are denigrating, and making a laughing stock of themselves, as supposed independent purveyors of truth, honour and justice?
Hugh Murphy

JOE DUFFY COULD ALSO BE A CONTENDER FOR THE HYPOCRITE OF THE YEAR STATUE.

A while back, in a Saturday's Irish Times {it's a different paper from Sunday Times, the News Review had an articles written by David McWilliams and Fintan O'Toole. I have personally raised the Belfast Docks scandal with them both - {in front of large audiences} and they refused to do anything about the cover up by SIPTU and ICTU. In O'Tooles article it would be hard imagine a more sly rendition of obfuscation to deny the Asbestos Truth - than that which his article contains.

Beneath a photograph of the German Writer Heinrich Boll and his Irish Journal - O'Toole's article has the heading: WE MUST ALL LEARN THE ART OF POLITICAL DENTRISTY and below this heading, is the by-line **"THERE IS NO SAFE DOSE OF FASCISM"**. O'Toole never printed a
truer word, I just wish he believed it - and he continues to quote Heinrich Boll. "It is in ordinary conversations, at work, in the cafe, on the bus, in the pub that toxic ideas are checked".

O'Toole relates how Boll was conscripted into the German army and was wounded four times - later he won the Noble Prize for Literature and spent his summer holidays in Ireland. O'Toole relates how Boll tells his friend Padric, that Hitler, was indeed a very bad man and just didn't go too far. Boll's wife agrees and encourages him to "pull out the rotten teeth of fascism".
Actually, due entirely to the deliberate blindness of O'Toole and his wealthy friends I have been put in a similar position to Boll.

I have been trying for 50 years to convince the Irish and brain-washed sceptics, about the existence of the Corrupt Union and Employers Fascism towards Belfast Dockers, but its like talking to a brick wall.

These educated people cannot and will not overcome their slave mentality and admit the Truth - even when presented with undeniable documentary facts from the Union and Employers Court. The truth of the matter is, that they are convinced of the corruption and censorship exits in Ireland, but know better than to admit it.

Time after time, in Pubs, Cafes and on Buses, I expose the details of the illegal corruption that rules Ireland but for self-preservation these enlightened people will not accept that disgusting Fascism controlled by the Wealthy exists in Ireland, today. And that this stems from the Asbestos Deaths in Belfast and from the censoring of my Belfast Play, 'The Judas Goat' Naturally this is ridiculed by intellectuals like Historian Diramid Ferrater, for to accept it his life will be censored and would go down the tubes. I wonder does O'Toole ever imagine what Heinrich Boll would Boll think of his abject corruption?

The proof is there for all to see. Dying Belfast Dockers and an unknown number of Belfast Citizens bear testimony to that. While the Union and Employers did not kill as many people as the SS, the very fact it ordered Dockers to discharge Asbestos without protection - makes them worse than the SS. I say worse because the SS never claimed to be a force for good, and on the side of workers. Besides the Asbestos the basic fact is… that it was the benefits that Connolly and Larkin's Union achieved for workers that made the Union a prime target for the Wealthy… and they succeeded in destroying it. In relation to the dangers of deadly Asbestos Dust, the Belfast Union chairman was corrupted, and knew full well of the dangers. Yet changed sides and ordered Dockers to discharge it or be sacked.

Besides this, the union and employers allowed Asbestos to be blown all over Belfast, and couldn't care less how many it killed. This is an undeniable fact, however, Fintan O'Toole does not "speak out" - like Bolls wife, instead he continues to pretend that the Employers and Union at Belfast Docks 'did not go bit too far'… He continues to deny the Truth that's before his eyes - that the Union in Belfast **did** go too far. O'Toole is not alone.

The catalogue of great names and independent thinkers In Irish Society, to whom I've informed of this atrocity is mind-blowing - and yet all have been fooled... willingly into silence.

This blindness by O'Toole and his people - is equal to Holocaust and Famine, deniers. Why and how are these Intelligent People fooled?

What lies are they and the Human Rights People in Ireland being told?

This example gives an inkling into the thinking of the Wealthy and their Lackeys. I just wish they'd take the advice of Boll's wife. Would some champion of Jurisprudence tell me how I can circumvent this Legal Atrocity?

I founded the Heart and Soul Theatre Company in to stage my play 'Daddy', which is a play about two sisters, survivors of child abuse. This play was staged in the large hall of the Teachers Club in Dublin, for five nights. Subsequently, the following year we staged 'The Grandeur of Delusions'. This play is a two hander and is about an Alcoholic interacting with him-self by talking to his delusion, a lovely young girl.

We had a short tour with 'The Grandeur of Delusions' ending up in the west of Ireland. My producer had also booked four nights in the Mick Lally Theatre. However this Theatre emailed our producer and informed her - that: "They had held a meeting and those dates were no longer available. Several years before Druid had asked me in writing not to tell anyone they refused to stage 'The Judas Goat', which I ignored.

Obviously the refusal to stage 'Delusions' was on the orders of Garry Hynds, and she took her revenge. I know there are decent Theatres in Ireland, just like there are decent reporters in the Irish Media, but the threat of being sacked for writing the Truth, or in Theatres, having funding withdrawn for staging a play that's not 'approved of', has stopped them. And thus - forcing them to engage in the most deplorable Act of Censorship?

In the homeless crisis, the Irish Times asked for people experiencing difficulties to contact them and printed their stories. "The responders speak about their fear and anxiety about renting, in a country that offers relatively little security of tenure and about the particular difficulty of finding an affordable place to live. In working class areas, homes for sale are snapped up by landlord's who outbid ordinary people, and rent them out for an astounding price, most of which is paid for by rent allowance.

This is just what the Wealthy in Fine Gael and Fine Fail wanted and knew would happen. This deceit forces people in employment, who can afford to buy, {whether they want to or not} - because the mortgage is a lot less than the exorbitant rent. But the ruling elite were too clever for their own good and it rebounded on them. Their money-making policies resulted in massive homelessness. At the next General Election they will be ignored in the Polls.

Many voters, who for years wanted to be like them - have been stung badly by their policies. They have seen that 'Greed is good', but only for the Wealthy, who get Richer while the poor get Poorer. Recent governments have welcomed Vulture Funds into Ireland to increase their profits and to divert attention from their own vulture like activities. As usual PAYE workers fund the life style of Wealthiest in Ireland.

Many others are also considering emigrating to find somewhere affordable to live. The Irish Times supports the institutions that foster these conditions, yet hypocritically - by reporting on them give the impression that they abhor them. Nothing could be further from the truth as reflected in an article by David McWilliams, which has the the by-line, **"EXPANSION OF THE MIDDLE CLASS IS IRELAND'S GREATEST FEAT"**.

Like a pathetic capitalist puppet he sings the praises of the Irish Wealthy.

He points out 'rightly' that, "It might be deeply unfashionable to champion the growth of the civic bourgeoisie, but the expansion of the middle class is a profoundly positive accolade". Anyone reading this nonsense knows from what perspective and for whom he is writing? He continues in this vein, stating, "In contrast to many western countries that are seeing their middle class shrink, the data tells us something we know already, when we compare our lives with our 'parents lives' and their parents lives: Ireland's bourgeoisie is in rude health". In that he is entirely right because it's dominated by lies from the Wealthy. He should try visiting the Homeless. In true journalistic fashion and to get the Reader onto his side – he claims that he's going against the tide of popular thinking, and makes this diabolical claim?

"Whether it is cool or not to admit, the middle class provides political ballast to a country, preventing lurches to the extremes. This is not a bad thing in a world with its increasingly demagogic flavour".

What madness caused him to write this? Again, he should try visiting the homeless, or children living in B&B's? Then the reason for this nonsense becomes clear. He states, "In international economics there's an expression for the collapse of the middle class. It is known as the Brazilificatioin of a country.

Brazil {and Argentina} used to have large middle classes with secure stakes in society. The civic bourgeoisie became the target of the corrupt right and the ideological left so much so that over the last 50 years, the middle has been squeezed by left wing and right wing populists, leaving the country, oscillating from one extreme to the other".

What McWilliams is doing here associating the ordinary middle class with the extreme Wealthy I.e those, who look down their nose at homeless people - and nothing could be further from the truth. No ordinary middle class family with a few kids wants to see children made homeless. His next pro capital utterance is. "The story of Venezuela, where the greatest humanitarian disaster in the Americas is played out in front of our eyes, speaks for itself.

Unforgivably, the assault on the middle class in Venezuela has been entirely ideological driven". Again in true Journalistic fashion he states, that "Five million people have left in the past two years. To put that in context five million people fled Syria over ten years.

But crucially in Venezuela there is no war, just monumental mismanagement based on a class war in the country with the largest oil reserves in the world". It all becomes clear. McWilliams is roping in and including 'ordinary middle class people with the Ultra Wealthy, obviously to get support for them. He continually talks up the benefits of the wealthy middle class but he ignores the fact - that in Ireland the ordinary middle class are the ones being screwed the most by the Wealthy?

Up to now the the People in suburbia who wanted to own their own homes were used by the Wealthy to get their Cronies elected. The Cronies played up the 'unspoken difference' between bought houses and working class estates. But the 'Pendulum Swings' and they have gone too far. The 'Elected Puppets' in the Dail by running the country for the benefit of the Wealthy- and treating everyone with contempt have "united the People".

The ordinary middle class are now as in as much danger of becoming homeless - as their working class neighbours. They see it could easily happen to them. If they miss one mortgage payment their loan can be sold to a Vulture Fund, their repayments doubled and bye bye house.

What would McWilliams say if he was homeless? This is happening to lots of middle class couples who divorce - because of the strain of living in perpetual debt? He continues with his diatribe.

"So when we look around we can see that the massive expansion of the Irish middle class is something to be extremely proud of and it comes from economic growth. Over the past thirty years - that is roughly the second half of the lifetime of the Republic - the growth rate of this country has been phenomenal". It surely has - but only for the extremely Wealthy.

I wonder why he didn't include the abuse of the Belfast Dockers, the Asbestos Deaths, the betrayal of Trade Unionism, in the growth rate? Why does he not mention the corruption and cover up by the Wealthy at Belfast Docks and the sell out of Trade Union Principles, as a "Positive?

This happened in his own home town and he can't claim 'ignorance' - because I personally told him this, to his face. He also negates to mention the plight one house Landlords? If he had a thousand houses he'd pay a pittance,but with one house he pays half of what he gets in rent to the government and the other half goes on maintenance.

For many single house landlords with an old property, it actually costs them money to rent it out. This is why when the government lifted the eviction ban that they're selling up. The consequence of this is... that thousands of children become homeless and have to live in B&B's?

David needs to get the Blinkers off and see Ireland as it really is - a Paradise for the Wealthy.
On the very next page to David's in that edition is a report from Kitty Holland entitled, A TALE OF TWO CITIES - POVERTY IN BELFAST AND LIMERICK.

Northern Ireland, where he comes from, "had the highest rate of child poverty in the U K and concerns are growing that more than 100,000 of the poorest families in receipt of benefits face a cliff edge of falling incomes from March 2020". No doubt David refuses to accept these facts and like a good little accountant will quote figures to sustain his arguments and may even claim that's a different country up there.

I wonder did David even bother to turn the page and read what Kitty Holland had to say about Limerick. It's not that David doesn't know the truth - it is that David doesn't want to know the truth? He should read her article which gives a true reflection on the under-class who are downtrodden by his attitudes and those of the Wealthy. While David and the Wealthy will talk up how great this country is - they see only what they want to see. This gives the lie to his Utopia.

He and they should go into an A&E {not a private hospital} and they'll think they are in Vietnam at the height of the war. While McWilliams is correct in saying, "Once the economy grows everything else grows from that. Without growth you can talk all you like about aspirations but nothing will ever be delivered".

No one is arguing with that fundamental truth - it is what the Wealthy do with this economic growth that is the problem?

Elected TD's "sock puppets" have been fooled for too long by the unelected puppets of the Wealthy into maintaining the status quo.

By hiding the truth they cover up for those who refuse to pay legitimate taxes on their Wealth - and hide it away in off shore accounts. Why do they not use it to build factories and create work to lift the poor out of poverty 'and' make a profit. It's the greed of the unfeeling and uncaring who have caused the poverty in Ireland by refusing to pay a 'just' tax on their Billions.

It seems that David has been to long with his spreadsheets to think objectively. Just how does the above statement about Brazil and Venezuela, tally with his lampooning of the Broadband fiasco? However, it tallies perfectly with my suggestion that he should run for the Dail.

Many elected TD's in the Dail have become involved in a Conspiracy of Silence. They will not speak out and point the finger at the mouth-pieces of the Wealthy. I do not make these charges lightly. The dead and dying Belfast Dockers and Citizens are proof positive of magnitude of this cover up. The veracity of what I say is contained in the documents at the end of this book. Truth, Justice and the Rule of Law in Ireland are at the beck and call of the Wealthy. They believe they are superior, vastly superior to the poor because of their money and believe they have a God given right to exploit the less fortunate.

Blinded by privilege they believe they have a right to exploit ordinary people for profit.
I use the word 'ordinary' to differentiate PAYE workers from the wealthy who will not pay tax. I don't believe there is such a thing as an "ordinary person" because every one of us is unique in our own way. If the Wealthy thought like this, they'd realise that given half a chance the so-called 'ordinary people'

people who never had the silver spoon in their mouths - are the backbone and the good people of Ireland.

The only ordinary people the Wealthy encounter are the hired help that clean their houses, and serve them in Luxury Hotels. They are truly aghast that the government puts homeless families in Hotels - believing that this brings down the tone of those establishments.

While they don't want to see children dying on the street, they don't ever want to encounter them in a hotel corridor either. Proof positive of their thinking is the fact they can ignore homeless children who don't even register on their conscience.Another bugbear of the Rich, is that asylum seekers are put up in holiday camps, and take over complete Hotels, when in one fell swoop they could deport the lot of them and solve the homeless problem.

This, obviously was before the war in Ukraine, which raises another question. Why are the Wealthy with their mansions and large estates not doing more to help? However, some Rich People have a conscience and have overcome their life of privilege.

They don't believe that money makes you happy' and hide their wealth by doing voluntarily work in Charities to help the less fortunate. This happens while most of their friends insist, "Many a good night has been ruined by beggars outside Theatres.

While this upstairs downstairs attitude prevails an unequal Ireland will remain the norm. Many Wealthy are not 'bad people', per se, but just ruined by money, privilege, and the pampered life style of their mothers and fathers. Most children of the Wealthy no matter in what country they reside - have inherited the snobbery and false belief, that money makes them better people? When the reverse is the case. What really surprises me is the Silence of the newspapers and why they will not expose the Union Hierarchy.

I believe, at least two of the Journalistic "champions of free speech" in Dublin are Eisenhower Fellows, and awarded, this honour for their courage in exposing wrongdoing. I wonder what happened to their principles? I don't know why they received this 'honour' - but I do know it wasn't for exposing Corruption in Ireland - or the elected being controlled by the unelected in the Dail? No doubt the mention of Belfast Docks has them reaching for the smelling salts.

In my condemnation of the media, i.e the upper echelons of RTE, the Irish Times and all newspapers - Fintan O'Toole stands out. He was Arts Editor for a long number of years and is supposedly a champion of Free Speech. However, he's proven, by ignoring SIPTU and the Wealthy corruption, he obviously has a deliberate blind spot where SIPTU is concerned.
A case in point is the now retired Jack O'Connor. While receiving a telephone number salary, and even after the membership rejected his advice, he was allowed to retire with his pension intact. This, despite the fact he covered up for the Wealthy by hiding the fact his own Union persecuted and sacked Belfast Dockers.

O'Connor well knows, avoiding Trade Union Principles {Re Belfast Docks} is not the same as breaking the law. The travesty of trade unionism is well known in the Dail through the cover up by Pat Rabbitte and his ilk. While the Labour Party prostituted its principles in covering
up for Pat Rabbitte they weren't going down the same route for Jack O'Connor.

The disgusting behaviour of these Union stalwarts is

compounded by the Irish Congress of Trade Unions. They also were corrupted by the Wealthy into covering up the Asbestos Scandal. This Deadly Dust was blown from Stormont Wharf towards Hollywood, Bangor and further afield. While from Sinclair Wharf it was blown in the other direction and covered the Shore Road, Whitehouse, Whiteabbey - and towards Carrickfergus. The dying Belfast Dockers and people infected by Asbestos - can rightly blame the greedy Irish millionaires and billionaires who refuse to pay tax in Ireland - and the lapdog Trade Unions for their industrial disease.

Actually, if the Union Leaders took a stand on this issue and dropped their sycophantic behaviour towards the Wealthy, Union Membership would increase and the Labour Party would make a start at regaining its Principles. They'd attract back the workers who see exactly what they've become. However to achieve this, they'll need to start blaming those responsible for the state of Ireland. The Wealthy think it's hilarious that the poverty stricken must financial contribute to their schools – and if they had an ounce of compassion would refuse to accept this money.

On the subject of the Rich and money, the Irish Branch of US Citibank, was fined, a half million Euros for breeching, its regulatory liquidly reporting, and for failing to apply discounts on cash-flows. This was before we exited the bail-out - when our government was literally, robbing the lame and the blind. Instead of taking money out of Bankers and TD's salaries they took it off the poor and Invalids. Justice in Ireland and the world is for sale.

Morgan Chase paid 13 billion and Bank of America 17 billion Dollars to stop investigations into the ripping off, of customers. And Goldman Sachs the multi Billion dollar World-wide financial institution is not above reproach. The main culprit was a Goldman Trader, one Fabrice Tourre, a French

National, who nicknamed himself the Fabulous Fab. During the US slump he made millions for one group of investors by playing them off against another group.

He was fined - one point one million dollars -
and the most disgusting thing is - In Court, Goldman Sachs was expressly forbidden by the American Government from paying the fine for Fabulous Fab.
While the fact that this stipulation was included, was of little comfort to the robbed. It must at the very least, question the morals of the Bank, and make all their dealings, suspect. Another bank that was up to nefarious dealings at the time was Barclay's who were found guilty of manipulating The Libor Rate. This Rate is used by banks to regulate the interest, which banks charge each other, and had been played fast and loose with by one unscrupulous Banker. At least in this case it was a bank robbing other banks. Unfortunately, and especially in Ireland white collar crime is rarely punished.

Across the board in legitimate Banking language, the term used for deciding what the price of gold should be, is called - 'The Fix' And one bank in London decided fixing the Fix would be a good idea. However, the regulatory authority had other ideas and the bank was fined £26
million pounds for artificially fixing the gold rate for ten years. In this instance, British Justice and Irish Justice were incomparable. The trader responsible for fixing the fix was banned by the FCA from holding any responsible position in the City and was also fined, Ninety Five Thousand, six Hundred Pounds.

And while the Truth is never slanderous, in Ireland today, it is getting people to speak it or print it - that is the problem. The profiteering Banks caused untold misery - while another Profiteering banker who worked for RBS was jailed for seven years, of which he served half, although it could have been much worse. He relieved his bank of only... one and a half billion, while he had 32 billion under his control.

And then there's the Big Octopus, or was it a Whale, a nickname given to Barney, something or other, I can't remember his name, in America, who lost four billion and his company covered it up. The US Senate said: the company lied to investigators and misled investors about the man's conduct. This happened, with the connivance of most major banks, and a Swiss bank was fined one and a half billion dollars for their part in skulduggery. Unbelievably, HSBC paid, almost two billion dollars to the US government for allowing their bank, to be used by Mexican drug barons. My reason for divulging the crookedness of world-wide high finance is to show how little they care about ordinary individuals.

They are a part of this world wide conspiracy and Non-Wealthy people are quantified, as just a profit or minus point on a spread sheet.RBS, after being out by the British taxpayer for over £45 billion - was fined15 million pounds by the Financial Conduct Authority. They said, RBS had serious failings in their advised mortgage sales business. The chief executive of RBS said... this was unacceptable and never should have happened.

In the US, Goldman Sach's was found guilty of contravening articles, 17-A and 20-B of the financial code of ethics, which deals exclusively with deliberate fraud. There may be honest bankers, but it seems like union officials, they are few and far between. I sincerely hope, after the announcement of Barclays Libor fine, which led directly to the setting up of a British Parliamentary Commission, that there has been a change in their Banking Systems.

In Ireland however, besides the Billions lost to greed of the Banks, why were unsecured Bond Holders - Gamblers, paid in full? There are people who made fortunes from the bank guarantee claiming that it saved the country from bankruptcy.

They would say that. Obviously the Wealthy claim that they acted honourably, and should not be questioned, as they saved the country.

To the ones in the 'know' this is laughable. Many people now believe the bailout was unnecessary, the country was *not* on its knees and the government was panicked into allowing the bail-out and the bank guarantee. The unelected advisers believed the nonsense that the ATM's would be empty. In fact: the so-called Bailout was an elaborate smokescreen to cover up the biggest confidence trick in the history of high finance, anywhere in the world.

Irish and European conmen with the connivance of Irish Lawyers pulled an elaborate stroke - that puts the 'double Irish' and all the other tax avoiding schemes in the ha'penny place. Far from being the rescue that the Wealthy, the tame media and present day pundits maintain, the so - called Bailout was, in fact, Legalised Thievery. The scare tactic of empty cash machines, and that the country was on the skids and broke, was nonsense. This generated hype was designed to fool well-intentioned people to do the con-men's bidding.

This was done solely, to make Billions for so-called speculators, while masquerading as a lifeline for the Irish People. Had this momentous bluff been called - Ireland would not and could not have been allowed to fail -
because it is part of the European Community. The EU would have supported and Guaranteed the Irish banks in all financial transactions.

This must have been obvious to even the most antagonist objector to the European Ideal, but scare tactics worked. The common currency was the benchmark that bound Ireland to the European Union, and therefore made the so-called bailout unnecessary. Because, had Ireland went down the tubes

Europe would have done so as well - and there was no way that would or could be allowed to happen.

The bailout for 200 Billion was fundamentally a confidence trick. The bank guarantee allowed Irish Bonds to be down-graded to Junk Status and sold for a fraction of what they were worth. Did none of the financial experts think to ask, "if we are being bailed out for 200 Billion, why do we need to sell off for a fraction of their value, our government bonds"?

Why not take another few Billion and keep them?
No con-man cares about the damage they do and they did massive damage to Ireland. Defenders of the so-called speculators say they took a big gamble and bought up, the "Junk Bonds" stating in retrospect that they could've lost a fortune. What nonsense. They ludicrously claim that they saved Ireland from bankruptcy. This is manifest lies. Firstly there was no gamble. It was money, buying money.
The so-called Junk Bonds were guaranteed by the IRISH GOVERNMENT AND EUROPE - and therefore could not fail - so the Wealthy and those in the 'know' increased their massive fortunes. This was the most serious and worst example of insider trading ever seen, and one supposedly not detected by the free press in this democracy of ours.

The proof of what I'm saying was confirmed when Greece faced similar financial problems. However they weren't too bothered about leaving the EU owing countless Billions and going back to their previous currency - but the ECB was. It stepped in and guaranteed their survival, not once but several times. Had it not done so, Greece's collapse would collapse the entire European Union and the trillions of Euros invested in it.

This proves that the Irish Bank guarantee was unnecessary and was an insider trading con trick by the Wealthy. They bought up government bonds for a fraction of their value -

and when things improved, sold them back to the government at their face value. Reaping a fortune. The Wealthy don't care who they use and abuse to make money. They are above the Law and just like at the Asbestos scandal at Belfast Docks many years before - it's the ordinary people who suffer.

To show that deviousness of unimaginably proportions happened in Ireland with the government bonds scandal - where is the supposed transparency and openness in financial matters that's supposed to exist?
When the proverbial money trail is followed it's impossible to find out who bought the so-called Junk Bonds and a blanket of secrecy has been thrown over the entire matter. Why can no-one find out who the supposed gamblers are and who bought the bonds, or even what nationally they claim to be? Do these "Benefactors" not deserve to be
"honoured" for their claim, that they saved Ireland in its time of need?

Why not erect a few Statues for their heroism? When further inquires are made the stock answer is – "that's sensitive information and is safeguarded because it could endanger future business dealings".

Which is utter nonsense. How...? Even if they made a fortune for rescuing Ireland why are they hiding? Was this not a win win situation?

Obviously by remaining hidden they feel they have something to hide - or a lot to hide? A sceptic could interpret this as a cover up of white-collar crime - and insider trading that was allowed by the Irish Government.

On a lesser scale, he same sort of con trick was pulled in Belfast. The Dockers were told if they objected to the piecemeal weekly sackings by the Union and Employers Court then the entire edifice of Decasualisation would collapse and they all would be thrown onto the Dole. This happened anyway in 1980 - the jobs for life lasted exactly eight years and they were all thrown back onto the Casual System.

However, had the Union and Employers Court insisted on the utilising the York Dock that was filled in during the late 60's and early 70's as a Container Park - to its full potential - many jobs could have been saved.

In both instances, massive amounts of money were involved, and it equates to moral and massive corruption by the Wealthy Financial Elite.

In every situation where money is involved, it is the ordinary people who suffer. Those involved in heinous crimes against the Irish People, with a fortune at their backs, who were pulling the strings will never be held to account. Especially after they cashed in their guaranteed Government Bonds for their True Value.

Apologists for the so-called speculators, cite the world-wide depression as a defence, however in this, not so little tax haven of ours, what beggars belief is, that despite the so-called crash, Irish bankers received large bonuses for doing a good job. One... got a pension worth 27 million and a bonus of one and a half million. And, over the course of one year his building society lost two and a half billion Euros. Ireland's banking system at the time was, hilarious and it seems that Ireland infected the British banking system.

The British Government's Parliamentary Commission, found, that, "the erosion of Banking standards and the culture of greed, was - "far removed from the interests of bank customers". Wonder why we didn't have a Government Commission?
Given free reign this would have exposed the "supposed

speculators". In Britain they needed a parliamentary commission to figure out what happened? They must have no dogs in the street over there.

It is history now, but our government believed, that many of the Bankers, who caused our calamity, should be retained, no doubt to protect them until the worst blew over - by pretending they were the best people for the job. The one who lost two and a half billion, was paid, for the last four months he worked, the sum of, two hundred and twenty one thousand, Euros. I would hate to see the worst of them. Our {unelected} government said they were contractually obliged to pay him. Apparently, these people seem to think that a contract means that you can do whatever you want, with impunity, instead of the reverse. It was not in his contract to to lose two and a half billion?

Anyone with an ounce of sense and every one of the {unelected} knows full well, that not sticking to the terms of the contract, in any way - will render that contract null and void. This is why contracts are agreed upon and signed in the first place. Someone should tell the builders of the new children's hospital this.

While the Bankers did what they do best, the Financial Regulator has a lot to answer for. The Banking system in Ireland was treated as a joke and the poor were trampled underfoot with their social welfare cut to the bone.

What the Bankers, so-called speculators and the regulator had in common was an old school tie - which allowed them to get away with pretty much anything. The Old Boys network was protecting its own, and as a matter of public record it has been done before with the FAS and DIRT scandals. Remember them.

Why does the government not say to the people building the

new children's hospital, when they want more money, 'you signed a contract either honour it or we will replace you and sue you'. This would put the price hikes out of their head. As usual, suit and tie works wonders?

The upper class Tax Farce is a sick joke. The Wealthy pay nothing and workers have their tax taken, every week, or month. Tongue in cheek the Wealthy claim - "the reason for this, is so workers don't have to fill out large complicated tax forms at the end of the tax year, so workers Tax is taken at source". What nonsense! This shows the thievery and abject denial of human rights on the poor by the Rich.

Obviously the Wealthy will become incensed at this statement and claim "We rob no-one". Obviously, they don't rob the Wealthy and I just wish this applied to PAYE workers as well. When it's pointed out, they don't use guns, but Tax Accountants, the Wealthy who have extremely thin skins get annoyed and proclaim: "Everything, we do is legal"!

When this is counteracted by charitable organisations, saying: "It is also legal, 'not' to charge Wealthy Irish Governments with conspiracy - for refusing to build social housing to drive house prices up? And its also legal, very legal to have thousands of homeless parents and children walking the streets all day to return to a single room in a hotel at night".

When faced with these 'realities' the Wealthy remain silent.

And that's not to mention the overcrowded hospitals where the poor die on trolleys, or worse, on the streets outside our Parliament.

Extremely angry at having to defend themselves the Wealthy protest at this criticism, claiming "that has nothing to do with us you can't blame us for the ills of Society". The very fact that they deny it means that the homeless dead have pricked their conscience... and what they'll do about it is... to fly out with their Wealthy non tax-paying friends to sunnier climes, in a millionaires paradise, where there are no homeless.

Here, foreign Millionaires and Billionaires and every multi-national under the sun, pay effectively nothing. The local Wealthy are allowed to drive a coach and four through the supposed tax regulations by using tax lawyers to avoid paying even the minimum required. Scandalously, the Wealthy 'who won't pay Tax' - justify the effectiveness and need for the PAYE System. Irish workers are treated like fools and cash-cows while every Irish government thinks and behaves like a state in the U.S - by privatising anything that can be privatised.
Unlike the American System, and every other system in the world where everyone pays tax, the Irish Government, allows these 'entrepreneurs' who risk nothing to pay nothing and live like Lords while Irish workers are strangled with PAYE and taxed to the hilt.

In America they'd be called, "Free-loaders". Irish workers are forced workers to pay for everything to support essential services. What Irish workers don't realise is -not only is this legalised Thievery but it's vilifying and denigrating every PAYE worker by labelled them... guilty of criminal intent. That is, intent ' not' to pay their tax. So they take it every week or month from working people.

Thus, in a sly and deceitful manner the Welfare State is paid for - solely by the people who use it - and the Wealthy know it? While refusing to pay for fundamental services, they obviously see no contradiction in making workers contribute 120 million to private schools every year. This is a disgusting perversion of the American System, which would not be tolerated in America. Here the Irish Rich have 'Privatised PAYE workers to make them pay for their Wealthy lifestyle. This "touching the forelock to Wealth must stop".

We need a government that will tell the Rich, you cannot have it both ways. Why is the champion of democracy Fintan O'Toole who teaches in America not railing against this system? If everyone {especially the Wealthy} and every multinational paid their fair share of tax the degradation inflicted upon the health system would be obliterated.
With the yoke lifted from PAYE Workers the system would be awash with money. We would have a Health Service to be proud of and poverty and homelessness would become a thing of the past.

Our Nurses and Doctors would not have to emigrate, to find a system that would honour their profession. The revamped health service would be decent scanning machines for unborn children, and the scandal of sick on trolleys in our hospitals would be obliterated. With an abundance of money - this is the very least that would be achieved if. No doubt, if this was suggested, the

Wealthy would react in typical fashion by claiming - that any change in the Status Quo would result in the entire financial systems collapsing. This is utter nonsense and would be used as a lever by the unelected in government to frighten the Dail, just like the bailout double talk. An obvious riposte to this silly statement is - why has it not happened in the US?

Unfortunately, the people at the coal face who have to manage the poverty driven Irish agenda are the over-worked doctors, nurses and well-intentioned Social Workers, who struggle to pay a mortgage. Their humanitarian feelings are spliced onto a system which knows they'll do countless hours of unpaid overtime, rather than abandon the distressed people in her care. Juxtapose this with their well paid managers. If workers complain about abuses visited upon the afflicted by their

supposed caretakers, they are rarely listened to.
This is evidenced by those wonderful dying women in the
Cervical Smear Scandal.

The Wealthy in Ireland have abandoned their conscience. They
pretend to have a moral compass but in reality only care about
themselves and their money. Instead of building high walls to
live behind - they should build a society where everyone has an
equal chance in Life? In the *'new'*
fair society the poor would not be ghettoised - and addiction
services { *which are the result of poverty*} given the resources
to educate the poor - so they would no longer will be poor or
addicts.

Obviously everyone would benefit but the Wealthy don't want
that. Actually, if everyone had to pay their fair share of tax, the
loudest proponents for safe-guarding the public purse, would
be the Wealthy.

The Rich claim that 'not' taxing multi nationals has created
work for the Plebs, and if Irish tax laws are changed, these
money making enterprises will up-sticks and leave. The 14
billion that Google is paying to the Irish government gives the
lie to that. Setting Google aside, where would they go? Asia
or South America are both to far away and too unstable. No
doubt the non-paying multi-nationals are well aware of Ford's
long abandoned car factories in the South American Jungle...
so they'll stay here.

The Tax situation has infected every level in the health system
as seen by the Executives large salaries.
These attract the kind of people who will obfuscate in the
extreme to save their own reputations and positions.

How could the HSE be paying for cervical testing services
in America and not know - that this 'outsourcing was being

outsourced'? They had no idea who was carrying out the tests they were paying for - just that they were cheaper. Previous to the 'Dying Women' anyone who complained was treated like a whistle blower, and pilloried. This culture of cover up affects every aspect of Irish Life and is effectively encouraged by the Wealthy.

Actually, this would never happen in a fully privatised system, like the American one - { *which I am not advocating for*} The disaster happening here is because the government is controlled by the unelected Secretary Generals - like Watt, who claim they could get more money in the Private Sector. With this mind-set they don't deserve to be in control of our so-called Health Service. The salaries these people get is an insult to the Doctors and Nurses who slaved during the Pandemic to keep the country afloat.

Don't get me wrong I don't want to see the welfare system abolished, I want to see in enhanced and used as a safety net for everyone who needs it. Let the dual system which the Rich have used for so long, like treatment in Private Hospitals be made available to everyone and to be the norm. So that the PAYE workers - the people who actually pay for running the country - can benefit from from being treated in the lap of luxury when they are sick.
Ex Belfast Dockers and God Knows how many Belfast People are dying from Asbestosis and not a word is reported in the Irish Media. Why? The answer is obvious but no-one will say it. It's because the unelected people who control every department and aspect of the government will not allow it. They also control the 'Free Press'.

Sickened and disgusted about the corruption and cover about the Asbestos Deaths and the Union and Employers Court, I recently I put an open letter on linkedin, addressed to both Law Societies and the police commissioner. I pulled no punches and fully expected a reaction. However, what I got was absolute silence. It's no wonder that the wealthy can get away with what they're doing, obviously I knew that the newpapers - who are bought and paid for would say nothing - however when not one TD, Left Right or Centre saw fit to raise this matter in the Dai, l was flabbergasted. See these letters on linkedin

In relation to the Asbestos at Belfast Docks after years long drawn out struggles large amounts of compensation was paid - in out of Court settlements. However, not a word about the involvement of the Union was mentioned. This was kept quiet so that cancer sufferers don't ask for an Asbestos Test. The corrupt controllers of Democracy have succeeded. They maintain that because it happened fifty years ago it is not relevant. Not so The Deaths and cover up are happening right now. {See the Doctor on the Asbestos video}

Obviously I believe that he uncaring Wealthy employers who owned the Asbestos, and he Union that covered up for them by sacking their own members, must be exposed and held to account. By their silence it seems that the elected TD's by agree with them. Or maybe it's Robert Watt and the other unelected back-room boy who won't allow them to speak out? I must admit, I'm puzzled - do we live in a Democracy or a Mickey Mouse Democracy unelected Robert Watt Democracy?

If it's a true Democracy, once the unelected cronies are replaced and to ensure that this Dictatorship never happens again - every department must have its own independent ' *elected by the People*' Ombudsman or woman. This, effectively would be a new government department and named the O.D.I. 'The Oversight of Democratic Institutions'.

The ODI would have an open format = and a simple phone call would guarantee every person in Ireland who has a grievance or complaint access to a solicitor. It's ridiculous that solicitors can cherry - pick and decide if they won't take on a case. Furthermore, if the citizen so chooses they can have their complaint acknowledged and investigated in a speedy fashion by the most relevant Ombudsman. Once the Ombudsman for every department was established, the first thing the one appointed for the finance department would do, is - investigate is the 81 thousand Euros that Robert Watt gave himself as a pay rise, when he changed departments.

The Ombudsman or women would cut out the bureaucracy and guarantee the electorate were listened to - and - that the elected Irish Government ran the country and not the Secretary Generals. More importantly the ODI would ensure that their power was severely contained. At present they effectually run the country by ' *not'* telling their 'elected minister' what they are doing. This must stop. They are civil servants must be made behave as they are supposed to - like servants of the Minister and not the other way around.

This ODI will investigate every aspect of the business of government and to suspend { *without pay*} anyone who is abusing their position, or has an ulterior motive. This wasting of public money, must end. If and when this policy is adopted, the 'elected' through the Dail, will 'really' run the country. The ODI would have a team of investigators and the power to bring to a standstill, immediately, all - and any unjust or corrupt action that is brought to their attention. A case in point is the refusal by the supposed Independent Public Accounts Committee on the instructions of the C&AG Shemus McCarthy not to allow me to appear in front of it. I wanted to give the committee a first hand account about the corruption at Belfast Docks.

And more recently the scandalous affair instigated by Robert Watt, which caused the resignation of Tony Holohan must never happen again.

The unmitigated abuse of power that general secretary Robert Watt wielded, and continues to wield didn't happen overnight. As General Secretary of several departments, this megalomaniac ran the country as he saw fit and paid himself what he liked.

His arranging of the moving of Tony Holohan to Trinity College at a cost of two million Euros a year, with a projected cost of twenty million – and telling no-one about it, shows the power this Secretary General has.

Then, when his swengalli like actions are disclosed he defends them and says he acted "legally and didn't have to inform the Minister for Health or the Cabinet".
Did no-one think to tell him, that this is supposed to be a Democratic Republic - and the Wealthy have no right to make him the King of it? The ODI will tell him - this is why we have elections - and to take off his crown.

The power of the ODI will not come without responsibility. Every week, it will be held to account in the Dail and made give the reason for any actions taken. For the sake of fair-play anyone accused of usurping Democracy would be invited in, to state their case. Any TD, general secretary or civil servant - who has overstepped the mark and behaved like a 'Dictator' will be given the opportunity - in a Democratic Manner - to justify their actions - or withdraw them or resign.

All positions on the cross-party ODI will be filled by genuine TD's i.e those not in thrall to the Wealthy and with a social conscience. E.g. Shane Ross would be questioned on his silence and what or whom made him go silent on his labelling of the payments to SIPTU - which he named, a slush fund, and, why union members got flown to St Patrick's Day in New York with their employer cronies?

In my own case, I should be able to question the C&AG why he saw fit to tell the Public Accounts Committee not to invite me to attend before them? I put an article on linkedin about this but as usual it was ignored.

This has to stop. When someone makes an allegation against any aspect of the Irish Government in Public - they must appear in front of the ODI to justify it or face the consequences. The silence in the face of allegations of government cover up must stop being ignored - and the Irish Government must be above reproach. If and when this new department is established, it will be for one reason only – and that is to make Irish Democracy behave like a Democracy. It stands to reason that with the 'new openness' emanating from the Oversight of Democratic

Institutions - the stranglehold the Wealthy have on this country through the unelected - will be stopped.

One case the ODI must investigate is - what genius or vested interests decided to place the new children's hospital where it is? Was it some rich far see seeing millionaire with a fleet of helicopters or the people who dug Port Tunnel?

How on earth are people going to get in and out Central Dublin to visit the children, because of traffic buildup, and that's not to mention the fleets of lorries which will be delivering to the hospital every minute of every day and night.

And what about the people who live beside it?

Maybe the genius's don't want to overload the M50 or to destroy those beautiful green fields beside Tallaght Hospital - which is on the Lewis Line.

Its been suggested that the children of the Wealthy who need specialist treatment, will 'not' have their own hospital entrance, but will have to use the main doors of the hospital. Here they will rub shoulders with ordinary people and their children, but once inside they can access the Private Suites. Firstly, do sick children actually care who they associate with - or is it their snobby parents who don't want them contaminated with a dose of reality. Obviously the Puppets who run the health service for the Wealthy - don't want their own children, or those of the very Wealthy rubbing shoulders with the children of the people whom they manipulate.

I.e the children of the people whose money actually built the Hospital?

In a ground-breaking and spurious attempt to make the HSE more feeling, hospitals were told to admit all mistakes and to apologise with kindness and in a meaningful manner when - wrongdoing occurred.

Correct me - if I'm wrong but if the people responsible for the wrongdoing 'have' to be told to do this - how genuine is the apology?

Why did the HSE feel the need to say this at all? Could it possibly have anything to do with the previous policy, i.e - that the HSE denied everything until the doors of the Court. The good is taken out of this new policy of open disclosures, by the fact, that the HSE can still claim legal protection - and their apology cannot be used against them in a court of law. Some apology.

CHAPTER FIFTEEN

Most people with the power to expose corruption have become nodding dogs to Wealth, because they know, if do otherwise they will suffer. This cover up is led by the national broadcaster RTE. Their present-day tribulations are exactly due to the airs and graces that the devious people who really run the country, bestowed on them. The wanton abuse and money that they wasted was incredulous to the general public.

While the stage-managed sacking of Ryan Tubrity was welcomed, the fact the he won't pay back hundreds of thousands he was paid - for nothing, beggars belief. Setting aside the fact that he is robbing the Irish Taxpayer a simple way of ensuring he refunds his ill gotten gains, is to instruct him - that next Monday morning he must present himself at RTE with a cheque for the full amount. Failure to do so will mean that the police are called in and RTE accuse him with 'obtaining money under false pretences'.
RTE would be well advised to take heed the of the Ancient Roman Scribe, Scurrilous. Five thousand years ago he lampooned the Senate for its duplicity – today he'd be in his element exposing newspapers and journalists who refuse to report the 'News' and the Truth.

E. g. When still Union President, Jack O'Connor personally

awarded the ex Belfast Asbestos Chairman who betrayed Union members and joined the Employers - his fifty year - Union long service badge. Talk about rubbing the Dead Dockers nose in it?

Belfast Docks is the only place in Trade Union History - anywhere in the world, where an Employer was a member of a Trade Union and entitled to attend - the only union meeting that was held every year, the AGM.

This also was the Chairman who ordered Dockers to discharge Asbestos without protection to save the Employers money. Why did the Union leadership so honour him? Was it because the Dublin Employers ordered them to.

I have put many letters on linkedin addressing the issue of censorship. A Scurrilous today is sadly missed although Kevin Myers was attempting to fill his shoes until he was sacked - for rightly calling single mothers "mothers of bastards". Whatever happened to 'I may detest what you say but I will defend to the death your right to say it'?

In a similar vein when I exposed the corrupt actions of Union Officials at Belfast Docks and the corrupt solicitors, whom I name - none of them, nor the retired Jack O'Connor, would sue me for defamation, which I dearly wanted? Also, why will Sunday Times Irish Times and others, seeing they are such 'champions of Truth' not expose this omission in their newspapers? Neither SIPTU officials nor Sunday Times will answer this. If I am not writing the Truth why have I not been summoned to a Court of Law to answer for my Defamation - of Libel and Slander? The simple answer is - I have spoken and written the simple unvarnished Truth.

The Sunday Times claims to be a newspaper of repute but is behaving corruptly and like all the others is engaging in the evil practice of Censorship. Where are the examples of the fine upstanding Journalism -

they claim to promote? Obviously this calls into question the multiple high ranking members of the legal profession who advise the Sunday Times and who engage in the wonderful defence of "Utter Silence".

One Legal Eagle stated at the start of an article entitled "A time to kill confidentially in harassment settlements", showed an incredible lack of understanding towards women who remain quiet about sexual assaults.

The abused women did not speak out because of the horrendous pressure they were put under, 'that their lives and careers would be ruined'. *[Not an idle threat].* No doubt the abusers solicitors swore blind his assault was a 'one off' and 'he promised never to do it again', to convince them to accept the settlement.

Hoping against hope that they were not complicit in another woman being attacked, and longing for the day when they'd be secure enough to be able to speak out – and be believed.

For this legal eagle and to say "without payment there would be no silence" is disgusting. The legal establishment has dressed up and hidden in legal jargon, the opinion, nay the fact - that the Law has been well and truly flouted. It is well known in legal circles that a barrister may be called upon to argue both sides of an argument, depending entirely on who is paying him.

So in this instance 'personal opinions' from this barrister is unwarranted and untruthful because he is being paid to say it. I wonder did any Feminist on Sunday Times object to this patronising and sly attack upon wronged women - especially Justine McCarthy, {who in relation to SIPTU's wrongdoing} has been as 'struck as dumb' as her male colleges. In a pathetic attempt to disguise what he is really saying, the contracted barristers says: "The problem arises when 'moving on with your life' means assaulting other women".

In the case of which he speaks and many others this is true, however the real problem is that the rich and powerful in Hollywood and elsewhere who were in the 'Know' covered up and facilitated what the abusers were doing - for the sake of an Oscar? This - was just moving on to the next vulnerable young actress.

After more muddying of the waters and bringing up a case from 1926 in England, the quoted barrister gets to the point.
"It is now mandatory to report child abuse. But when an adult is sexually harassed, new legislation would be needed to prevent an Irish superstar from buying civil immunity. Such a law would be difficult to draft, since you would be balancing the right of one actual victim to settle in private with the rights of future victims to know". And now the crux of the matter is. "It is equally important to educate attitudes. It is easy to forget, that in cases of criminal conduct, your first call should be to the police and not to a lawyer".

This Barrister has shown just how much empathy he has for young women threatened and blackmailed into keeping quiet - none whatsoever. Especially in view of his parting shot. "This is not something you will learn from watching legal thrillers".

I would rather have heard from this educated gentleman - what possible legal ramifications would fall upon the heads of women who accepted money and then spoke out? Could the abuser from his prison cell legally demand his money back for breach of contract? Would any jailed abuser have the audacity to pursue such a disgusting claim? Or indeed what would happen if it was the abused woman's best friend who broke the silence and reported the abuse? The Hypocrisy by the champions of Jurist Prudence in Ireland is stunning.

In the Belfast Docks case the Sunday Times legal eagle, its Editor and Journalists all know about the censorship and the blind eye employed by their own newspaper.

They are also well aware of the cover up of corruption that took place at the legal conference chaired by Judge Peter Kelly - because I told them about it. I have also highlighted this in my articles on LinkedIn hoping that an honest Barrister would take on my case Pro Bono. But nary a peep from any of them so the cover up continues.

Seeing the quoted Sunday Times barrister was public-spirited enough to bestow on readers the benefit of his legal training - why does he remain silent on wholly preventable Asbestos related Deaths? And also - the existence of the Union and Employers Court and the Union's diabolical behaviour. This is confirmed by Belfast solicitor John O'Neill of Thompson McClures - and should have ruffled his legal feathers - but apparently not?

Jack O'Connor had engaged John O'Neill to "sue the arse off me. Needless to say, in a normal Democracy a Trade Union Chairman cannot form a Union and Employers Court for persecuting Union Members – but this is exactly what happened? Anyone who showed contempt for the Court by not attending when summoned - was sacked. For documentary proof of the Court see facebook, twitter numerous posts on linkedin and www.siptupresidentjackoconnorexposed.com –

A historian who also cherry-picks the truth is Diramid Ferriter I have told him several times about this atrocity but he chooses to ignore it. The last time I did so - was publicly in an open letter on linkedin. This occurred when he sycophantically reviewed Fintan O'Toole's new book.

Both he and O'Toole cover up what happened at Belfast Docks. As a historian he will have no trouble looking up the case of

"Quinn verses Leatham". This went to the house of lords and is quoted in a book entitled 'THE RISE
OF THE IRISH TRADE UNIONS', by Andrew Boyd. He was a Belfast Writer who first published this book in 1972.

What transpired was - in 1901, the North of Ireland Operative Butchers' Society, a local Belfast Union was involved in a lawsuit that has become world famous. It has been studied by generations of lawyers in many countries". **But apparently not in Ireland.** The case arose out of an attempt by J Quinn and other officials of the union to compel Leatham, a flesher operating in Belfast Abattoir to employ only union labour.

The case is listed in the law records as Quinn V Leatham. Leatham refused to dismiss some of his workmen who had been expelled from the union for not paying their union contributions. He tried however to encourage them to rejoin the union and even offered to pay the arrears for them.

But the union rejected this offer and in the course of the dispute that followed - Quinn and colleagues persuaded Munroe, a meat retailer, not to take supplies form Leatham.

When Munroe stopped buying meat Leatham brought an action against the union officials, on the grounds that they had conspired together to injure him - and that as a result he had suffered material damage.
The case was tried by a judge and jury who found for Leatham and awarded him £250 damages. The union appealed against this decision and took the appeal to the House of Lords.

The Lords upheld the jury's verdict. The Quinn V Leatham case was established – and this is presumably where it is of interest to lawyers". *[Not the bought off Irish ones]*

The house of lords ruled. **"If two or more persons combine**

together, without legal justification, to injure another and by doing so cause him damage, they are liable to an action for conspiracy".

Years later at Belfast Docks The Union and Employers 'did' obviously combine together, but it wasn't over meat it was over Asbestos. How can the Tame Historian, Ferriter and the denier of Corrupt Trade Unionism - Fintan O'Toole argue with these facts and this ruling?

In an attempt to put Legality onto their actions and to fool the Dockers, The Union and Employers Court put everything in writing. This is plain to seen from their summons letters and is why the Irish Times and its award winning Journalists will not report on this scandal. How could they bring into disrepute the Irish Employers who were acting "illegally" for the Wealthy, and put their own positions in danger? This is why the self-proclaimed cherry-picking Historian plus a multitude of 'nodding dogs' in TV and print media turn a 'Blind Eye' to the 'Culture of Privilege' that controls Ireland.

Leading this litany of shame is RTE, the State Broadcaster which has it claims - several cutting edge Investigative programs. What a joke. The reporters on these programs are well aware of the magnitude of this scandal and will do nothing about it. When are they going to stand up and be counted - among the true Investigative Reporters of the World? I often wonder is it because of shame and not wanting to be "washing Irelands Dirty linen in public" - or - that the exposure of the Wealthy will expose their own cowardly shortcomings? Do they think that having ignored this scandal for so long - they'll be 'Tarred with the same Brush' for allowing it?

Why will they not 'Publish and be dammed' and allow Ireland to be exposed as a corrupt third world country that pays lip service to anti-corruption legislation. The Free Press and media should've exposed this years ago, but they don't want exposed on the world stage as absolute LIARS AND SYCOPHANTS. All they have to do is report on the house of lords ruling - and state why they are doing so. While I can understand that the people who run Ireland { *the unelected like Robert Watt}* don't want their undemocratic behaviour exposed, what is stopping the supposed unfettered media?

If Ireland is ever to be regarded as a Democracy, everyone involved in covering up this Corrupt Scandal must be charged with Covering up Corruption.

50 years ago the trade union that fought to free Ireland in 1916, was corrupted by the Wealthy at Belfast Docks.
When this eventually gets out, past and present day leaders of SIPTU will have some explaining to do. **{Take note Jack O'Connor}**. Obviously this will sully the Republic's Image on the Democratic world stage - but they can claim innocence and rightly state that they weren't around then? However their cover up actions today and in previous years, since they were informed of the Truth - makes them worse, far worse than the original Union and Employers that ordered Belfast Dockers to discharge Asbestos without protection and sacked Union Members who would't do so.

The original corruption at Belfast Docks with the Asbestos, pales into insignificance when compared to the lengths they've gone to - to prevent this from becoming Public Knowledge? When viewed through the lens of Democracy. The Union and those in government right now who cover up this atrocity, must be sacked and stripped of their pensions. The megalomania of the Unelected and the Union must be exposed and stopped. The longer this scandal is buried the more it stinks and the more people it sucks in to cover it up.

Asbestos killed a lot more people in Belfast than the Dockers who discharged it. This was well known at the time but totality ignored by the Wealthy - the Docks Employers and disgustingly - the Union and ICTU.

They were supposed to be concerned about their members well-being? But obviously had been bribed into silence.
At the time, while human rights were in their infancy the ITGWU was well established and had over 250 thousand members. This must have terrified the Wealthy - who in one fell swoop nullified, corrupted and took revenge on Connolly and Larkin's Union. This was particularly pleasing for them. Besides taking revenge on the Union, for its part in securing Ireland's independence, the bribes amounted to 'chicken feed' compared to what would be paid in Asbestos Compensation.

To this end they established the unbelievable Union and Employers Court which they named "The Joint Disciplinary Committee" and stood Connolly and Larkin's Trade Unionism on its head.

As related earlier, to cover up the Union and Employers Corruption - the Wealthy had to Corrupt the Lawyers. This started with Norman Shannon and because there is an unlimited amount of money behind this corruption - both Law Societies in Ireland do their utmost to keep this Pervasion of the Law hidden.

In all sincerity I ask this question - **IS THERE AN HONEST LAWYER IN IRELAND** who will expose this cartel of Wealthy Employers, Government, Heartless Union Officials and the Silent Free Press? If not, where are the Professors of Law in the Universities - not to mention the supposed Law Makers? Obviously they are all too scared to admit that the Law in Ireland is Corrupt - and for sale to the highest bidder?

Thus, the scales of Justice outside the Four Courts should be replaced with a large Euro sign. Many Belfast people
died believing, they were unlucky in life and had contracted a 'run of the mill Cancer'. Not for one minute did they believe that their Deaths were due to the Wealthy Irish Employers and a bought off Legal System.

The people who orchestrated this scandal can easily be identified.They are the Wealthy to whom the unelected government at the time reported.

Probably the only one's still alive with any in-depth knowledge of this are Jack O'Connor and Pat Rabbitee. They must be questioned 'under oath' as to why they covered up this scandal? O'Connor in particular must be asked why he allowed the ex Union Chairman in Belfast to remain a Union Member - and then to honour him knowing full well about his crimes against Belfast Dockers.

This is beyond comprehension and puts the Deaths from Asbestos into another catalogue altogether? Because of prior knowledge of what Asbestos can do - the deaths of Belfast citizens was not Corporate Manslaughter but Corporate Murder.

Even today - besides the Wealthy controlling the unelected Secretary Generals - why will the C & AG, the PUBLIC ACOUNTS COMMITTEE and the JUSTICE COMMITTEE not allow me to appear in front of them?

Does the Truth not matter to them? Why have "they all" engaged in this cover-up? The very least they can do - if they don't want to be judged alongside the orchestrator's of Asbestos Deaths - is to get ex Union President Jack O'Connor to answer - why he didn't expose this scandal?
Obviously it is the Truth they are afraid of.

While its too late for the full force of the law to be brought down on this matter, if any of the many Human Rights groups demanded an investigation into the Belfast Docks Asbestos scandal, they couldn't be ignored? However, will they do so?

They fear the Back Room establishment and Shadow government of Robert Watt, as much as the TD's in the Dail. Watt rides roughshod over democratic principles and his cohorts and have the power to silence any free-thinking Journalist or individual who may wish to break ranks and expose them. Hence the Human Rights people would be afraid of losing their funding so they keep quiet and look for a worthy case thousands of miles away.

While the puppet TD's and Irish Human Rights are happy to be silenced - I cannot ignore the Union in Belfast forming the Union and Employers Court - because I was one of the persecuted Dockers sacked by the Court. A while back a barrister had a humorous article in The Sunday Times, This told, how a 10 year old misspelled Terraced as Terrorist and claimed to be living in a Terrorist House.

Much more subtler - was the point at the end whereby "the courts have resisted attempts by the state to criminalise normal behaviour", and he gave several excellent examples. His point I assume was to suggest, that questioning this boy about his spelling mistake could actually encourage him to behave in the manner suggested. Now to get to my point - this was from an Irish Barrister - so it's acceptable for me to believe that this barrister *must* believe in the Rule of Law. Therefore I'm assuming that - seeing he was a *part*-t *ime* journalist he knew nothing about the Belfast Docks and the Censoring of my play, 'The Judas Goat', by the Theatre world.

However, I believed - as a legal practitioner when made aware of this scandal he would be obliged to do something about it. Especially as he was writing on points of law in the Sunday Times. So I set about informing him. And low and behold he did nothing about it. While Sunday times readers will claim, why should he put his own career in jeopardy when this transpired many years ago?

My point is - as a practising Irish Barrister, who took a oath to uphold the law - he now knew about the persecution of the Belfast Dockers and the cover up today. To put this in context, it's comparable to Doctor refusing to help a dying man who has collapsed in front of him. Only this is far worse. The Union Chairman and the Union, stood on its head what Connolly and Larkin fought all their lives to achieve.

Even if he saw fit to ignore the betrayal of Trade Unionism, I thought as an educated and enlightened individual - the censoring of my play, would have caused some consternation within him.
I had informed the Barrister of this, several times but he wasn't interested. In an attempt to pique his interest I informed him of a more recent legal scandal that related to the upper echelons of his own profession.

This I mentioned earlier about me having I gate crashed a Legal Conference held to discuss the changes to the Defamation Laws, in 2010, chaired by High Court Judge Peter Kelly and attended by the crème de la crème of high ranking Lawyers in Dublin, but he still wasn't interested. Obviously The Sunday Times barrister and the entire legal profession are not interested in Justice – so I asked him, "will you sue SIPTU for me, pro bono, because I cannot afford to pay for Justice in Ireland".

However he declined, not verbally but with silence. Disgusted I advised him "to stick to pontificating in The Sunday Times

- but asked him, "would you at the very least – and in the interests of Justice, ask The Sunday Times editor why he will not report and expose this travesty of Trade Unionism? And while you're at it, ask him what happened to the Sunday Times Philosopher who was going to write about the ethics of a Trade Union sacking its own members, for and with the employers. He went on holiday, never returned and has ignored my emails".

As a parting shot I advised the Barrister, "if you're going to take refuge like all the other professional people I've contacted, in silence, then please stop writing for The Sunday Times, because like them you're making a Liar and a Hypocrite out of yourself".

It gives me no pleasure in saying this - because it shows without doubt - from the facts I've related here, that - **THE IRISH LEGAL SYSTEM IS UTTERLY CORRUPT.**

Hopefully there is a decent lawyer in Ireland who will prove me wrong.

President Michael D Higgins rightly lambasted Ireland over its housing policy. Government Ministers were furious and stated that he'd overstepped the mark and had no right to involve himself in Politics.

What a joke. If they involved themselves in Politics and didn't jump through hoops for Vulture Funds Ireland's homeless would not be on the streets. Hopefully, now that Michael 'D' has refused to listen to his advisers and told the Truth - he will now be as forthcoming about the Belfast Docks betrayal of the Dockers. I have emailed the details of this to him many times and just received the usual standard reply.

Not only does the entire Irish Legal profession engage in censoring the Truth, the ruling body of the Arts does as well. I posted an article on linkedin complaining about the censorship I'm experiencing and also sent it to Aosdana, and was ignored. As they can only be contacted through the Arts Council Offices I'm unsure if they received it. The article includes my points about Censorship. I felt I had to make them to Aosdana, who are supposed to be the 'Conscience of Principled Artists in Ireland'. I may as well not have bothered. Obviously Aosdana don't care about the corruption in the Arts either and have been literally bought off.

While in control of the Abbey, Fiach McConghaill broke ranks and railed against the unseen and unknown people who really run Ireland. Whether he was ordered to do so by the Billionaire who funded his "We the Citizens Farce" or this was own grandiose plans for a political career I'm not certain.

He was an unelected Senator at the time and by association used this position to promote the Billionaires activities, and his own. As leader and chief spokesman for the 'We-The-Citizens' farce he was laying the groundwork for a new Democratic Party, as yet un-named but was definitely going to have "Citizens" in it. While emulating 'the grand ole duke of york', he led his followers around the country, at the behest of said American Billionaire.

At huge meetings, in large Hotels, 'it was the same people who attended them all'. I discovered this when I attended the last one. held at the Maldron Hotel in Tallaght. I was amazed to see how a crowd of strangers were getting on so amicably - and questioned the people at my table, saying they were getting on like old friends. To my surprise, they laughed and said they were indeed friends, as they and everyone else had met at the first meeting - and had attended them all. These people were all from South Dublin and were great supporters of the Arts.

They praised McConghaill to the high heaven and outlined the wonderful things his 'we the citizens' would achieve. Every person had a different viewpoint of his greatness, and only I knew better I would have thought I was about to hear a Messiah speak.

As the old friends interacted and moved from table to table, I soon ascertained there was only one person from Tallaght present, myself.

Before I could comment on this a rumour spread like wildfire that the Billionaire who was funding this enterprise was present, though incognito.
After the free soup the McConghaill called the meeting to order and spoke pure drivel for a long time. At the Q&A I stood with my arm raised for ten minutes. Obviously he remembered me from the Abbey.

I had been standing for so long that eventually people saw this and kept silent. Due to embarrassment only, McConghaill eventually nodded to the girl with the microphone and I was allowed to speak. When given the microphone I immediately raised the matter of McConghaill's censoring of my play 'The Judas Goat' at the Abbey and the Union sacking its own members at the Belfast Docks.

I got all of two minutes before he ordered several young ladies to wrestle the microphone from me. I shouted into it "Am I not a Citizen and entitled to speak", to which McConghaill, replied, "We are pressed for time and this meeting is not about the Abbey".

Several people with South Dublin accents accused me of being anti - Trade Union. This surprised me as South Dublin in not a hotbed of trade unionists, to which I replied, "No, I'm anti Corrupt Trade Union, and say that after you see my play". I appealed to them to see the 'big picture and asked, "why is a Billionaire paying for these hotels, employing all these nice students from Trinity College and giving away 'free soup'? Is it because the Billionaire has ulterior motives for this undemocratic farce, where the Poor get screwed by the Rich and it cannot operate - without the vital ingredient of, a Tame and Greedy Trade Union Leadership.

Needless to say I was ignored and MacConghaill continued praising the audience for attending.

The 'We the Citizens' merry go round has faded into oblivion, for which I take the credit. I opened the Billionaire's eyes to MacConghaill's censoring of my play 'The 'Judas Goat'. No doubt the Billionaire asked to see my censored play - and was astounded. Obviously he was equally astounded to learn that it was the same people who attended all their meetings around the country. Plus the glaring fact that I was the only person from the working class area of Tallaght, in attendance.

This would have resonated with the Bilionaire who is 'a self made man'. I'm sure and certain that the Billionaire went onto my linkedin site and got his eyes opened. He could also confirm I spoke the truth because the meetings were all video recorded and he could identify the same Dublin People.
When ITGWU changed its name to SIPTU it became a willing Puppet of the Employers and did their dirty work for them. I.e, covering up the Asbestos scandal and the Union and Employers Court. Obviously this corrupt behaviour denigrates the existence and blackens the soul of every genuine Trade Unionist. This needs to be reversed and will only be - when the people at the top of the Union are paid the same as those at the bottom. Everyone in the Irish Media including Fintan O'Toole know this but are afraid to report it.This makes a sick joke of the National Union of Journalists.

Telephone number salaries and the name SIPTU must be

abolished and the proud name, the Irish Transport & General Workers Union re established. This would see the Union returned to its place as a refuge and protector for workers and their families, as envisaged by James Connolly and Jim Larkin. Neither of these workers champions would have allowed Employers - and the Union they founded - to order Union members and their families to their deaths? Indeed they would be apoplectic with rage if it had done so when they were alive. The stoic acceptance of persecution by The Union - on ordinary union members at Belfast Docks and the inevitable, 'Black Humour' was a symptom of helplessness. It was easier to laugh at wrongdoing, and ignore the Union with their "Employers Hat" on - rather than stand on principle and be victimised.

Needless to say, neither the Employers nor the Union ever heard the sarcastic and funny remarks spoken about them.
When I exposed their corruption in the Dockers Voice - intelligent people advised me to desist from naming the wrongdoers - because they would 'get me'. But I believed that the Truth had to be told - and when it came to a showdown the Dockers would not be lacking.

I believed they would have the moral courage that Larkin put into the Belfast Dockers in 1907. I was wrong and was sacked. This was largely due, in the 1970's to the non-action by the ICTU who obviously agreed with the sell-out. {See their letters} This scandalous behaviour and cover up is continuing to the present day. The leadership of ICTU is well aware of this scandal. I told Patricia King this to her face - on the back of a lorry in Belfast at a Mayday Parade. She actually put her arm around my shoulders and said, "you have made your point". In saying this she has made a liar out of herself. If I had made my point she would've exposed the past corruption of ITGWU, SIPTU and ICTU and done something about it. Instead she made mealy mouthed platitudes in line with ICTU's cover up of corruption.

What working class Irish Person could say the name - Irish Transport and General Workers Union - and not feel proud of its History. This history was forged in conflict during the Dublin Lockout to protect workers from the Dublin Mounted Police. Ultimately this led to the Union
- as The Citizens Army marching to join the Rebels in the GPO at the start of the Easter Rising.

Only when this great name is reinstated outside Liberty Hall, and the disgusting letters of SIPTU, thrown into the Liffey - will the workers of Ireland reclaim their heritage able to hold up their heads again.

The first motion carried by the reinstated Irish Transport & General Workers Union should be a unanimous vote on action to be taken. I.e that is every Union Member and their families in a peaceful demonstration gather outside Liberty Hall and bring Dublin to a standstill.

With the eyes of the world on them - they can demand that - the one hundred twenty million euros given every year to wealthy schools from the wages of workers is stopped. Only when this happens will the cowardly so-called Historian's take off their rose tinted glasses, and have the courage to condemn - what happened at Belfast Docks.

Obviously, ordinary members don't like the unwholesome fact that SIPTU and ICTU leaders denigrated and prostituted our Union founder's working class principles, so to curry favour with the wealthy employer class, and actually became worse than them?

Future students of history will judge the 'silent historians, the great and the good in the Irish Media, like Fintan O'Toole for their deliberate sycophantic behaviour. They will ask, "Where were their Principles"?

How could investigative journalists ignore this usurping of the Courts, the Law of the Land and their own moral compass? The silence imposed by the Wealthy has ruled the Ireland for too long. Hopefully, in the not too distant future, when the cloak of censorship has been lifted and the Truth is told - it will be as commonplace to read about their betrayal of Connolly and Larkin's Union - and the cover up by Jack O'Connor and his ilk - as it is now to read, that William O'Brien sacked Jim Larkin from the Union that he founded and replaced him as Leader of ITGWU.

Any right thinking person, given that Ireland has such Draconian Libel Laws, would surely have expected me to be charged, convicted and jailed for making 'wild, hysterical, unscrupulous and perverted accusations against named Lawyers, DCC Officials,Trade Union Leaders and Journalists'? Why do they not demand an apology and that I be metaphorically flogged in the media for making such dastardly and disgusting accusations? The reason this not happened is because I speak The Truth, and will repeat it in any Court of Law and rightly claim "it is fair comment". Instead, the Wealthy and the Tame Journalists have organised a news blackout which amounts to 'Cancel Culture' to stop the Truth being told.

Only one media organisation that will print the Truth about the massive cover by that exists in Ireland - and that is "Linkedin". They print my articles because, they believe in Freedom of Speech. Unlike, the willing fooled who control and write for the supposed 'Free Press'.

While masquerading as 'reporters of the truth' they have no

doubt meticulously scanned my articles on Linkedin and the documentary proof in the corrupto'connor website - searching for some morsel of contradiction - but can find none. The truth in the documents from the Union and Employers Court, and the sell out by the Belfast Chairman cannot be denied.

Neither can the documentation which proves that ICTU and the human rights bodies, know all about the Trade Union Corruption that took place in Belfast, and will do nothing about it? At best the Union head office in Dublin covered it up -'at worst' were part of it. So instead of a case in a 'real court' that would expose their involvement, the Union - the employers and the Unfree Press use Corrupt Silence to hide the Truth.

No doubt, the well paid SIPTU Lawyers have told the Union's Leaders, "we cannot deny the evidence that Union in Belfast sacked paid up Union Members, it is too well documented. And even if it didn't exist, the letter from the Docks Receiver says it all". He states that **"Mr Murphy was removed from the Docks Industry by a Joint Disciplinary Committee consisting of members of the holding companies in Depo - and of members of the Irish Transport and General Workers Union".**

They say, how can we cross-exam the Truth, and hope to get anything but the Truth".

This is why SIPTU was in such a quandary and bent over backwards to meet me - and set up a series of meetings with the sub-committee they established. Obviously to buy me off? The National Executive Council that runs SIPTU and who jump through hoops for the Wealthy should be ashamed of themselves.

Had their predecessors and those in ICTU, stopped this corruption Fifty years ago and owned up to this scandal instead of denying it, this Trade Union and employers Atrocity would be ancient history.

However, had they done so, this would also be a different country - because once admitted, the employers Lap Dogs in the Union would've been driven out and genuine trade unionists, of the ilk of Connolly and Larkin would've taken over. With them at the reins we wouldn't have had the recent financial scandals, because things would never have been allowed to get so bad. The Sunday Times, Irish Times and the joke of a "free press" won't rock the boat on trade union and employer corruption.

Silence on my accusations and censoring of my play 'The Judas Goat' - keeps hidden their 'Strange Bedfellows' and their dictatorial behaviour.

Obviously, this Cancer in the Union started many years ago, when William O'Brien and his Union cronies saw the danger in Larkin's return from Jail in America, and set out to destroy him.

O'Brien's mind-set continues unabated to this day with their tongue in cheek claim to honour Larkin's memory - while trashing everything he believed in.
The Union Elite over the years have reaped the benefits of joining with employers and the Wealthy. They keep unrest to a minimum and wages low with assistance from the un-free press and tame human rights people. Through them they control every aspect of Irish Life.

This Dictatorship is enthusiastically promoted by Fintan O'Toole, who, in America trumpets his working class roots, while in Ireland leads the charge in Censorship and covering up for the Irish Times and the wealthy. This scandal has spread to social media. Any articles I post on supposed freedom of speech websites, are rapidly taken down, or not posted. The "Free Press" and Fintan O'Toole have insidiously controlled legitimate protest in Ireland. The fact that most Irish People don't know about the scandalous Trade Union behaviour at Belfast Docks – shows just how effective the censoring of the Truth has been.

The Wealthy have also corrupted every human rights group in Ireland, in particular IHREC by feeding them false information through the willing offices of Michael Farrell, a prominent human rights lawyer. Obviously Farrell and the Wealthy will deny this - but only on the quiet so not to give publicity to what has been covered up for years.

The facts I related earlier prove this. John Devitt of Transparency International should not only be sacked - but should be prosecuted for corrupting the organisation and bringing it into disrepute. These facts speak for themselves and the human rights lawyers plus O'Toole, the Irish Times and all other Journalists who cover up this scandal - are in fact, as corrupt as the Union and Employers Court in Belfast.

No doubt these Journalists once had principles - but a wife and children made them embrace the status quo. So - to advance themselves they acquiesced and adopted a slave mentality. They saw the only way to survive was to become a nodding dog. Over time, however, and usually caused by promotion - to justify what they had become, the slave mentality of these Journalists hardened into establishment beliefs.

Their thinking today, overrides the long abandoned desire to be fair and above board in their journalistic activities. They push the big questions to the back of their minds. Questions about clouds of Asbestos dust blowing over Belfast. The dead and dying Dockers, plus an unknown number of family members and afflicted Belfast People. This - never even costs them a thought.

While they make sure to pay their union dues to the NUJ, the hypocrisy of a Union Employers Court that sacked Union Members is not even on their radar. They obviously comfort themselves with the 'group think' of the Censors. I.e. "who is ever going to know - and if they find out - what can they do about it"? Hopefully when this scandal is exposed, a Solicitor or Barrister in Ireland 'with principles' {there must be one} will take on the case and sue the lot of them. Stranger things have happened.

If a Lawyer, Journalist, or SIPTU Official who is in 'the know is ever prosecuted, to protect themselves - they will divulge all and point the finger at those who were pulling the strings.

I have realised I made a mistake. When Jack O'Connor set up the sub-committee which was "**not**" to investigate the corruption I had exposed.

I should have participated and allowed them to buy my silence. Then when I received the cheque, ignored their 'non disclosure agreement' by never cashing it - photo copied it a thousand times and sent it all the newspapers in Ireland and Europe. This would have given me leverage to expose the Union Corruption. In retrospect I realised I was 'played' by the Wealthy who control the Union.

They knew me better than I know myself. By sending the letter from Martin Naughton, dated 3rd May 2006, they knew there was no way I would or could participate in the cover up - and would do as they wanted. By refusing to attend the sub-committee meeting and the many others they set up. I had in fact stopped myself from taking the matter any further.

Many of the dead Dockers were really nice people, especially the two Browne brothers. The description of Sean Browne by his wife - and their life together, related in the TV programme, Death Trap on the Docks, by UTV - would bring tears from a stone. A similar program made my Northern Visions named Dying Dockers is a bit harder on the Union.

However both video recordings show the utter contempt the Union had for the dying Dockers. Many people were appalled at the Dublin Union Officials refusal to help dying Belfast Dockers - but what else could they do? It was on Dublin's orders that the Joint Disciplinary Committee ordered the Dockers to discharge it. And it was the ex Union Chairman, Jim Austin, for the Employers, who did the ordering. On pain of getting sacked the Dockers complied. He repeatedly said and I quote, "It's only dust, how can that kill you".

Because of the arrogance, outright lies and seemingly un-ending salary increases paid to Robert Watt, John McGuinness TD castigated the refusal by government to reply to a report compiled by two powerful committees. The finance committee [of which he is the chair] and the PAC. This investigation was into the rise in salary of Robert Watt. And other relevant matters.

John McGuinness said: "The appointment of Secretary Generals is unique in public and private life. Watt and the other secretary generals have no boss. Bankers have bosses, judges have bosses, politicians have SIPO. [Standards In Public Office Commission] and the people. Everyone is accountable except for secretary generals". This is a scandalous state of affairs, however, I took John McGuinness at his word when he said, SIPO has oversight regarding the actions of Politicians.

Therefore, I emailed SIPO to find out - why the Public Accounts Committee - and the Justice Committee will not investigate the cover up by SIPTU, ICTU and the IHRC - as it was when it refusd to investigate the Union Corruption then - and even now refuses to see this corruption as a denial of Human Rights. I posted the article on linkedin. I was surprised when SIPO replied to me, stating in no uncertain terms that they **did not** have oversight of TD's in the Dail.

They conveniently did not comment on the matters I wished these committees to investigate? I asked them to inform John McGuinness of their "non oversight" statement. Several high ranking TD's including Michael Martin accessed my post on linkedin. This begs the question, who {does} have oversight in the Dail? It's obviously not the various elected committees that Watt treats with disdain. However it's a bit rich for John McGuinness to 'rightly' complain about the lack of Democracy in the Dail - when the PAC the C&AG and the Justice Committee cherry-pick which scandal to investigate and - who appears in front of them?

Why do these powerful commitees ' *also*' not want the Union Corruption exposed. This is where my proposed - Oversight of Democratic Institutions, ODI would come into its own. It could investigate everyone in the Dail and government both elected and unelected, who, for whatever reason - were not acting in the best interests of Democracy.

While SIPO were quick to clarify that they do not have oversight over TD's, its obvious they don't have oversight over Robert Watt and the other Secretary Generals either, who are not elected - but they are in Public Office so SIPO ' *should*' be able to control them and their behaviour'. Watt's 'snout in the trough Dictatorship' shows that his
'Public Office' has deplorable Standards. Why is this behaviour tolerated?

Are SIPO afraid of the consequences if they upset him? SIPO should immediately live up to its name and launch an investigation into the scandalous behaviour of Robert Watt towards the elected TD's and the elected committees. If SIPO flexed its muscles in this way - in one fell swoop it would also put manners on Robert Watt, by showing that no-one is above the Law.

However, seeing that SIPO will not do this and the undemocratic behaviour of Robert Watt is obviously upsetting John McGuinness, why doesn't John organise a cross-party protest to suspend the Dail until "King Watt" is informed that Ireland cannot stand for his dictatorship and longer. While he cannot be sacked he must be to obey the houses of the Oireachtas and act in a truly Democratic manner?

While the housing and hospitals scandals get worse, children, who should have been operated on years ago are suffering in agony, and face a lifetime of incapacity, because of the delays in treatment. I have a suggestion that in one fell swoop would alleviate years of pain for these children and get them the treatment they deserve. As good Irish citizens the well paid Secretary Generals and every TD should be compelled to donate a year's salary to pay for the necessary operations in the US - for all children on a waiting list.
I will tell you now - not one of them will object - and before one cent is paid - every child who needs an operation will get it in Ireland.

A glaring example of our Sham Democracy is this. Before the IHRC acquired the {E} which instead of Equally should stand for Employers, it refused to hold an inquiry into the Belfast Docks scandal. At this point I didn't know that Michael Farrell of Flac was then involved with IHRC.

This would have explained a lot - and more to the point would reflect their true nature of slavishly adhering to 'Orders from Above'. Farrell and those who act in the 'best interests' of the Wealthy are a disgrace and purport to represent 'Irish Human

Rights'. While these unsavoury facts must be anathema to right-minded people, they must be brought into the light and not swept under the carpet any longer. The Law Reform Commission could do this but will not be allowed to?

Of course no-one wants to attack SIPTU unfairly, but as ITGWU it joined forces with the Belfast Employers to persecute union members - this must be exposed. I repeatedly told head office and ICTU [see letters on website] that the Union had joined with the Employers, and was forcing the Dockers to discharge Asbestos without protection, but was ignored.

Actually, in my final letter to the Union, after I was sacked by the Union and Employers Court - I related again the actions of the Union and how they were behaving worse that the Dublin Employers did during the lock-out. I asked the then general secretary, Michael Mullen, 'how can you sleep at night knowing of his betrayal of Larkin and Connolly' beliefs and that Asbestos Dust is being blown all over Belfast'? In his reply dated 15th July 1974 he said: "Many things keep me awake at night but never the contents of your insulting letters"... This says it all. And shows just how much the Union of 50 years ago considered the well-being of union members - the Irish People, and its own antecedence. Not at all.

See also the letter from Jack O'Connor dated 25 July 2005 whereby he sympathises with me but claims that 'nothing' can be done. Because of my insistence he eventually agreed - but it was to silence it.

This is also why the solicitor and chairman of FLAC, Michael Farrell [originally from Belfast] told blatant lies in his attempts to cover up for Norman Shannon. I've been told there's a family connection but at this remove cannot prove it. The Law Societies, North and South, know full well that they have corrupt solicitors in their midst and will do nothing about it.

This shows they're more concerned with protecting their own reputations than with the Rule of Law. If proof were needed that a "cover up" will always spreads to encompass a lot more than the 'initial and original corrupt action'.

Michael Farrell is it. In one letter of several, he states, that "he could not speak for the IHRC".
I only found out years later that he could do nothing else - because at that time he was both a solicitor for them, and a high-ranking member of it. Ignoring the corrupt actions of Norman Shannon and Michael Farrell, has led to the corruption of both Law Societies.

Belfast solicitor Martin Hanna and City Hospital Doctor Joe McMahon gave devastating testimony on the UTV Video, DEATH TRAP ON THE DOCKS about the dangers of Asbestos. While the doctor stated it could take fifty years to kill infected people.

There is a can of worms here that needs to be opened. I believe - the reason why was the ex Union Chairman turned Labour Controller was allowed to remain a Union Member - and actually rewarded received his long service badge was because he Blackmailed Jack O'Connor? This redeemed his reputation in Belfast. Had O'Connor not acquiesced then the ex union chairman would've blown the whistle on why the Union ordered Belfast members to their deaths.

This would've ensured that the entire Union Leader ship and ICTU, the plus the employers who owned the Asbestos {any who were still living} would be charged with Corporate Manslaughter. While this would have been the least, 'legally wise' they should have suffered - the damage to the Union and to their Reputations would have destroyed the Union?

It would have also destroyed it both Norman Shannon and Michael Farrell, who are still alive and know who bought them off - and if faced with a jail sentence will tell all. This corruption and cover up continues to the present day with the Both Law Society's fully aware of what transpired and are ignoring it. This is not Justice - this is Legal Corruption to protect their own so-called Legal Reputations. The magnitude of these facts prove that the cover up that originated at Belfast Docks, is continuing in the Dail. Without its silent approval none of this, nor Fintan O'Toole's control of the unfree Press, media and Democracy could take place.

Just what are our elected TD's in the Dail afraid of? In fact John McGuinness has supported my arguments. He claimed - that senior civil servants have taken over the running of the country, and cited the annual report by the TLAC, the Top Level Appointments Commission -
which shows that no private sector workers were appointed to the highest paid civil service positions.

McGuinness has promised to bring the TLAC in front of his Finance Committee to explain this, seeing that the number of private sector applicants was twice the number from the previous year. He publicly stated "The people in the top jobs appoint the same people to the top jobs, and politicians are reduced to the status of mere **"Sock Puppets"** . Continuing he said: "It's almost as though there appears to be some pact where the civil servants take all the power and jobs so long as they keep their political 'master' out of trouble". At least in McGuinness we have a TD not afraid to upset the Wealthy by calling a spade a spade.
I wish more of our elected Politicians in the Oireachtas had more to say about running the country. Its refreshing to have a politician like McGuiness speak the Truth. He exposes the real power behind the façade of a Democratic Government. I look forward to John demanding an Inquiry into the cover at Belfast

Docks?

However sometimes the scandalous manipulations of the 'unelected' brings them out of the woodwork. Robert Watt attempts to defend the indefensible saw him 'going public'. Obviously he wasn't happy at not being given given the recognition he deserves for running the country.

So, when appointed to his new position he awarded himself a massive pay rise - and more importantly refused to attend the Finance Committee to be 'grilled' over this - and the manipulations which led to the resignation of Dr Tony Holohan.

John McGuinness has seen the danger that Robert Watt presents. If he is allowed to continue to flout the democratic process. In fact it may already be too late. He has established himself as a man who does what he wants and gets what he wants - and no TD elected in the Dail can stop him. In the eyes of the Wealthy, no-one would make a better Taoiseach. However, I believe that Robert Watt With his megalomania has set his sights higher. Just running Ireland is not recognising fully his talents and would be only the start. With his undoubted dictatorial ability to control the democratic process - he could easily be the President of Europe.

However, at present unelected bureaucrats led by Watt and the other Secretary General's are the 'defacto' government and declare them - selves as "The State". They decide on the best way to run the country - and not the 'Sock Puppets'. Hence, "The State has no plans to disown the report of the Commission of Investigation into the Mother and Baby Homes". Also, "The State" will argue 'against' a series of judicial reviews taken by survivors, saying that the commission was '**not**' "independent".

'The State' to give themselves an 'out' and to explain the

discrepancies between the written statements of survivors and the 'doctored' final report - says "when it comes to the executive summary of the final report, that - this is not and could not be expected to be, a complete account of the commission's investigation". This gobbledegook evasions and double talk.

Why then was the commission instigated and established in the first place - if not to find and publish the Truth? Obviously, the commission was set up just to take the heat out of the situation and when this was achieved, it was stopped and wound up? It also was an attempt to **'not'** show Ireland as a backward Priest Ridden country that murdered innocent children.

Even 'The State' cannot deny the skeletons of at least 800 babies in one Cesspit. They and the Wealthy are trying to protect the Catholic Church from the scorn of the outside world? The first hand accounts given by women abused by the Catholic Church are not unreliable, they are the Truth.
This shocking example of Ireland's corrupt past, and its behaviour must be exhumed - in all its grisly detail. There must be no more cover ups.

Obviously, however a cover up was the aims of the unidentifiable and - dictatorial "State", who can do as they wish, hence their report. However, with Watt coming out of the woodwork a face has being put on the "Unelected State"?

Why is he allowed to impose his dictatorial will on Democracy? Because of this prime example, many hypocritical elected government TD's support the unelected 'State' and cherry-pick History.

To expose where this thinking comes from, I put the following letter on Linkedin.

TO IVANA BACIK THE HYPOCRITE

Ten Days ago the new leader of the Labour Party, Ivan Bacik had a letter in the Irish Times. This letter harked back to the glory days 100 years ago when 'the people' the poor of Ireland believed in the Labour Party. This letter was no doubt an attempt to inspire Trade Unionists to come out in force for a show of strength on May Day. It failed dismally and showed just how much workers today believe in trade unions. No doubt, the saying 'it takes one to know one' is very relevant to Bacik and the leaders of SIPTU, seeing it is the largest trade Union.

The sight of the great Jim Larkin on the SIPTU banner was particularly disgusting and shows the duplicity of their thinking. How can they claim they follow his beliefs when they betray everything he believed in. In their defence SIPTU will claim that times have changed, which is perfectly true - the extremely wealthy have found many new ways of keeping the Poor, poor.

However what can never change is the diabolical fact which is ignored by SIPTU and Bacik - is that the Union which now proudly has him on their banner SACKED Larkin from the Union he founded for being too militant. While ignoring this shocking and abject fact of Labour History, she cites many other Labour Victory's of 100 years ago - to disguise her hypocrisy.

The first was the General Strike in 1922 - "which was organised by the Labour Party and the Trade Union Congress, as a protest against the growing militarisation of both sides of the Treaty divide". This was obviously was a good thing - which as we know made no difference. She continues, stating: "The threats their military activities posed were against working men and children" I think even the most stupid and silly multi millionaire in Ireland would contend - that no-one intended to make war on children.

She continues in this revisionist vein, stating, "we have been well conditioned in this nationalist- dominated state to believe that the broader labour-movement played no role in the events before, during and after the foundation of the southern state, but this is untrue." and she does not elaborate on this preposterous statement.
How can the leader of the Labour Party make such stupid and diabolical utterances? There is no evidence to suggest what she is suggesting and actually its to the contrary. No-one in Ireland - Right, Left or Center has ever air-brushed, denied or attempted to play down the actions of James Connolly and the Citizens Army.

I presume she has heard of James Connolly - whom she negates to mention? Obviously playing up to her middle class voters.

I am astonished at the behaviour of Ivana Bacik. If these statements from her are meant as a rallying cry for Labour she should go back to the drawing board. If she continues in this vein Labour is dead in the water and will never rise again? She goes on to mention several other campaigns and victories and strikes by Labour, over 100 years ago. I.e "The Labour Party was instrumental in organising, the strike against conscription in 1918 - and another victory during the War of Independence in support of hunger strikers, which forced the British to release the prisoners". But she mentions nothing more recent?

How sad is this - talk about living in the past - with nary a mention of sell-outs in later years that shattered Labour's working class base and decimated the numbers in the Dail.

Seeing she's now the Labour Leader she could champion the

cause to remove the 100 million subsidy that the poor pay to Rich Schools?

On this, she knows she's a dyed in the wool Hypocrite but will not upset her wealthy neighbours. The old saying 'those who live in glass houses shouldn't throw stones' is relevant here.

I must point out to Ivana, that she is wrong when she says "Everyone is feeling the pinch". To even describe the deprivation that families are suffering as a 'pinch' shows just how well insulated from reality she and the other wealthy people are today. In particular not feeling the 'pinch' are the parents whose children are the benefactors of the 100 million in 'sports facilities'. On this point, a few years back the principles of the schools that receive this largesse from the Poor, insisted that the schools themselves "didn't benefit" and that the money was only used to pay the salaries of Teachers.

From this nonsensical statement from the 'educated' it's easy to see just where their students get their sense of Privilege from.

In her letter she states: "Labour has always been criticised for being either insufficiently nationalist or radical" - and again cites Labour party activities of 100 years ago. However, for Ivana I will just go back 50 years - and she know about this because I have emailed her several times and sent her the details. I publicly ask how could Ivana, in her mining of labour history ignore the achievements at Belfast Docks 50 years ago. Here, under the guise of abolishing Casual Labour the ITGWU entered into an unholy alliance with the Employers and sacked its own members.

They achieved this Trade Union Atrocity by forming a Union and Employers Court which they named the 'Joint Disciplinary Committee'. The banner heading on the summons letters was:

NORTHERN IRELAND FEDERATION OF EMPLOYERS

AND IRISH TRANSPORT & GENERAL WORKERS UNION JOINT DISCIPLINARY COMMITTEE

This was a world first when Union committee members sat with employers and persecuted its own members. As Ivana well knows, this committee also ordered the Dockers to discharge Asbestos without protection, to save the employers money.

The simple reason why Ivana won't claim these victories is - by doing so her wealthy neighbours and her friends in the Law will never speak to her again. She knows just as well as I do, that the Joint Disciplinary Committee at Belfast Docks was the fore-runner and a 'try out' for Partnership which was introduced in Dublin a few years later. The only difference was - with Dublin Partnership the Union's didn't sack their own members. Plus, because the Asbestos Dust was blown all over Belfast there could be nasty legal complications if it ever got out, that it was instantiated in Dublin.

If Ivana and the Labour party want to be a fundamental player in Irish Politics she will expose this cover up by the Wealthy and their trade union cronies. However, for Ivana to do as I suggest and be an "honest leader for the Labour Party" - is I believe beyond her capabilities.

This would expose the higher echelons of her own profession who cover up this illegal scandal. The large file that I'm attaching to this letter [I hope it goes] is documentary evidence of the cover up by ICTU and ITGWU at the time. Here is the web address. If its not posted, see it at www.siptupresidentjackoconnorexposed.com - facebook, twitter and linkedin. And I welcome the people, especially the solicitors who are well aware of the Law - like Norman Shannon, who sat on my case against the Union and Employers for seven years, until it became Statute Barred, to sue me for defamation.

These Lawyers know just as well as Ivana Does, that the Truth is not - and never can be Defamation. As a professor of the Law, if Ivana took up this challenge and exposed this "Legal Corruption" - the Labour Party would be guaranteed a permanent say in running the Irish state and Government for years to come. However to do this she must show she's her own woman and not afraid to stand up to the controlling men in the Law. In so doing she would be declaring herself as "in the pocket of no-one" but would be exposing the cronyism, sycophantic behaviour and "illegality" of her own profession in Ireland.

If Ivana stood up as a champion for women, she would also expose the self-censoring of the Truth by the Irish Times and the Un-free Media? This includes RTE, our so-called National Broadcaster whose motto laughingly is - THE TRUTH MATTERS.
If Ivana, as leader of the Labour Party refuses to expose these corruptions then she and the so-called Labour Party will continue to dream of past glories which happened 100 years ago - as they again go down the tubes.
Hugh Murphy

Below is another letter I recently posted to a Labour Party Senator.

AN OPEN LETTER TO LABOUR PARTY SENATOR REBECCA MOYNIHAN

Rebecca, I note that you've called for housing Minister to publish his report into various matters that have taken place in An Bord Pleanala - regarding a conflict of of interest that has occurred. This is a very serious matter.

Among other things, you said and I quote, "I'm calling on

the minister to publish the report in full immediately and convene an Oireachtas debate upon its return in September. Transparency and fairness are the bedrock of any democracy and trust in the planning system is completely vital, and the public must be satisfied that the minister will outline specific to address any system failings.

Rebecca, obviously you didn't clear this statement with the Labour Party Leader? She would have told you to keep quiet and don't embarrass yourself. What world are you living in when you think Ireland is a Democracy.
Surely recent events which prove the "Unelected Secretary Generals" led by Robert Watt do run Ireland - and they don't care who knows it.

However, seeing that you are not like Ivana and prepared to speak out - ask her why she will not expose the fact that she covers up for SIPTU who in turn cover for the Wealthy and ITGWU. I will explain. 50 years ago at Belfast Docks the union influenced by the Wealthy and supported by Head Office and ICTU formed a Union and Employers Court for sacking Dockers. Many, myself included were sacked by this Court because we wouldn't discharge Asbestos without protection. This is a fact and documentary proof is on www.siptupresidentjackoconnorexposed.com

Your leader Ivana knows all about this and ignores it. See the open letter I sent her on linkedin when she was elected. If you ask a question about this you will be sidelined blacklisted and put out of the Labour Party. So do yourself a favour and don't mention it to anyone - and do a 'Pat Rabbitee on the matter.
Hugh Murphy

I have always had an antenna - and objected strongly to wrong-doing and felt the desire to confront it. This stems from my childhood. Along with two of my brothers we suffered horrendous beatings during childhood, from our father.

We were whipped with a leather belt until we bled like stuck pigs, while my mother and sister banged on the bedroom door screaming. This resulted in the family tragedy which I related earlier - and is the reasoning behind my quest for justice - for the underdog.

Because of my childhood I went off the rails and for a long time and abused alcohol as a means to forget. While I have relapses - at least - now I know the reason for my behaviour. This puts me back on the straight and narrow. It was a Nun in Cuan Mhuire, in Newry that wised me up to the destructive terrors that blacken my soul. Over a period of five months she lifted the fog from my brain.

Many others are not so lucky. They live a terrible existence, shunned by society and die sad and lonely deaths.
As I mentioned before because of Facial Recognition when I go into a shop the security staff are hovering around me - no doubt so their superiors can see what a good job they're doing. The worst culprits are the Library, McDonalds, Lidel and Centra. The original corrupt RUC
Policeman, who allocated to me a lengthy violent criminal record which I had nothing to do me, follows me to this day.

This plus the Criminal Behaviour of the RUC in refusing to believe that an obviously deranged woman stabbed me - and instead prosecuted me for an assault on her. This juxtaposed with the fact that she stabbed her husband in the heart - must call into question their competence? No doubt they were relying on the false criminal record to justify their illegal actions.
I am calling on the Police Commissioner Drew Harris who comes from the RUC - not to cover up for them but investigate

the serious matters of a falsified criminal record and get it abolished.

The few issues of wayward behaviour I engaged in - in the 1960's were because of the brutal treatment I received as a child. The tragic death of my brother proves that. The few drunken offences were more a cry for help rather than Criminal Malfeasant behaviour. These have no relevance to the person I am today. To this end I have attached three of my plays 'The Judas Goat' - 'Daddy' and 'The Grandeur of Delusions'.

The last two were staged by Heart & Soul Theatre Company - but ignored by the Dublin intelligentsia - no doubt instigated by Fintan O'Toole. After some changes I've renamed them 'Betrayed' and 'PSYCHO-LOGICAL'. Here is a brief synopsis of both. Also attached is a large file which contains the documentary proof of the Union and Employers Court at Belfast Docks. Plus evidence from the Union and ICTU showing that they were aware of this travesty of trade unionism and did nothing about it.

The Grandeur of Delusions
Renamed
PSYCHO-LOGICAL

This is a semi autobiographical play about an alcoholic who tries to sort himself out by talking to his Delusion, a lovely young girl.
This was staged by Heart and Soul Theatre Company, at The Civic Theatre,Tallaght, for three nights - The Mill Theatre Dundrum, for four nights - and two single nights, one in Drioght and the other in Westport Town hall. This play deals with circumstances surrounding the
downward spiral that alcoholics inflict upon themselves - and on their families. It shows exactly how and why anyone – given inappropriate childhood circumstances can become addicted

to alcohol or indeed to any mind-altering substance.

The delusional aspects of 'Terry', the alcoholic in the play, not only affects his thinking, but also corrupts the thinking of all who surround him. Unless treatment is sought there can only be one inevitable end, and because Addiction knows no class or age barrier this play will reach every spectrum of society. Nothing buried can be cured - it must be dug out and dealt with no matter how painful - and with sobriety - eventually overcome. Uniquely this play is both a duologue and a monologue, which is an obvious contradiction. It shows 'Terry' the alcoholic talking to himself through the medium of his Delusion, a young woman. To most people a Drunk on the street is a disgrace. Very few question what brought them to the state of degradation.

The two actors earned a well-deserved standing ovation on the last night.The play shows, that because of learned behaviour, when a child from an early age, is exposed to destructive drug and alcoholic trauma, they are almost guaranteed to form an addictive personality.
Thus, when adults they become addicted to some form of escapism rather than face the rigours of life. This is not a concious decision but rather the learned behaviour of a child seeking relief from the trauma they've experienced-like sticking their fingers in their ears and pulling a duvet over their heads. In the past this was not sufficiently recognised.

However, to be fair, Young Children's Agencies and the 'powers that be' are now aware, and are doing much to prevent this from happening. Many people who suffer from Addiction, {because of horrific trauma in their own lives} are recognising that addiction breeds addiction - and by abstaining, can prevent the cycle from continuing down the generations.

Obviously, this is easily said but a lot harder to do. By living a

sober life and happy life, where love and respect is the norm, their children -
because they have a loving family and a happy childhood behind them will have the moral courage to resist all mood and mind altering drugs.

Heart & Soul Theatre Company had hoped to take this play into schools to show our children, in a dramatic fashion just what addiction can lead to. However, Fintan O'Toole and Nolene Blackwell with their Right Wing Censorship in refusing to see the play limited its possibilities and showed their true colours.

DADDY
Renamed Betrayed

This play started out as 'Daddy' and gives a horrific glimpse into the lives and minds of two adult sisters who were abused by their father. This shows, because of the abuse how their adult lives and the lives of their children are controlled by the abuse. I'd originally written with two male characters, but some people reckoned it would work well as a result I now have two versions. The play opens with a dramatic scene over the coffin of the abuser - where the mother finally realises the harm that was done to her daughters.

Fintan O'Toole refused to review this play - even after I left a copy of the script into the Irish Times for him. This is corruption personified. How could an enlightened author and Irish Times Arts Critic allow the warped perceptions of the Wealthy - to override his reviewing of a play about child abuse. No doubt he was well aware that this play received a Rehearsed Reading from Tinderbox in their first Festival Festival of New Irish Writing.

THE JUDAS GOAT

This play is shows the terrible conditions at Belfast Docks. The name is one I coined for the corrupt Union Chairman, and printed many time in 'The Dockers Voice'. This was because the Chairman sold out and left the Union - and joined the Employers as Labour Controller. It also shows the corrupt Union and Employers Court in action.

This has had several readings but has never been fully staged. I believe this is because of the control of the Right Wing who control Theatre and the Irish Times - and it speaks for itself. The play shows the dictatorship the Union on the Belfast Dockers. This was what led the Dockers to accept The Union and Employers Court. This play is an Irish On The Waterfront. See many examples of the Union's dictatorial behaviour in the corruptoconnor website below.

The JudasGoat Stage-play.pdf

BETRAYED.pdf

PSYCHO-LOGICAL.pdf

www.siptupresidentjackoconnorexposed.com
©

www.ingramcontent.com/pod-product-compliance
Lightning Source LLC
Chambersburg PA
CBHW060235100426
42742CB00011B/1536